HOPE RISING

HOPE RISING

Me, Kee, and the AT

RICHARD HUBER

HOPE RISING, LLC

Hope Rising
Copyright © 2025 by Richard Huber
All rights reserved, including the right to reproduce
distribute, or transmit in any form or by any means.

Except as permitted under the U.S. Copyright Act of 1976, no part of this book may be reproduced, distributed, or transmitted in any form or by any means, or stored in a database or retrieval system without the written permission of the authors, except in the case of brief passages embodied in critical reviews and articles where the title, author and ISBN accompany such review or article.

While all the stories in this book are true, some names and identifying details have been changed or omitted to protect the privacy of the people involved.

For information contact:
ducttape96atthruhiker@gmail.com

authorrichardhuber.com

Published by:
Hope Rising, LLC

Cover and interior book design by
Francine Platt • Eden Graphics, Inc. • edengraphics.net

Cover photo by author

Stock images by Adobe Stock
The Pink Panda, Matty Symons, Big City Lights, and Apiwan

Hardback color ISBN 979-8-89454-049-8
Paperback color ISBN 979-8-89454-050-4
Paperback black & white ISBN 979-8-89454-077-1
eBook ISBN 979-8-89454-051-1

Library of Congress Control Number: 2025906324

Manufactured in the United States of America
First Edition

To the loving memory of Grandpa
and a life well lived.

Also, a big thanks to my parents.
Without your support, none of this
would have been possible.

INTRODUCTION

I HAVE ALWAYS had this innate desire to see what is around the next corner. Just ask some of my friends and relatives, and they will tell you how I would drive them to near madness and exhaustion as I would rally their spirits to go just a little farther. It was somewhat selfish on my part, this constant urging to push on, to unlock the mysteries hidden around the next bend. To venture into the wilderness is exhilarating for me, not unlike a treasure hunter searching for undiscovered riches. This profound curiosity drives me, still to this day, to seek out the hidden treasures, those pockets of natural beauty that take your breath away and leave you humble in the presence of a divine Creator.

Initially, I was certain that this book would be an epic adventure story. But, as I look back with clarity, through the eyes of time, I realize this is supposed to be a message of unifying hope. Enjoy the journey.

PROLOGUE

MY DAD SERVED in the Military Intelligence Corps while in the United Sates Army. Honorably discharged in 1960 and desperate to find work, he took a security job at a power plant in Joe City, Arizona. There he met my mom, a stunning beauty, the likes of her made a man's heart skip a beat. He will tell you that after taking a crisp second look, he had to ice his neck.

Mom was on a liberating journey with some girlfriends to break from the shackles of domestic abuse, to find hope, and to see America.

With his chiseled good looks, Dad carried himself with the rebel air of the 1950's actor, James Dean. While stationed in Kassel, Germany he traveled extensively in Europe, acquiring a wealth of knowledge making him even more attractive to my mom. She put her travels on hold, and as they say, "the rest is history."

Chapter 1

Phoenix, Arizona

One summer evening in 1991, I took my girlfriend, Hannah, home from a date. As we walked toward the courtyard gate, the heat radiating from the blacktop felt like a furnace.

A brand new, red Jeep Cherokee slowly rolled by in the dimly lit parking lot. It passed premium spaces and circled around to the far end of the lot. The dark tinted windows prevented me from seeing the Jeep's occupants.

My first instinct was to rejoice in the driver's new ride, but something was nudging me that all was not as it appeared. The jeep casually idled our way, and then suddenly, a Hispanic man jumped out, brandishing a machete. Sparks flew as he ran toward us, dragging the blade on the pavement, yelling, "Give me your wallet, Mother F#%@*#." and then he started swinging.

Something inside me died that night.

I thought, *How in the world did I get here?*

So, let me back up a little to give you an idea of how events in my life set me on an unexpected collision course with these rebellious young men, and why I sought an adventurous solution to find my answers.

Chapter 2

In the Beginning

I GREW UP IN HOLBROOK, ARIZONA. My earliest memories were of my two native American friends Buzzy and Tweety Maktima. I don't know if those were their real first names, but we didn't care about race, names, or any such nonsense back then. We spent a lot of time playing in the neighborhood doing the things that most kids do, and occasionally, I would talk them into exploring the surrounding hills with me. I enticed them with stories of what I had seen exploring cool caves I had found. We would venture into the sagebrush-covered hills on the north side of town, catching lizards and horny toads every chance we had. We were not competitive, but it was always "game on" to see who could spot the most jackrabbits, cottontails, or coyotes. On one of our ventures, we found a cave that appeared somebody was living in. While we never saw the person or persons, we felt their presence. We saw where they had relieved themselves after we ventured into their hideout and found it equipped with a relatively new mattress, some bedding, and miscellaneous cookware next to the fire ring.

On another occasion, we found a hobo camp next to the Little Colorado River on the outskirts of town. It was just out of sight of passing trains. We visited the hobo camp on several occasions, always cautious of the rumored quicksand in the area. We would scour the campsite looking for clues to figure out how these people lived. We found coffee cans that doubled as a stove, miscellaneous eating utensils, makeshift shelters, and sometimes torn and discarded clothes.

We visualized that the occupants were hanging their clothes in the trees and bushes to air out, and that in our wild imaginations, the characters might be returning. We always double dog dared each other to stick around and spy on who might show.

But our mothers' warning to be home before dinner always took precedence over a late evening spy operation.

I hustled a buck, even before I knew the value of money. All I knew was that I had to work in exchange for money; then I could buy something I wanted. At that time, it was candy from the local Pow Wow Trading Post where there seemed to be an unlimited supply of my favorite Snickers candy bars.

The summer before my kindergarten year, I got permission to sell the excess produce from my parents' garden. Cucumbers were growing like weeds in our backyard, so I'd pick them and peddle them to the neighbors; five cents for one or three for twenty-five cents. For some reason, I always came back with a lot of quarters.

The following summer, I delivered the *Holbrook Tribune* and received five cents per paper for my efforts. One summer, I made the mistake of thinking my dad was cool mowing the lawn, and I wanted to be like him, so I asked if I could try it. With great effort, I finished that lawn under my dad's approving eye and earned the privilege of maintaining the yard from that point on. That experience gave me the confidence to go down the block, mowing the yards of neighbors willing to give me a chance.

Early on, my mother discovered just how headstrong I could be. I don't even remember the argument, but I'm pretty sure it had something to do with limiting my freedom. I was so upset at the time that I decided to run away. Obviously thinking ahead, I grabbed a frozen chicken, stuffed it in my treasured football helmet, headed out the door, and slung my helmet over my handlebars.

With my jaw set, I rode off into the sunset, determined to figure it out on the fly. That is, until I reached the end of the block and realized that in my haste I had forgotten matches. I went home and walked through the back door. My mom greeted me with a knowing smile, took the frozen chicken from my helmet, casually put it back in the freezer, and then put another plate on the table.

Holbrook is located near Arizona's Painted Desert and Petrified Forest. It was a great place to grow up if you had an adventurous spirit and an insatiable curiosity. Otherwise, since the wind never ceased, it was a kite-flying mecca.

Dad was a letter carrier for the U.S. Post Office, and midway through my fourth-grade year he took a transfer to a Phoenix station. With the overtime, he could nearly double his salary and open up a world of possibilities for his five kids. The move was bittersweet for me, as I said goodbye to my friends and teachers. Still, I looked forward to being closer to all my cousins, and the whispers of adventures we would share. We would be close by the Bradshaw Mountains, the Mogollon Rim, and the Superstition Mountains; to name a few.

It was intoxicating.

Our excitement was palpable as we crested the hills of Black Canyon City on Interstate 17 and dropped into the Valley of the Sun. Its warming thermals filled our car with the sweet scent of orange blossoms. We knew we were within minutes of seeing our cousins when we passed through the first orange grove, where the temperature would drop noticeably. As our anticipation grew, we hardly noticed the chill bumps that formed on our sweat-soaked skin. No one ever had to insist we spend time with our cousins, and we always seemed to pick back up where we had left off, as if time had scarcely passed since the last we were together.

We eventually moved into a small three-bedroom, two-bath, ranch-style house just north of Turf Paradise, a horse racing track, and officially on the outskirts of Phoenix. Being the new kid in school is always challenging, and if it hadn't been for my size and natural athleticism I probably would have struggled trying to fit in. On one of my first days in fifth grade at Village Meadows Grade School, the school bully snuck up behind me and tried to throw me to the ground, underestimating the strength of the skinny new kid. When I broke away and turned to face him, he lost his nerve and backed away while his little gang looked on. They were obviously disappointed that there wasn't any bloodshed, namely mine. That same kid was killed two weeks later while playing chicken on his minibike with passing cars. I can't say there were a lot of tears shed by his classmates, but I remember feeling sorry that our relationship never progressed from unspoken mutual respect to a true friendship.

Seeing the horses training daily at Turf Paradise and having a neighbor who owned horses fueled my imagination about the possibilities of being a cowboy and roaming places less traveled with my faithful steed. The problem with this dream was I had to convince my dad—so I told him I wanted to be a cowboy and then asked if I could have a horse.

Dad was always so practical. "Sure, son, get a job so you can buy one and then afford to take care of it." The third of eight siblings and the son of a Great Depression iron worker, he knew how to rein in a boy who loved to dream without crushing his spirit. Only this time, it was different. I desperately wanted a horse and was willing to do whatever it took. To me, a horse was a noble creature, and I dreamed of the adventures and freedom ahead. I would ride in the wild country like the mountain men and cowboys of the past, free as the wind.

It was a magical lure that, for me, held endless possibilities.

Dad always made me believe I could do whatever I put my mind to, so his suggestion sounded reasonable. There aren't many jobs available for fifth-grade kids with big plans. After searching high and low, I realized babysitting wasn't steady enough, and mowing lawns was seasonal. I needed something with serious earning potential. Almost losing hope, I came across a want ad in the *Arizona Republic* looking for paperboys. I couldn't believe my good fortune. Shortly after making that initial inquiry, I met with the District Supervisor. The interviewing process was new and exciting but also a bit unnerving. A great weight was taken off my shoulders when the supervisor asked my parents to participate in the meeting.

I have always been eager to establish my independence but

knowing I could count on my parents to keep me from crashing and burning too hard as I tried new things was comforting.

During the interview, I noticed the Super's facial expression softened when he learned about my goal. He told me about the responsibility of getting up at four am, seven days a week, and about the monetary potential as I quickly figured out how long it would take me to be a horse owner. He then convinced me that a savings account sponsored by the paper company was a good idea. It was supposed to be an early college fund, which was the farthest thing from my mind. All I knew was that this college fund was testing my youthful patience, and it would take me a little longer to get my horse.

Within the hour, I signed a paper carrier contract while Dad beamed, and Mom tried to conceal her concern.

Three months later, I heard about a Quarter Horse/Morgan mix who was no longer needed as a pony horse for the thoroughbreds at Turf Paradise racetrack. It was rumored that if nobody bought him, he would be auctioned off and more than likely sold into the pet food industry. With that information tugging at my heart, I went to see him. He was in the desert on the west side of Turf Paradise in a makeshift corral, situated under some mesquite trees. Down on his luck, his owner, or trainer was camping next to the corral.

That horse wasn't much to look at. His ribs were showing, and his mane and tail were matted, but the scars, scabs, and open wounds on his neck were what caught my attention. Then he looked at me with eyes that had a sadness to them, touching me in an unfamiliar, visceral way. He nuzzled up to me as if he was pleading for a new lease on life, and I knew at that moment I couldn't let him down.

As I gently ran my hand over his battered neck, his owner said, "They were collateral damage, bites from the high-spirited thoroughbreds that we're running."

"How much?"

He looked over at my dad and then turned to me with a sigh and a knowing nod, "He's yours for seventy-five-dollars."

I shook his hand, got a bill of sale, and thanked him, knowing I would've used my entire savings if I had to. But, as luck shined favorably on a kid with a dream, I had enough left to get the tack I needed.

"Dad, what should we name him?"

"That's on your shoulders, son. Don't worry. A name will come to you."

With the help of the neighborhood horse whisperer, Karen "Squeaky" Schillings, a self-professed cowgirl whose voice squeaked when she talked and seemed to know everything there was to know about horses. We nursed that horse back to health, applying a medicated salve morning and night. As he healed and packed on weight, he no longer plodded but pranced with his tail up, his neck arched, snorting and tossing his head, a real vision of power and beauty. I could scarcely believe he was the same horse.

He would follow me around like a big dog, and when he put on his beautiful silver winter coat, it had a smoky sheen that shimmered when the sun hit it just right. He must have noticed me watching him, because he walked over and playfully nuzzled me. I rubbed his forehead and looked him in the eye. "Hey, big guy, how's Smokey sound for your name?"

He bobbed his head like he knew what I was talking about. "All right, Smokey it is."

As usual, Squeaky had a pulse on everything related to horses, especially anything happening around the racetrack. She knew I needed tack and told my parents about an upcoming auction sponsored by the Western Saddle Club. Attending that auction was a little strange, as I was the youngest person in the smoke-filled room. People quit bidding once they realized that I was bidding on the same items, and I was able to get completely outfitted for less than $100.00. Within an hour, I was officially in the horse business and ready to ride.

The summer between fifth and sixth grade, I was a boy with a horse, and a long way from being an accomplished horseman, let alone a cowboy. But a lot can be done with determination and encouragement from parents who believe in you.

Over the next several months, I rode every chance I got, and by the time spring rolled around, I was a pretty good horseman. It had been a wet winter, and everything was green and blooming. Early one morning, when I rode into the desert, it came alive with the sound of songbirds, doves, and my favorite, the Gamble quail with its haunting mating cry.

I rode at a canter, wanting to cover some ground before the midday heat forced most animals to seek shelter. Riding as one, Smokey and I moved quickly through the Creosote bushes, avoiding the Jumping, Barrel, and Prickly Pear Cactus, as well as the Spanish bayonets and Ocotillo plants. Even with the dangers, the desert had a rugged beauty, filled with attention-getting flora and fauna. An inattentive misstep could get one pierced or poisoned, either guaranteed to put a damper on your day.

As we rode, dodging dangers, we passed a Palo Verde tree in full blossom that was buzzing with activity of a beehive. Smokey bolted as if something in that tree had bit him, and we were off at a full gallop within seconds. He seemed to scarcely notice the bit, as if his mouth had turned to stone. I pulled back on the reins and gave him the command to stop, but it was ineffective. I contemplated bailing, but quickly changed my mind when the cactus became a blur as we flew past.

We were out of control, and I began to panic as I envisioned us going down in a heap if he stepped into a prairie dog hole, maybe snapping a leg or, at the very least, tripping and catapulting us into the waiting thorns. Picking cactus out of our hides seemed inevitable.

I realized we were heading toward some cliffs on the banks of the Cave Creek Wash at breakneck speed, and a cold sweat ran down my back. Disaster was less than two football fields away, and Smokey wasn't responding to neck reining.

I knew I had to get him turned.

With adrenaline blasting through my system, I tugged on one rein with all my strength, turning his head so he could see me with his left eye and see where he was running with his right. His ears were pinned back, and his eye was full of sheer panic. Leaping over cacti and busting through the brush, we were quickly running out of real estate. Miraculously, somehow, we avoided all the snake holes and the shallow burrows of the prairie dog towns, barreling toward our personal buffalo jump and the river rock below.

Whether he tired of running with his head turned or he finally started to trust me remains a mystery, but we came to a dusty stop a mere fifteen feet before blasting through the last of the brush and launching into the rocks below.

I jumped off, glad to have my feet on solid ground, and exhilarated that I had a rocket for a horse. I accused him of trying to kill us both, but that only seemed to make matters worse. I began petting him and coaxing him in a steady voice. "Easy boy, easy."

His sides were heaving, his nostrils flaring, and he was snorting, but his ears were no longer pinned back, indicating that he was attentive and listening. When he calmed down, I wondered what it was about those bees that got him so spooked. Is it possible that animals suffer from some form of PTSD as well?

For the next four years, my day would begin at four am delivering papers. Feeding, grooming, and mucking out Smokey's corral were done before catching the bus to school. Then afterward, I'd head straight to football, basketball, or track practice, depending on the season. Mom would pick me up when I was finished.

No matter how my day went, Smokey was always there to greet me, showing off with his enthusiastic neighing and prancing around the corral. I petted and talked to him, and he listened as if he understood what I was saying. I'd muck out his stall and feed him before heading in to eat myself. After dinner, I'd do my homework and then turn in for the night, ready to do it all over again the next day.

During that first year, a neighborhood friend of mine had an unexpected litter of puppies sired by a very athletic German Shorthaired Retriever. In a scramble to find homes for the puppies, he asked me if I wanted one, and not one to turn down a good deal, I took one off his hands and named him Buckshot. He was built like his dad, with the mottled markings of a German Shorthaired Retriever; he also had the black and white coloring of his Australian Shepherd mom, along with one light blue eye and one brown eye. He was perfect.

When he was old enough, he went with me daily on my paper route. He hated to be left behind and would howl if he thought Smokey and I were going on a ride without him. The three of us were inseparable.

One day, we came across two hungry coyotes who took turns trying to lure my rambunctious pup, barely a year old, away from us. He would chase one off and come back to us, and then the other would come in just close enough that Buckshot had to give chase. For him, it was a game, and I thought it was funny until he came in dragging his tongue, and the coyotes were barely winded, both aggressively closing in on Buckshot with their teeth bared. I didn't know if we could close the distance in time, but Smokey seemed to sense the urgency, and when I reined him in their direction, yelling "Hah. Let's get 'em, Smoke." He rocketed toward them, scattering those coyotes as they ran with their tails tucked, barely out of reach of his thundering hooves. We circled back, and I loaded Buckshot on the saddle with me. Smokey pranced off as if he knew he had saved the day.

I built my paper route up to one of the biggest routes in Phoenix, earning me honors as paper carrier of the month and year. Many of my customers also became lawn-mowing clients in the summer, and the additional income allowed me to buy a horse trailer and help pay for veterinary and farrier bills.

Smokey, Buckshot, and I were the Three Amigos. We would ride out of our backyard into the desert, exploring the Cave Creek area where the coveys of quail would explode from underfoot by the hundreds. Smokey wouldn't bat an eye, but Buckshot would lose his mind trying to chase all the birds at once, but he always seemed to come back with a smile on his face.

We were living the dream, exploring the rugged desert in search of her many hidden treasures. Rides north of the Deer Valley Airport into the Carefree Valley were always fun, and occasionally, we would find a herd of javelina, wild pigs, that could disembowel a dog with the flash of a tusk. For the sake of all, we always gave them a wide birth. Often, I would spend hours sitting in the saddle watching planes take off and land, dreaming of what it would be like to fly with the freedom of a bird.

One of our adventures found us riding in the mountains around Flagstaff. Riding right up to a herd of elk or deer wasn't uncommon as they continued to feed undeterred by our four-legged presence. We fished Mary's Lake, Kinnikinic and Ashurst Lake, Mormon Lake, and Stoneman Lake. Oftentimes I fished from the back of Smokey, catching rainbow trout and monster pike on a regular basis while Buckshot waited patiently for us to drag the next fish on shore.

Our fourth year together was another adventure-filled summer until one dreaded Saturday. It started like any other day. Buckshot and I were up at four am, and we raced through my paper route, which covered roughly ten miles. Buckshot was an incredible athlete and in peak shape, every muscle rippling as he moved. He could easily jump our nine-foot block fence and would do so if a dog was in heat within smelling distance. This was a problem because having your dog neutered or spayed wasn't even an option, I was aware of, so I was forced to chain him up in the yard.

That morning, I clipped him into his tether and then fed Smokey, and I went back to bed; every fiber of my being was exhausted. I remember listening to Buckshot's barking and whining as he strained against his collar. It sounded as if he was choking, but I couldn't be sure if I was dreaming or not. Deep sleep overcame me, so I was startled when my mom shook me awake with tears streaming down her face. "Rick, you need to check on Buckshot."

I jumped out of bed, ran through the house, passing my distraught baby sister on my way out of the back door. The taught chain disappearing over the top of the fence and into the neighbor's yard was more than I could take; my legs buckled.

I got up and ran toward the wall with tears streaming from my face, yelling, "Nooo. Oh God, no." I scaled to the top of the fence and found my beautiful dog with his tongue hanging out and bloody streaks on the block wall where he had tried to scratch and claw his way back over, coming up short by an inch. I was too late; he was already starting to stiffen up. Overwhelmed with grief, I knew I had to give him a proper burial.

I immediately saddled up Smokey and laid Buckshot over his neck for one last ride into the desert. I buried him on top of a mountain overlooking our hunting grounds, saying some last words of gratitude for his friendship. I think God created dogs to show us what unconditional love is.

The ride home that day was the longest of my life. We were the Three Amigos no more. The whole family went up the mountain to pay their last respects the next day. It was pretty emotional as each family member reminisced about a favorite moment with Buckshot, and that's when my baby sister, overcome with guilt, apologized for lengthening his chain; she just wanted to give him more room to roam. She was only five, and to see her agonizing over the loss of a family member was more than I could bear. All I could do was hold her. "It was an accident, Sis. Everything is going to be all right."

Chapter 3

Growing Up

TRANSITIONING INTO HIGH SCHOOL was an anxious time, but my fears were eased as coaches and teachers made me feel at home. My freshman year was a blur. I continued to deliver papers at four am, took care of Smokey, went to school, and then to practice. Mom would pick me up every day and take me home so I could feed Smokey and muck his stall, eat dinner, finish my homework, and fall into bed exhausted, only to do it again the next day. I didn't have time to get in trouble, much less think about it. That year, I played football and basketball and ran track. I was getting burned out toward the end of basketball season and knew something had to give.

Time in the saddle with Smokey became less and less. School was getting more challenging, and sports demanded more of my time. Between Saturday morning practices and Sunday morning Church with the family, my weekend time riding Smokey was limited and unfair to him. It broke my heart, but I had to get out of the horse business. I sold my best friend to an Idaho outfitter running a trail-riding business in the Cave Creek area. When I said goodbye, I felt like I was letting Smokey down.

I didn't want to grow up.

I quit delivering the *Arizona Republic* once the sale was finalized, to dedicate more time and energy to the sports I had a growing passion for.

To this day, when I hear a creaking saddle or smell leather mixed with the musky aroma of a horse, I'm taken back to those childhood memories and the adventures we shared.

Within days of retiring as a paperboy, a papergirl who delivered the evening paper for The Phoenix Gazette disappeared, never to be found. This ultimately ushered out the last of the bicycling paperboys' era. Adults took over the routes, using their personal vehicles to deliver papers. Ironically, I later discovered that one of my customers had a son, Bob, who lived with his mom and was a few years my senior. Bob was arrested for committing twelve burglaries. While in prison, he heinously executed a fellow inmate, earning him the nickname Bob "Bonzai" Vickers in reference to the tactic used by the Japanese during the Pacific War. While I don't know all the extenuating circumstances leading up to his "Bonzai" attack, I was thankful that he always hung in the shadows when I collected payment from his mom.

WEST DIVISION
RICK HUBER
Rick Huber attends Deer Valley Junior High and is active in sports, student council and received the "all-around outstanding seventh grade boy" award this past year. The son of Mr. and Mrs. Richard Huber, Phoenix, Rick enjoys hunting, fishing and riding horses in his spare time. He has been carrying the paper over two years.

The summer following my freshman year, I attended an Alvin Adams & Paul Westphal basketball camp in Prescott, Arizona, and it was a dream come true to be instructed by members of the Phoenix Suns franchise. I remember being in awe of Alvin's height and grace. Paul's ball-handling skills were magical, and he was like a machine at the free-throw line. While blindfolded, Paul sunk ten free throws in a row, demonstrating what hard work and practice could accomplish. I was determined to be like them someday, but first, I had more pressing needs as I approached the legal driving age.

I knew without asking that if I wanted to drive anything but mom and dad's green Ford Station Wagon, I would have to get a job. As luck would have it, our parish priest got me a job as a hod carrier, working on the early stages of building St. Paul's Catholic Church. The night before my first day, my dad pulled me aside and gave me some advice, saying, "Son, do not stand around. Ask your boss what he would like done, and get it done correctly and as quickly as possible. Then keep asking him what else he would like done. Drive him nuts with the questions. Keep moving, and don't hang out at the water cooler."

Mom dropped me off the next day, and I marched over to the Job Trailer looking for the construction foreman. Russ Peterson, the owner of Sun Masonry, was a mountain of a man accustomed to hard work, with a rhino hide that had been bronzed from working countless seasons in the unrelenting Phoenix sun. I shook his hand and was shocked at his grip strength and how calloused his hands were. It felt like, without giving it much thought, he could have crushed my hand. He sized me up, and his look had me second-guessing how tough I really was. I certainly didn't feel as invincible as I had when I first walked through his door. He introduced me to his laborer and told me to shadow him and try to keep up with him if I could. Those first two weeks, I was so nervous working with a bunch of grizzled old guys that I didn't smile once. We would break for lunch, and I would devour two sandwiches, a bag of cut vegetables, and a banana to keep me from cramping, and these guys would smoke a bowl of opium or chase some speed down with a swig of Coke or Pepsi; it was their way of self-medicating so they could power through the evening despite chronic back, wrist, elbow, and shoulder pain.

All day long lifting an eight inch by eight inch by sixteen-inch slump block that weighed up to ninety pounds, was a great way to stay in shape for football, but I knew if I didn't take care of myself, it would cripple me. I didn't want to end up like them, but I marveled at their gruff humor. One of the lead block layers saw me crack a smile at one of his off-colored jokes and asked, "How old are you?"

"Fifteen," I responded.

"Fifteen," he bellowed. "I thought you were a natural-born killer the way you never smiled." I didn't dare tell him I was scared, but because they knew my age, I was forced to work extra hard to earn their respect. After a month, I received a check for my first two weeks of work.

Russ pulled me aside. "I bumped you up two dollars an hour. Keep up the good work."

I was now making eight seventy-five an hour. I was rolling in the dough, and none of my friends were making that kind of coin. I knew I was destined to get a sweet set of wheels soon. My aspirations were checked once again by unsolicited parental wisdom. My mom and dad wanted me to stay focused on school and athletics. They advised me not to get a vehicle for the upcoming school year so I wouldn't be burdened with insurance and maintenance costs. It made sound economic sense at the time, but it was the heavy dose of necessary patience that I struggled with. That summer, we finished the structural part of the Parish Hall and would have our first service there before Christmas. I knew this new building would give people a renewed spiritual opportunity, and everyone attending would be super excited. Imagine my surprise during the first Mass in the new building when I saw people showing up late, the guy next to me looking at his watch, parishioners going through the motions, looking more like zombies, showing no emotion, and not singing (the original lip singers).

Some were gazing out the window, failing to be present in the moment, and they were leaving before mass was over. Had our priest not been an excellent homilist, I could only imagine how much worse things could've been.

Nothing had changed, and our church was still full of hypocrites.

It was disappointing to realize that the building couldn't stir up some emotion, excitement, or gratitude, anything that would indicate a sincere desire to be there, a tangible change of heart instead of checking an obligatory box. Those changes would have to come from deep within, a revelation I was certain to learn the hard way.

Summer tryouts for football were still a couple of weeks away, and I still had time for one last adventure. All summer, my buddy, Earl, and I had been dreaming of escaping the heat and heading north into the mountains to do some trout fishing, so when this small window of opportunity presented itself, we jumped at it.

With youthful enthusiasm, we quickly devised a plan to ride our bikes from Phoenix to Lake Mary, just outside Flagstaff. My parents agreed to drive support and catch up to us with food and water. We set off on the one hundred and twenty plus mile journey at two am with youthful vigor to beat the heat. The cool breeze on our faces was invigorating as we flew down the empty streets, climbing steadily out of the Valley of the Sun toward Fountain Hills.

We made great time and were already past the turnoff to Roosevelt Lake on the Beeline Highway before the morning sun began torching the land, sending the temperature north of ninety degrees. The heat waves radiated off the pavement and played tricks on our eyes with mesmerizing vistas of standing water on the road, only to vaporize the closer we got. We were getting dangerously low on water as the temperature soared above one hundred and fifteen degrees, but we peddled on, hoping my parents would catch us soon to refill our water bottles for a third time.

As a desert-dweller, this was not the first time I had gotten behind on my hydration, so to pass the time and ease my misery, I began to fantasize about the cool water they would bring and how it would slake my thirst as it cooled me from the inside.

Our climb began in earnest on the Beeline, a narrow, winding, two-lane highway that rose from the desert of Fountain Hills to the pine-covered mountains of Payson and on up the Mogollon Rim.

I was in a zone, riding the six inches outside the white line, when a blaring horn from behind spooked me back into reality as a truck with a cab over camper shot past me. The overextended side view mirror clipped my left arm nearly causing me to pile up in the roadside cactus. It was then that I realized Earl was no longer behind me. I pulled over in the shade of a solo saguaro, nursing a newly earned raspberry on my left triceps, and waited for Earl. I heard plodding as Earl appeared from the bend below, pushing his bike with labored effort. Earl always had a flare for the dramatic, and when he reached me, he collapsed on the highway and curled up in the fetal position in total resignation. "I want my mommy."

"Dude, put on your big boy pants and get out of the road before you get run over!" I yelled as I dragged him and his bike to the shoulder.

The things Earl would do to make light of a situation always made me smile. His summer job in the pizza shop had not prepared him to endure such harsh conditions as mine had, and he hadn't trained as he had professed. We were seven miles short of riding into Payson when Dad pulled up and offered us a ride. Earl wholeheartedly agreed, refusing to go any farther before I could weigh in on the conversation. Admittedly, I don't think my butt could have taken any more time in the saddle. Wearing only lightweight running shorts left me with some undeniable saddle sores.

Seeing how stiff we were the following day, my parents suggested they would gladly shuttle us up the Mogollon Rim to Lake Mary. Earl and I were thankful it felt like their idea, and we didn't have to grovel. They dropped us off, and we packed our food, camping, and fishing gear into Dad's seventeen-foot Coleman aluminum canoe and headed across the lake into an evening squall. The wind quickly whipped the waves into three-foot high white caps, threatening to swamp us if we continued on our cross-lake course. We turned the bow into the wind, tacking slightly toward the opposing shore. The bow sliced through the oncoming waves, and the spray soaked us, but we never felt more alive.

We spent a week camping on the shore of a lagoon on the back side of the lake, feasting on the fish and crawdads we caught. There is something deeply satisfying about being able to not only survive but thrive in the wild. I often wondered if ancient man felt that same sense of satisfaction and if we weren't still hardwired the same somewhere in the deep recesses of our DNA. Perhaps then his satisfaction came solely from the essence of a full belly, but I have to think that at some point, he had to realize that he was pretty good at providing and, in doing so, stroked his ancient ego.

In my sophomore year of high school, I discovered girls, or maybe they discovered me. I don't know if it had anything to do with me being the starting quarterback on the JV team or getting moved up

Returning from a week long camping trip on calmer waters.

to varsity basketball, but it did amaze me how playing a game could attract so much attention. Playing basketball with guys three years my senior was a great challenge and much more physical. An errant elbow caught me square in the chin during the Christmas tournament, breaking my upper right canine so that it was barely hanging on by the enamel. With seconds left, I was fouled and sent to the free throw line for a one-on-one. We were down by one, and I had to make the first to tie the game. Our opponents called a time-out to ice me.

In the huddle, coach tried to distract me by making light of the pressure shot I was facing.

This is my chance to be like Paul Westphal, I thought.

I stepped up to the line, spun the ball in my hands, bounced it three times, swallowed a little blood, looked up, and stroked it, nothing but net. Another time-out was called. Coach was all smiles as he upped the ante and bribed me with an ice cream cone after the game. The place was going wild, but as I took the ball from the ref, everything went quiet; I wasn't aware of anyone else in the gym—just me, the ball, and the rim.

I swished the second shot.

Total pandemonium broke loose, and my team carried me off the court. Win or lose, there is no greater feeling than knowing you gave it your all, along with your brothers. I finished that game swallowing blood until it stopped bleeding. After the game, I smiled and pushed my tooth out with my tongue. Coach almost passed out.

He was also my biology homeroom teacher, and he knew that I had a crush on Robin Hale. He would always make a point to tell all the guys in the room to stay away from girls because they would give us weak knees. None of us were buying it, but I knew coach was trying to keep us focused.

Robin was a sweetheart. She was kind and had a super bubbly personality that rivaled her beauty. She was a cheerleader and way out of my league, but I asked her to the Sweetheart dance, and to my shock, she said, "Yes."

Elated as I was, sheer panic washed over me as I turned and walked away. I didn't know how to dance. I must have watched John Travolta in *Saturday Night Fever* and *Grease* a dozen times, trying to perfect those disco moves. I was oblivious to my rhythmic inadequacies, so I was failing horribly. Because nothing is sacred or secret in my family, once word got out that I had two left feet and no inherent rhythm, two of my aunts conveniently showed up. They turned on the music, and the kitchen dance lessons commenced. They taught me how to waltz, two-step, and jitterbug. All I had to do was take those short, choppy, jitterbug moves and make them smooth and flowing like Travolta.

Mom handed me a corsage and the keys to the family station wagon. I drove off with feigned self-assurance. I picked up Earl and his date before going by to get Robin. She lived in the very same highfalutin part of town where Alice Cooper lived.

For all the time I knew this part of town existed, it never occurred to me how differently people with money lived. However, it became painfully evident when I picked up Robin at her parent's Moon Valley Country Club estate, which I dubbed a castle. Robin was a princess, and she seemed excited when I opened the door of my humble green chariot for her. I was so self-conscious at that moment but shook it off and decided to make the best of it. The four of us went to dinner at a steakhouse where Earl managed to dump his mashed potatoes and gravy into his lap, momentarily revealing his nervousness despite his calm exterior persona.

I wasn't the best on the dance floor, but I held my own, and we had the time of our lives. As much as I cared for Robin, I knew I couldn't give her what she deserved or had grown accustomed to. We continued to be friends, and I remember the pain I felt when I saw her drive out of the Thunderbird High School parking lot with some college guy who had a new sports car. That was the moment I knew I needed to break free from the middle class, and sports could be my ticket out.

The summer after my sophomore year, I bought my first truck, a used, red Mazda pickup with a rotary engine and manual transmission. It was a great work truck and perfect for getting me from point A to point B, which is what I needed it to do when I started to work for Sun Masonry again. I would work all day, then go to open gym at Thunderbird and play full-court basketball games until they kicked us out. On nights when there wasn't an open gym, we would close the parks down, playing full-court games with some of the best high school and college talent in the valley. The only rule; "No Blood, No Foul." It was like playing tackle football with no pads. My band of brothers could hold our own on most nights. We even had some ASU football players who wanted to hustle us for beer money, and that's when things got really serious.

One of them laid me out with the hardest pick I'd ever endured. One second, I was running full speed across the key, looking for a lob pass, and the next second, I was bounced out of the lane like I had hit a wall. I landed flat on my back, wondering what truck hit me. After I got my breath back, we outhustled them, never letting them get a solid piece of us again. They reluctantly paid up, but that didn't matter to us as we had just beaten some legit college athletes.

Pre-season football started in August, and the heat and humidity would take its toll. It was a suffer-fest for those who didn't take their conditioning seriously. There was a lot of retching and puking on the sidelines as bodies were pushed to their limits. The heat never bothered me after working all summer, and it felt good to run and stretch my legs. Honestly, practice felt like a vacation compared to what I had endured at work. After earning a starting position, I turned my attention to academics, reestablishing old friendships and creating new ones.

People-watching has always been one of my favorite pastimes. I love it. They come in all shapes and sizes from various socio-economic backgrounds, and somehow they connect. Sometimes, those connections are lasting and very meaningful. I believe they are more than mere coincidence. I experienced such a situation in an elective PE class called Systematics. It was an exciting class where you could explore different sports, from weightlifting to tennis. Most kids thought it was an opportunity to get an easy physical education credit.

One such student was John, a senior, who was taking it at his counselor's suggestion. John had a permanent scowl and was facing suspension for knocking two students out for looking at him the wrong way. He was built like a tank and used the weightlifting segment of the class to establish himself as an alpha amongst his peers. While I took notice, I chose not to associate with him because of his reputation as a troublemaker, and my coaches made it very clear that we were to lead by example, academically and socially, or run the risk of being kicked off the team. John and I kept our distance from each other. We casually acknowledged each other, but nothing more—until the wrestling segment where we all learned about different wrestling moves. For the final class grade, we had to wrestle with the person Coach matched us up with. I hoped to be matched with one of my friends; however, I began to panic a little when I realized Coach's strategy for pairing us up. When John and I were the only ones left, Coach moved to the center of the mat and announced, "And for the final wrestle-off, we have Rick and John."

I looked at Coach and thought, *Coach, what were you thinking? There's a reason my nickname is Rick the Stick. He's got me by twenty pounds, and he's a senior.*

Nobody else's match lasted more than three minutes, and with thirty minutes left in the class, my day of reckoning was upon me. I would have to use my tall, lanky frame to my advantage. I would spread out knowing leverage was my friend. During the match, John spent a tremendous amount of energy trying to roll me onto my back, and it became a test of will as neither of us would give in to being pinned. Just as one of us was about to pin the other, we would dig deep and find just enough energy to pull off a reversal. We fought for control, not understanding the depths of stubborn pride engrained in our DNA. We wrestled until the end of class, and every muscle fiber felt as if it were made of lead. Coach called it a draw. We both rolled onto our backs, gasping for air as classmates dragged us off the mat. I had never been so tired in my life. When I looked at John and smiled, I knew our fledgling friendship had been bonded in mutual respect.

Our friendship grew over the next couple of years, and I realized just how significant a father's influence could be when developing character. My whole life, I took for granted the value of having a dad who loved me and wanted to be involved in my life. John did not have this anchor in his life, which was catastrophic for his childhood. My dad recognized this deficit in John's life and filled in as best he could, becoming that anchor for John at a crucial time.

One evening, we were playing a friendly basketball game called Horse, and John was busting out his latest trick shot to even the score when Mom yelled from the front door, "Dinner's ready, and John, you're more than welcome to join us."

We quickly hustled in, cleaned up, and joined the rest of my family at the table. We all bowed our heads, and my dad led us in a blessing. Halfway through the blessing, I snuck a peek at John to see what he was doing. He was wide-eyed, looking around as if he were having an out-of-body experience. After eating, he thanked my parents, and as we walked out the door to resume our game of Horse, he whispered, "That was different."

His family rarely gathered at the same table while he was growing up, and saying grace (blessing before a meal) was something he had never experienced.

Over time, as John opened up about his past, I would shake my head in disbelief.

How many other guys like him are out there who have never had a chance?

For starters, he had been expelled from South Mountain High School for fighting and was allowed to live with his uncle, who lived in the Thunderbird District. Living under his uncle's roof came with a set of rules. He had to stay out of trouble, maintain good grades, and hold a job. He wasn't familiar with accountability, but there was something deep within him that wanted more out of life.

What that was continued to escape him. John grew up fighting because that was encouraged by his dad. For example, when his dad saw a kid of color walking down their street, he would drop everything, round up his boys, and ask, "Who wants to earn some ice cream?"

He would point his children in the direction of the intruding kid of color and say, "Teach that kid that it's not okay to walk down our street." Then he rewarded them by taking them to the local Dairy Queen. On other occasions, he would load the boys up in the back of his truck and drive the alleys in various subdivisions, scouring people's backyards for anything of value. The boys would signal him to stop by beating on the cab's roof. They would then take turns jumping over the fence and throwing anything that wasn't bolted down to their waiting brothers. It would take them less than thirty minutes to get a good load, which they took to "Park and Swap" and sold their loot while their dad went to the local tavern. The boys ran the risk of a beating if they hadn't sold everything when he returned at closing time.

John buckled down and did as his uncle requested. He rode his bike to school, and after he would ride to Denny's, where he would close the restaurant down, working an eight-hour shift washing dishes. Somehow, he managed to attend my home football games, where you could hear him cheering above the crowd. He told me he lived vicariously through me when I was on the field. We both knew that if things were different, he would have been out there with me, and we would have been unstoppable.

Thunderbird High missed out on the inherent talent of a real hard-nosed, tough guy. Through it all, John managed to keep his grades up, and just when it was wearing on him, he saw the girl of his dreams on campus and vowed that he would give her the life she deserved. John would ride his bike the ten miles to her house to visit until he had saved enough money for his first car. He was so proud when he showed up to school in that orange AMC Gremlin Hatchback.

John would often come over to my house during the summer, wanting to play basketball or go fishing. On one occasion, he came over, and I was busy painting our fence. I felt a little like Tom Sawyer when I convinced him that two sets of hands could finish the task quicker. Reluctantly, he agreed, and we proceeded to paint together. We would pass the time by telling stories of memorable exploits and dream about future adventures. Before our friendship, there was a stark contrast when we spoke about our past experiences. He would look at me as if I had led an unusually sheltered life, but I could tell he was a bit envious as he told me what normal was for him. He told me about his dad, who bragged about hiding under dead bodies to survive the oncoming Vietcong while serving in Vietnam. His dad knew how to work the system and bragged about the months of free rent he could get until the sheriff evicted them. John told me about camping at Lake Pleasant, north of Phoenix, and having to shake the scorpions out of his shoes and bathe in the lake twice a month.

I would ask, "How did you guys afford food?"

John said, "We would go to a scrap yard in Black Canyon City under the cover of night, where we would meet other families. Our parents would talk while the smaller kids would break down whatever was in the big bags and put it in smaller bags. The older kids were responsible for weighing and writing the weights on each bag. When we were done, we would go our separate ways."

In disbelief, I would comment about his dad's ethics or lack thereof, and that's when he would say with a feigned boastful air, tempered with a degree of disappointment, "That's nothing. Wait till you hear this one."

John began his next story. "The summer before we were evicted, my dad noticed the neighbor working in his backyard garden. When the plants began to leaf out, my dad would sneak into the garden in the dead of night and spray a little bleach on the leaves. It wasn't enough to kill them, but enough to make the leaves turn brown. When he saw his neighbor looking over his garden with concern, he would casually stroll over and make small talk until the neighbor would mention the mysterious brown spots or withered leaves on his plants. Dad would say, 'I saw that a lot over in 'Nam, and I know just what to do for it.' With a concerned look, he would return to his garage and act like he was mixing a special concoction for this brown leaf rot. He would combine the contents of several unidentifiable bottles of water into a gallon jug and charge his neighbor twenty dollars. If the neighbor continued to use his product, his plants would recover. But, as soon as the gardener thought his plants were cured and stopped buying the product, the rot would mysteriously appear again."

I would shake my head, disgusted at the dishonesty and lack of integrity. Simultaneously, I would marvel at his dad's sheer creativity. If only he would have channeled that creativity into something positive.

While most of John's siblings preferred incarceration over life in the real world, John continued to distance himself from that life and ended up marrying his high school sweetheart before enlisting in the Army. There, he became a Culinary Arts Expert, creating fanciful, delectable delights for the upper brass. After an honorable discharge, he was phenomenally successful in the insurance industry.

My junior year was a fun and successful season, playing on the varsity football and basketball squads. My most memorable game in football was against the Paradise Valley Trojans. All the coaches warned us about one of their star players, Dave Pasanella, a senior running back. They stressed that if we wanted to win, we would have to swarm tackle Dave as he was the Teenage Power Lifting Champ of the Nation. At age seventeen, Dave could squat 575 pounds, deadlift 545, and bench press 340. He weighed 220 pounds and was rumored to have thighs the size of Earl Campbell, who played for the Houston Oilers. He was an animal with the running style of Larry Zonka, a fullback for the Miami Dolphins, who would just as soon run over you as around you.

That particular game was the Trojans Homecoming. We executed our game plan perfectly on defense for the first three quarters, with at least six guys involved in every tackle where Dave was carrying the ball. We were like locusts flying to the ball. We were shutting them out 14-0 until the final minutes in the fourth quarter when

Dave rallied his team and began running with a vengeance. He was determined not to be shut out on their home field. With time running out, they were poised to punch it in from the fifteen-yard line. The play was a handoff to Dave, and he ran my way. My job as an outside linebacker/defensive end was not to lose containment. I was required to force the run to the inside so that we would make a "Dave sandwich" between myself and my inside support (middle linebackers and defensive linemen). My inside help never came. As I strung Dave out, he turned up field with a full head of steam, running a little upright and carrying the ball with both arms, cradling it against his chest. I took a couple of steps forward and met him in the backfield. I planted my facemask on the cradled ball.

Holy Crap!

It was like I had just hit a Mack truck; I felt every vertebra in my spine pop, and I was driven to my knees. Dave's forward momentum stopped cold, and the ball squirted into the air. After a mad scramble, we recovered the ball, cementing our victory in a shutout. The visiting stands erupted in wild celebration. As I came running off the field, one of the assistant coaches met me on the sideline and screamed above the crowd's roar, "Son, that is one of the finest high school games I have ever seen any kid play."

He gave me the shirt off his back, and I still have that shirt to this day.

We began to gel as a team during my second year of varsity basketball. We won most of our games and made it to the playoffs. Midway through the season brought a unique challenge for us as we were scheduled to play our archrivals, the Greenway Demons, and, in particular, their six-foot, eleven-inch center, Brad Lohaus. The game plan was simple. I was to keep Brad out of the key at all costs. I had to play the defensive game of my life, always staying one step ahead of him, blocking every route into the paint, and forcing him to take a lower percentage shot from the outside. It worked brilliantly, and we held the lead for the entire game. While this was our Homecoming game, and our fans were as loud as ever, there was not a soul on either side of the court that wasn't anticipating a spectacular dunk from Brad as he had given us an incredible demonstration of his repertoire in the pre-game warm-up. Toward the end of the third period, Greenway stole the ball and lobbed it to Brad on a mid-court breakaway. He had five steps on me, but I was determined not to let him show off at our house. I sprinted the court and elevated as he launched for a "Tomahawk dunk." I pinned my elbow against the rim for leverage and slammed the ball and Brad to the floor. He landed on his back and bounced, momentarily knocking the wind out of himself. I checked him to ensure he was okay, then looked into the roaring fans and saw my football team going crazy with the high fives and fist pumps.

This is absurd; this is supposed to be just a game.

But deep down, my ego was getting stroked once again, and I was starting to like it. The next game against the Greenway Demons was on their home court, which resulted in our loss by a narrow margin. Brad's teammates did an exceptional job with the pick and roll, lobbing to Brad inside the key where he was unstoppable. Brad was a McDonalds All-American and then went on to play for the University of Iowa before the Boston Celtics drafted him.

I trained harder than ever the summer before my senior year. My day would begin at five am with a three-mile run to the Thunderbird High School Stadium, where I would meet a basketball teammate, Don Webber, then do a mile and a half of two hundred and twenty-yard sprints followed by three sets of twenty "stadiums." One set consisted of hopping twenty times with one leg to the top of the stadium and then repeating with the other leg, then twenty times on both legs. We would finish the workout by running home. Don and I played open gym basketball every day and even played in a couple of summer leagues in the evenings. When I wasn't playing ball, I was running North Mountain, Shaw Butte Mountain, and Squaw Peak Mountain with forty pounds of tire chains in a daypack. On weekends, I would add sprints in the sandy sections of Cave Creek and then push my truck around the block while my cousin Bob steered. My standing vertical increased six inches that summer, and I could run without effort and not tire. Dunking from a stationary two-foot takeoff was now part of my game.

One particularly hot and humid summer day, we were scheduled for a game in Shadow Mountain's Gym. Their team showed up in force, and the only ones that showed from our team were me and our point guard, Don Webber. Faced with a forfeit since we didn't have a minimum number of four players, we recruited our cousins, who had tagged along to watch the game. Neither of our cousins was in shape to play a full-court game, and on top of that, my cousin was asthmatic, so we devised a plan for them to work the defensive side of the court while Don and I ran the full court. After several quick pulls on his inhaler, my cousin Bob stepped onto the court with a determined look, and I knew we could count on him. He had been faced with asthma-related issues most of his life, but there was no quit in his game. Don and I outran our opponents, and we shot the lights out. Our hard work paid dividends as we could elevate the same on every jump shot, giving us the same consistent release every time. It didn't hurt that we were both in a zone and playing the game of our lives; almost every ball we put up went through the net. We won that night and walked out of the gym, giving congratulatory high-fives to our cousins as the opposing coach had a butt-chewing session with his players. To this day, Bob relives that game as if it were yesterday.

Coach Clark had stepped down as head football coach from Tulane University and accepted a head coaching position at Thunderbird High. We were very fortunate to have someone with his experience and love of the game leading our program. He recruited me to play quarterback, knowing that I had a rifle for an arm. He said I reminded him of a guy named Elway who was playing at Stanford. At that time, I didn't know who Elway was, but I was willing to play whatever position it took to win. Our receivers had a tough time catching what I was slinging. The ball would whistle, hit them in the hands, and bounce off their chest pads or face masks. Coach insisted that I continue to throw with heat, and he would find someone that could catch it. It didn't pan out. After re-evaluating our personnel, coach had me play tight end, outside linebacker, and all special teams. Any passing I got to do was reserved for trick plays and long yardage.

My senior year was a blur. Every game brought more attention from colleges expressing interest. Senator John McCain sent me an appointment letter to the Naval Academy to play football; this piqued my interest until I found out my eyesight didn't qualify me to fly fighter jets. Flying with uncorrected vision of 20/225 wasn't something the military was willing to entertain, especially at those speeds and pulling G-forces with an aircraft north of sixty-six million, that was 1980 prices. It was a major inconvenience when I would get a contact lens knocked out of my eye on the field and would have to go to the sideline to pop in a spare, so I understood their concern regarding my eyesight. There was no room for error, but it didn't sit well with me being told that I couldn't do something because of a physical disability.

Playing through pain was inherent to playing the game, and my senior year was plagued by minor, annoying injuries. Two dislocated big toes (Turf Toe), a sprained finger, and a sprained neck were just collateral damage for playing a game you loved. The worst was when I contracted ten plantar warts on the bottoms of my feet. Apparently, that virus thrives in warm, moist locations like locker rooms, and I unwittingly caught them walking barefoot in the showers. It was as if they strategically manifested in an area where the cleats on my football shoes pressed on the soles of my feet. Every step was painful, but if you want to play, you must train yourself to ignore and override the pain.

Overall, high school made me feel like I had a charmed life. Girls were actually showing interest in me, and I even got to date some absolute sweethearts. My grades were excellent, I was nominated Homecoming King, and we made it to the state playoffs in football. I earned Arizona All-State and All-Star honors and was invited to play in the North vs. South All-Star Game at the NAU dome at the end of the school year. None of my successes would have been possible without the ten other guys on the field, doing their best on every play. Life was good, and I was looking forward to the upcoming basketball season where I hoped to make an even bigger impact.

Since the playoffs had extended the football season, I only had one week to practice with the basketball team before our first game, and it became apparent that the warts on my feet were getting worse, and I didn't think I could tough it out the rest of the season. Surgery was scheduled, and they had to scrape the growths from around my bones, leaving some gaping holes. The doctor assured me they would close up with time. I missed the first three games of the season before coach asked me if I thought I could play despite not being able to practice. I agreed to give it a try. He taped half-inch thick pads to the soles of my feet, and we decided he would use me only if he needed me. Coach tapped me shortly after the opening tip-off. I played a solid quarter before I felt the wounds open from the quick starting, stopping, and pivoting. I could feel my socks getting wet. I looked down to see blood squirting out of the breathing holes in my shoes. By this point, my footsteps were leaving a trail of blood on the court. This forced the refs to call a timeout to clean the floor. We narrowly lost that game, and our season was off to a dismal start. With each game we came up short, I knew my scholarship opportunities would diminish. After each game, like any good leader, Coach praised our work ethic and perseverance. Then he turned white as a ghost and wretched involuntarily when he cut the tape and pulled the pads out of the craters in my feet. I never did get back to my summer form. We went on to have a winning season and made the playoffs, but we fell short of what I had hoped and dreamed for. Don would go on to play basketball at the next level without me.

In the spring of 1981, I opted not to run track and got a job at Waldo Pepper's Pizza Company for extra spending money and to help maintain my Ford Grand Torino. It was a muscle car that loved to guzzle fuel and smoke tires at the slightest hint of lead in my size thirteen foot. Spring break was in April. While most of my friends were on vacation with their families, I hustled to earn a buck, making pizzas and delivering them for tips. I worked with a guy named Allen, who was going to ASU and studying to be a pilot. He was a full-time student who worked part-time and washed planes at Deer Valley Airport to earn flight time. We were both closing the restaurant, hustling through our cleaning duties while jamming to "Free Bird" by Lynyrd

Skynyrd, dreaming of a future with unlimited possibilities.

I was on top of one of the tables doing a guitar solo with my broom when I got the call from my dad that my cousin, who was a freshman at my high school, had been hit by a car and wasn't long for this world. If I wanted to say goodbye, I had better get to the hospital soon. In shock, I dropped everything and broke some land speed barriers as I let that Torino roar to life. I ran into the hospital just in time to hear the attending physician tell my aunt that Andy was brain dead and that we should say our final goodbyes. My aunt's hysterical wailing haunted me as we filed past the remnant of my cousin, saying our last goodbyes.

He had been riding home from school when an inattentive driver struck him. The driver continued to drag Andy until he became lodged in the wheel well, crushing the base of his skull. The sadness was gut-wrenching as I tried to make sense of it all. He was an incredibly talented kid who was already sparking interest from the Professional Soccer League. Where was the fairness? Why do bad things happen to good people? I struggled with the sheer weight of the moment. The funeral was a somber occasion. While it was sad that a gifted kid's life was cut short, somehow it didn't seem like a "goodbye," but more like "until we meet again."

A week later, Allen approached me at work, and in an effort to lift my spirit, he asked me if I'd be interested in going for a ride in an open cockpit bi-wing stunt plane called the Red Baron. Allen had been washing that plane in exchange for flight time, and he'd gotten permission to fly out of Deer Valley Airport. I agreed with youthful vigor, never once entertaining caution. I'll never forget that brisk spring morning, walking out on the tarmac, putting on a leather helmet, goggles, and a headset with a microphone. I settled into the front seat and strapped on the shoulder harness and waist belt. Allen gave me a quick run-down on how to use the stick and we were off. As we climbed from the airport, he gave me one last bit of advice, "Let me know if you need to puke, and I'll take it easy on you."

I fired into the mic, "Bring it on, I'm game." I momentarily second-guessed my level of bravado as we rocketed straight up into the air, my back pressing deep into the seat cushion, and my cheeks pulled back toward my ears. His first attempt at making me sick was the Hammerhead maneuver. This is accomplished by flying the aircraft vertically to near stall speed, which results in a feeling of weightlessness. The aircraft is then pushed forward and rolled so the nose points straight down. Now, you are free-falling, gaining speed with every second. I had to scrunch down so the windshield would shield me from the buffeting wind. I could sense the glee in Allen's eyes and that mischievous grin as he called out the different maneuvers from his position in the rear seat as if I knew what to anticipate. We descended down, down, down. It felt perilously close to the ground when Allen finally pulled up at the last second, sling-shotting us into a double loop-to-loop. I wondered if our wings would hold up under the stress. He put us into a dizzying amount of barrel rolls and then combined the barrel rolls with the loop-to-loop. As the coup de gras, we went into an inverted loop, and at the apex, so much blood flowed into my head that it felt as if I was going to black out. After a couple more inverted loops, we dove down, leveled off, and flew back toward the airport in the CAP (California Arizona Project) canal (before they filled it with water). There was scarcely two feet clearance between the wing tips and the concrete banks of the canal. Back on the ground, there were a lot of high fives and adrenaline-laced gratitude for the experience of being able to fly with the eagles. This was also mixed with a bit of sorrow, knowing I could never fly fighter jets. Maybe someday I'll be able to go for a ride-along.

Out of all the schools that showed interest in me playing football at the next level, I opted to sign a letter of intent with NAU since they had one of the top ten forestry programs in the nation. Yes, I wanted to be "Ranger Rick" and hedge my bets in case football didn't pan out, as a career-ending injury was always in the back of my mind. It was surreal when NAU's head football coach, Dwain Painter, and his defensive coordinator met my parents in our living room. He explained the football program, touting the school's academics, and reassured my parents that I was in good hands. My parents watched proudly as I signed that letter of intent, shook hands with the coaches, and agreed to show up a month early for pre-season practice. They told me they would be at the All-Star game on their way out the door. Nothing like a little extra pressure.

I loved it.

The All-Star game brought the best players from across the state to showcase their talent. We had a two-week training camp to prepare us for the big game. The first day of practice was a brief meet and greet with all the players and the coaching staff. The head coach, Coach Putman, introduced himself and all the assistant coaches, saying, "I'm Coach Putman…"

One of the players leaned over and whispered, "I think his nickname is Tiny."

I instantly liked him because he was sincere and respectful and was anything but "Tiny." He was a mountain of a man, measuring six feet six inches, and weighing three hundred plus. His stature commanded attention, but his genuine love for the players and straightforward approach to the game commanded respect. He informed us that we had much to do in the next two weeks before we were ready to play as a team. He said, "Football teams are not about great players, but teams that play great. Now check into your dorms and report back in one hour suited up for full contact drills. It's our way of getting to know you." Talk about putting egos in check—we hit the ground running. After two weeks of full contact, two-a-day practices, and countless hours of skull sessions, we were as prepared as possible before playing the South All-Stars.

Just before we left the locker room for the big game, Coach Putman huddled us up and told us, "Win or lose, <u>ALWAYS</u> play your best. Now go have some fun." Even though we lost a close game, I had the time of my life. I caught a touchdown pass from our quarterback Trent Hutchinson, had a bunch of tackles on defense, and even made several tackles on Vance Johnson, the South's star running back. Vance would go on to play for the Denver Broncos and was a part of the infamous "Three Amigos." I didn't learn until later what a genuinely humble and good-hearted man Coach Putman was. When he was younger, he was drafted into the Army and served in Korea.

After that, he was a fifth-round draft pick for the New York Giants and played with Frank Gifford, Tom Rote, Tom Landry (a player/coach), and Vince Lombardi (an assistant coach at the time). He believed people were good and always strived to improve young men by using football to help us discover ourselves. His motto was, "Winning was a bonus," as character building was his main reason for coaching. Coach Putman understood his players and had an innate ability to recognize their inherent strengths and how to motivate each individual to be his best. He really was a mountain of a man, especially in ways that matter, and the guys loved him. You couldn't ask for a better role model.

At the end of summer, my parents took the family on one last vacation to my grandparent's cabin on Mormon Lake before I had to report to training camp. The cabin was just thirty minutes from the NAU campus, but it was worlds away at the same time. We did some hiking. We explored the bat caves hidden in the cliffs on the lake's western side and fished every day. We ate a lot of what we caught, and my grandma, one of the best cooks I've ever known, would always prepare a delectable meal with whatever we brought home. I always felt absolute satisfaction in being able to contribute to feeding my family with what I could harvest from nature.

As luck would have it, the folks at Mormon Lake Lodge were sponsoring a fishing tournament. Once I caught wind of the competition, I knew I had to recruit my baby sister to enter with me. She is one of the luckiest people I know, and I'm confident she inherited my grandma's love of fishing. We fished hard that day and ended up with the heaviest stringer. We won some money and lodging, but more importantly, we shared a memory and a love for fishing that I still have with me today.

Dad had to get back to work, so the plan was for my grandparents to drop me off at NAU the following day. After a brief goodbye and some final words of encouragement, Mom and Dad loaded the family into the car. As they pulled away, arms stuck out of every window waving goodbye, with my dad honking the horn and my mom yelling, "Don't forget to write."

I watched their car until they disappeared from sight. I was excited, but a little nervous about this next chapter in my life, and at the same time, it felt like a part of me was driving away with them.

My grandparents dropped me off in the Tinsley Dorm parking lot with all my worldly possessions: a trunk and a duffel bag filled with clothes, a hot plate, some eating utensils, and a few cooking utensils. As the last of my family drove away, I remember feeling a little homesick, but I didn't have time to dwell on it since I had to get settled into my dorm and get to the Skydome for orientation by high noon. Walking onto the field as an official NAU Lumberjack was exhilarating. While mingling with some of the players I met during my recruiting trip, I overheard some grizzled veterans voice their concerns while looking at us rookies. One shouted with disdain in his voice, "What did coach do, sign a bunch of basketball players?"

I had a tempered air of bravado and thought, *I don't know what you're talking about; I'm six four and one hundred and ninety-five pounds with a thirty-two-inch waist and six percent body fat. I'm a lean, mean fighting machine.*

Little did I know that I had a lot of room for improvement and that a diet of meat and potatoes and a serious weightlifting regimen would pack on an additional thirty pounds of lean muscle. I refused any "Power Packets" they handed out to players who wanted to maximize their performance. Our coaches didn't consider you in good football shape until you could bench press twice at the end of a workout, at least one hundred pounds over your body weight, and squat two hundred pounds over your body weight. The coaches discouraged athletes from performing a one-time max weight repetition out of concern that guys would blow out a shoulder or knee. With a proper diet and an elevated intensity in the gym, I achieved those goals in less than three months. The meals at our training tables were glorious, especially for those of us who were on the skinny side. I had only experienced feasting like this on special occasions, not on a daily basis. Bulking up was awesome, but it destroyed my accuracy with a basketball. As it happens, the linebacker coach advised me against trying out for the basketball team. If I got hurt playing basketball, it could jeopardize my scholarship. His concern was more than a little ironic, especially since he coached us to "take people out." We would work on proper tackling technique daily with him barking, "I want you to stick him with your face mask in his solar plexus, wrap him up, drive your head up his sternum into his chin. Lift him and plant him in the ground."

I had this done to me during practice, and even at half speed, it would leave a raspberry on my chest. Bumps and bruises, cuts and scrapes, and even an occasional broken bone or dislocation are inherent to the game. I was conflicted about the game I loved when the coach continued teaching us how to make the highlight reel with a sensational "Decleater tackle" (a violent tackle that intends injury). I continued to practice these techniques with respect for my coaches and an understanding they were paying for my education. So, I resolved to play hard and never intentionally take out one of my brothers; a brotherhood is exactly what we were. There was no room for prejudice of any kind if we were to be a cohesive team with winning as our singular goal. Every play required each player to execute their responsibility flawlessly. If someone missed their assignment, the play would fail. Enough missed assignments, and you would lose a game or, even worse, set someone up for a career-ending injury. I have an indelible memory of a missed assignment during a game where the fullback missed his kick-out block on the strong safety as the safety came torpedoing in with reckless abandon. He broke up the play just as our pulling guard planted his foot and turned up field to seal off the middle linebacker. In that horrible instance, an audible crack could be heard above the roar of the crowd. A direct hit from the safety's helmet blew our guard's knee straight back. As our guard tried to get up, his lower leg swung in unnatural directions as if his skin was the only thing holding the leg together. This vision reaffirmed a guttural instinct that this highly recruited senior's career was over. All those years of intense training were vaporized in a flash. Seeing that event reinforced the daily risk of playing a game we loved. This Decleater culture was common in Pro football at the time. It was secretly incentivized with lucrative bonuses.

It took a while, but the practice was eventually banned.

Another leap in football safety was the new concussion protocol, which was ushered in 2011. This advance has gone a long way in ensuring the safety of players. Gone are the days when guys were compelled to play through the pain of having their bell rung and suffering from CTE (Chronic Traumatic Encephalopathy). Blacking out and choking back the puke with each additional hit was something you endured to gain respect amongst your peers and coaches. There is nothing worse than gutting it out with an intense headache and nausea, trying to focus so you can see straight, to prove how tough you were. I remember one head-to-head collision that literally knocked the snot out of me and left me with a bent face mask. Seeing stars and willing myself to get back up on wobbly legs as the other guy blinked a couple of times, shook his head to clear the cobwebs, and said, "Good hit."

Then we wobbled back to our separate huddles. One of my teammates asked if I was okay. "I'm good."

"Then clean the snot off your grill."

We used to joke that we were modern-day gladiators and thankful that we didn't have to fight to the death. One coach used to profess with a psychopathic stare, "This game is organized chaos and war in a controlled environment." While there was a degree of truth in his statement, I was still a little surprised. *Wow, I thought it was just a game.*

We struggled, winning a little more than half our games that first year, mainly because we were a young team. While nobody likes losing, there was hope in the air as we all knew we would only get better as we matured and grew as a team. Before the end of the fall term, Coach Painter pulled us together in a team meeting and told us to schedule our spring classes early in the morning so we could practice during the evenings. We all complied, and the entire coaching staff was fired before we started spring ball. The new coach came in from Cal Poly, reassuring fans and boosters that; "His players were students before athletes." During our first team meeting, he told us there would be two-a-days during spring practice, and all were expected to attend. This schedule change meant I would have to skip my morning classes, rely on friends' notes, and work with the instructor to schedule make-up exams. My grades started to fall, and panic set in. I began attending classes and skipping morning practice. That didn't last long, and Coach Joe called me into his office. He said, "Rick, I expect you to be at morning practice, and if you need me to talk to your teachers, I will."

I responded, "Coach, these are the classes that are in my major and the reason I had decided to attend NAU in the first place. And besides, you're the one who said we were students before athletes."

He replied, "Look son, this is a business I'm running, and everyone on the team is making this sacrifice."

Immediately, the hair on the back of my neck stood on end. I could hear my dad saying, "Just because everyone else is jumping off the cliff doesn't mean you need to."

I walked out of his office and into an unknown future. My mind was made up, I knew I wasn't going to play for that guy. I quickly learned that NCAA rules prohibited players from transferring from one university to another without sitting out a year. This was to keep coaches from stacking their teams. This dose of reality was a real gut check, and I began to second-guess my decision. My aspirations and everything I had worked so hard for seemed to be ending abruptly.

I had grown up in a family environment where integrity was ingrained, and your word was gold. Real anger began to course through my veins for the first time in my young life as the reality of this betrayal set in. Fortunately, news travels fast, and I received a call from Ken Stites, the Head Coach of the Phoenix College Bears.

He informed me that he had a scholarship for me and insisted that I could play for him and meet the NCAA requirements since they were a Junior College. Coach Stites had a real knack for lifting guys up and helping them become the best versions of themselves, both on and off the field. He was a real players' coach. His players loved him and would go to extremes to play for him. The ultimate example was played out each game by our middle linebacker, Scott. He had two bad shoulders that the trainers would wrap and strap so he couldn't lift his arms above shoulder height, minimizing the potential for dislocation. Inevitably, he would walk back to the huddle several times a game with one or both shoulders hanging in unnatural positions. He would have that familiar grimace on his face, where you are mentally trying to transcend the pain, and asked if we could pop his shoulder back in so he didn't have to leave the game. We would grab an arm, sometimes both simultaneously, and give it a firm, quick downward tug. The relief was instantaneous, and he would proceed to call the next play with all of us marveling at his sheer grit. It inspired us to push past preconceived limitations.

We made the playoffs that year. There was a three-way tie for first place, and during the final game, our opponents threatened to score. Their quarterback was picking our secondary apart. Coach called a stunt and sent the two outside backers. The fullback had consistently tried to take my knees out with chop blocks—this time, I anticipated it and, at full speed, dove over him into the back of the QB as Jersey Joe, the other stunting linebacker, hit him in the chest. The crunch was audible over the roar of the crowd. He crumpled to the ground as if his legs were noodles. Everyone took a knee as the paramedics rushed to his aid and began to work quickly to stabilize his head and get him strapped to a board as the ambulance drove onto the field. They loaded him up and hauled him off. We went back to playing the game but with less reckless abandon. I couldn't shake the thought that I had possibly ended a brother's career. We never heard how that quarterback made out, and not knowing only intensified the pangs of guilt. I tried to rationalize that accidents happen and that we all accepted the inherent danger of playing a violent game. But still, I couldn't shake the guilt.

We had a successful season, and my first semester at Phoenix College ended with a congratulatory letter from the College President, William E. Berry, on making the President's Honor List. I would be lying if I didn't admit a little redemption toward Coach Joe's willingness to hamstring his players academically and to treat us as collateral damage in the name of business. Division-1 scholarships came in, which turned into partial ones once they realized I needed to sit out a complete year and wouldn't be able to attend spring training.

That was the final straw, and I walked away from a game I loved.

I got a bagger/carryout job at Bashas' grocery store and continued attending school. Initially, it was a very humbling experience, but I quickly moved up the ranks. One day, while working as a clerk/cashier, a prominent lady came through my line and asked if I was new. I didn't have the heart to tell her she never acknowledged me as I frequently bagged and carried her groceries to her car. Instead, I smiled and said I'd been here for a little while. This event prompted me to wonder if I treated people the same way. If I failed to be present to those around me as I hurried through life. I was promoted to Liquor Manager during my first Christmas season at Bashas. Eddie Basha, the owner, came in and casually conversed with me. He asked me what I was studying, and when I mentioned wildlife biology, his eyes lit up as he told me of a nine-day lion hunt he had recently returned from. As he spoke, I felt I was in the presence of greatness, possibly an Arizona version of Teddy Roosevelt. While he never ran for the presidency, he ran for the gubernatorial office in 1994. He didn't get elected, and I couldn't help but think that his work ethic would have served Arizona well.

Chapter 4

1990 Phoenix, Arizona

The Seed

I WAS QUICKLY PROMOTED to assistant grocery manager at Bashas'. As the new guy in management, I was responsible for many of the closing duties. Bashas' Grocery was a home-grown store that began in the early 1900s and had grown to over fifty stores by 1990. Their success was not due to always having the lowest prices like the big chains. Instead, their exceptional customer service policy got them through their start-up years and helped them flourish during the competitive times when there seemed to be a store on every corner. I was proud to be associated with an outfit that went out of its way to treat people right.

One evening, a customer notified me of a bum panhandling outside. I immediately went to the front of the store to tell the vagrant that he couldn't harass our customers and would have to move on, or the police would be involved. From a distance, he looked like any of our casually dressed customers sporting well-worn faded jeans and a reasonably new flannel shirt. I quickly discerned from the price tag hanging from his collar that he had stopped at the nearby Goodwill before poaching our parking lot.

The man was bent over, rifling through an ashtray. I approached him, "Excuse me?"

He stood and tucked a cigarette butt behind his ear as he turned to face me. His grungy undershirt collar and excessively worn boots confirmed my suspicion that he was living on the streets.

I looked him in the eye and told him, "You can't harass our customers; you'll have to move on."

He responded with a smile. "Do you have any spare change?"

I looked into his clear blue eyes. I thought, *You've got to be kidding me*, but I said, "I can't give you any money, but I can buy you a meal."

He followed me to the deli and when he put his order in, the clerk rolled her eyes at me. I reassured her with a nod.

Eager to know this man's story, I asked him to sit with me while he ate. With a congenial nod, he agreed, and we sat at an inconspicuous booth in the corner. His appearance was that of a man who had slept many nights on the ground. A streak of black ash, probably from the previous night's fire, adorned his face. His red cheeks were barely discernable under a week's worth of stubble, dirt, and grime. Whether his cheeks were sunburned, windburned, or caused by excessive alcohol consumption, I couldn't be sure.

While he ate, I asked him questions, and he surprised me with his articulate responses. He was obviously educated and began mesmerizing me with his stories of the beauty he had seen as he walked this great nation. He spoke about the tranquility of crystal-clear streams meandering through alpine meadows. He mentioned the healing whispers of a gentle breeze through trees. He gave witness to the power of rivers and cascading waterfalls and spoke with awe as he described the beauty hidden within canyon walls. He reminisced about swimming in high mountain lakes that mirrored the majesty of autumn-cloaked mountains and climbing those mountains for the sheer joy of beholding the beauty below.

He didn't eat like a ravenous animal. Instead, his focus was on reliving his adventures. He had a sparkle in his eyes, and it was apparent that he was at home, sleeping under the stars. What I found most unusual was that he looked eerily similar to the Santa Claus of my youthful imagination. We shook hands, and he went on his way. As he walked into the night, I felt an adventurous curiosity rekindle inside me that had long been dormant.

A clerk approached me as the man disappeared and asked, "Who was that?"

"That was Sam, an adventurous soul."

Chapter 5

Reality Check

My brother-in-law, Tim, called in the summer of 1989. He told me someone had left a flier on his windshield offering two free lessons in the martial art of Kenpo, which is an Americanized Karate.

He said, "If it's free, it's for me. What do you think?"

I quickly jumped on that bandwagon, suggesting we could be like Steven Seagal in the movie *Above the Law*, fighting the good fight.

Above the Law had just shown that spring, giving us a hero to emulate. We were shown some cool self-defense moves within the first two weeks of instruction. We learned how to disarm a knife or gun-wielding assailant. It was enough to keep us interested and dangerous at the same time. We were filled with a false sense of confidence that didn't come from years of disciplined practice, but, more accurately, from inflated youthful egos.

Shortly after our Kenpo initiation, I walked my girlfriend, Hannah, across a dimly lit parking lot toward the apartment she shared with her sister's family. Hannah's sister, Carol, and her husband, Dan, were the proud parents of four rambunctious children and one on the way. I loved to visit them every chance I could because the boundless energy of those kids reminded me of the chaos that I grew up with in a big family. Plus, if I wrestled with them long enough, Carol would invite me to stay for dinner. She was an exceptional cook, and I could only hope that Hannah had inherited some of her culinary genius.

As we walked, a cool night breeze breathed life back into anyone who survived another day of sizzling triple digit heat in Phoenix, Arizona. It was not uncommon to hear the locals boast about a dry heat that was capable of sucking the last bit of moisture from any life form. The intensity of the heat could melt your shoes, particularly if you stood on the pavement for any length of time. I remember when I was a kid, I tested the local "hotter than Hades" lore by frying an egg on the hood of Mom and Dad's car. In hindsight, I should have used a nonstick cooking spray because it baked into the hood and blistered the paint.

While reminiscing and savoring the cooling breeze against my sweat-soaked skin, I noticed a brand new, candy apple red Jeep Cherokee with dark tinted windows pull into the parking lot. As it cruised slowly by, I wondered:

Who could be the proud owner of this new ride?

Hannah and I were nearing the gate to her apartment complex when the jeep turned at the far end of the parking lot and drove in our direction. Subconscious red flags popped up for me as they drove past several empty spaces at the far end of the lot.

I quickly brushed it off to the phenomenon I like to call the *"Have a car will not walk far"* parking technique. You see it all the time when people burn a tank of gas searching for the optimal parking space near their final destination. I also wrote it off to the chance that they were making a second pass to get another look at Hannah. It wouldn't have been the first time a guy had taken a second look when I was with her.

The red flags turned into fire alarms as a Hispanic man in the back seat jumped out of the jeep and moved quickly toward us. He was dragging a machete on the pavement. The sound of steel grinding into asphalt caused me to view our assailant in disbelief and with a feeling of déjà vu. I realized I had seen a similar scene in the movie *Black Rain,* starring Michael Douglas and Andy Garcia. I quickly wondered if this assailant had seen the same movie.

But suddenly, I felt a surge of panic as I remembered Mr. Garcia's demise. In the movie, the motorcycle gangster drug his samurai sword on the pavement for effect, before he lopped off Andy's head while Michael watched helplessly from the other side of a fence.

My mind reeled, *This really couldn't be happening.*

My incredulous denial was deeply rooted in a sheltered upbringing where I was taught to always trust and believe in people. Your word was worth something, and a handshake sealed a deal. It was a naive reality that was about to be shattered by a stranger brandishing a machete. Little did I know that a part of me would die that night.

He quickly closed the distance between us and brought the machete up into a threatening posture so there would be no confusion about his intent.

He began yelling, "Give me your f#@%*#@ wallet, mother @#$%&*, now."

My mind went into warp speed, and everything that followed seemed to move in slow motion. I dropped my gym bag and simultaneously pushed Hannah behind me.

She ran for help.

I tried to convince myself that this was a practical joke that went too far. I wouldn't put it past some of my football buddies to concoct such a realistic scheme. Frozen in my tracks as if paralyzed, I wondered if the instinct to fight or flee had been bred out of me through generations of civility. Feeling like a third-party observer in a surreal setting, I was shocked back to reality when he lunged toward me, forcefully swinging the machete. I sucked my stomach in as I watched the blade narrowly miss my abdomen.

On the second pass of the blade, I envisioned being eviscerated and seeing my intestines spill from my body, uncoiling as they fell. Stunned and still immobilized, as if my legs were made of lead, he swung again, more determined than before. Enough was enough. My disbelief turned to a rage that shocked even me. He swung with such force on his third attempt that he over swung. His mistake afforded me a brief opportunity to move in and pin his arm against his chest with my body. With adrenaline coursing through my veins,

I wrenched the machete from his grip as he tried biting my shoulder. In that brief moment, I marveled at how easy it was to disarm him and how fortunate it was that my brother-in-law found that Kenpo flier on his windshield. I remember inwardly chuckling *Holy crap, this stuff does work!*

It seemed I could do what I wanted in this slow-motion realm, and for a split second, I thought I needed to negate this threat with a quick snap of his neck, well, that's what Steven Seagal would have done. But something deep in my subconscious wouldn't let me go there. Instead, I stunned him with an elbow to his face. As he crumpled to the ground, I sensed danger from behind. Turning, I faced his two accomplices, closing in on me. They were stunned to see me rise and meet them, brandishing the machete in front of me defensively, daring them to come closer.

Their shock was apparent, and I felt the momentum turn. There was a momentary standoff as they appeared puzzled, wondering how they should handle the unexpected turn of events. The larger and obvious self-appointed leader calmly lifted his shirt and exposed a handgun tucked into the front of his pants. He brazenly brandished the pistol with newfound confidence and pointed it in my direction.

Scarcely fifteen feet separated us. I felt a little foolish sporting a big knife in a gunfight, and my mind flashed to the scene in the movie *Raiders of the Lost Ark* when Harrison Ford casually pulled a gun out of his pants and shot the sword-wielding bad guy, unimpressed by his sword-handling display.

Unbelievable!

Swollen with a bully-like enthusiasm, the big guy yelled, "Give me your f@#$%^&* money."

I spun and grabbed the first attacker who was getting back up and attempted to use him as a shield as three shots were fired in rapid succession.

Later, Hannah told me she raced to her apartment and screamed, "Dan! Rick is getting jumped!" She said she heard the shots and was sure I was dead, she collapsed on the floor. She told me that Dan was barefoot, but he ran past his pregnant wife and disappeared through the door.

During the volley of shots, my mind raced through past experiences, trying to process where I had heard the familiar sound of a discharging pistol. Looking back, I remember being a kid at age five or six, sitting in the back seat of Mom and Dad's blue Ford station wagon at a drive-in movie theater in Winslow, Arizona. We were watching the movie *Patton*. George C. Scott portrayed General Patton, and in one scene, he described how he savored being on the front lines, listening to the buzzing bullets fly by. I could think of better ways to get an endorphin rush, but hey, to each his own.

I also recalled walking through the woods during hunting season as a kid and hearing the sound of a giant bumble bee fly by and slam into a nearby tree. With wood chips raining down on me, I realized it wasn't a bee but a stray bullet. Still, after rifling through my memory, I couldn't find a satisfactory connection with any experience to compare my current situation. I wondered if I was too close to hear the bullets fly by and was astounded that he had missed. He certainly hadn't hit my human shield as he neither shrieked nor recoiled.

Then it dawned on me. I had heard that familiar "pop, pop, pop" sound at track meets during high school. I was willing to bet it was the sound of a starting pistol. I instantly dropped the first thug and went on the attack. The foiled assailants raced to their stolen jeep and smoked the tires as they sped off.

I sprinted alongside the jeep. By the time I reached the driver's window, my adrenaline was raging, and I broke all the windows on the driver's side with the butt of the machete. I hoped it would make it easy for the police to identify.

When I smashed the window, I made a concerted effort to check my swing and not follow through, which would have ended in a possible decapitation of the driver.

Shards of glass pelted the driver and landed on the passenger. I saw fear wash over his face as he white-knuckled the steering wheel and stomped on the accelerator with a newfound urgency. I saw Dan fearlessly sprinting after the first assailant. The fugitive made it to the right rear passenger door and was hanging on for dear life as he was drug through the parking lot by his buddy driving the jeep, who was more concerned about saving his own skin.

Dan's feet barely touched the pavement as he sprinted. He tackled the guy hanging on the door and wrestled him to the blacktop. I chased the fleeing jeep out of the parking lot but could only get a partial license plate number before they disappeared into the darkness. I returned to assist Dan with the struggling Hispanic man. He continued fighting to free himself while yelling that he was going to sue us. I encouraged him to do so if he had the chance. He changed tactics and told us, "You can't hold me. I'm Chief Ortega's son."

Humored but unconvinced, I told him, "Well, your dad's going to want to know about this."

The black of night turned to daylight as a police helicopter appeared. It's spotlight illuminated our ongoing struggle. I noticed a conspicuous teardrop tattoo on the corner of the man's eye.

Later, I learned that particular tattoo meant the owner drew blood or killed someone as part of his gang initiation rite. The cavalry came charging in as three cop cars roared to the scene, power sliding to a stop. Amidst the smoking rubber appeared six apparitions yelling over the chopper wash, "We'll take it from here."

The hardheaded assailant continued to struggle. The more he did, the more the police officers made a human pretzel out of him. They used strategic pressure holds to subdue him. After "cuffing and stuffing" him, that's police jargon for assisting him to the confines of the squad car, one of the policemen pulled me aside to get my statement. All the while, the "perp" continued to curse me and my heritage. He swore that when he got out, he would kill me and my family. I couldn't help but marvel at his spontaneous creativity and briefly wondered how different his life might have been had he used his talents in a more positive way.

While sitting on the hood of a police car, the interviewing officer asked me point blank, "Why didn't you give the assailant your wallet?"

My response was, "First, he didn't give me a chance, and secondly, I work too damn hard for my money."

He then told me that since they had used deadly force against me, I had every right to defend myself, and if I had killed one of them, not a court in the land would have convicted me. Seeing that I was visibly shaken from the ordeal and coming down from the most intense adrenaline rush of my life, he jokingly asked me, "Why didn't you at least lop off an appendage?"

I appreciated his stab at humor. I was embarrassed about my quivering voice and my body, which was shaking out of control. I had never experienced that kind of adrenaline dump before.

While in custody, the Hispanic man began complaining that his head hurt. Two EMTs checked him and assessed that he had a mild concussion. They reassured him that he would be fine. As they returned to their fire truck, they glanced my way and gave me a subtle thumbs-up sign.

Before they visited the Valley of the Sun, gang activity wasn't a problem in Phoenix as far as I knew. I soon learned these three desperados were gang members from Los Angeles enjoying a crime spree in Phoenix. Their rap sheet consisted of robbery, convenience store holdups, and auto theft, to name a few. They each wore teardrop tattoos as a badge of honor. The police found the Jeep Cherokee abandoned in South Phoenix with all the driver's side windows busted out but were never able to find the other two assailants.

The first assailant was prosecuted, and he did time. During the court proceedings, I overheard a relative or friend tell him, in Spanish, he was a dumbass for messing with a big cowboy. I smiled and again thought to myself what a waste this was. There were no winners here.

How can we help guys like this reach their full potential before they walk down this path of no return? I thought.

How do we prevent evil from being parasitic on the good?

Chapter 6

Life Goes On

I returned to work the very next day with a great tale to tell, but hidden behind the bravado was uncertainty about a safe future, and I found myself looking over my shoulder with growing frequency. Undeterred, Hannah and I made future plans to move back to her home state of Colorado so she could be near her parents and two other sisters. Our dreams quickly became reality shortly after the sentencing of machete man.

I was at work when a longtime customer, frail in stature and sporting a permanent sour demeanor, came in with a chip on her shoulder. She shuffled up to the customer service counter with her usual scowl and a squint in her eye. It felt like the second coming of the shootout at the OK Corral was imminent. She complained about life in general, faulty transportation, and the fact that she could not find the advertised sale item. I informed her that today was Wednesday, the beginning of the new ad campaign, but since she couldn't make it in by Tuesday to get the previous week's ad items, I would happily honor those sale items. She left diffused and happy.

The next guy in line gave me his card and told me, "Well done, please give me a call." Coincidentally, that guy was Jeff Farstad, a gas and oil tycoon who owned Farstad Oil in Minot, N. Dakota, and just happened to be in the neighborhood playing golf with many of his clients.

I did call him. "Jeff, I know nothing about the intricacies of the gas and oil world."

He assured me, "Don't worry, Rick. The most important component is to be personable.

The energy industry can be learned if you are coachable."

"Now you're talking my language."

Within a week, I found myself flying with Jeff in his personal jet to Minot as he laid out his plan to open an office in Denver. Wanting a fresh start with great potential, I agreed to hire on. I insisted he give me a month to make housing arrangements in Denver, get packed, and give my two weeks' notice. I flew back to the Scottsdale airport with an enthusiasm fueled by opportunity.

Hannah was ecstatic about getting far away from any potential threats in Phoenix. While very nurturing but not enabling, her parents agreed to let her move home and stay for as long as she needed while she found an apartment for me. She was practically packed by the time I had landed. At our first opportunity we moved her to her parents' place in Parker, Colorado.

Before I left, I asked her dad for permission to marry her. He shook my sweaty hand and smiled. With a twinkle in his eye, he said with an assured southern drawl, "Yes, we look forward to you being a part of our family."

It felt like I was stepping into an extension of my own family. Hannah's parents had made me feel right at home from day one, and it was incredibly heartwarming to see how they showed love to their four girls and their extended families. I was blessed to be accepted into such a warm and loving family. Our future together held such promise.

A short week later, I was running the nightly numbers report at work and got a phone call from a hysterical Hannah. Between the tears and uncontrollable sobbing, she told me she had met some friends at a party and was driving home when she was run off the road in a dark, rural section of highway between Denver and Parker.

Two guys had forced her into the ditch and ripped open the right rear passenger door before she could get it locked. They pulled her over the bench seat and had their way with her. She didn't go down without a fight, but they beat her senseless. When she regained consciousness, she explained this horrific event as a helpless, out-of-body experience as they took turns with her.

With tears streaming down my face, I turned to my store director, Tom Swanson, and explained what had happened and that I had to go. He told me not to worry, that he would finish my reports, and that he and the other managers would cover my shifts until I could return. I quickly thanked him and left as another wave of nausea washed over me. I knew I had to be there for Hannah, and within three hours, I was on a red-eye flight destined for Denver and the unknown. When I got to her parents' house, Hannah was just getting home from the sheriff's department. The rape kit, subsequent interview, and report left her feeling revictimized. Bruised and battered, she collapsed into my arms, and I held her until she quit shaking. Anger welled up inside of me, and I was consumed with a desire for revenge.

I've never been one to tolerate life's injustices directed by bullies toward the vulnerable of society.

There was a time in college, while out listening to music at a club with my roommate, three of our female friends approached our table and asked if we would dance with them the rest of the night because two guys kept trying to drag them out onto the dance floor without asking.

These guys were pretty full of themselves and needed a reality check. We were honored that the girls had asked us to run interference. At the night's end, my roommate and I escorted the girls out of the club safely to their car while the two scorned guys glared at us. Emboldened by liquid courage, the hooligans proceeded to give us a verbal lashing. I heard as much as I could handle when I got to the girls' car. I walked over to the two guys who were sitting in their jacked-up four-wheel-drive truck with the windows down and politely told them, "You guys seem to have it all wrong calling me gay. Maybe your memory has failed you, but I danced all night with three beautiful ladies, and now I'm escorting them to their car because they didn't feel safe around you guys. Have a good night. I hope you enjoy each other's company."

As I turned to leave, Linda, one of the girls ran up and asked, "Rick, what are you doing?" Before I could answer, the driver yelled, "Take that whore with you."

Usually, I would avoid a physical conflict, but this time, I looked up into the air, let out an exasperated sigh, and shook my head in disbelief. I turned, reached through the window, grabbed the driver's head, and proceeded to slam it into the steering wheel with enough force to get his attention but not enough to destroy him. "You need to treat women with more respect and learn some manners while you're at it."

His buddy had long flowing blonde hair, and looked like Fabio, an Italian actor/model and self-professed ladies' man who appeared on the cover of dozens of romance novels. He jumped out, ran around the truck, and put on an impressive display of martial arts mastery.

Oh crap, I may be in over my head was all I could think.

I had barely processed that thought when he flew at me with an impressive jump kick. There's nothing like a potential swift kick aimed at one's head to motivate oneself into action. Slightly moving my head out of target range, I felt his boot fly by. I pinned his leg next to my head with one arm and grabbed his "boys" firmly with my other hand. Looking him in the eyes, I tightened my grip. I asked, "Do you want me to finish this?"

He whimpered, "Nooo."

"Good, because the cops will be showing up soon, making their closing rounds." I released my grip.

"I don't want any part of that."

I thought he was serious and turned to walk away. Call it intuition or second-guessing, I knew he would attack from behind a split second before he jumped on my back and tried to choke me.

Instinctively, I leaned forward, grabbed a handful of his golden locks at that sensitive nape of the neck, and threw him over my shoulder. As he scrambled to get up, I missed with the left hook but caught him with a right uppercut, and he crumpled.

Thankfully, an attentive Linda was hanging on the driver's back, yelling, "Rick, he's grabbing a pipe."

I ran over and grabbed his wrist as he was pulling a pipe from the bed of his truck.

Obviously dejected, he dropped it. "I just want to load up my friend and get out of here."

"Great, have a good night."

He gathered his friend as we walked off, and then he tried to run us over on his way out of the parking lot.

All these years later, man's inhumanity towards humanity was a flash point that left me infuriated once again. I wanted justice for Hannah, and it was probably a good thing that the sheriff's department hadn't quickly apprehended anyone connected to Hannah's rape because it gave me time to cool down and realize that justice was better served by the law, no matter how much the movies glorified vigilante justice.

Hannah didn't want to stay in Parker. We decided she would return to Phoenix until I could finalize the move to Denver. We didn't want to live together unless we were married, so with the help of her family, we put together a wedding in three days and exchanged our vows in a small chapel in Loveland, Colorado. Sometimes, you will do whatever it takes to protect those you love, even if it means ignoring that intuitive voice telling you something is wrong.

Regardless, and with stubborn idealism, I married a frightened and diminished version of the woman I knew. I hoped that love and time would be enough to heal wounds I couldn't understand. My only regret was that my family, especially my mom and dad, could not attend due to the short notice. The shock and disappointment in my mother's voice broke my heart.

We eventually made the transition to Denver. We found an apartment in Bear Valley near my office, and I hit the ground running. My job was establishing new accounts, developing relationships, and brokering transportation for oil and gas products to retail and construction accounts. It proved to be both challenging and rewarding, but it wasn't all work and no play. Our office put together a fishing tournament at Navajo Lake in Southern Colorado. It was a huge success. The fishing was great, the food prepared by a local chef was spectacular, and the comradery of a bunch of good old boys having some fun was something I could get used to.

Initially, my job required lots of road time, a sacrifice I was willing to make to "get ahead." Little did I know how much this sacrifice would cost a young marriage. Hannah was not the "stay-at-home" type. She needed to find something to occupy her time, or she would dwell on the horrors of her not-so-distant past. She got a job waiting tables at a local restaurant. As a new hire, she was expected to take on the bulk of the closing duties. We had hoped that keeping busy would keep her from spiraling into the depths of darkness, but each commitment put an additional strain on a relationship that was more tenuous than either of us cared to admit. Still, we clung to the hope that time would heal all wounds.

Six months later, with our office in the black and everyone working toward a prosperous future, we convened in Vail, Colorado, for an energy conference touting Senator Ben Nighthorse Campbell as our guest speaker. I was looking forward to spending time in the mountains, learning what I could from the industry giants, and trying my hand at golf with our other sales reps.

Hannah and I loaded up and headed to paradise, nestled in the heart of the Rockies. After checking in at the Marriott in Vail on Friday evening, we had dinner at Grouse Mountain Grill in Beaver Creek. My boss, Jeff, dropped over ten grand on dinner for all the sales reps and their spouses. The food was exquisite, and as the wine flowed, I thought I was living the American dream. The next day, Jeff and all the sales associates went golfing in Eagle-Vail while our wives went shopping in Vail, where even window shopping can be expensive. As the water hazards claimed the better part of my box of golf balls, I vowed that I'd have to take this game a little more seriously so that I didn't lose so many.

The decadence surrounding this conference was surreal and excessive for this son of a U.S. letter carrier. My grandmother was a product of the great depression and one of the most frugal people I have ever known. Had she been there, she would have been astounded at how the privileged lived.

On Saturday evening, we went to an amazing banquet and listened to several guest speakers, along with Ben Nighthorse Campbell as the keynote speaker. There was no doubt in my mind that things were looking good for Hannah and my future. As we were checking out of the hotel Sunday morning, Jeff pulled all of his sales associates from the various offices across the nation into a room and dropped a bomb on us. He said he was pulling the plug on all satellite offices and that Farstad Oil would be changing course in its expansion efforts.

As I was processing the magnitude of what had transpired over the last thirty-six hours, Jeff pulled me aside and told me that he really liked me and that he would find a position for me in Minot.

I told him, "Thanks, but I can't leave these mountains."

He understood and told me my severance check would be in the mail. Heading down to Denver to help close the office, I wondered if I had just made the biggest mistake of my life.

The following two weeks Hannah started coming home later and later. She said they had to do a super clean as part of their closing duties. It sounded reasonable, but something told me she wasn't being entirely truthful. Living in a state of denial for too long can have devastating results. One evening, she never came home and remained missing for three days. Her family and I filed a missing person's report and searched local hospitals. Her manager verified that all closing employees were always gone by nine or ten pm. She called at the end of the third day, wanting to come home. She had been partying and self-medicating to ease the emotional pain and had lost track of time. I told her that we couldn't go on like this and that we needed to get help.

I suggested that she pick a counselor, preferably a Christian one. She picked out a female Christian counselor, and our first meeting went well with a call to action on both of our parts. Unfortunately, her part was more than her fragile mental state could handle. While I was at work the next day, Hannah was heading out the door to follow the Grateful Dead and a life of self-medication.

We got a divorce by corresponding through the mail. When Jerry Garcia died and the band quit touring, Hannah was so far removed from her previous life and engrained in her fun-loving, free-spirited lifestyle that she readily transitioned into the Rainbow Coalition Organization and found a sense of belonging from her Rainbow family, something that we all desire.

Chapter 7

Ski Bum

During this time of great loss, I also went looking for some semblance of happiness, but before I could do that, I needed to get a job as the bills kept coming and the severance check wouldn't last long. I answered a help-wanted ad for sales associates for an upcoming ski sale called Sniagrab, which is bargains spelled backward. It was an opportunity to sell fun for an outdoor sporting goods store called Gart Brothers, and that was just what I needed.

After brief training clinics with the various ski, boot, and binding representatives, we put on a successful sale for the budget-conscious skier in the covered parking lot at "The Castle," which was the main superstore for Gart Brothers in downtown Denver. People would camp out overnight for this annual preseason sale.

I soon discovered that my passion for selling fun and giving people a quality product at a bargain price overcame my lack of experience in the field. After all, being a bona fide desert rat with only thirteen days of skiing under my belt didn't qualify me as an expert in the industry. I was asked to be on the traveling sales team once the sale at The Castle ended. The travel team loaded semi-truck trailers with ski hard goods and soft goods equipment to completely outfit anyone's skiing needs. We set up our sales in Colorado Springs and Boulder, with equal success. Most of the traveling team was offered permanent employment at one of the Gart Sports stores. I chose a little satellite store in the heart of the Rockies, in the little ski town of Vail, Colorado.

My fellow Vail employees were from Washington State, Oregon, Alaska, and upstate New York, with a few local extreme skiers thrown in for good measure. Many of them were ex-college racers or on the pro-bump tour. I was the token desert rat they took under their wing and instructed me on the finer aspects of throwing caution to the wind and "letting 'em run." We literally ran on adrenaline from the moment we went to the annual Warren Miller ski film to the end of the season. Skiing top to bottom without stopping. We relished the freedom of the cold, crisp wind on our faces while enjoying some of the most stunning natural beauty I had ever seen.

We worked hard and played harder in one of the planet's most incredible outdoor recreation meccas. It didn't hurt that my first two years as a ski bum were epic snow years. I learned to ski in champagne powder, and it was like flying down a mountain on a bottomless cloud. Mogul runs were filled with hero bumps, soft forgiving snow that would explode on impact. They would forgive technical errors and reward you with cold, fluffy face shots. At times, it felt like I was reliving my childhood and having more fun than an adult should legally have.

Hanging with my new-found thrill-seeking friends sometimes pushed me past my comfort zone. One day, after several weeks of continuous storms, we woke up on a Colorado Bluebird day with an additional four feet of powder. The total storm accumulation was over ten feet, and we made sure we were first in line to bag the most untracked runs before the crowds carved them up. The snow was so deep that if you weren't on steep enough terrain, you would come to a dead stop, and in this kind of snow, stopping on moderate slopes was disastrous. You had to seek out the steepest terrain to keep your momentum going to a groomed run that led to a lift. Hiking in the flats was not an option this day.

I dropped in on a double black diamond run in the back bowls and completely submerged on each turn. The snow billowed over my head, obliterating my vision and normal breathing. I would grab a quick breath as I resurfaced in chest-deep snow before making my next turn. Skiing the "skinny ski" those days—with a width of about three and a half inches—was a lot of work, and midway down the slope, I had to bail off to the side, gasping for air. As I recovered, I noticed a tiny spec above me drop in on my run.

This skier disappeared and reappeared in the same fashion as I did, with one exception. He never stopped. When he blasted past me, I noticed a snorkel in his mouth.

Seriously?

Note to self: *Extreme conditions require extreme measures, next big dump—bring a snorkel.*

At the end of the day, we would wait at the top of the mountain until the crowds dispersed, and we soaked in the grandeur of the Gore Mountain range. In the 1850s, the Gore Mountains were named after Lord St. George Gore, an Irish aristocrat who came to the American West for a three-year hunt. He lavishly camped in what is today the Dakotas, Montana, Wyoming, and Colorado. He claimed to have killed more than two thousand buffalo, sixteen hundred elk and deer, and one hundred bears that he left to rot.

Native Americans, Mountain Men, and even the U.S. Calvary were angered by his unsustainable slaughter. However, in their rush to name things in the pre-Gold Rush era, early cartographers affixed Gore's name to the range based on word of mouth and hand-drawn maps that indicated this was Gore's range. Federal naming criteria were instituted around 1889 by the United States Geological Survey. Qualifying to have a federally recognized feature, such as a mountain range named after you, required that you are no longer among the living. Additionally, someone would need to prove that the person was an exemplary community member for an

> "A peculiar virtue in wildlife ethics is that the hunter ordinarily has no gallery to applaud or disapprove of his conduct. Whatever his acts, they are dictated by his own conscience, rather than that of onlookers. It is difficult to exaggerate the importance of this fact."
>
> ~ **ALDO LEOPOLD,**
> *A Sand County Almanac*

extensive period of time. Perhaps one day, these majestic mountains will get a name that honors their grandeur.

I always loved the last run. It gave tourists time to get to the bottom, and it gave me time to be in the moment and soak up the beauty of creation. A snowstorm approached late one afternoon and threatened to block the waning light. A stranger, by the name of Dan Schons, skied up with one of my Denver Sniagrab buddies. He was a likable guy, and at the time, was an electrical engineer who had just finished an internship with Siemens in Germany. He was here to unwind and have fun.

After one ski run and a few beers at one of our local hangouts, Dan, who at the time was not a great skier, was convinced that this lifestyle was just what the doctor ordered. He was a talented college athlete, and it didn't sit well with his competitive nature to struggle with runs that everyone else flew down looking like poetry in motion.

I didn't know it then, but we could have been brothers and were destined to be best friends. Snow conditions would dictate our last run of the day. If the snow conditions weren't optimal, we would make high-speed GS (Giant Slalom) turns on the corduroy groomed runs. If it was a powder day, we would rip it down a PPL (Prima, Pronto, Log Chute) bump runs followed by a well-earned après ski at the Red Lion or whichever pub was running a special at the time. Other options would be to ski the Minturn Mile off the back side of Vail and end up at the Minturn Saloon, where a plate of nachos and a cold beer jived with a ski bum's budget.

Lastly, dropping off the cliffs on the East Vail chutes down to Garton's Saloon for a cheap meal and drinks was always a great way to finish the day.

The first time I launched off of an East Vail cliff, I had a conversation with myself on the way down. I questioned my sanity and willingness to hang with a bunch of invincible adrenaline junkies who were always looking to take their bravado to the next level. They were the modern-day cowboys mixed with a little James Bond, always chasing the perfect storm of the frozen North.

Vail was always hopping. Continuous sporting events such as

World Cup skiing, Half Pipe competitions, X Games events, Nordic skiing races, Ice Hockey, Figure skating, or Freestyle Mogul contests were going on somewhere. It truly was a Winter Wonderland.

My roommate, Gary, all five feet four inches and one hundred and forty-five pounds of him, was a professional bump skier. His nickname was Bamba due to his fearless skiing style. With a jump that defied gravity, he won the big air segment of the 1994 Red Bull Pro Bump Tour in Vail. I didn't think it was humanly possible to sail that far, land that hard without having a yard sale, and still find your line and launch the second jump in one piece. He went on to win the event the following year, and Dan and I triumphantly hoisted Bamba on our shoulders while he was awarded the champion's check. I love an underdog story, and Gary was proof that big things come in small packages.

That was the same year that Shane McConkey was disqualified for going inverted off one of the jumps. He later did a naked protest run. He executed his trademark backflip perfectly with an Iron Cross off the upper jump and then fearlessly nailed a Spread Eagle off the bottom jump. Shane then calmly skied into the waiting crowd like it was just another day at the office. He was the free-spirited Michael Jordan of the slopes with more talent than most, and way ahead of his time regarding pushing the envelope on what was humanly possible.

Shane was killed while Big Mountain skiing in the Dolomites of Northern Italy. He launched off the two-thousand-foot Saspardoi cliff, performing his iconic double backflip with the intent to release his skis and then fly like a falcon in his wingsuit to the valley below. His skis didn't release. He left behind a wife and young daughter.

When I heard the news, I remember feeling sad for his family's loss and that the world would never know what an incredible skier he was. Eventually, a movie was made about him as a creative innovator who helped shape the ski industry. It is appropriately titled *McConkey*. Shane inspired people not to take themselves too seriously. He dared to be authentic with himself and those around him. His motto was, "Live to die happy."

He died doing what he loved, and there is something admirable about that.

Winters and the opportunity to ski in a world-renowned destination resort brought me to Vail, but the summers kept me there. The hiking, biking, mountain climbing, fishing, and white- water rafting were world-class. I felt like a kid in a candy store with unlimited possibilities.

Traditionally, the spring and fall mud seasons were downtime for business. But for outdoor enthusiasts, there was always something to do. If you were not an outdoor person, this wasn't the place for you.

My second year in Vail required me to offset the high cost of living by taking a waiting job at the Eagle-Vail golf course restaurant in the evenings. In addition, to help supplement our grocery bill, my ski buddies and I decided to go hunting before the ski season kicked into high gear. We had pre-scouted a big elk herd before opening day and knew exactly where to be opening morning. Overly confident in our potential success, we played cards until the early morning hours and headed out in whiteout conditions. As we drove higher to where we had seen the elk the day before, the snow kept getting deeper until we were pushing snow with our bumper. When we got to our honey hole, the snow had stopped, and early morning light revealed an empty valley. The snow had started the winter migration, and the elk had already headed for lower elevations. It was anyone's guess as to how far of a head start they had.

We each took a different drainage and started down the mountain. Travel was slow going. After a few hours, I found fresh elk tracks but lost contact with my hunting party. For hours, I trailed the elk. Steaming piles of scat indicated that I was getting close. The mid-day sun was overhead, and I knew they had to be getting ready to bed down. Their trail led me to a north-facing bowl filled with dark timber. I was getting close to their bedroom, so I slowed and cautiously worked my way down a steep slope, side hilling as I approached. To my surprise, they were bedded down just as I suspected. I belly-crawled the last two hundred yards and was about to take a shot when the whole herd jumped up in unison and stampeded up the drainage.

Exhausted, I cleared snow off a rock and sat down to eat lunch, wondering what had gone wrong. Had the wind swirled? Had my approach been spotted by one of the satellite bulls hanging on the periphery? Just then, out of the corner of my eye, I spotted some movement about fifty yards below me. Initially, all I could see was fur moving through the bushes, and it was huge. Grizzly bears in this part of the country were killed off years ago. Was I seeing the last surviving grizzly, or maybe this was the fabled Big Foot of backwoods lore?

My imagination was in overdrive. Mesmerized, I waited as it approached an opening. I was relieved when two black bears—a giant boar and an enormous sow—stepped into a clearing.

They were oblivious to my presence as they had other things on their minds; at least the male did. I felt like a voyeur as the male tried to mount her, but she would roll over on her back and slap him upside the head, and they would playfully wrestle. They didn't have a care in the world and continued to play and feed until they came upon a big pine whose trunk was curved. It grew vertically for the first fifteen feet and then horizontally for about ten feet before extending vertically again. They climbed to the horizontal section and settled in for a nap. They were only thirty yards away. The boar started to snore, and just as I was ready to leave them in peace, the boar rose from his slumber. He stood bow-legged with the hair on his neck standing up. He huffed, then growled, and looked in my direction. I don't know if he saw me. I stayed motionless, but the swirling midday winds gave me away. After a couple of minutes, he laid back down and resumed snoring as if any perceived threat had vaporized on the shifting wind.

I quickly threw my partially eaten lunch back into my pack, and as I slung the pack over my shoulder, I heard the huffing and growling noise again. Motionless, trying to become one with the rock, I slowly looked up and saw him looking directly at me as if he were the king of the forest perched on his throne. It seemed like an eternity before he relaxed and began snoring again. I didn't want to play that game again, so I backed away, careful not to disturb him.

As I circled to a position forty yards below the slumbering bears, I could hear a herd of elk casually dropping over the ridge. The crack of breaking branches and the thud of hoof against a log or rock indicated that they were moving through the timber in the direction I was heading. My elation at another possibility to fill my tag was cut short by a noise behind me.

I looked over my shoulder just in time to see the big boar shuffle down the tree with authority. In his hurry, shards of bark flew as his claws raked the trunk. He hit the ground and quickly moved away from me. A sense of foreboding came over me as he stopped at the rock I sat on and began to sniff around. He walked around several bushes and trees with his nose to the ground. The hair on my neck stood up as I realized those were the same bushes and trees that I walked around on my way out. He was tracking me.

A cold sweat took hold of me as I realized *Wow, that's not normal. Bears are supposed to be afraid of people.*

As he closed the distance, I wished I had a bear tag. He followed my trail precisely. I nervously marveled at how keen his sense of smell was and wondered what he was thinking. I didn't want to shoot him, but if he kept coming, I'd have no choice.

He stopped about twenty yards from me. We stared each other down and sized each other up. I tried to make myself look imposing by holding my hands over my head and calmly talking to him. Determined not to show fear, I was careful not to make too much noise and risk scaring the herd below me. I mentally kicked myself for not shooting sooner because if he charged at this distance, I would only be able to get one shot off before he was on me. My mind raced through the probable outcomes of the scene playing out before me, and if it weren't a well-placed shot, I would have to beat an enraged bear off with the butt of my gun. Pulling my knife would be a last resort.

I barely completed that thought when he charged and quickly closed the distance.

CRAP!

I put pressure on the trigger, but before it broke, he stopped ten yards away and stared at me. I could hear my heart pounding as I stared back into those beady black eyes that showed no emotion. I kept my finger on the trigger, grabbed a hefty branch, and threw it, hitting him in the shoulder, and he whirled around and ran off.

My victory celebration was cut short when he abruptly stopped, turned, and squared off with me once more.

Unbelievable.

He charged again. This time, he stopped about six yards away. Keeping my rifle trained on him, with steady trigger pressure, I reached down and grabbed a rock slightly bigger than a softball and threw it with everything I had. The rock smashed into his head with a thud that sounded like a watermelon getting thumped. He shook his head and ran off, not stopping this time. He circled and went into the trees roughly where the elk had dropped in from the ridge above and showed no sign of slowing down. If he stayed on that trajectory, it would put him in the vicinity of the elk, where I was heading.

I halfheartedly snuck through the woods. I wondered if Hugh Glass, a famous mountain man, had a similar adrenaline rush right before a grizzly bear mauled him. I feigned looking for elk because, in reality, all my senses were on high alert, expecting an ambush.

To make light of my situation, I recalled a family vacation in Yellowstone when I was fifteen. I was reading about the recommended use of bells and the proper use of pepper spray on an information sign when a park ranger walked up and gave me some insightful information. "Son, do you know the difference between a grizzly bear and a black bear?"

I gave him a brief description of their physical differences, and he nodded in agreement. He asked if I knew the proper evasive measures when confronted by either species. Before I could respond, he said with a wistful smile and a twinkle in his eye, "You can climb a tree, and the bear that climbs up after you would be a black bear, and the one that knocks it over would be the grizzly."

He explained their scat's identifying features, saying, "The black bear scat has the remnants of fur and berries, and the 'GRIZ' will have bells in it and smell of pepper spray." Humor has long been my solution to anxiety.

Colorado Baptism

As a transplanted Desert Rat, water was a novelty to me. The idea of having cold, crystal clear streams and rivers teaming with fish right out my back door was a dream come true. My fly rod was always with me, and I would fish at every opportunity, no matter the season.

One day, in the spring of my second year in Vail, I was on my way to work. As I went through Dowd Junction, I noticed fish swirling everywhere at the confluence of Gore Creek and the Eagle River. I had an hour to kill before I had to be at work, so I threw on my rubber waders and walked into the icy waters. Chunks of snow and ice were floating by, but the water warmed enough that a Stonefly hatch was going off, and the trout were voracious. I caught six within the first twenty minutes. My seventh fish was a monster. It launched into the air several times, trying to spit the hook out of its mouth before diving deep and running into the fast current while stripping line as he went.

There is nothing like the sound of your drag screaming as you try to turn a fish before he spools you or snaps your line. I walked downstream, focused on my line as it headed for the log jam below. I was thinking about the story I could tell the guys at the ski shop

if I landed this hog. The bottom dropped out as I stepped into a hole. With the current pushing me into the icy depths, there was no backpedaling. I went under in the blink of an eye, and my waders instantly filled up, making it difficult to move. Panic swept through my veins as I remembered the log jam below and knew I had to get out before I was pinned against the waiting log strainer by the force of the water and not seen again until the spring runoff was over.

I bounced helplessly on the river bottom in the main current. Eventually, I was bumped into a slight eddy and was able to start crawling toward what I hoped was the direction of the nearest shore. I emerged shivering, still holding my rod. I looked like the Michelin man as I struggled out of the water carrying close to eighty pounds of water with me. I raced home with teeth chattering. I was reminded again that Mother Nature is indifferent, and inattentiveness can be costly. This realization only heightened my love for wild places.

By the end of my second year in Vail, I had already won many of the sales contests put on by the different vendors and had completely outfitted myself with ski boots, GS, Slalom, and Bump skis and bindings.

The year-end contest offered two round-trip airline tickets anywhere in the continental U.S. for the highest-grossing salesman. I won, and the company's president came to our store to see why our little mountain store was continuously outperforming his Denver superstores. It didn't hurt that we were in an optimal location and had wealthy clientele from all over the world shopping at our store. Sometimes, I had to pause for a moment to try and count the many different languages being spoken simultaneously. This was indeed a sport that brought nations together. What's more remarkable is that the renowned ski town of Vail didn't exist until after WW2, "discovered" by two members of the Tenth Mountain Division. They arrived with a vision and turned it into white gold.

While winters were lucrative, summers were brutal to scratch out a living selling fishing lures and hiking equipment with a base salary plus a 1percent commission. If I wanted to continue to live and flourish, I would have to find another way to make a living in the land of plenty.

In the spring of 1993, I was hired as an "extra" for a Disney movie called *Tall Tales*. It starred Patrick Swayze as Pecos Bill, Oliver Platt as Paul Bunyan, Roger Aron Brown as John Henry, Catherine O'Hara as Calamity Jane, and Gary Sinise as Jonas Hackett, who was the father of Daniel Hackett, played by Nick Stahl. The Vail Valley was buzzing with the news that a portion of the movie would be shot at the Gilman Mine between the nearby towns of Minturn and Red Cliff. The Gilman was a gold and silver mine in its heyday and had previously been closed to the public, but as extras, we were to get special access to the lower reaches in the bowels of the canyon, along the Eagle River. Curiosity to legally venture past the no-trespass signs was at a fever pitch.

The thought of meeting Patrick Swayze along with the rest of the cast was tantalizing, especially after the massive success of the 1990 blockbuster movie *Ghost,* in which Patrick starred along with Demi Moore. It was fascinating to see all the creativity behind the scenes that goes into a movie production. The logistics are monumental. First, they supplied costumes for over two hundred extras, and then everyone had to go through makeup. I walked into the hair and makeup designer's tent and walked out looking like an 1800s miner with a mustache, goatee, and fake coal dust on my face and hands.

They gave us sledgehammers, picks, and shovels. They spread us out on the rocky hillside so that it looked like we were all doing hard labor with taskmasters walking through the laborers, cracking their whips, and forcing people to "put their backs into it." After they did a couple of takes to capture the overall misery of the place, they rolled cameras from the perspective of the son searching for his father toiling in the mine. Before they zoomed in on the father, we were told to make our work look realistic, so we swung our sledgehammers with intent. Gary and I stood beside each other, swinging our hammers and breaking rocks. I broke three hammer handles before realizing that prop hammers weren't the same quality a tradesperson would expect. The handle on the third sledgehammer snapped, but not before sending a rock shard into Gary's cheek, causing him to bleed. I thought the blood trickling down his face made the scene more realistic, but the director cut the scene, and Gary went down to the medic's tent. He was cleaned up, and they stopped the bleeding so they could reapply coal dust to his face before the final scene was shot. In the final scene, the son discovered his father working his fingers to the bone with the rest of us. The son called out, "Pa. Pa," as he realized he may be too late to help save his father's farm from a greedy land baron. Gary finished the scene as a consummate professional, and the director thanked us for enduring the occasional snow showers and long hours.

After working a weekend as an extra, my eyes were opened to the creative complexities of getting a couple of scenes right and the enormous teamwork needed to take a production to the big screen.

Chapter 8

Planning

*If you tell enough people,
your dreams will become a reality.*

The Rocky Mountains provided a rugged buffer from the outside world, and the Vail Valley was a welcome distraction as a Mecca for outdoor recreation. However, we didn't live in an insulated bubble. I was haunted by the evening news that constantly reported the worst in humanity. I found myself getting twisted up inside and increasingly agitated. I questioned whether I was overly sensitive to the negativity because of my experience with the three gangsters, even though I felt they were inherently capable of good had they grown up in an environment that cultivated positive decision-making skills. Something deep inside me wanted to investigate if this continuous barrage of stories about man's inhumanity toward his fellow man was the norm in America. I would have to risk leaving my small-town bubble where people interacted with each other, looked me in the eye, smiled, and waved.

Initially, I wanted to hike the Appalachian Trail from Maine to Georgia and then walk across southern America. I would finish my trek on the Pacific Coast Trail at the Canadian border. I thought I needed to go that far to answer my question. Admittedly, it was a huge undertaking, especially since I had never hiked more than twenty miles in my life. I came to find out that a guy by the name of Peter Jenkins had already done it almost a quarter century ago. Things, however, could have changed drastically in those last twenty-five years. I was undeterred and felt that comparing today's America with Peter's experience might prove which direction our country was heading. I even went to one of Peter's book signings in Denver and discussed my idea with him. He felt it was a great idea, and his words of encouragement were all I needed.

Now, I had to turn the concept into a reality. This was easier said than done. The daunting logistics were overwhelming, but I was resolved. I quit my sales associate job with Gart Sports and said goodbye to my ski bum lifestyle as I took a more lucrative job in construction.

I don't know if I ever entertained the thought of guardian angels, but I did find it amazingly coincidental that Dan Schofield, the guy who tackled "machete man" several years before, happened to walk into Gart Brothers looking for something. We agreed to catch up over dinner at the Jackalope Saloon. It was next door and a favorite hangout for the locals. My fellow ski bums wanted to blow off some steam and enter the Sumo wrestling contest that night, so I met Dan for dinner and a beer. He informed me that he was awarded a contract to remodel the Marriott in Vail and wondered if I would like to join his crew. We sealed the deal with a handshake and agreed that I would start after I gave my "two-week" notice. Dan left, and the rest of us closed the place down. We wrestled Sumo style for a chance to win a dinner for two and free beer. It didn't take much to bring out our competitive nature, and we beat the snot out of each other for little more than bragging rights.

In the spring of 1995, we began remodeling The Marriot in Vail. We did all the steel stud framing, hanging drywall, tape, and texture. We did the lobby, offices, restaurant, conference rooms, and spa. It was hard work, but the pay was good. We were putting in long days, and everything went together with military precision until one fateful day.

We were hanging drywall on the ceiling in the restaurant. We didn't know the sprinkler system in our area was fully charged. As we were hoisting a twelve-foot-long sheet with all the necessary cutouts made, I started to say, "Watch out for the sprinkler…"

Mike slammed his end of the sheet up to the ceiling; he broke the sprinkler's head off. Immediately, water started gushing at five hundred gallons per minute. Thankfully, the concrete slab was pitched to the perimeter, and we soon had a waterfall cascading into the outdoor pool. Mike panicked and tried to save the day by running into the downpour with an empty five-gallon bucket and quickly earned his nickname "Rain Man." By the time I located the shut-off valve in an adjacent stairwell, at least five thousand gallons had poured into the pool.

The Sante Fe Crew

For the next year and a half, I worked long hours remodeling the Marriott in Vail, a hotel in Steamboat Colorado, and another one in Santa Fe, New Mexico. During this time, I pitched the idea of hiking the Appalachian Trail to my girlfriend, Sandrine LeClair. She was a spunky French woman, an avid snowboarder, and an adventurous world traveler with a stamped passport from most countries. She required very little convincing. Although, in hindsight, I think she thought it would be a romantic excursion. I don't think either of us fully comprehended the physical hardships and level of commitment required to complete such an arduous trek. It also became inconceivable for us to leave our beloved dog, Kiana (pronounced Keeanna), behind for the five to six months it would take to finish the trail. Kiana was an athletic, three-year-old, half-Alaskan malamute and half-German shepherd with an easygoing disposition. She had the black and tan markings of a German Shepherd, a Malamute head, and a bushy, curled tail indicative of her native Alaskan Arctic heritage. Initially, people were alarmed by her size but warmed up to her quickly once they realized how friendly she was. She was a gentle giant with a big heart. Our decision to take her on the trek with us was a no-brainer.

Within a year, I had banked enough to finance the trip, and Gart's sales prize of two roundtrip airline tickets was a fortuitous bonus. After finishing the last hotel in Santa Fe, I returned home to Avon, Colorado, intent on telling friends and family about my upcoming adventure, which subconsciously forced me to follow through with what I had started.

Sandrine and I went to the nearest Recreational Equipment Incorporated (REI) store to buy the last of our gear, Kiana's first pack, and dog booties to protect her feet until they toughened up. Over the past several years, we had bought enough gear to outfit a small army. As I looked at the mounds of equipment in my living room, it became apparent that it would not fit in our packs, and we needed to eliminate unnecessary items. After trimming down to what I thought was necessary, we loaded everything up, put our new boots on, and went into the mountains by Vail Pass to test our gear. Although it was a short excursion, we were confident everything worked as advertised. In retrospect, we were naïve but returned home eager to begin the journey. The final logistical nightmare was to purchase enough food for the trip and estimate the food and miscellaneous supplies we would need in each mail drop. For this crucial element of the expedition, we went to Phoenix, Arizona, and recruited Mom and Dad, knowing they could be relied on. As I unraveled our plan to them, emphasizing their importance as our support team, I could see the quizzical look on their faces. They tried to be supportive but didn't understand why I wanted to attempt such a trek. My dad didn't have to say anything. I knew from past experiences what he was thinking. He was old school. He had an ingrained thought process, "If you want to make something of yourself, you need to keep your nose to the grindstone."

While there is truth in that adage, I had heard it a thousand times while growing up, and I knew what he was thinking without him saying a word. The tension level was rising, but seeing that I was determined, Mom pulled me aside and asked, "Son, why on earth do you want to do this?"

Area residents Rick Huber, Sandrine Le Clair and their dog Kiana hike a waterfall in East Vail Thursday. They are off Saturday to hike the Appalachian Trail with hopes of continuing across America to do a comparison of today's America compared to a quarter of a century ago when the author of "Walk Across America" made the traverse. Be sure to wish them good luck.

I reassured her that I wasn't losing my mind or going through an early midlife crisis; it was simply something I had to do. Of course, I had to back that statement up with something concrete. So, I asked her, "Mom, do you remember when I was four or five years old and we lived in Holbrook, Arizona?"

She hesitantly said, "Yes," obviously wondering where I was going with this. "Remember when I was younger, how I always asked you to pack me a lunch so I could explore the hills surrounding Holbrook?"

"Yes."

"Well, didn't you think it was odd that I always wanted to explore my environment, to see what was around the next corner? Mom, I have always been inquisitive and wanted to test my physical abilities while growing up."

She knowingly agreed while we reminisced about some of the adventures I concocted as a youth. Hair-brained as they might have been, they were times when I really felt alive and was able to establish a sense of independence. She was horrified as I divulged some of my life-threatening experiences that she chose to forget or never knew. One example was when I persuaded a good friend to join me on a canoe trip. During the flash flood season, the deluge of rain had converted Cave Creek, AZ, usually a dry wash, into a raging torrent. Armed with Dad's seventeen-foot Coleman aluminum canoe, a couple of wooden paddles, and a youthful invincibility, we scouted out the biggest rapids we could find. As we put in, I asked my buddy if he knew how to paddle. He assured me he did. It quickly became apparent that he didn't know a thing about paddling a canoe, and he could not discern my commands over the roar of the water. We sliced through the muddy, raging water, ricocheting off exposed boulders as we went. You could hear the rocks grinding under the churning water, pulverizing each other at the mercy of unbridled power. We passed a half-submerged, crumpled canoe pinned against a car-sized rock. Undaunted and entirely at the mercy of the water, we raced on until we reached some slack water at the river's edge. At that point, we could eddy out into a road intersection where only the top of a stop sign could be seen. With youthful invincibility and adrenaline coursing through our veins, we decided to try that section again. We ironed out our mistakes during the portage upriver and reviewed proper paddling techniques. The second and third runs proved to be every bit as exciting, except we were more in control of our destiny. Our seaworthy vessel didn't fare so well. It required a lot of pounding with a rubber mallet to get the dents and dings out so that it resembled a canoe once again. To my dad's discerning eye, it was evident that we hadn't floated calm waters. The lecture that ensued involved topics covering personal safety, recklessness, and responsibility. Then he posed the question, which he always knew the answer to. "Was it fun?"

Dad was always an adventurous soul and encouraged us to learn from our mistakes but would have preferred us to use a little more caution and good ole' common sense. As we discussed numerous other adventures, I saw my parents begin to soften and wistfully understand.

My family rallied as they joined me on a shopping spree at Sam's Club, a warehouse store stocked with large bulk items. The excitement intensified as the mounds of food, spices, toiletry items, photo film, Ziploc bags of varying sizes, and dog food filled the carts. We checked out with six super-sized carts loaded to capacity, two more carts filled with almost one thousand pounds of dog food, and six large boxes of biscuits. Since I had a horse for a dog, I figured she would eat five pounds of food a day, and I hoped the journey would take less than six months, leaving me with a little extra in case she required more. We all laughed as we stared at the enormous piles of food and supplies that had taken over Mom's family room. Like a seasoned drill team, we dove in and sorted everything into breakfast, snack, lunch, and dinner items. Then, we sorted those categories into similar items. After the sorting, we packed our first two mail drops and sent them off labeled General Delivery; please save for AT Thru-hiker Rick Huber, and then the respective location and zip code it was going. Seeing my name associated with AT Thru-hiker seemed rather boastful, but I went with it since the AT data book suggested it. The first mail drop was sent to Abol Bridge Campground, which had enough supplies and dog food to last a worst-case scenario of ten days to get through the hundred-mile wilderness. The second mail drop went to the post office in Monson Maine, and had enough supplies to get us to Stratton, Maine. We promised to call home and update everyone on how the wilderness section went when we arrived at Shaw's Hiker Hostel in Monson. From there, we would let them know what we needed more or less of and where to send the following mail drops in correlation to our estimated arrival time. With our family rallying behind us, the trip was already a success. The exuberant support from family lifted our spirits as we drove back to Colorado on cloud nine.

Chapter 9

Travel Logistics

Feeling confident that we had a rock-solid support team we had little left to do except arrive on time at the airport with all our gear accounted for. It would be Kiana's first flight, and we gave her a sedative to calm her nerves. In Portland, Maine, we waited at the baggage carousel as everyone else retrieved their luggage. As the conveyor belt spit out the last bag, a temporary wave of panic washed over me as horror stories raced through my head about unfortunate travelers arriving at their destination without their luggage. Could this be the end? Anxiety welled up inside me as I wondered if one of the straps on our packs hadn't been secured properly and had become entangled in the conveyor system at the airport. I envisioned several baggage handlers chuckling between themselves as they placed bets on which pack would survive the longest as the savage belts shredded our backpacks and all the contents into their rudimentary beginnings.

At the baggage claim counter, I was greeted by a pleasant woman who smiled coyly, obviously picking up on the stressed look on my face. She assured me that our packs had arrived on a previous flight, and she went to retrieve them. Relieved, I wondered how that could happen when you and your luggage checked in simultaneously. Fortunately, a slightly frazzled Kiana was waiting with our packs. Boy, it was obvious she was happy to see a familiar face.

After grabbing our gear, we rented a car and headed north on

Interstate 95 with the windows down, deeply breathing in the thick, salty air of the East Coast. We stopped at Tiny Bigman's seafood shop for lunch, near where the fishing fleets offloaded their precious cargo while opportunistic seagulls waited for scraps as they squawked and hovered in the slight breeze. Tiny was a rotund, jolly man who spoke with a distinct New England accent. We were astounded by the inexpensive prices of lobster. Back home, you would be lucky to find a one-pound lobster for $15.99. At Tiny's, they sold for $4.99/lb. And soft-shell lobster for $3.00/lb. Tiny proudly showed us a ten-pound bug (lobster) in one of his tanks that marine biologists estimated to be one hundred and ten years old. As landlubbers, we were astonished by the huge lobster claws hanging on his wall that dwarfed the ten-pound lobster in its entirety. The monster claws belonged to what was thought to be a forty-five-pound granddaddy lobster. It amazed me that the cockroaches of the sea could attain such sizes if given the opportunity and a fertile environment. Our taste buds rejoiced as we ate our fill of some of the freshest seafood I had ever experienced. I thought I had died and gone to heaven, and it was with mixed emotions we bid Tiny farewell as we headed north to Bangor.

En route to Bangor, I noticed that almost every vehicle had a canoe strapped to it, and I felt a little out of place, like a kid showing up to a baseball game without his glove. I'm confident that the hearty souls of Maine are avid outdoors people, and the canoe is their chosen secondary mode of transportation. Especially since the navigable bodies of water far outnumber usable roads the farther north you drive. It seemed we had entered the territory of adventurous souls, and my inner child screamed with excitement and wonder about what experiences were about to unfold in the land they called Maine. As we ventured north of Bangor on our way to Millinocket, I noticed an increased frequency of cautionary moose-crossing signs. Maine was beginning to feel like the outdoorsman's paradise that I had heard so much about. Before reaching Millinocket, we were treated to a monster bull moose crossing the interstate as if he owned it. He quickly disappeared into the dense foliage as we approached. It is incredible how such a large, gangly animal can move so gracefully through such an overgrown jungle and virtually disappear. This sighting fueled my imagination. I wondered what we would see as we hiked the trail in Maine. Upon arriving in Millinocket, we checked into the Pamola Motel. Karen, the front desk clerk, kindly pointed us toward a good seafood restaurant since we felt obligated to indulge in a lobster feast as our last meal before hitting the trail.

While walking to the restaurant, we noticed a few small but persistent black bugs feasting on us. I laughed out loud as I realized that these were the notorious black flies that we were warned about. I viewed them with contempt, thinking they were no match to our deer flies back home, which could take chunks of flesh and leave a distinct mark. Underestimating their ability, these minuscule black vampires would come back to haunt me.

At the motel, sleep eluded me as I thought about taking the first steps on the adventure of a lifetime. Meanwhile, Sandrine slept soundly as I continued to toss and turn, rehearsing the final logistics. This was more my dream, and I could only hope that Sandrine would be able to appreciate it half as much as I did. After a hearty breakfast, we took Kiana to a veterinary boarding kennel and said goodbye. Dogs are not allowed in Baxter State Park, which made it difficult to explain to Kiana why we were leaving her again. With a great deal of reassurance, she calmed down and seemed to understand. After saying goodbye, we went to the post office and mailed her dog kennel home. There was absolutely no turning back now.

Hiking the APPALACHIAN TRAIL
2160.4 miles

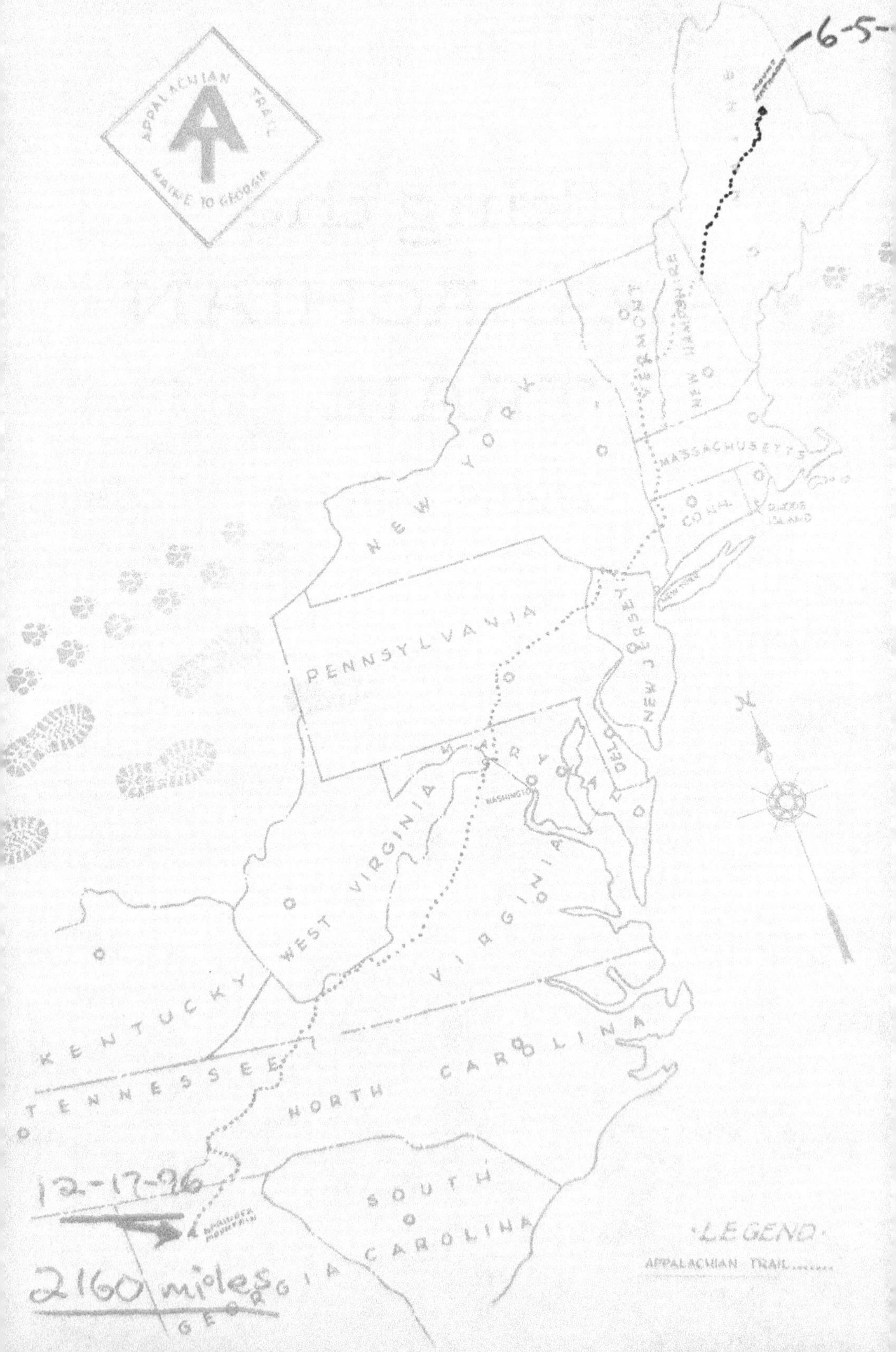

APPALACHIAN TRAIL
MAINE TO GEORGIA
-6-5-
NEW HAMPSHIRE
VERMONT
NEW YORK
MASSACHUSETTS
CONN
NEW JERSEY
PENNSYLVANIA
DEL
WASHINGTON
WEST VIRGINIA
VIRGINIA
KENTUCKY
TENNESSEE
NORTH CAROLINA
SOUTH CAROLINA
GEORGIA
12-17-96
2160 miles
LEGEND
APPALACHIAN TRAIL.......

Chapter 10

Maine

> "Remote for detachment, narrow for chosen company, winding for leisure, lonely for contemplation, the Appalachian Trail beckons not merely north and south, but upward to the body, mind, and soul of man."
>
> – HAROLD ALLEN, *Thru-Hiker's Handbook*

Finally, we were on our way to Baxter State Park, and I detected a slight hint of excitement in Sandrine. Upon arriving, we quickly set up the tent in a light drizzle at the Daicey Pond Campground. Sandrine had agreed to stay behind while I returned the rental car in Bangor. She was a little hesitant about me leaving but was reassured when she saw rangers on duty at the ranger station. I had another run-in with a moose during my two-hour trip to Bangor. This time, a young bull refused to get off the road. We continued to play a cat-and-mouse game for a couple of miles until he finally grew weary of it and stepped aside to let me by. After dropping off the rental car in the middle of nowhere, I approached the attendant and inquired about reserving a taxi to get a ride to the bus terminal.

He shook his head. "You're better off saving your money 'cuz by the time the taxi gets here, you could have walked there."

After getting directions to the bus stop, I thanked him for the advice and walked two miles along a country highway to catch the bus, hoping I would be on time since it was the only one heading north for the day. I arrived with over two hours to spare. The additional two-hour bus ride was uneventful, except for my conversation with one of my fellow passengers. He was an odd, quirky, vertically challenged guy who was overly protective of his carry-on bag. He would open his bag occasionally and peer inside as if to reassure himself that everything was intact. He caught me looking quizzically at the exposed contents and proceeded to tell me his life story and how he loved to "collect" license plates. Hundreds of them were in his bag, and I wondered what his real intent was. Oh, how I longed to be on the trail. When we arrived at Medway, I excused myself and made a hasty retreat for the nearest cab.

Oblivious to posted speed signs, my driver and I raced into the foggy night. At times, I wondered if the cab was on autopilot as the death-defying cabby continued to converse casually while turning his head to look me in the eye. He must have noticed the frantic look in my eyes as he calmly told me he had driven this road countless times and knew it like the back of his hand. At ten pm and in a heavy downpour, we zoomed into Baxter State Park. The cabby screeched to a halt as if to signify the end of the road. Sensing that he was hurrying to get home, I politely asked if he wouldn't mind taking me the rest of the way into Daicey Pond Campground. Agreeably, he slammed the car into gear, and we were off to the races again. We narrowly missed a magnificent white-tail buck as it crossed the road and disappeared into the darkness. After violently swerving to miss the deer, I braced for impact as we seemed destined to power slide off the road and into the tangled forest. My driver's reactions would have made any New York cabby envious. He corrected his steering and gunned the throttle, shooting up a muddy rooster off his tires and fishtailing back and forth several times before streaking like a missile to the campground. That's what a fifty-dollar cab ride would get you in 1996. Safe at last on solid ground, I watched as the headlights illuminated our tent, and a relieved Sandrine poked her head out, inquiring why it had taken me so long. Feeling slightly hen-pecked but thankful to be alive, I paid the man, and he quickly disappeared into the darkness with the pedal to the metal.

We chose to begin our hike at Mount Katahdin, the trail's northern terminus, to avoid the crowds starting at Springer Mountain. We hoped to walk in solitude and achieve a quality wilderness experience. Due to its remote location, I underestimated the logistics of getting to Daicey Pond in Baxter State Park. A southern start at Springer Mountain would have been much simpler once you factor in the complexities of boarding a dog before you start and then retrieving your pet once you were out of Baxter State Park.

> "I went into the woods because I wished to live deliberately, to front the essential facts of life, and see if I could not learn what it had to teach, and not, when I came to die, discover that I had not lived."
>
> – HENRY DAVID THOREAU, *Walden: Life in the Woods*

We were lulled to sleep by a steady rain and woke the next morning to gray skies and a cool, invigorating bite to the morning air. In the excitement of taking our first steps, I don't even recall eating breakfast, let alone preparing it. We hurriedly packed, signed in at the ranger station, and were off to hike the 7.6 miles to the summit of Katahdin. Mt. Katahdin is the tallest mountain in Maine, with more than 4000 feet of climbing to reach the 5270-foot summit. Penobscot Native Americans called it the "Greatest Mountain." According to Penobscot tribal legend, Mount Katahdin was inhabited by Pamola, a thunder god and protector of the mountain. Henry David Thoreau noted in his 1846 exploration of the area, "Pamola is always angry with those who climb to the summit of Ktaadn."

Before leaving Colorado, I had hiked several fourteeners and countless trails in the Eagles Nest and Holy Cross Wilderness areas. All these hikes had originated at an elevation of eight thousand feet or higher, so I wasn't too concerned about hiking a mountain that would have been considered a hill back home. With fresh legs and lungs used to higher elevations, we climbed with relative ease to the summit. On the way up, the clouds thickened, and animals would take on a ghostly appearance and disappear as the clouds swirled around us, moving with a noticeable intensity the higher we climbed.

Birds brave enough to venture out in the growing fury would appear, struggling to fly, and then quickly disappear into the clouds. We wondered if they ever reached their destination or sought refuge and survived to fly another day.

Northern terminus — only 2,160 miles to go

I knew we were getting close to the summit when we reached the ladder section constructed of rebar embedded into a rock face. We climbed straight up that ladder and vanished into the moisture-laden veil of fog. We didn't know how long this storm would last but knew of Katahdin's reputation. If we turned back, there was no telling when we could safely summit again. We moved quickly across the "tabletop flat," weaving our way around boulders that would seem to vaporize into the misty shroud. The wind started to howl as we neared the summit sign. The gray skies quickly turned black and buffeted us with gale-force rain. As the ambient temperature dropped, we stopped long enough to take photos at the Katahdin summit sign, signifying the beginning of our journey south—only 4,583,000 steps to go. I could only hope that my camera worked properly in the driving rain. I relished testing my grit against the forces of nature, and then I noticed a sliver of fear in Sandrine's eyes as she began to shiver. I stepped in close and yelled, "We need to get off this mountain, *now!*" With the wind screaming at forty to fifty miles per hour, the rain quickly turned to quarter-sized hail, pelting us with relentless stinging blows as we scurried down to the safety of the trees. So, our journey began. We were humbled by the forces of nature and the mountain called Katahdin.

We continued to hike in the rain all the way back to camp and were treated to our first trail sighting of a giant bull moose casually feeding in Daicey Pond. At first, I detected a slight movement from what I thought had been a rock about forty feet offshore. Upon closer inspection, "the rock" was actually the shoulders of a moose that transformed into a massive bull as he raised his head from the depths below and exposed an enormous set of antlers draped with the plants he was foraging on. Delighted in our discovery and because we were concealed in the shoreline vegetation, we watched as the magnificent creature fed on succulent water plants, oblivious to our presence. I could have stopped hiking right there and been completely satisfied, but the adventure was just beginning. The trail beckoned for more discovery. Silently, we left the undisturbed ungulate and wondered to ourselves what else would magically unfold as we headed south.

We Feed Them Tourists

The rain stopped while signing out at the Daicey Ranger Station, and the black flies came out in force. We had researched bug repellants and took stock in Avon's Skin So Soft. It became apparent that we had fallen prey to their marketing genius that claimed their product would repel bugs and be better for our skin than a product with DEET. Their ploy made sense to me, but the black flies thought it was barbeque sauce and continued to feast. I imagined them relishing our flavor as they smacked their serrated jaws in anticipation. As I swatted like a madman, trying to fend off the ensuing attack, I noticed that the rangers, Gabe and Marsha, didn't seem bothered by the swarms of veracious female flies seeking to nourish their developing eggs with a high-protein blood meal. I knew I had to have whatever they were using. I calmly asked, trying not to look desperate, "What are you guys using to keep the black flies off you?"

With smug smiles, they responded in that thick upstate Maine drawl, "We just let them feed on the tourists."

I stood there staring and thinking, *What a warped sense of humor.*

I sheepishly smiled and nodded my head in an understanding gesture. Who was I kidding?

I would have said the same thing if I were in their shoes.

Marsha finally relented and offered, "It's pretty much a state of mind; you just don't let them bother you. But if you're going to be in one place for a while, use a citronella-based repellent and always wear long sleeves and long pants."

Some herbalists suggested that a few garlic cloves would work as a repellent. But, after seeing how they were unphased by Skin So Soft, I wondered if these bugs preferred the extra flavor. It seemed that even the mosquitoes had developed a longer and stronger proboscis that could penetrate up to two layers of clothing if it was tight to the skin. After a brief conversation with the rangers about what the trail was like on the way to Abol Bridge Campground, Sandrine and I made a hasty retreat to the safety of our tent. Bitten but not beaten, we settled into a deep slumber, dreaming with anticipation of tomorrow's adventure.

We were awakened by the haunting cries of loons at four a.m. Eager to get started, I crawled out of the tent, trying not to disturb Sandrine. Honestly, I didn't know how she could sleep through the eerie, piercing cries of the loons. There is something about the loon's cry that adds to a place's wild mystique. I found myself wandering in the pre-dawn light around Daicey Pond and discovered three more bull moose appearing from within the thick fog blanket that shrouded the pond and surrounding trees. With the sound of the loons in the distance and the grazing apparitions ahead, I was momentarily transported into a realm that ancient man shared. I was thankful for the foresight of the late Governor Percival Baxter and his generous donation that established this state park. No zoo could hold a candle to an experience like this.

Back in camp, as I prepared a gourmet oatmeal breakfast, a covey of grouse ambled through camp with their fuzzy little chicks scampering in hot pursuit. While marveling and giving thanks for our feathered guests, I hollered for Sandrine, "Come and get it before I throw it out." She rallied, energized by the additional sleep, and ate like a ravenous animal. I didn't know whether to be shocked by her appetite or be pleased that she enjoyed my cooking.

After walking 15.2 miles on our first day, we were excited about the 7.5-mile walk to Abol Bridge Campground and our reunion with Kiana. We looked forward to hot showers, picking up our first mail drop, and reevaluating our pack weight before entering the 100-Mile Wilderness. We shouldered our packs and hiked south into the rain. Our gear provided perfect protection from the steady downfall, black flies, and mosquitoes but caused us to overheat as we struggled with uncomfortably heavy packs. Sandrine and I agreed that we would have to eliminate some weight if we were to survive the wilderness section. This was a learning experience that we would continue to hone as we hiked. We opted to hike with our rain gear and head nets on instead of slathering Skin So Soft barbeque sauce on ourselves. Self-preservation forced us to choose between overheating or being eaten alive by the black flies. Covered as we were, those pesky little flies found a way into our head nets, and Sandrine suffered the most. Within an hour of leaving Daicey Pond, Sandrine had been bitten countless times on her neck and looked like she was sporting a puffy, pink necklace. She looked miserable but never complained. I felt horrible that I dragged her into such a ruthless environment and offered to duct tape her head net to her rain jacket. This seemed to help, and she marched off with a newfound determination. With Sandrine in the lead, we came around a corner and found ourselves face-to-face with a young bull moose. In the ensuing standoff, we looked at each other, unsure how to handle the situation. Thankfully, the moose whirled around and trotted down the trail, stopping occasionally and looking over his shoulder to see if we were still in pursuit. For the next mile, he continued to trot down the trail until he was out of sight, and once we came into his view, he would repeat the sequence all over, refusing to step aside. Finally, he grew weary of us tagging along, and he ventured to the safety of the trees. He seemed curious as he watched the strange-looking two-legged creatures with large humps on their backs walk by.

Ecstatic and careful not to quell Sandrine's newfound enthusiasm for the trail, I warned her that we had been lucky not to walk upon a mother moose and her calf. Emphasizing caution, I told her how I had been chased up a tree by a protective cow moose while fishing on the Kenai River in Alaska during the summer of my eighth-grade year.

We had been hiking in a steady rain since we left Daicey Pond, and then the clouds unleashed an impressive deluge. I had not witnessed a torrential downpour like this since I was a kid. In Phoenix, the monsoons quickly dump several inches of rain, causing the neighborhood streets to flood. In my youth, I would take full advantage of the monsoonal flooding and float the family canoe down the raging streets in pursuit of adventure on the high seas. As I reminisced about my childhood, we came across seven people standing on the shore of Foss Brook. They were extremely nervous about crossing the Foss since the combined effect of the spring runoff and the heavy rain had transformed the brook into a swollen, roaring force to be reckoned with. Refusing to be deterred, I grabbed a dead lodge pole pine long enough to straddle the opposing banks. The other hiker's thought it was a great idea and elected me to be the guinea pig to see if it would work. We lodged the opposite end between two trees and secured our end between two boulders. After crossing, I left my pack on the shore, returned to the slightly skeptical onlookers, and offered to carry their packs across. Seven trips later, they became believers and crossed one by one, using the tree as a handrail. I positioned myself downstream with another long branch, prepared to pluck anyone out if they couldn't hang on and got swept. Sandrine and one of the other guys, who were slight in stature, had their feet swept, and a look of pure terror came over their faces. I prayed that the flexing pine they used as a handrail wouldn't snap. Refusing to panic, they both clung to the tree and, with renewed determination, pulled themselves hand-over-hand to the out-reached grasp of the others. In an instant, total strangers had come together in a victorious bonding experience.

We successfully crossed the Knowlton Brook in a similar fashion. As we reached Katahdin Stream, the storm increased in intensity, and the rain came down as if someone had opened the flood gates from above. Crossing the Katahdin Stream became treacherous as we watched the level of the stream rise before our eyes, with no indication of slowing as the deluge continued. We forged ahead, crossing in pairs for stability before the stream became impassable. Sandrine and I made it across as deafening thunder roared overhead, and a simultaneous lightning bolt struck thirty yards downriver. Startled and in awe at the increasing fury of Mother Nature, I turned to see the others scrambling for cover under a few sparse trees on a small island in the middle of the stream. They were extremely exposed and vulnerable on that stretch of real estate. It was apparent that the rising water would soon swallow that patch of land and force them to swim. I motioned for them to finish the crossing, but they were frozen like deer in headlights. I quickly crossed back to the stranded hikers, throwing caution to the wind, hoping that lightning wouldn't strike twice in the same vicinity. We had to work fast as the water continued to rise, and we were able to get everyone safely ashore. With renewed enthusiasm, we hiked the remaining mile to the Abol Bridge campground and set up camp in the rain. As we were putting up our tent, I couldn't help but envy other campers enjoying the luxury of their motor homes, trailers, and pop-up tent trailers.

After a soggy dinner, Sandrine and I went through our packs with a fine-tooth comb, eliminating anything we had not used or considered a luxury item. With the 100-Mile Wilderness looming ahead of us, we were forced out of self-preservation to cut weight drastically from our packs. We were both amazed at how quickly everything added up. We mailed clothes, books, a Swiss army knife, unnecessary items from our cook set home, and letters telling everyone back home that we were still alive and enjoying our adventure. Duplicate items from our first aid kit, spare filters for our water purifier, repair kits for our stove and tent, town clothes, and personal hygiene items went into a floater package we mailed to our next town stop in Monson, Maine. Amazingly, we reduced our combined pack weight by almost twenty pounds.

To my surprise, our first resupply box had a few letters from home along with the necessary provisions to get us through the 100-Mile Wilderness. I carried a letter from my best friend for the entire AT length and referred to it often when the going got tough. It read:

The winner is always part of the answer,
The loser is always part of the problem.

The winner always has a program,
The loser always has an excuse.

The winner says, "Let me do it for you."
The loser says, "That's not my job."

The winner sees an answer for every problem,
The loser sees a problem in every answer.

The winner says, "It may be difficult, but it is possible."
The loser says, "It may be possible, but it's too difficult."

Rick, I know you're a winner. The experiences we've had are tucked away in memory, and the future ones will just have to wait a few months. Always remember that living out your dreams is the ultimate reward in life… God bless you, Sandrine, and Kiana on your journey, and don't forget Cindy and I are always here for you… JR

The following day, we were awakened at four a.m. by a Meadow Lark singing at the top of his lungs. It gave a whole new meaning to the saying that the early bird gets the worm. He proudly sang his song until he successfully woke every bird in the neighborhood. This resulted in a beautiful cacophony that I would grow to prefer over the noise pollution of the mechanized world. I stayed nestled in my sleeping bag until 5:30 AM, listening to the sweet chorus while Sandrine slept blissfully through the increasing crescendo. When she woke, I asked her if she was having a good time, and she responded without hesitation, "Ah…No."

She isn't going to make it, ran through my mind.

She didn't complain much and was trying to make the best of it, but it was apparent she wasn't enjoying the outdoorsman's paradise of Maine like I was. Sandrine's pack weight had been reduced to thirty-five pounds, and we were optimistic that the reduced burden would enable her to focus more on the intrinsic beauty of the trail instead of any physical discomfort inherent to hiking long distances. I could only hope that she would discover her adventurous spirit as the mysteries of the trail unfolded before us.

After breakfast and a quick shower, Sandrine decided to hang back while I went to pick up Kiana. When I left the campground,

I encountered some anglers catching salmon from the Penobscot River. It took great restraint on my part not to join in, forcing myself to stay focused on retrieving Kiana from her kennel in Millinocket. Even though Kiana was a 120-pound half-Alaskan Malamute and half-German shepherd mix, she was an incredibly gentle and faithful dog who often suffered from separation anxiety, so I was compelled to hustle into town, vowing to try fishing another time. This was going to be my first attempt at hitchhiking. I walked for two hours and six miles on the road to Millinocket. I saw twenty-one moose, and had only seven cars pass me; I wondered if I had the proper technique. With another twenty-four miles to go, I knew I had to figure this hitching thing out, or I wouldn't make it to the veterinary's kennel before they closed.

I tried holding my thumb in different postures. I looked the oncoming drivers in the eye and pumped my thumb in the direction I wanted to go. Nothing influenced the speeding cars to pick me up. Just as I resolved myself to walk the entire way into Millinocket, a car rumbled by and stopped. Shocked but thankful for the opportunity, I ran to the open window and asked for a ride to Millinocket. The smell of cheap liquor permeated from within, and the driver responded cheerfully, "Sure, hop on in."

He didn't slur his words and spoke coherently, so I took a chance and jumped in, knowing that the odds of catching another ride in this remote stretch of backcountry highway were slim to none. The driver, a hulking young man and an offensive lineman for the local high school football team, informed me that carrying my pack would increase my hitchhiking success rate. This would set me apart from being misidentified as a vagrant. I thanked him for the advice and chuckled to myself as I realized everyone else in the car was suffering from intense hangovers. They had partied like rock stars and were now paying the price. They dropped me off in Millinocket, and I quickly caught another ride from a long-time local. Thankful that my hitchhiking karma had improved, I listened to the man talk non-stop all the way to the Northwood Veterinary Clinic.

Speaking for the first time, I thanked him for the ride and said goodbye. Kiana greeted me with boundless enthusiasm, smiling and wagging her tail in circles as she pranced around the vet's office while she waited for me to settle her bill. She knew we were going somewhere and didn't care where, as long as it was out of there.

On my journey into town, I didn't see a single car heading back to Abol Bridge Campground. So, instead of tempting fate, I called a cab. During the cab ride, the driver informed me that the local economy was in a slump due to the paper mill's automation. Many folks in the area were laid off and lost their homes as a result. She mentioned that homes were selling for half of their appraised value or best offer. Despite the economic downturn, she remained optimistic that things would turn around with renewed efforts to develop tourism. To promote the area further, she informed me that the crime rate was really low and that the last homicide in the area was back in 1982. Unlike other rural regions of America, she said, "The biggest offenses around here are the kids with too much time on their hands and not enough creative outlets, so they turn to drinking, resulting in frequent DUIs."

100 Mile Wilderness
06/08/96

Kiana was an instant celebrity with Linda, the owner of the Abol Bridge camp store. She had recently lost her dog to old age, and Kiana eagerly took all the love and praise Linda showered her with. I sometimes wonder if dogs don't intuitively sense sadness, pain, and loss and if they are there for us unconditionally to help us through the difficulties we all endure. Linda gave us some topical medicine for Ki's tender belly to help ward off the black flies. We said our goodbyes, and we headed toward the 100-Mile Wilderness.

I looked back one last time to see Katahdin in all its majesty, basking in the morning sun, daring adventurous souls to test their mettle. I wondered how my Northbound comrades would feel once they emerged from the 100-Mile Wilderness after hiking over twenty-one hundred miles and could see Katahdin in all its glory. I could only imagine the gauntlet of emotions that coursed through their minds, reinvigorating them to push their trail-hardened bodies to the summit of Katahdin come hell or high water.

We dove into the 100-Mile Wilderness to the sound of Sandrine's bear whistle banging against her Nalgene water bottle. Did I mention she was petrified of bears? Before we reached Hurd Brook Lean-to, a three-sided camping platform, we came across a ton of moose sign and some very fresh bear sign. It seems that the local wildlife frequently used the AT. Sandrine reminded me of a problem bear the rangers were trying to trap. They mentioned that they would relocate it if it had an ear tag. But the one they were looking for had a tag on each ear. This meant it had become habituated to humans and lost its fear of people. It was on a rampage, harassing campers for a "Yogi" snack.

Braving the inevitable mosquito swarm, we stopped briefly at the Hurd Shelter to duct tape some hotspots on our feet and to patch a cut I'd gotten on my foot during one of the earlier stream crossings. We signed in on the ledger and snapped a couple of pictures of all the unnecessary gear that hikers in survival mode had jettisoned. There were cast iron skillets, ropes, water jugs, axes, big knives, and giant fishing lures, to name a few of the extravagances people thought they needed. It reminded me of stories about early pioneers discarding their treasures from their wagons as they headed west.

In a rush to escape the savage swarm, we hurried to the log crossing on Hurd Brook. I was the first to cross, and about midway, my boots slipped on the wet logs and shot out from under me. I plunged into the Brook, getting my first AT baptism. After crawling out the other side, I searched for a hiking stick to stabilize me for future crossings. I found a stout hickory that appeared sturdy enough to make it to Springer Mountain.

We were hiking along Rainbow Ledges when Kiana bolted out of the peripheral shrubs and passed me on the trail, hell-bent on staying ahead of the constant drone from the ensuing black cloud of insects. Panic set in as I realized she had ditched her pack along with her six-day food supply somewhere in the forest while trying to escape from the bloodthirsty winged mob. I only had another five days of dog food in my pack. Knowing Kiana's appetite, there was no choice but to head into the woods in the direction she had come from, making circles into the forest on either side of the trail, hoping to find her pack. Fortune shined on us as I found her pack fully intact in a tangled thicket about two hundred yards back down the trail.

We made it to Rainbow Lake and were the only ones there, except for a couple of guides fishing out of canoes with their clients. I thought the bug problem in Baxter State Park was terrible until we stopped to set up the tent at the designated site. The black cloud grew increasingly loud as reinforcements joined the onslaught. Kee was madly running around the camp, diving into the bushes, trying to find solace, but none could be found. It's one thing to suffer because of choices you have made, but it is incredibly disheartening when you see innocents suffering. I'd heard rumors that Maine had the most moose/auto collisions this time of the year. The moose were reported to run mindlessly, trying to escape the blood-sucking onslaught. After witnessing Kiana's reaction, I do not doubt that the sheer numbers could drive the largest moose mad. The black flies were crawling like ants through Kee's fur. I quickly brushed her down and put her in the tent with us. She didn't move a muscle and looked content as she fell fast asleep. On the other hand, I lay on my back, watching through the mesh ceiling of my tent as at least three hundred mosquitoes gathered on the underside of my rainfly. The hum of winged bloodsuckers intensified as more gathered under the rainfly. Drawn like a moth to fire by every breath we exhaled. The inside of my tent had dark spots where we killed the black flies and blood spots where the mosquitoes met their demise. It sounded like a light rain pelting the rainfly as they bombed our fortress. Our bug repellent was starting to run low, as *someone* had been re-applying continuously throughout the day. I was beginning to think that I drastically underestimated the intensity of the bugs of Maine. We had to ration the repellent and hike with head nets, long sleeves, and long pants as the heat of June started ratcheting up. Duct taping all cuffs and the perimeter of our head nets to our shirts, we saved the repellent for our exposed hands. We went to bed in an itchy mess and were frequently awakened by the haunting cry of Loons. Then, a Great Horned Owl found a perch above our tent and waited to hoot until we were soundly resting. Sleep didn't come easy between the loons and the Great Horned Owl. In the predawn hours, a band of raccoons visited us. Thankfully, we had taken the time to hang our food correctly, and they made quite an unsuccessful ruckus trying to pillage our camp for food. Kee slept through it all.

06/09/96

Before breaking camp, I took an icy plunge in Rainbow Lake. The cold, crystal-clear water was incredibly soothing on all my bites, and I found temporary refuge where the bugs could not follow. Coming back to shore, the first wave of bugs was ineffective as they contacted my wet skin and became immobilized. I hoped they were drowning.

As I put on my hiking clothes, I noticed movement in the shoreline ripples, and to my amazement, there were numerous big, fat, cigar-length leeches prowling the waters. They must have been attracted by the vibration in the water from my morning swim. I couldn't help but feel sorry for the moose that tried to find refuge in the lakes while foraging on aquatic vegetation, only to be subdued by these parasites. What a rough way to eke out an existence. While breaking camp, I noticed that the rigors of the trail were already taking a toll on Sandrine, and I wondered how long she would last. As hard and uncomfortable as this was, it was far easier than the construction work I had done to get here. Perspective and a positive state of mind would get us through the rigors of walking through Maine.

As we hiked along the lake, we came across *huge* granite boulders covered in green moss, dispersed intermittently, probably resulting from an ancient glacial retreat. The stunning variations of green foliage were not lost on this transplanted desert rat. The rotting decay from the dense foliage gave the forest a rich, earthy aroma, all signs of a fertile and healthy ecosystem. I found myself unconsciously breathing deeper, trying to take it all in.

We made it roughly ten miles and were camping near Pollywog Stream. The bugs were making it challenging to cook and do any camp chores. The mosquitoes weren't as bad, but the black flies had shown up with reinforcements, creating a humming black cloud that followed our every movement. Nobody wanted to jump in the creek and run the black fly gauntlet back to the tent, so after dinner, we dove into the tent tired, sweaty, and stinky. Waiting for sleep's sanctuary as the pitter-patter of kamikaze black flies pounded the walls and the tent fly, lulling us into a guarded sleep. This certainly wasn't the romantic walk in the woods that Sandrine had envisioned.

06/10/96

In the morning, we broke camp in a refreshing rain with no bugs. Ecstatic, we hiked all day in wet clothes. As we climbed Nesuntabunt mountain, we kept hearing sounds like a Harley motorcycle starting up or somebody playing the drums, and it wasn't too far from either side of the trail. Upon closer inspection, I sneaked up on a Spruce grouse drumming on a log. He was trying to call in the ladies. He wasn't alone, as rival males were sounding off around us. Combined with the singing of other birds, it was nature's orchestra at its finest. Especially the drum crescendo, where everyone is trying to outdo each other. At the top of Nesuntabunt, my shoulder strap snapped. The extra forty pounds of dog food combined with my normal pack weight was too much for my Jansport external frame pack, but it was nothing that a little paracord and duct tape couldn't fix.

We spent the night at Wadleigh Stream Lean-to, and Sandrine was borderline paranoid about bears. She never went anywhere without her bear spray and whistle; she even slept with it. She went to the outhouse armed for battle. It's been a week since we climbed Katahdin, and we were cherishing the simple things like a brisk swim, a sponge bath, a cold drink of water, a hot meal, and a place to lay our heads down safe from insects. What we tend to take for granted in this modern day with all of its conveniences is amazing. We truly are spoiled here in America.

06/11/96

While we walked along, I noticed most of the streams had an abundance of brightly colored red-orange Wood frogs. During winter hibernation, this fascinating frog is known to survive the winter without a beating heart, as most of its body is frozen.

We made it to the newly constructed Pataywadjo Spring Lean-to. It's a beautiful L.L. Bean-sponsored shelter with a log table and benches. There were also dispersed tent sites as well. These luxuries are unheard of out west, but I was starting to get used to this. I went to get water from the nearby freshwater spring and noticed a bunch of worms crawling around in the sand at the bottom of the spring. Some were already encasing themselves with tube-like homes woven out of silk and grains of sand. Caddis fly larvae are susceptible to pollution and are the canary in the coal mine of freshwater insects. A healthy population of these bugs was an excellent indication of good water quality. I probably didn't need to filter the water, but I did it out of an abundance of caution.

06/12/96

On the way to Cooper Brook Lean-to, I stopped to let my feet cool off in a stream. I pulled my feet out just as they were starting to ache from the cold, and to my surprise, I caught a huge leech on my big toe. It didn't want to let go, and when it did, it left a sensitive red mark. Why do leeches have such an affinity for blisters or pre-blister hot spots? How did they sense those weak spots? Did they prefer dessert before the main course, where pus is the crème brulee, and blood is the entree? We certainly couldn't let our guard down in these woods.

There had been a storm brewing all day, and we hoped it would bring a reprieve from the bugs. It caught us as we were crossing a stream. I felt the air being charged, and my hair stood up with static electricity. Then there was a deafening, almost simultaneous *flash & crack*. Fear permeated my core as I questioned the wisdom of an external frame pack. We dove into the trees on the far side of the stream, ditched our packs, and waited until the thunder and lightning subsided. We made it to the Cooper Brook Falls Lean-to and were able to go for a quick swim before another storm started rolling in. We got the tent up as the evening sky flashed and thunderous booms echoed, unleashing another impressive downpour.

06/13/96

We were almost halfway through the 100-Mile Wilderness when we met Wild Bill, a Baptist minister, his wife Cindy, and their son Travis, who were also traveling south. Cindy had twisted her knee and was moving gingerly, but it was the least from which she suffered. Her neck, face, wrists, and hands were bright pink and swollen. Her hands and wrists looked like she had elephantiasis and were ready to split. She didn't complain and kept putting one foot in front of the other. There were no other options; the nearest phone or services were fifty plus miles away in Monson. We came across another young couple, Dove and Rebecca, who were doing their best to commune with nature while hiking south, but the constant onslaught of bugs disrupted their Zen-like Walk in the woods. We forded the East Pleasant River and set up camp, hoping Wild Bill and his family would show up. They came in late and chose to stay another day and rest. The East Pleasant River campsite was anything but pleasant. The bugs were ferocious.

06/14/96

We were forced to run the gauntlet every morning to take care of business. We would dig a cat hole, drop our pants and pray that this was a quick deposit because, within seconds, our legs and butt would be covered with black flies and mosquitoes wanting an easy feast. No one dared to bring reading material to the morning ritual. Sandrine is at her breaking point; she's depressed, and tears are streaming down her face. My hands and wrists are swollen; my ankles and lower legs are swollen. I don't dare let on that I'm miserable. There is no choice but to march on.

While in Millinocket, before we started our hike, some locals told us a story about this local kid who went to solo hike the 100-Mile Wilderness. The bugs drove him crazy, and he broke into somebody's cabin and stole some food before disappearing into the woods. Luckily, the owner found his cabin had been broken into, and the authorities located the kid several days later sitting under a tree, dazed, with bugs crawling all over him. His whole body was swollen, and he was near death. Initially, I thought it was a tall tale, but now I wondered if there wasn't some truth to it.

We made it to the top of White Cap Mountain as the wind started screaming, pushing massive black thunderheads in our direction as lightning clapped, illuminating the voluminous clouds. White Cap was rugged and every bit as tough as the SOB trail in the Black Canyon of the Gunnison River back in Colorado. Once I had done it, I knew why they call it the SOB trail because it is two thousand feet straight down. This section of the AT was made more difficult with a snarl of trees; many snapped off and piled higher than a house on the trail, creating the world's largest jungle gym. We had to crawl over them and belly crawl under them. Going around these massive piles was nearly impossible as the forest was so thick. The winds that caused this jumbled mess had to be impressive. We snapped a few pics at the summit and dashed to the safety of the trees as Mother Nature unleashed her fury.

We made it to the Sidney Tappan Campsite, and the bugs were horrendous, so I made a campfire. The damp wood created a smoke shield that kept the bugs at bay. As long as the wood was wet, we opted to smoke ourselves and gear so our bug repellent would last. The clouds finally cleared, and we were treated to a brilliant star-studded night sky. Then, the fireflies came out in mass, and we watched as thousands of green lights blinked everywhere. The forest glowed a luminous green. This was the first time I had witnessed the firefly mating ritual, and it was spectacular.

I couldn't get my Whisper Lite stove to work. I tore it apart and cleaned it, but it still wouldn't light. Dove and Rebecca's Whisper Lite wasn't working as well, so I cannibalized parts and got one of them to work. We finished dinner around 10 PM and collapsed into the tent, only to be treated to a blinking green light show from all the fireflies on our tent fly.

06/15/96

I woke up to take care of the Dutchman's Deuce and realized our toilet paper supply had nearly vanished. We still had four days of hiking before we arrived in Monson. I did some investigating to see if it had been misplaced or lost. I came to find out that Sandrine had been using it to clean the bug splatters from the inside of the tent instead of using a wet hanky. The rest of our supply was going toward her monthly hygiene. Crap, we may have to resort to using leaves.

We hiked past Screw Auger Falls, and we stopped long enough to get a few photos and dunk our heads in the cooling water. Before climbing up Chairback Mountain, Sandrine was swarmed by bugs. They attacked her abdomen through her buttonholes. She snapped, her eyes teared up, and she started taking her top off in a panic to get at the black flies. She was oblivious to the black cloud that hovered above her head, waiting to finish her off. I had to yell at her to put her shirt back on and smash the ones already inside. She looked at me with tear-filled eyes and hesitated; she was teetering on the edge.

I firmly told her again, "Put your shirt back on."

This time, it registered. She finally did and began furiously killing all the bugs inside with a vengeance that startled me. That was a close call. I imagined her dropping everything and running crazed through the woods. I wondered if the swarm wasn't caused by her period. Regardless, we had to keep moving to stay ahead of the onslaught. She remained edgy throughout the evening until we reached Chairback Gap Lean-to and got some food into her. It seemed that she passed out as soon as she had taken her last bite of food. She woke up in the morning smiling as if nothing had ever happened. Come to find out, she hadn't been snacking throughout the day for fear of lifting her head net. She had bonked and was beyond "Hangry" when her meltdown occurred.

We were sitting around the campfire fantasizing about what

everyone was going to do and eat while in Monson when a guy came racing into camp, swatting madly at his winged assailants. He certainly didn't read the room as he continued to rant about the bugs. He said he had heard of a study that some college students had done on some of the black fly populations nearby. They found thirteen different DNA samples of the same black fly species, inferring that the pesky little blood suckers were adapting and mutating incredibly fast while building up a tolerance to bug sprays. Fact or fiction, I couldn't tell you, but it certainly added to their legendary reputation. If all else fails, feed them tourists.

06/16/96

After camping at Long Pond Stream Lean-to, we had to ford Long Pond Stream, which was running high. Rebecca, one of the hikers, lost her canteen mid-stream. I had to run about a quarter of a mile downstream to fish it out. After crossing a couple more streams, we encountered a guy named Greg. He had just graduated from college and was section hiking from Stratton to Katahdin. He had just resupplied in Monson and was hanging out by the stream, relaxing and grabbing something to eat. He asked us how our food supply was, and I responded, "We're doing all right."

Then he said, "Well, you know what? I bought five extra Snickers bars for any South Bounders coming out of that 100-Mile Wilderness."

He gave each of us a Snickers bar. You would have thought we found a pearl of great value.

Unexpected Trail Magic certainly lifted our spirits.

06/17/96

Our final camp of the 100-Mile Wilderness was at Little Wilson Stream. After dinner, I went swimming to cool off and gashed my big toe on a rock. I let it bleed to sanitize the wound site and then duct-taped it. We were treated to another spectacular firefly display. The forest was alive with thousands of dancing, blinking lights. It was magical.

Sandrine crossing Big Wilson Stream

The next morning, I stopped to get some photos of the spectacular Little Wilson Falls, and Sandrine kept on motoring. I think everyone was anxious to get to Monson, but I worried that if Sandrine didn't stop to smell the roses, she would miss much of the intrinsic beauty of the AT, and only the difficult struggles would be etched in her mind.

With four miles to go before we were out of the wilderness; we came across a sign that read:

CAUTION – There are no places to obtain supplies or help until you reach Abol Bridge – 90 miles North. You should not attempt this section unless you carry a minimum of ten days' supplies. Do not underestimate the difficulty of this section. Good Hiking.

The 100-Mile Wilderness is no joke, and I wondered how many southbound thru-hiking dreams were crushed.

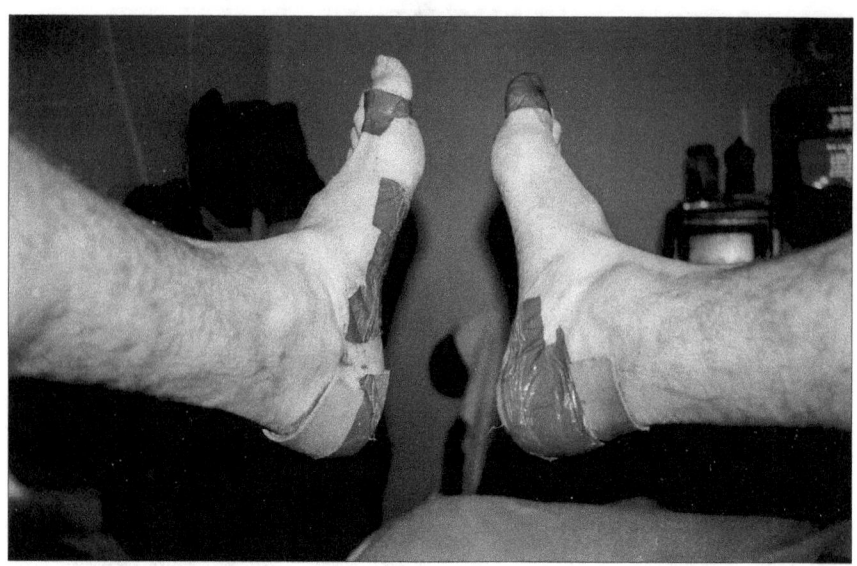

Collateral damage from the 100-mile wilderness

06/18 & 19/96
Shaw's

We made it to Shaw's Hiker Hostel, which was owned by Pat and Keith Shaw, where hospitality was second to none. We were welcomed with open arms and a knowing smile as we walked through the front door. It felt like I had walked into my grandma and grandpa's house. For dinner, the Shaw's put on one of the most incredible spreads consisting of baked chicken, meatloaf, mixed vegetables, broccoli, cauliflower, potatoes, salad, and apple fritters for dessert. As we were sitting around the family dining table, Keith announced, "This is all you can eat. If any of you leave the table hungry, it's your own damn fault."

True to his words, nobody left hungry, and it was a culinary sensation that even my grandma would have been proud of. The next day, I was able to fix my stove with parts Keith had on hand. He then showed us around town (population 500), where everyone seemed to know him, and then ran us into Dover so we could resupply with groceries. Only in Maine can you get a lobster sandwich at

Pat and Keith Shaw

McDonald's. It was incredible. When we got back, ol' mister Shaw, at seventy years of age, challenged me to a game of horseshoes. I quickly learned that this wasn't his first time. He was a ringer, and he smoked me 21-4.

Shaw's is under new ownership with the same zeal for hospitality. Kimberly and Jarrod Hester (Hippie Chick & Poet–'08) are former thru-hikers who understood the needs of hikers. Not much has changed in Monson since 1996, except for the population, which has skyrocketed to 609.

06/20/96

We woke up the following day at 5:30 AM to the smell of breakfast cooking, making it all the harder to leave the "Shaw comfort zone." Wild Bill and his family made it to Shaw's as we prepared to head out. They decided to stay until they had healed, promising they would catch up sometime soon.

We never saw them again.

Keith took all of us who were ready to the trailhead. He shook all the guys' hands, hugged all the girls, said goodbye, and gave us some last words of advice: "If anyone gets hurt, give me a call, and I'll get there as soon as I can and get you out so you can get treated."

Keith Shaw was small in stature but big in heart.

The trail heading south was relatively flat, with a few rolling hills. It felt like a walk in the park after the wilderness trek. Everyone walked in silence, most likely lost in thought and suffering from the "Shaw Blues." Kianna was the only one full of energy and raring to go after sleeping for almost two days and eating an abundance of table scraps with her dog food. We couldn't ask for a better day to hike; the bugs were minimal, and the rain was off on the horizon.

06/21/96

We tentatively broke camp because the clouds were getting darker with every passing moment. The problem was that if we holed up and waited out every threatening storm, we would never finish the trail. It started to sprinkle, and within the hour, the heavens opened up, and it felt like someone was continuously dumping buckets of water on our heads. I don't care how much rain gear you have on; you will get soaked when it comes down like that all day long. Hiking in those conditions was treacherous. I went down several times, stepping on slippery rocks. My feet would shoot out from underneath me, and I would stick my arm out to break my fall. It would bury up to my shoulder in the mud, packing my ear full of black gold. I would free myself from the pack and then pull it from the sucking sounds of mud as it resisted giving it back to me. Covered in mud as I was, it wasn't long between the downpour and fording the West Branch of Piscataquis (pronounced "Pis-cah-tah-kwis") River and Bald Mountain Stream, a couple of fast-flowing rivers before I was cleaned. Sandrine chose to butt-scoot across a log on the Piscataquis. The current did catch Kee by surprise, sweeping her quickly down the river before she swam free of its grasp, easily making it to the other side. I marveled at what an athlete she was. The wind started picking up, and we were shivering by the time we reached Moxie Bald Lean-to. We were greeted with a warm smile from an old guy named Herb, who had been intermittently hiking the Appalachian Trail for twenty years and was on the Maine AT crew. He had a young kid with him named Phil. An absolute Greenhorn, according to Herb. It was Phil's first backpacking trip, and he was excited about the adventure. I commended Herb for passing on his knowledge to the next generation.

06/22/96

"Lucky" LeClair

The rain hadn't let up; it had been raining hard all morning. Sandrine LeClair left the tent door open, and we had standing water inside, earning her trail name *"Lucky" LeClair*. Exhaustion and limited caloric intake can cause lapses in judgment and, at the very least, be the source of discomfort. The rain finally let up at 10:30 AM. It was still overcast, and the air had a bite to it, making me regret sending my fleece pants and gloves back home. Any view from the summit of Moxy Bald was hopelessly lost in the thick clouds. We were lucky to see fifty feet in front of us. We hadn't been bothered by mosquitoes and black flies all day. Hallelujah. I'll take hiking in the cool mist of clouds any day. On our way down Moxy Bald, we walked through a cave that looked like somebody sheared off some massive granite slabs and set them on top of huge granite boulders, creating a granite walkway. Whoever mapped this trail did an amazing job.

It was raining again, and all the puddles were alive with thousands of polliwogs. Knowing the life cycle of frogs, I wondered how many would develop first and end up feasting on their siblings. I imagined what it would be like to be chased down in a shrinking pool of water until there was nowhere to hide, only to be eaten alive.

I used to collect polliwogs as a kid during the rainy season in Holbrook, Arizona. I'd load them into my red wagon and bring them home. Once they had eaten all the algae and baby mosquitos, they turned on each other. The ones that grew legs first had the advantage, and their brothers became their source of protein. I even witnessed a tadpole swimming furiously with his intestines trailing behind him as those with legs closed in for a meal. Nature can be ruthless, void of emotion.

Climbing Bald Mountain made Moxy Bald seem easy. There appeared to be an endless number of false summits, and at times, it felt like we were salmon heading upstream, fighting rapids in the trail. Hiking in the rain all day really sapped our energy. Heading down Bald Mountain was treacherous. It was steep, and there was a massive maze of twisted roots to negotiate. I stepped on a root that was covered in dirt. The dirt gave way, and my boot slipped as if I had stepped on a greased pole. My downhill foot continued to slide down a granite slab while my uphill leg twisted unnaturally behind me. Mid-slide, I knew this could be a hike-ending injury. Miraculously, I slid to a stop virtually unscathed with only a minor knee strain. Somehow, everyone escaped, taking a severe digger off the steep slopes of Bald Mountain.

LeClair kept things interesting as we neared Pleasant Pond Lean-to when she slipped off a bog log that seemed to have been greased with clear silicone and pitched sideways into the black goo. Her whole left side was transformed into a black swamp monster. She came up smiling despite having that distinct rotten, earthy scent. Thankfully, showers awaited in Caratunk, Maine.

The Kennebec River crossing was wide and deep in places. The AT handbook warned that the river could rise and surge any time since a dam upstream released water automatically when there was a power need. It went on to warn hikers not to underestimate the power of this river, reporting that a less fortunate section hiker had drowned in 1985. While it looked doable, we opted to play it safe and take the ferry across. Rene, the River Master, provided shuttles across the Kennebec. Rene gave us some fresh butter lettuce from his garden before we boarded his canoe. Fresh produce is something we craved, and we devoured it while it was still crisp. Rene flashed a smile of approval before we shoved off. On the fifteen-to-twenty-minute ferry ride, Rene gave insight into what we might find on the trail.

He said, "Don't hike the trail looking for silver and gold; there are far more rewarding riches to be found in the people you meet and the experiences you have."

All the rain had created a supersaturated ground, and at times, it felt like we were hiking the swamplands of Florida or a tropical rainforest with mud trying to suck our boots off. The mosquitoes were out in force, swarming with intent. Sandrine panicked, ripped her pack off, grabbed a flask of Ben's 100% Deet, and poured it on any exposed skin as if we had an unlimited supply. Those bloodsuckers won't bother her for a while, at least not until she sweats it off.

Rene the Kennebec River Master

As we crossed Sandy Stream near the middle Carry Pond inlet, Sandrine insisted on removing her boots instead of stepping on the slightly submerged rocks and relying on her waterproof boots to keep her feet dry. Sometimes, I thought she had had enough and was trying to sabotage our hike. Lately, I had wanted to ask her if she wanted to quit. Part of me would be relieved because she was definitely slowing me down, and at the rate we were traveling, we wouldn't finish before Spring of next year. I was carrying all the food, stove, cookware, and tent. My pack weighed eighty plus pounds. I didn't mind the extra load and clung to the hope that she would enjoy this trail to some degree.

06/24/96

We hiked fourteen miles. Most of it was flat but very slippery. There were many mud bogs to cross, and the mosquitoes swarmed by the thousands.

At some point, every thru-hiker has to hike their own hike, or they run the risk of burning out or injuring themselves. Toward the end of the day, we decided I should forge ahead and get camp ready. I made it to West Carry Pond, pitched the tent, and got a smoky fire going to keep the mosquitoes at bay. I filtered water from the lake for our evening meal, and then I went to look for Sandrine. She came hobbling into camp with tears in her eyes. She had a nasty blister on her heal. It was bloody raw and needed attention before it got infected. After cleaning the site with biodegradable soap and water, I made a thick donut from moleskin and then duct-taped it into place. The donut kept the pressure off her blister, so she could hike the next day comfortably.

Shortly after dinner, the black clouds that had been building all evening unleashed another relentless deluge and didn't stop until halfway through the next day.

06/25/96

I didn't get much sleep between the storm and Sandrine scratching madly throughout the night. Everything about this trail is challenging, and it is only exacerbated when your hiking partner is miserable and you're running on three hours of sleep. Everyone we have run into says this is one of the wettest seasons they have ever seen, and the trail is flowing like a stream. Some days, we had to listen to our bodies and take a short day. We only hiked a little over six miles before stopping at Little Bigelow Lean-to.

06/26/96

On our way up Little Bigelow Mountain, I found myself feeling exhausted. The rain and bugs were wearing us down. Sandrine's suffering weighed heavily on me. Not seeing the sun was depressing, and the mountaintop views were non-existent. Just when I was feeling sorry for myself and the circumstances we were in, along came Slow Joe, a northbound section hiker. At seventy years old, he had overcome triple bypass surgery and was finishing the last 100-mile leg of the AT.

Synchronicity? Coincidence? Whatever you call it, it was the shot of inspiration that we needed.

The skies cleared on the way up Little Bigelow, and we could see a panoramic view of Flagstaff Lake and the surrounding mountain ranges. We could also see Mt. Katahdin on the northernmost horizon. We've hiked one hundred and seventy-four miles, and it was humbling to get a view that enabled us to gauge the distance we had traveled in comparison to the vastness of this mountain range. From our vantage point, we could see the wind whipping the white caps on Flagstaff Lake to boat-swamping size. Avery Mountain was shrouded in dark clouds, and they were heading our way. It wouldn't be long before the light breeze on Little Bigelow would intensify. We made it to the top of Avery Peak, and the winds were more furious than anything we have experienced so far. The clouds were ripping past this mountain with a hypnotic swirling, increasing in speed as they passed. It was howling up there. I was lifted and moved a couple of feet off the trail by a surprising gust. My backpack rainfly was ripped off my pack and acted as a sail with one strap tethering it to my pack. Reeling it in before it broke loose, I glanced behind me to see how Kiana and Sandrine were doing. A look of panic was etched on Sandrine's face, and her eyes seemed to telegraph her disbelief in the power of the wind. With her lower center of gravity, Kiana was struggling less than the rest of us. Her ears were blowing straight back, and her lips were peeled back and flapping, exposing her teeth as if she had her head sticking out of the truck heading down the highway at sixty plus miles an hour. Our hands were beginning to hurt as the cold penetrated past flesh and settled into bone. There was no chance of starting a warming fire; we had to get off this mountain and get something hot into us soon. We scurried down the trail as safely as we could. The wind gusted and blew a tree over a couple of steps in front of me. The wind let up, and the tree sprung back to its natural upright state. A little farther down the trail, another gust came at us, roaring through the trees. This time, we were watching and ready to spring out of the way. I stepped on a mossy section of the trail that looked like a carpet, and the whole thing lifted as a snarled root system was ripped from its home, slamming the trunk to the ground. I jumped off the roots before they went perpendicular to the trail. I thought a tree slamming to the forest floor would make more noise, but not when it was muffled by the roar of the wind. Trees in this area were at the granite mountain's mercy and could not grow deep roots.

The closer we got to Horns Pond, the trail turned into a solid carpet of moose droppings; we couldn't take a step without stepping on a pile. Add a lot of rain, and this section turned into a moose shit slip and slide.

06/27/96

After spending the night at Horns Pond Lean-to, we hiked five miles to where the trail intersected Highway 27. We didn't have any luck hitching, so we walked the additional five miles into Stratton, Maine, where we decided to take a couple of zero days at the White Wolf Inn and wait for the Fourth of July celebration on the weekend. The fireworks show was excellent, and the grand finale was spectacular.

07/02/96

Two zero days turned to four as it took Sandrine longer to heal. By the fourth day, we felt eager to get on the trail, and Kiana pranced around as we loaded our packs. She had become an amazing trail dog, and part of me wanted to do the happy dance with her. We've been feeding her a diet of Purina Puppy Chow, which seems to have given her a spring in her step. She could barely hold still long enough for me to strap her pack on. I may have to sneak some of her puppy chow into our trail mix.

As soon as we started up the trail from town, Kiana began to punish us. That puppy chow gave her unbelievable energy, but the drawback was that she had the worst gas known to man. If we could bottle this, we could win wars. If she continued to fumigate us, we may have no choice but to let her sleep outside. I don't think the black flies and mosquitoes stand a chance. Thank God, by the time we had hiked fourteen miles to Spaulding Mountain Lean-to, Kiana was burning clean again.

We met our first father-son hiking team at Spaulding Mountain Lean-to. Bob, or "Old Man of the Mountain," was about to turn seventy-five, and his son, a schoolteacher, was hiking with him so he could witness his dad finish the last 100-mile section and officially complete the AT. Bob was incredibly agile, and I asked him what his secret was. He said, "A loving wife who feeds me well and an active lifestyle."

07/03/96

We woke up, and Sandrine was bitten a couple of times by a spider. There was no evidence of the spider in her sleeping bag, but whatever it was, she had a startling reaction to it. Her leg looked like it had the early stages of Elephantiasis. She didn't have any pain or pus associated with the bite. We waited around for a couple of hours to see if it got any worse, but it didn't, so she shrugged it off and hiked the next eight miles to Piazza Lean-to, and the swelling subsided in the process. We thought it was likely a Wolf Spider bite, and she was having an allergic reaction to the venom.

On our way to Piazza Lean-to, we hiked mostly in the clouds and then above the clouds as we summited Saddle Junior, The Horn, and Saddleback Mountain at forty-one hundred plus feet. The view of the surrounding mountain tops protruding above the clouds looked like islands in the sky. They say you can see as far north as Katahdin and as far south as Mount Washington on a clear day. I'm sure we saw Katahdin, but to the south, Mount Washington was obscured in clouds. If the prevailing winds continued, it seemed inevitable that we were destined for more weather. On the way down Saddleback, we dipped back into the clouds, and visibility was reduced to ten yards or less for most of the day. At one point, we heard something splashing to the side of the trail.

The clouds thinned enough for us to glimpse the apparition of a giant bull moose feeding in a pond fifteen feet from us. When he lifted his head, he had water plants hanging from his massive rack, and the water cascading off his palmated antlers sounded like someone had turned on a landscape fountain.

Shortly after that, I had a grouse attack from my right flank. She came hissing from the undergrowth so fast that I jumped, not knowing what it was but expecting a snake. She then went into a broken wing diversion tactic, luring me away from where she had burst from the undergrowth. I looked back just in time to see a bunch of fuzzy baby grouse disappearing into the bushes. I heard a cluck from above and got a picture of a male Spruce Grouse perched in a tree, watching like a sentinel as we passed below. His camouflage was so good that I don't think I would have spotted him without his brilliant red eyebrows. As we left his family safely behind, he clucked a couple more times to signal that the danger had passed.

07/04/96

Fourth of July Grandeur

Shortly after leaving Stratton, I found an M100 firecracker on the trail and planned to set it off on the 4th. I wasn't sure it would be very effective with all the moisture in the air. It rained throughout the night, and there had been a steady downpour since we left Piazza Lean-to. As we rolled into Sabbath Day Lean-to, the rain intensified, so we opted to stay in the shelter instead of our tent. The view of the lightning and thunder far exceeded the Stratton celebration. Clouds would light up for miles in every direction, and the thunderous booms would shake our shelter, leaving us humbled with shock and awe. The *crack and sizzle* arcing erratically across the sky took your breath away. Lighting that M100 firecracker seemed foolish. To this day, I have not witnessed a better 4th of July display.

07/05/96

With all the recent rain, Bemis Stream was running swift and deep where it forked around a small island. We found a skinny log, down river, that had fallen across a narrow section of Bemis. Everyone was nervous to carry their pack while crossing the log. One slip and a hiker could be swept downstream. The log felt like a highway to me, so I volunteered to carry their packs, including Kee's. It flexed a great deal under my weight as I carried five hikers' packs, one by one, over the raging narrows. Sandrine butt-scooted across safely to the other side while I kept Kiana from following. We searched a couple hundred yards upstream, where the stream was much broader and swimmable without any strainers or log jams for Kiana to get trapped in downstream. Kiana launched from my grasp as Sandrine called for her. She made great progress until she entered the fast current, and the swiftness with which it carried her downstream was alarming. She swam harder against the current, trying to reach Sandrine upstream, and was swept further away. Sandrine froze and didn't run downstream, calling for Kiana to *swim*. I couldn't call her back, knowing she was running out of real estate and risked getting caught in a log jam, slightly upriver, close to where we had crossed. Kiana seemed to realize her effort was in vain, so she switched direction and ferried directly toward the opposing shore. She broke free and swam quickly across the slower moving middle section and was swept again in the deep bend of the far bank, but she swam with powerful strokes that mocked the clutches of the current, shaking free on dry land, safely upstream from the waiting log jam. I crossed Bemis one last time on the limber log, my heart still racing and wondering if this was worth the risk.

We just finished climbing Bemis Mountain and were crossing on the flat top of Old Blue Mountain when we ran into a solo hiker. She was sixty-eight years old and moved effortlessly through the mud and rain. I warned her about the stream crossing at Bemis. Undaunted, she thanked me for my concern and hiked on as I marveled at her mettle. Her indomitable spirit was made of the same mold as Grandma Gatewood, who had a family of eleven kids and twenty-two grandkids before she became the first woman to thru-hike the trail in 1955 when she was *sixty- seven*. The AT certainly attracts hearty souls. Despite her determination, I couldn't help worrying about her out there alone.

On a side note, don't waste your money if you want to hike in the Amazon or a tropical rainforest. Just come to Maine, let it rain for three days, and you will have all the elements of a tropical rainforest: mud up to your knees and water everywhere.

07/06/96

Every northbound (NoBo) hiker we passed warned us of the difficulty of hiking Moody Mountain. Pay attention when a thru-hiker who is trail-hardened and seems to move with effortless grace tells you there is an arduous ascent and descent in your near future. Going up Moody was challenging but doable. While going down Moody, Sandrine wrenched her knee and hobbled to Sawyer Notch, where we were able to hitch into Andover. We stayed at the Pine Ellis B & B, which Paul and Ilene Trainor owned. While there, we met an engaged couple, Sue and Dick, who were also avid hikers. Sue (White Glove) had thru-hiked with her father (Pole Dragger) in 1989, and, for her wedding, planned to have her father walk with her and Dick to the summit of Mount Washington, where they would exchange their vows. Despite the wind and cold, they had their summit wedding on September 28, 1996.

We agreed to reconnect once we got to North Woodstock, New Hampshire.

07/07/96 & 07/08/96

Sandrine's knee needed a break, so we took a zero day and then slack-packed (carried a day pack) the next day. With the lighter packs, it felt like we were floating, which made the 17.7 miles from Sawyer Notch to Grafton Notch seem easy. We stopped briefly for lunch at Hall Mountain Lean-to, and I read through the trail register. It was filled with helpful information about trail conditions, hardships endured, must-see landmarks, great food and sleeping establishments at the local town stops, and occasionally some newsworthy tidbits from the outside world. At the back of the register, I discovered a poem section and found one that mildly summarized our experiences.

> "Mosquitoes and dirty socks, aching knees and slippery rocks.
> I'm the tired backpacker that the mountain mocks.
> On my way to town for my next food box."
> – Lone Wolf '94

07/09/96

Paul shuttled us back to Grafton Notch so we could continue our southern trek. As soon as he drove off, I realized my belt pack containing my voice recorder, toothbrush, harmonica, and power bars had slipped off my pack belt, along with a Nalgene water bottle. I had to hike/hitch to the town of Bethel, seventeen miles one way, to make a phone call. Ilene answered and found the missing items on the floorboards behind Paul's driver's seat. She mailed it to our next mail stop in Gorham, New Hampshire. Three hours later, I made it back to the trail, and by the end of the day, we pulled into Speck Pond Campsite. It was a beautiful alpine pond with fish jumping everywhere. The detour and the actual AT miles combined for my first unofficial twenty plus mile day. It wasn't too late to go fishing, but I was tired and beginning to wonder if I shouldn't jettison my fishing gear at the next town stop when Sandrine, looking behind me with wide eyes, said in a hushed but firm voice, "Don't look. People are running through the woods naked."

Instinctively I turned my head as I heard the splashes of naked people jumping into Speck Pond.

I turned back toward Sandrine, knowing that the ruckus in the pond had ruined any chance of catching a fish, and suggested, "Maybe I should go fishing."

She glared, and I laughed inwardly. I proceeded to make dinner, confident that netted fish wouldn't define this evening's meal as I had hoped.

07/10/96

We were breaking camp as the forest came to life when I suddenly heard the most beautiful violin music floating through the trees, surrounding us with ethereal beauty. I dropped everything, grabbed my camera, and went in search of this gifted soul. I found a guy sitting on a log in a small opening, so involved with his music that he didn't even notice me watching from the shadows. He had long hair and a chest length, bushy beard. Andy Johnson wore a brown beanie, purple t-shirt, and brown pants tucked into his calf-length socks protruding above his logging boots. He looked like someone perfectly at home in the Maine woods, yet he played magnificently. I found myself wondering how this was possible, and then I realized, when faced with this paradox of a person, that I had fallen prey to judging him by his looks and a preconceived notion of what a master violinist should look like. In the self-examination that ensued, I wondered how I had allowed this judgmental behavior to latch onto my soul. I didn't used to be that way. It must have happened slowly enough for me not to realize. How had I been indoctrinated to view my brothers and sisters so superficially? I didn't have answers as to how this judgmental bias had crept into my being, but I do remember vowing to try harder even though I didn't think it was humanly possible.

I thanked Andy for playing and hoped my voice recorder awaited me in Gorham in case our paths crossed again.

Andy Johnson-backwoods violinist extraordinaire!

Mahoosuc Mayhem

We were about to hike through the Mahoosuc Notch, the toughest mile of the AT. The Mahoosuc Arm is a steep descent into the Notch. Every kid, both young and old, should have the chance to climb, squirm, and crawl through the AT's biggest jungle gym. During the Ice Age, a receding glacier created a jumbled mess of huge granite boulders, piled as high as a house and wedged together in a mile-long ravine or notch, as it is called out east. It was hot and muggy as we dropped in; we could hear water running below, and the farther down we climbed, the cooler it got. There was ice under the bottom layer of rocks, and if we loitered for too long, we would get chilled. I had to really help Kiana through this section, either pushing her up to a ledge or pulling her up by her pack. She slid down a rock at one point and wedged her pack between two rocks. She was stuck swimming in the air about three feet off the ground. She turned her head to look at me as if to ask for help or maybe, "How did you get me into this situation?" Either way, she wasn't hurt, and I couldn't help but chuckle as she continued to slowly crawl through the air.

Sandrine slid down another section, banged her shin on the way down, and wedged her boot between two boulders. I had to shimmy down headfirst to untie her boot with one hand so we could pull her foot out. I feared the Mahoosuc Notch was the final straw for Lucky LeClair. We put most of her pack's contents into my pack, and she hobbled another eleven miles to Gentian Pond Campsite, officially hiking all of Maine.

Rock Cairns on Goose Eye Mountain.

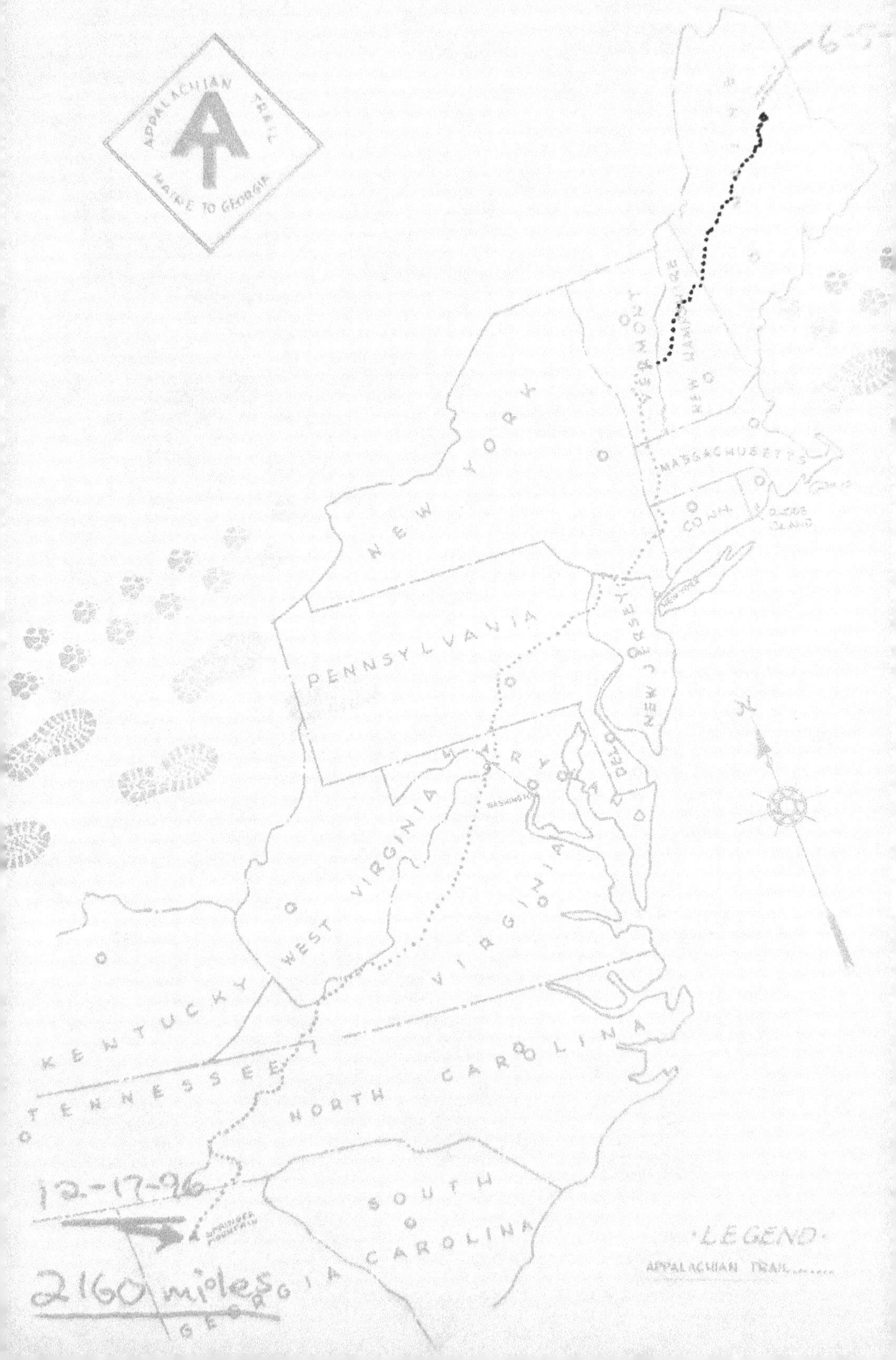

APPALACHIAN TRAIL
MAINE TO GEORGIA
NEW YORK
VERMONT
NEW HAMPSHIRE
MASSACHUSETTS
CONN.
RHODE ISLAND
PENNSYLVANIA
NEW JERSEY
DEL.
MARYLAND
WASHINGTON
WEST VIRGINIA
VIRGINIA
KENTUCKY
TENNESSEE
NORTH CAROLINA
SOUTH CAROLINA
GEORGIA
SPRINGER MOUNTAIN
12-17-96
2160 miles
·LEGEND·
APPALACHIAN TRAIL.......

Chapter 11

New Hampshire

07/11/96

I woke up the following day, and Sandrine was moving a little slow, so after breakfast, we decided to have her hike ahead while I packed up camp. When I started out, I came across a giant black snake that was having a hard time slithering off the trail, and I noticed that it had two large things sticking out of its mouth. I thought I may have discovered a buck-toothed, fanged snake. On closer inspection, I discovered that the monster's fangs were legs protruding from its mouth. I grabbed my camera and tried to push the snake back onto the path with a stick. He panicked, and to get away, he disgorged a huge frog. The poor frog was still alive but traumatized. It was still able to hop around but had part of its intestines hanging outside of its belly. The snake waited patiently in the shadows of the nearby bushes. I reluctantly walked on, confident how that scene played out, knowing that nothing would go to waste.

Shortly after that, I caught up with Sandrine, and we came across a mother grouse that started squeaking at us like she was wounded. As I approached, she flew a short distance away and then started her wounded act again. It was a very believable routine, but I wasn't buying it after she miraculously flew the first time. I looked around, and sure enough, half a dozen fuzzy chicks were cowering in the trailside bushes. I didn't even bother taking a picture and kept moving so Kiana wouldn't be tempted to grab a fuzzy chew toy.

It wasn't long, and we were in a zone hiking with a steady rhythm. We were walking around a small bog right before Dream Lake when I suddenly found myself within five feet of a bull moose chewing on a bush. He was as startled as I was. He jumped and took a couple of steps away and turned to look as if to make sure I wasn't a threat.

Sandrine thought he was charging, and she froze in her tracks. Run-ins with moose can go south quickly if you ignore their body language and the position of their ears. If their ears are pinned back, you had better retreat.

I had flashbacks of when I was fifteen, being treed by a cow moose defending her calf, near the Kenai River in Alaska.

Thankfully, this guy and I had a bit of a standoff until he walked about fifty feet away, turned, and watched us. What an adrenaline rush.

I'm glad there wasn't *another* cow moose and her calf.

Only 6.9 miles into New Hampshire, and it didn't disappoint. I was so looking forward to seeing what the rest of the state had to offer.

We crossed the Androscoggin River (Eastern Abenaki, meaning "river of cliff rock shelters") and into Gorham, New Hampshire. We holed up at the "Hiker's Paradise," AKA Colonial Comfort Inn, with high hopes that some zero days, a hot shower, and some hearty food would help Sandrine heal. We got caught up in the world and local news during our stay. We talked with other hikers and were dismayed to find out that the FBI had been posting fliers up and down the trail looking for information about two women who were killed. The women had been discovered by Shenandoah National Park Rangers on June 1 in central Virginia, near Skyland Resort. Just when I thought we had found paradise on the AT, news of the murders was a chilling reminder that the trail life was a microcosm of society.

I called home to check in and request that my next supply box be shipped to the North Woodstock, New Hampshire, Post Office. It can be a bit daunting knowing that there is an elevation change of approximately 464,500 feet throughout the entire Appalachian Trail. That's nearly ninety miles of ascending and descending, enough to have climbed Mount Everest (29,029 ft.) sixteen times from sea level to summit. This next seventy-five-mile leg through the state of New Hampshire would take us through the White Mountains and over the Presidential Range, which is the highest of the Whites. When we left town, we would be climbing from seven hundred and ninety-four feet to the exposed arctic tundra in the Presidentials. This section had a reputation for being difficult, so I planned eight days of food, hoping it would only take us six or seven to complete.

Before hanging up, my dad let me know that my grandpa wasn't doing well. The decision was made that he would need home hospice soon and that he should finish his days under my aunt Annie's care since she was a registered nurse with decades of experience. I was at a loss for words as memories came flooding back. Gramps always had the time to take us grandkids fishing during our family's summer vacation to their cabin at Mormon Lake, Arizona. He taught us how to tie our lures with an improved clinch knot, and honestly, I didn't know how his big sausage fingers had the manual dexterity to tie such a knot. He was a quiet man with the patience necessary to take four grandkids out in his fishing boat at once. I found it curious that he would always bring his favorite fishing pole along but never use it. I think he enjoyed all the excitement playing out in his boat every time one of us hooked a fish. He didn't have time to fish between untangling snags and snarled lines, unhooking fish, putting them on the stringer if they were eating size, and driving the boat. I don't think it mattered to him that he didn't fish, as he smiled approvingly, urging us to keep our rods up and our lines tight as we battled our next trophy. I knew I had to be there for him and asked, "Do I need to come home now and say my goodbyes?"

Dad replied, "Not yet, son; I'll let you know."

Conflicted, I hung up the phone with a heavy heart.

07/12 thru 07/17/96

We stayed for five days, and Sandrine's shin wasn't getting any better. The hike out probably didn't help, but we didn't have much choice. It looked like she had a stress fracture in her tibia, and she had decided to take a couple of months off and recover at her parents' place in France. She wanted me to go with her, and I was torn. It would have been incredible to spend two months in France. Meeting her parents and hanging out in their vineyard sounded like bliss. I knew in my gut that if I went, I wouldl not return to finish the trail or be able to see my grandpa before he passed. My decision was not received warmly, and there was a great deal of tension when she boarded the bus to Boston, even though she suggested that she would meet me in the Shenandoah Mountains when she returned. With one last look, she set her jaw, flipped her long, flowing brown hair, and hobbled onto the bus.

Jump on the bus, you fool!

That was what my heart said, but my head wouldn't let me, and neither would Kiana. She pranced around with her tail held high in anticipation of the adventure ahead. Loneliness set in as I returned to the hotel, and I questioned what I had done.

I stretched out on the bed, thankful for a hot shower and another night of blissful sleep in the comfort of clean sheets and a pillow. Settling in for the night, I grabbed the remote and flipped the TV on, only to discover *Breaking News*. A TWA Boeing 747 had blown up sixty miles off the coast of New York en route to Paris, killing all 230 on board.

I could not get ahold of Sandrine and didn't have her parents' number. My mind raced through her possible travel timeline, and it seemed unlikely that she could have taken the bus to Boston, hopped a connecting flight to New York, and been on that ill-fated flight. I was unsure, but I thought she had a direct flight from Boston. Sleep would not come easy, wondering if Lucky LeClair's fortune held while praying for the unfortunate souls of TWA flight 800.

Thursday 7-18-96

I didn't have time to dwell on the ramifications of hiking solo. I had a list of things to do before I headed out. I had to finish my laundry, waterproof my boots, purchase some last-minute supplies, and mail my floater package to North Woodstock along with postcards briefing family and friends of the turn of events. Then, I had to get both mine and Kiana's packs loaded and ready for the next day's early departure.

07/19/96

Just Me and Kee on the AT

I set out early, determined to either lose myself or find myself on the AT. There was very little traffic that morning, so I hiked the three and a half miles out of town to the trail head, suffering through double glute cramps as I went. Distracted by my continual cramping, I found the trail and continued hiking along without seeing any white trail blazes when I came across a bridge on the Rattle River. I crossed the bridge, scanning the abutments for white blazes, and not paying attention to where I was walking. My left leg fell through a hole, and I caught myself as wooden splinters dug into my thigh above my knee. A couple more inches and that could have been disastrous.

> Call on me in the day of trouble; I will deliver you, and you shall glorify me.
>
> - Psalm 50:15 (NIV)

As if that wasn't enough, the extended town rest and cool morning air had Kiana feeling extra frisky. She raced ahead; her muscles rippled under a glossy coat as she effortlessly loped down the trail. I marveled at her athletic grace and watched helplessly as she ducked under a branch and caught her pack, blowing it apart. I put it back together with duct tape and a prayer. It wasn't pretty, but I hoped it would get us to the next road crossing at Pinkham Notch. We would have to hitchhike to the nearest town with a sporting goods store and hope they had dog packs in stock. Otherwise, I may have to search for thread and needle. It hadn't been a good day, and I was kind of missing ol' LeClair.

It had to get better.

07/20/96

Careful What You Wish For

We spent the night at Imp Campsite, and as I was finishing breakfast, the wind picked up, and it started to drizzle. The longer I hiked, the storm became more intense. It wasn't long before the storm's rage was evident, sounding like a locomotive bearing down on us. Every gust would reach a deafening roar, snapping tree tops off and toppling others over. Sheltering in place was not an option. We had to push through, dodging trees as we went, and hoping to make Carter Notch Hut before dark.

A gust blew Kiana over a small ledge, and she gracefully landed ten feet below on all fours. I scrambled down and helped her back up the ledge and onto the trail. Adrenaline coursed through my veins, and I planted my feet firmly in place. I leaned into the wind, and screamed at the oncoming *roar*, "Bring it on!"

I had no idea how much more we could endure or how long our luck would hold, but at the same time, I had never felt so alive. For the first time in my life, I felt like I was living as if I was dying. A peacefulness washed over me as I let go of my need to be in control of the circumstances. Instead, I trusted. The light was fading, and leaning into the wind we pressed on, not knowing how much farther we had to go. Just as dusk turned to dark, we rounded a bend in the trail to see the warm lights of a hut. Not just any hut, but one of sturdy rock built in 1914.

We ducked inside where Carter Notch Hut felt like a solid rock cave, capable of surviving the fury outside. The Hut Croo leaders, as they are officially called, were mostly collegians, and they offered to let me do a work-for-stay option that they traditionally offer thru-hikers.

"We've had some cancellations, and you're the first thru-hiker to show. So, if you don't mind sweeping floors and washing dishes, you can hang here for the night."

The smell of warm lasagna wafted through the dining room, and I felt like one of Pavlov's dogs agreeing to his terms before he finished speaking. What a glorious meal it was. Due to the cancellations, they had many leftovers and insisted I eat my fill. I must have eaten a whole pan of some of the most delicious lasagna, garlic bread, and salad my thankful tastebuds had ever encountered.

After finishing my kitchen duties and sweeping the dining room floor, I grabbed my pack and Kiana from the foyer, and we scurried to the bunkhouse. The trees danced in the light of my headlamp as if some unseen force was shaking them violently. The bunkhouse was a wooden structure that was set on concrete piers. I settled in on a bottom bunk, and Kiana curled up on the floor beside me. The storm grew in intensity. Kiana paced and whimpered throughout the night as the hut began to vibrate and hum. It soon turned to a high-pitched whine, like a jet engine powering up right before takeoff. None of us hikers slept as we half expected to be blown off that mountain. The wind ceased sometime during the predawn hour, and an eerie calm hung in the silence.

I jumped out of bed and scrambled outside to see if we were in the eye of the storm or if it had passed. I was shocked when I had to climb over and through the branches of a huge white birch tree that had narrowly missed the corner of our bunkhouse. The wind was so loud during the night that I never even heard it fall. Humbled, it was a stark reminder of who was really in charge.

I couldn't thank the Croo leader enough for bending the rules under the circumstances and allowing Kiana and me a safe harbor to ride out the storm.

07/21/96

Ambushed on Wildcat Mountain

I finished my morning chores early and quickly packed up as the tops of the trees began to rustle. I brushed it off as "nothing to be concerned about" and stayed focused on hiking up and over Wildcat Mountain's peaks A & D. The humidity hung heavy in the air. The morning sun illuminated the hardwood canopy, casting an ambient green glow that nurtured my soul. From the depths of the forest came the lonely calls of the Whippoorwill. Nuthatches flitted here and there, searching for food on the underside of branches. A single robin appeared out of the green canopy and landed beside a puddle, bobbing and chirping excitedly. The forest floor soon became a whirlwind of activity as plump robins hopped around, slurping half-drowned worms with reckless abandon as if it were their last meal. Squirrels scolded us as we walked past their nut caches hidden alongside the trail, nervous agitation apparent in the twitching of their tails. Fresh deer tracks in the mud came to a sliding stop before changing direction, indicating the owners must have sensed our approach before we saw them.

Suddenly, everything darkened. The surrounding bushes and ground sounded like hail falling with increasing fury. The soft rustle of feathers grew louder as the canopy overhead morphed into a moving entity. Thousands of blackbirds flew with stealth fighter speed through the tangled foliage, dropping bird bombs, not hail, with stinging, pinpoint accuracy.

A half-smirk replaced Kiana's confused look. The acrid smell of ammonia hung heavy in the air, forcing us to humbly hike on. With tails tucked and looking like we had been peppered with paintballs, we begged for a cleansing downpour.

There was a slight drop in the temperature as we climbed. The rain started, and the wind got blustery just as we summited Peak A. Once I was washed clean, I stopped long enough to don rain gear to protect myself from the heat-robbing wind, fearing what might be coming.

"Come on, Kee, we have to hustle!"

We had to cover two miles before we would summit Peak D of the Wildcats and then another three miles before we were in the relative safety of Pinkham Notch. Ditching the trail and bushwhacking to a lower elevation through the trees seemed like a suicide mission, so we marched on with renewed passion, Kiana faithfully on my heels constantly watching out for a crushing tree. As we crested Peak D, the trees began to dance to the roar of the wind, whipping violently.

I barked at Kee, "Come on, girl. We have to move!"

She followed, glued to my heels. It was steep going, and the cliff faces were extremely slippery in the rain. My hands were beginning to freeze, not that the rain was that cold, but the wind sucked all heat from exposed skin. I thought the day before winds were intense, but I had never experienced winds like this before. My face felt like it was being sand-blasted by the wind-driven rain. Down we climbed, steadily down, over an exposed rock face. A gust of wind pinned me against it, humbling me once again, as I imagined this must be what it felt like to be an insect stuck on a fly strip.

The wind ebbed and released me. My pack rain cover flapped violently, threatening to disown me. I reeled it back in, and was thankful the wind wasn't blowing in the opposite direction. Down we climbed, staggering as the wind buffeted us, mocking our efforts. Still, we persisted down into the sanctuary of buffering trees with their hidden dangers. Wildcat Mountain has over two thousand feet of elevation in less than a mile and a half, with the last thousand feet dropping precariously in that half-mile stretch where I was pasted to the rock.

The Lodge at Pinkham Notch Camp was full of hikers seeking shelter. I was able to find a pay phone and get a ride back to Gorham, where all the inns were full. We waited out the storm in "The Barn" at the Gorham House Inn, owned by Maggie Nutt and her partner Paul. Both were section hikers and understood the rigors of the trail. The Barn was simply a barn attached to the inn and had a bunch of mattresses in the loft reserved for hikers. We waited two days for the storm to pass, and I was grateful to have a roof over my head. Before leaving town, I purchased a new Jandd pack for Kiana, and she seemed excited when I strapped it on to make sure it was a good fit. She didn't want me to take it off, so I let her parade it around town on our way back to The Barn.

07/23/96

Paul was kind enough to give Kee and me a ride to Pinkham Notch. Enroute, he handed me the morning paper and plastered on the front page in bold print was:

Wind wallops the mountain.
Record blast on Washington

On the day we had hiked down Wildcat, Mount Washington was blasted with 154 mile- per-hour gusts, shattering the previous July record of 110 mph, set in 1933. That same year the mountain set the world record wind speed of 231 mph.

I was the first to sign in at the Great Gulf Wilderness Area on my approach to Mount Washington. The sun was coming up on my right as I hiked, which could only mean I was heading north. Did I make a wrong turn? I pulled out a Topo map to verify my location. I marveled at the AT creators' route-finding genius and the effort it took to put together a trail of discovery with all of its twists and turns along the spine of the Appalachians.

The recent storm had wreaked havoc on the trail. I lost track of the blowdowns, and our progress was slow. This would rival the Mahoosuc Notch in difficulty. The Appalachian Mountain Club (AMC) would have their work cut out to get this cleared anytime soon.

The skies were almost clear blue, with a few light clouds. Four miles into today's hike, we had to cross the West Branch of the Peabody River on a suspension bridge. Kiana didn't want anything to do with that wobbly bridge and kept trying to go down to the river's edge to swim across. She's a very headstrong dog and is determined once she decides to do something. There might be some truth to studies that suggest dogs take on their owners' personalities. Why else would they be man's best friend? It took a lot of coaxing and treats before she overcame her suspicions and trusted me enough to cross that bouncy bridge.

We'd been heading north since leaving Pinkham Notch. We hiked a circuitous route around the Great Gulf Wilderness on our way to Mount Madison, then headed in a southerly direction past Mt. Adams and Mt. Jefferson before we reached Mt. Washington. There was no wind, and only a very slight breeze could be felt on my damp skin. The climbing began in earnest as we headed up the Osgood trail, which the AT followed. I could see Mt. Clinton Road off in the distant western horizon, snaking its way up to the summit of Mount Washington. No cars were traveling up or down the road, and I wondered if crews had to clear debris. I hadn't seen a person all day, and I thought I had the park to myself.

What a glorious day. The views from Mt. Madison (5366 ft.) were stunning, and I could only imagine what it would be like on Mt. Washington (6288 ft.), the highest peak in New England. While pausing on Madison to take in the grandeur of this incredible mountain range, I spotted some movement at the Madison Spring Hut, five hundred plus feet below.

Having my first human sighting of the day felt like a post-apocalyptic novelty. I hadn't realized the popularity of hiking in Eastern America until I hiked the next six miles to Mt. Washington. People seemed to morph out of the rocks. The closer I got to Mt. Washington, the more the ridges seemed to have conga lines of people, and at those vast distances, appeared to be the size of ants working their way through the rocks, descending or ascending from the great ant hill called Washington.

Near the summit, a caution sign read,

"The area ahead has the worst weather in America. Many people have died here, even in the summer. Turn back now if the weather is bad."

I could've used that sign back on Wildcat Mountain.

It was just another reminder of the genuine consequences you can face, and I was no stranger to the wild fury of nature.

Everyone I met was enthusiastic about being in such a special place. It really seemed like people were glad to be alive.

They would ask, "Are you a thru-hiker? What's your trail name? What's your dog's name? How far have you hiked so far?" At first, I felt like a "Rock Star," and then after being asked the same questions a couple of hundred times, I *still* felt like a Rock Star. It really was incredible. At first, I would answer that opening question with a false sense of bravado. I felt like an actor who, after traveling three hundred and thirty plus miles, could only feign legitimacy. Who would have thought that hiking could garner so much attention?

On the summit of Mt. Washington with Mt. Madison in the background

I stood on the summit, trying to soak in the immensity of the place. These are the kinds of views that leave you feeling insignificant and appreciative simultaneously. I looked north, and if I strained my eyes, I thought I could pick out Mt. Katahdin from the farthest mountain range. This view certainly helped bolster my sense of accomplishment until I looked south. The expanse of mountain ranges appeared as waves in an endless ocean, humbling my very essence, leaving me wondering if I had what it took. Part of me yearned to discover, and then that little voice would creep in, trying to convince me of the absurdity of this daunting task. Guilt weighed heavy as I entertained the thought of abandoning this foolhardy mission to be at my grandfather's side.

Choosing not to dwell, I decided to play tourist myself and got someone to take a photo of Kee and me posing by the summit sign with the weather station in the background. I overheard someone mention that they thought the recent weather events were probably caused by Hurricane Bertha, which made landfall in North Carolina on July 12 as a category two storm. I guess it was possible, but I think this mountain range creates its own weather when warm air rises from the valleys below and meets with the cold air of the mountain tops.

The sun was beginning to set, so I hustled down the 1.4 miles to Lake of the Clouds Hut just in time to snap some pictures as the sun dipped behind distant mountains, lighting up the sky with vibrant reds, oranges, and yellows before fading to dark. I sure hoped that the rhyme for sailors' warning held true.

> *"Red sky at night, sailor's delight;*
> *red sky in the morning, sailor's warning."*

Lake of the Clouds Hut was a busy place. All ninety beds were spoken for, and even the "Dungeon" was stuffed with six hikers and all their gear. I had no choice but to move on.

Sunset from Lake of the Clouds Hut

With a headlamp, I found my way to Lake of the Clouds and went for a short, frigid swim. It almost took my breath away. I will never again take hot running water for granted. Hiking up to where I'd left the AT, I could see the Lake of the Clouds Hut shining like a beacon in the night, calling me back like a moth to light. If I listened closely, I could hear the faint laughter of fellow hikers. The joyous sound beckoned me to join in their revelry. I so wanted to join in, but something nudged me to continue hiking on in the sanctity of silence, yearning for peace and clarity. Mizpah Spring Hut and Nauman Tent Site were five miles away. Chances were, they were also full, and I didn't want to miss seeing anything by hiking too far in the dark.

We slept on the first flat section of the trail so we wouldn't impact the fragile Alpine Tundra. Listening to the soothing sounds of a bubbling brook, exhaustion overcame discomfort, and I dozed off contemplating the title of Thru-Hiker. It seemed an audacious notion, knowing that there were many miles to go, and anything could derail that goal.

I was awakened by the singing of a Slate-Colored Junco that stuck around waiting to see if there were any crumbs to be had after breakfast. The Junco and I had a staring contest as Kee gobbled her breakfast while I shoveled down instant oatmeal. The morning was crisp and clear with a layer of clouds building down below. I stowed my sleeping pad and bag, put my rain cover over my pack, and lashed my rain gear on top so it would be available at a moment's notice. I questioned the validity of the sailor's rhyme. It doesn't look like it will hold water in the Whites. I spent most of the day hiking in the rain. Distant views were nonexistent. My view corridor was fifty feet at best. I wondered what beauty I was missing. I hiked on, slipping and sliding down the Webster Cliffs. As I crossed the Saco River, I spied a note on the bridge that said:

> ***To all Thru-Hikers — Help yourself to get some soda;***
> ***it's under the bridge, in the stream, in a bag.***

As cold as I was, that soda made a difference, energizing me like rocket fuel. I couldn't believe the thoughtfulness of this stranger. I made it to Ethan Pond Campsite. I was soaked, and I looked forward to drying out in my tent, but not before heeding the posted bear warnings and securing our food on a highline. I was too tired to deal with a hungry bear and I would rest easy knowing Kee would warn me if danger came lurking.

07/24/96

Slickers & Snickers

I broke camp in the rain, and it didn't look like it would let up. My goal was to make it the twelve miles to Galehead Hut and see if they had room in the Inn. I was hoping that since they were so remote, the work for stay would still be available. If not, I would have to hike another three miles to Garfield Ridge Campsite.

We stopped briefly at the Zealand Falls to grab a snack and enjoy the cascading water. I wasn't able to take any photos since it was still raining. We had about fifteen hundred feet of elevation to climb in the next four miles before we would reach the summit of Mt. Guyot. Hallelujah, it had stopped raining, and the sun poked through the clouds. I might be able to get a view from Guyot yet. It was a bit hazy, but the clouds lifted, and Kee and I stopped long enough for a photo. She seemed to relish the views as much as I did. I may not have been an official Thru-Hiker, but I was starting to think like one. Thoughts of the possible culinary delights waiting at the Galehead Hut propelled me forward like a puppet on a string. I hoped I could make it there before all the positions were filled.

I pulled into Galehead Hut in a pouring rain, and as luck would have it, they had plenty of room. I would have gladly washed dishes and swept the floor for a warm, dry place to lay my head.

So, when they told me that baked haddock was on the menu, I felt like I had won the lottery. I ate like a king, and they encouraged me to eat my fill as they had weather-related cancelations and didn't want leftovers. I astonished the entire Galehead Croo with the quantity I could comfortably consume. They say that when we're hiking the distances we were doing and carrying the loads we had, we were burning the equivalent calories of running two marathons per day. That would explain why I was continuously hungry and still losing weight. I slept like a dead man that night and dreamt my mom made pancakes when I woke to the unmistakable smell of batter on a hot pan. I easily ate three large stacks of pancakes, did my morning chores, and thanked the Croo for their hospitality. Even though I couldn't take in the "never-ending views" that Galehead is noted for, I headed out into the driving rain with buoyed spirits and my faithful dog.

I had been hiking for hours in the rain. Thoughts of my grandpa seeped into my mind, and I began to formulate a plan to get off the trail at the next highway. I envisioned hitchhiking to the nearest town, grabbing a cab or a bus to the closest major airport, and using my open-ended return flight ticket to get to Phoenix while I could still get some quality time with him. I thought about our shared passion for the game of football and how he often spoke fondly about his younger days playing the game. He talked about the camaraderie and what it was like to play as a unified band of brothers. I realized how tough he had been when he told me about playing with a leather helmet without a face mask and how they used nails in their shoes for traction. That was an old-school toughness that I always wanted to emulate. I sensed that I was running out of time, and panic started to set in. Frustrated, slogging through the constant rain, I prayed.

Lord, can you help me out with this rain? Show me a sign that what I'm doing here is not in vain.

Within minutes, it stopped raining.

That's odd.

Part of me wanted to brush it off as coincidence, and part of me wanted to believe that God had the time or cared enough to do something. Regardless, I couldn't be certain, so I settled for being thankful for a reprieve in the rain and powered on, certain that I would be back in Phoenix by week's end. The clouds weren't breaking up, so I continued to hike in full rain gear.

I made it over Mt. Garfield (4500 ft.), the wind was picking up, and the clouds were getting thicker. It didn't seem to be raining, but the air was dense, and moisture that condensed on my rain jacket ran off as if it were drizzling.

The Franconia Ridge is supposed to be the most scenic of the entire Appalachian Trail, and I couldn't see anything. I felt cheated, especially since I was used to the epic views out west. Hiking in the east, we really had to earn our views. At lower elevations, the hike goes through dense hardwood forests where the canopy can block out the sun, creating the semblance of hiking in a "Green Tunnel." The best views can only be had from mountain tops.

The clouds continued to close in; I couldn't tell if I was climbing a mountain or on an undulating ridge. I climbed one false summit after another, or were they mountain tops? I couldn't be certain. At times the clouds were so thick, it seemed I was hiking along a knife edge with the terrain plunging precipitously into the veil of the clouds on both sides of the trail.

I moved with intent, focused on the trail, hoping to spy an intermittent white blaze to reassure me that I was still on the right course and not on a connecting side trail. I hiked on— squish, squish, squish. The only sound was the wind and mine and Kee's footsteps in the mud. The light was fading, and urgency quickened my step. Again, we climbed higher into the thinning clouds, and as I came around a bend, the wind seemed calmer, and I was surprised to see someone squatting on a rock. He was about fifty feet away and seemed to be just hanging out. As I closed the distance between us, I was fully aware that he didn't have a pack or even a water bottle.

I called out, "Hello!"

He was perched on a rock about four feet in diameter, and the way he was squatting, we were practically eye to eye. He was wearing a yellow rain jacket and commented on the beautiful day. I cordially agreed and attempted to make small talk when he looked up from under his hood.

He produced a king-sized Snickers bar. "Here, I want you to have this."

I politely declined. I had plenty of food in my pack, including some bite-sized Snickers. Still, as hungry as I was all the time, I couldn't believe I was turning down food, let alone my favorite candy bar.

He looked me in the eye. "No, I insist. You need it more than I do."

He was persistent, so I took it but felt a twinge of guilt. "Thanks. Have a great evening."

"You as well."

I started to walk away, took five or six steps, and turned to talk to him while I was still within easy speaking distance. I wanted to thank him for helping me with a decision I was struggling with, whether I should get off the trail.

He wasn't there.

I bolted to see if he was hiding on the other side of the boulder. I found nothing. There were no tracks in the intermittent mud except for Kiana's and mine. I scanned the perimeter of clouds where I could see about fifty feet before rocks became obscured in the gray veil. Is it possible that he could have sprinted that distance and disappeared into the clouds before I turned? At that speed he would have been able to run an amazing 4.4 in the forty-yard dash. I'd only seen that from our fastest guys in college, and if he could do that over uneven terrain, then why didn't I hear him splashing?

Maybe he jumped off the back of the rock? No, I would have heard him bouncing, possibly busting rocks loose. I walked away from the rock. Nothing made sense.

My mind spun. *I have lost it! I've been in the woods too long.*

I took one last look at that rock as I proceeded down the trail. Shaken, I tried to convince myself that nothing weird had happened. I walked for a long time, replaying the events in my mind, and had all but convinced myself that I had experienced some kind of delusion until I realized I had a firm grip on something in my hand.

I glanced down at the king-sized Snickers bar, and my heart practically jumped out of my chest. I knew I hadn't packed anything so extravagant, and to make sure I wasn't going crazy, I ripped open the package and took a bite. It was the real deal, and I had never tasted anything better. The rest of the way down Franconia Ridge, I struggled to wrap my head around what had transpired. Once I got to Franconia Notch/US3, I hiked the .7 miles to the Flume Visitors Center, found a payphone, and called to check on Grandpa.

Dad answered. "He's doing great. He's keeping food down and seems to have more energy. Even the Hospice nurses are hopeful."

"Dad, that's awesome! Should I come home?"

"I don't think so; keep going, Son."

"All right, then send my next package to the Post Office in

Hanover, New Hampshire. I have roughly seventy miles to cover before I'm there."

"Will do. And Son, we're proud of you."

"Thanks, Dad. Make sure you tell Grandpa that I love him. Give Mom and everyone a big Huber hug for me."

My next call was to White Glove, who I had met roughly one hundred and twenty miles earlier in Andover, Maine. A deep, gravelly voice answered, **"Hello?"**

I was caught off guard. It sounded like a grizzly bear had answered. I knew it wasn't White Glove's fiancé and guessed it must be her dad.

Our Appalachian Trail Code talk went something like this:

"Is this Pole Dragger?"

"Yes?"

"Pole Dragger, this is Dr. Ducttape. I met White Glove in Andover, and she wanted me to give you a call."

"Ducttape! I've been expecting your call. Where are you?"

"I'm at the Flume."

"I'll be right there."

Click.

Holy crap, what did I just get myself into?

Kee just looked at me and did her little spin move, signaling me to take her pack off and feed her. She finished up just as an elderly man pulled up in a truck and climbed out.

He was slight in stature, sporting a gray beard and with every move, his muscles rippled like a highly trained athlete. There wasn't an ounce of fat on that guy. He was spry in step and moved with a surprising agility that belied his seventy-five years of age.

He shook my hand. "Let's get you loaded up. You can stay with us tonight, do your laundry, get a hot shower and a home-cooked meal if you'd like. If you need anything, I can run you around town tomorrow."

His enthusiasm was contagious. "I'm in, let's do it."

True to his word, he and White Glove finished preparing dinner while I took a glorious hot shower. After a dinner of spaghetti, chicken, baby carrots, and salad, we talked late into the night. They took me in like I was family. They were sad to hear Sandrine had to leave the trail, and they absolutely loved Kee.

I had to ask, "Pole Dragger, how do you stay so fit?"

"I mountain bike, train with a fifty-pound pack filled with wrenches, and try to eat healthy. During rough weather, I'll hike my stairs."

He obviously didn't let the dust settle on his boots, and I marveled at his old-school toughness.

I soon learned that I was in the presence of local celebrities. Pole Dragger and White Glove were the first people from Lincoln, New Hampshire, to hike the Appalachian Trail, and the town had acknowledged them with a party and a plaque to commemorate their achievement. It felt like hiking was an integral way of life celebrated by a community rejoicing in the triumph of the human spirit and simultaneously promoting a healthy lifestyle. I was beginning to see how vital outdoor recreation was in the vicinity of the Appalachians.

Was there a correlation between activities in nature and the increased overall sense of well-being in mind, body, and spirit? I pondered.

Pole Dragger and some of the other elderly individuals I met seemed to suggest there was.

White Glove cooked pancakes in the morning as she and her dad inspired me with stories of the trail magic they encountered. He drove me around Lincoln and North Woodstock, proudly showing me a local's perspective of his hometown until the post office opened at 1:30 pm.

I got my packages, organized them, and mailed what I didn't need in a floater package to my next town stop in Hanover, New Hampshire. He then took me to a store to get some last-minute necessities and then to the trail, where he handed me some of his secret recipe muffins. As we said our goodbyes, it seemed to me that a part of him wanted to go with me, and I was surprised at how connected I felt to this amazing kindred soul and his daughter.

Thru hikers White Glove and her dad, Pole Dragger

With the late start, Kee and I only hiked three miles to Lonesome Lake Hut. We were welcomed by the Hut Master, Emma, and her Croo, Anthony the Greenhorn—he made up for his lack of experience with heart and hustle. Becky, who kept everything running like a well-oiled machine, and Karen, a good-hearted volunteer who loved everything about this mountaintop hut and the hearty souls that found their way there.

At Lonesome Lake, they catered to families and their children with a lot of different programs for kids. On nature walks they learned about the local flora and fauna while touching on the basics of conservation. There was even a pond study which is an ecosystem unto itself. The kids all seemed to love learning about the food chain in the pond and how the trout was at the top of that chain. They even took kids out on a bat watch at dusk.

The overwhelming hit topic was about carnivorous plants that dined on mostly insects and occasionally small amphibians and mammals. These flesh-eating plants could kill insects within fifteen minutes and digest them within a week or two. It was fascinating to see the different techniques that they utilized. Sundews (flypaper plants) have long sticky tentacles protruding from their leaves. The tentacles have a gland that secretes sticky drops resembling dew drops. Bladderworts look like yellow Snapdragons that float on the water and have sticky pear-shaped bladders on their stems that suck in aquatic insects. Purple Pitcher plants trap insects inside the sticky base of their pitcher-shaped flower. All these remarkable plants were nature's way of keeping the ecosystem balanced. I didn't think I harbored any ill will toward mosquitoes, but the thought of these plants liquifying their prey comforted me with a sense of justice. Truthfully, they were my favorites as well.

Kiana and I went down to the scenic lake, and before I knew it, she found a big stick and wanted to play fetch. For a dog that was half German shepherd and half Malamute, she loved to swim. Kids gathered around to watch Kee launch off the dock or off the shore to retrieve a far-flung stick. Kee was in her glory and put on a tireless display of athleticism to the delight of many wide-eyed youngsters.

Kiana in her glory—Lonesome Lake

We finished the evening sitting around the dining table, sharing tales of the trail and feasting on the most amazing beef stroganoff I have ever had.

The Appalachian Mountain Club should be proud of the people and its hut system in the White Mountains of New Hampshire; it's a testament to what people can do when they work together.

Anthony hustling to feed the hungry

07/28/96
First Father and Son SoBo Team

It was raining when we headed out in the morning, and it continued to rain all day. It was a tough slog getting over the North and South Kinsman Mountains. Slipping and sliding made for hair raising descents, and we grabbed for trees to slow our slide. Kee fared much better with her four legs and claws. When we stopped at Eliza Brook Shelter for lunch, Kee fell fast asleep. It was still raining, and I didn't have the heart to wake her and continue, so I called it a day after only six miles. The swimming yesterday had taken its toll.

The storm blew in a couple of guys from Jersey, Jay and Archie, seeking refuge in our shelter. They offered to help if we needed assistance and were within an hour's drive. It was beautiful to see how people were willing to help a stranger.

A couple of hours later, I met some more southbounders who were also attempting a through hike. They were a father-and-son team from Georgia that looked like a couple of drowned rats. They decided to wait out the storm before moving on. Thunder Snow, the father, was a professor of Education at Kennesaw State University in Kennesaw, Georgia, and his son Fox had just graduated from the University of Georgia and was taking a sabbatical from his job at Walmart, where he worked for spending money primarily to fund his hike.

I asked Fox, "So, why are you hiking the trail with your dad?"

He responded with that southern drawl that quickly put me at ease, "Dad took me hiking when I was in high school, and I became fascinated with the idea of through hiking, wondering what it'd be like.…You know, all those miles, the people and places I could see." He smiled.

"So, your dad kind of stoked your curiosity, and you wanted to see if you were up for the challenge?"

"Yeah, I guess so."

I gave him a knowing nod and thought, *How cool is that? Never underestimate a dad's influence to nurture your innate curiosity and challenge your adventurous side.*

A flood of memories overtook me as I remembered adventures shared with my dad. One of my earliest memories was when he and Uncle Jerry took my cousin and me on our first backpacking trip deep into the Superstition Mountains. We camped at the base of Weaver's Needle, where legend claimed the Lost Dutchman's Gold Mine was supposed to be near. Sleeping on the ground and seeing this fabled landmark silhouetted against the night sky only fueled youthful imaginations, conjuring images of the Dutchman leading his donkeys laden with gold to the vicinity where we were camped.

Thundersnow and his son Fox

Humbled

The trail seemed to take us straight up and down North Kinsman and South Kinsman mountains, and it was tough climbing. As we descended Mount Wolf toward Kinsman Notch, I could see three people the size of ants far below. They were running up the mountain, hopping from rock to rock as agile as mountain goats. As they drew near, I was shocked to see the leader had long white locks and a flowing white beard. His name was Merlin, and the three called themselves the "Three Amigos." They were all retired professors, and the youngest was a spry eighty-one years young. With a spark in their eyes, their exuberance defied their years. It was as if they had found the fountain of youth on the Appalachian Trial.

We made it nine miles to Beaver Brook Shelter, where the views were extraordinary. Summits with views implored us to pause and try to soak in the majesty of the surrounding mountains. I could see Mt. Lafayette on the Franconia Ridge to the north, a mere twenty-four trail miles away. Any sense of accomplishment was put into perspective while gazing at the immense vastness of the Appalachian Mountains that stretched as far as I could see, effectively taking the air out of any inflated ego. Unlike views out west, those in the east were hard-earned and never guaranteed.

At 12:30 AM, I was startled awake by the urgent and desperate sound of a bleating fawn. Its frightened cries reached a desperate crescendo, followed by muffled, fading cries and then abrupt silence. The silence was followed by a gusting breeze, the rustling of leaves in the trees, and the gentle popping of my tent walls. Unmoved by what transpired, the rhythms of nature continued on without missing a beat.

07/29/96

The father and son team left Beaver Brook Shelter at the crack of dawn. Kee and I weren't far behind and looked forward to climbing Mt. Moosilauke (4802 ft.) first thing that morning. Clouds were starting to form, so I had to hustle if I was going to earn the five-state view that could be seen from the summit on a clear day.

On the way up, I stepped on some moss at the apex of a huge granite slab. The moss broke loose and my traction with it and pitched me headfirst down the other side. I slid about ten feet and came to a stop against a tree. Wedged upside down, I felt like a turtle on its back. Kee was quickly at my side, licking my face to ensure I was okay.

I was good—other than a scraped leg. I had to release my hip belt and spin out of my shoulder straps to get back upright. I pulled my pack back up the slab to the trail and continued climbing with a little less gusto.

We caught back up with Thunder Snow and Fox as they had stopped along the trail to grab a snack. If we didn't stay ahead on fuel, these mountains would crush us. Once fueled up, we powered to the top of Moosilauke and captured a wonderful panoramic view that stretched to the distant horizon in every direction. There was something very satisfying about experiencing an incredible view for the first time. It's magical as you try to take it all in, imprinting on your mind the artistic beauty that was beyond reproach or compare. So, we lingered and drank it in as if it were necessary for survival itself.

Before we left, we shored up plans to meet at the Atwell Hilton that evening. According to the *AT Thru-Hiker's handbook*, the Atwell Hilton was a house owned by the National Park Service that was closed, but the yard was available for tent camping.

Dizzy Bee and Dr. Slow Jive

The Atwell Hilton was a run-down old house on the verge of being condemned. I was surprised at how many hikers were tenting out in the yard, which was overrun with Blackberry bushes. I had to tramp down the weeds to claim my stake at the improv Hilton rendezvous. I guess northbounders had gotten word that a previous thru-hiker, Dizzy Bee, was going to bring refreshments for all on this fortuitous evening.

She didn't disappoint, showing up with gallons of water and cases of beer, along with her harmonica-playing boyfriend. I knew we were in for a treat when he pulled out a suitcase full of harmonicas, one for every occasion. There were over twenty people there that night. If statistics are worth the paper they are written on, then only four or five from a group that size would finish the entire trail.

Northbounders and southbounders gathered around the campfire, listening to the lonesome sounds of a harmonica played by a master. As I surveyed the ruddy faces of those around the fire, it seemed that this same scene could've played out in the early 1800s before heading west into the wild frontier. The only exception was that these rugged characters wore Thinsulate, fleece, and Gortex instead of buckskin and fur clothing.

There is something primal about sitting around a campfire, listening to the wood crackle and pop, watching the dancing flames lick at the night sky. It is mesmerizing until the smoke shifts, chasing the most hardened individual into retreat.

Those northbounders could drink like fish, and Dizzy Bee made another beer run to keep the party alive. It gave everyone an opportunity to loosen up and swap trail stories of hardships endured, equipment failures, budding trail romances, must-see places, and top food stops. These were always secondary topics to Trail Magic. What made Trail Angels the number one topic on the AT? I believe the magic happened because people were genuine and cared about helping hikers be the best they could be and maybe help make a dream a reality in the process.

I tried to get to sleep at 11 PM, but those northbounders were whooping it up with one southbounder, Dr. Slow Jive. He was an ER doctor on sabbatical from the stresses of his profession. He was a real hard charger and could hang with the best the northbounders could muster. They kept getting louder and louder, staying up until 2 AM, hell-bent on not letting any beer go to waste.

What the Hilton lacked in creature comforts, Dizzy Bee and her boyfriend made up for in hospitality.

07/30/96

I woke with the birds singing at 5 AM, struggling to clear the cobwebs; I made a mental note to buy earplugs on my next town stop. I had every intention to hike the seventeen miles to Trapper John Shelter but only made it twelve miles to the top of Smarts Mountain, where I met my first brother team, Shoofly Pie and Tree Trunk. I'm not sure how Shoofly ended up with his trail name, but he did say, "If you haven't had Shoofly pie, you haven't truly lived!" With his deadpan sense of humor, I couldn't be sure if he was sincere or speaking with youthful bravado. Regardless, just the thought of that delectable delight activated my salivary glands.

One look at Tree Trunk, and you knew it was a great trail name for him. He had the quads of Earl Campbell, a crushing downhill running back for the Houston Oilers. It didn't look like the weight of Tree Trunk's pack phased him much. He had just earned his Eagle Scout badge, and he and his brother decided to take the summer and hike the trail.

Shoofly Pie & Tree Trunk

07/31/96

Life on the trail was starting to take on a natural rhythm along with an incessant need to cut pack weight. I found myself falling asleep as dusk turned to dark, effectively minimizing my headlamp usage and eliminating my need to carry spare batteries. Waking to the serenade of birds every morning and regularly paying attention to the sun's position in the sky made me even question the need for a watch.

While heating water for my instant oatmeal, I noticed Kiana intently watching a section of the forest floor. Following her gaze, I saw an Eastern Newt (terrestrial eft- adult stage). It was bright orange, and I was able to head Kee off before she got too close and decided to play with it. Newts release a neurotoxin (tetrodotoxin) from their skin and can kill a pet within hours. Newts, like the reptiles of my youth, have a remarkable regenerative ability. They can regenerate missing arms, legs, tails and parts of their eyes, intestines, jaws, heart, brains and spinal cord. *The newt's only natural predator is the garter snake, which has built up a tolerance to the amphibian's poison.

National Geographic – Newt healing factors unaffected by age and injury-July 12th, 2011.

Kee and I stopped to filter water at the Trapper John Shelter, and I took a photo to honor the M.A.S.H. character it was named after. We had been hiking in the clouds most of the day. It wasn't raining, but the condensation was collecting in the trees, and every time the wind whipped through the canopy, it felt like a sudden downpour. The temperature was dropping, and I could see my breath. I had to constantly move to keep from shivering.

Kiana thrives in the cooler temps, trotting along, stopping long enough for me to catch up while she seemed to be analyzing interesting scents with her nose in the air. She never stopped, and I could only imagine the stories she could decode as she deciphered who had been where and how recently.

Trapper John Shelter

Occasionally, we would have a steady drizzle, and visibility would be down to less than forty feet. That which was hidden behind the veil only added to the mystique of the trail and beckoned me to see what was around the next bend of this endless green tunnel. We found our stride with the cool weather and covered twenty-two miles. We made it to the Velvet Rock Shelter as it became too dark to see without a headlamp. About a half mile before the shelter, we came around a bend to find the trail and the surrounding area alive with hundreds of orange newts. It was a vibrant contrast to the green tunnel, and we had to choose our steps carefully to avoid crushing them.

08/01 to 08/02/96
Panarchy Frat House

We were able to stay in the Panarchy Frat house at Dartmouth for a nominal donation. Initially, the college guys were a little intimidated by Kiana's size, but they quickly fell in love with her wagging tail and easy-going disposition, and before I knew it, she was the queen of their frat house.

While waiting for laundry and hanging out in the downstairs living room, two other southbound hikers walked in. Leapfrog was a spunky, college-aged strawberry blonde who bubbled with enthusiasm and had spent some summers in Glacier National Park. She had a fascinating story of a grizzly stalking her. I shot Fox a glance, and he didn't even notice; it was as if we had all vanished for him except for her.

Dr. Slow Jive casually walked up and rolled his eyes toward Fox and Leapfrog. "Ahh, to be young again. Anyone want to go grab something to eat?"

He reminded me of Friar Tuck in Robin Hood's legendary band of outlaws. He was built like a tank and had an affable sense of humor. Despite his trail name, he had an incredible quick wit.

We ate like kings at EBA (Everything but Anchovies) and bonded over a couple of beers. The next day, we toured the campus and ended up going for a swim in the Connecticut River down by the boat houses where the athletes kept their sculling boats. We watched the rowing teams practice, moving as one, skimming effortlessly up and down the river. They were poetry in motion. Kiana wasn't happy to just hang out on the floating docks and watch the teams. She somehow found a tennis ball and insisted we all take turns throwing it into the river so she could retrieve it. She was always present in the moment and made the best of every situation.

Personal hygiene was a premium during town stops. Guys would shave, and some would get haircuts. I even snapped a quick picture of Thunder Snow looking at his reflection in a car window and trimming his eyebrows. Town stops were critical opportunities for guys with the Chia Pet eyebrows to trim them back before they became the AT Crazy Brow that morphed into a unibrow. Why is it that when men age, the hair on their heads thins or falls out but then grows like weeds out of their noses, ears, and backs? God sure has a sense of humor.

I couldn't thank the Panarchy guys enough for giving us a place to take showers, do laundry, and a place to hang our hats for a couple of nights.

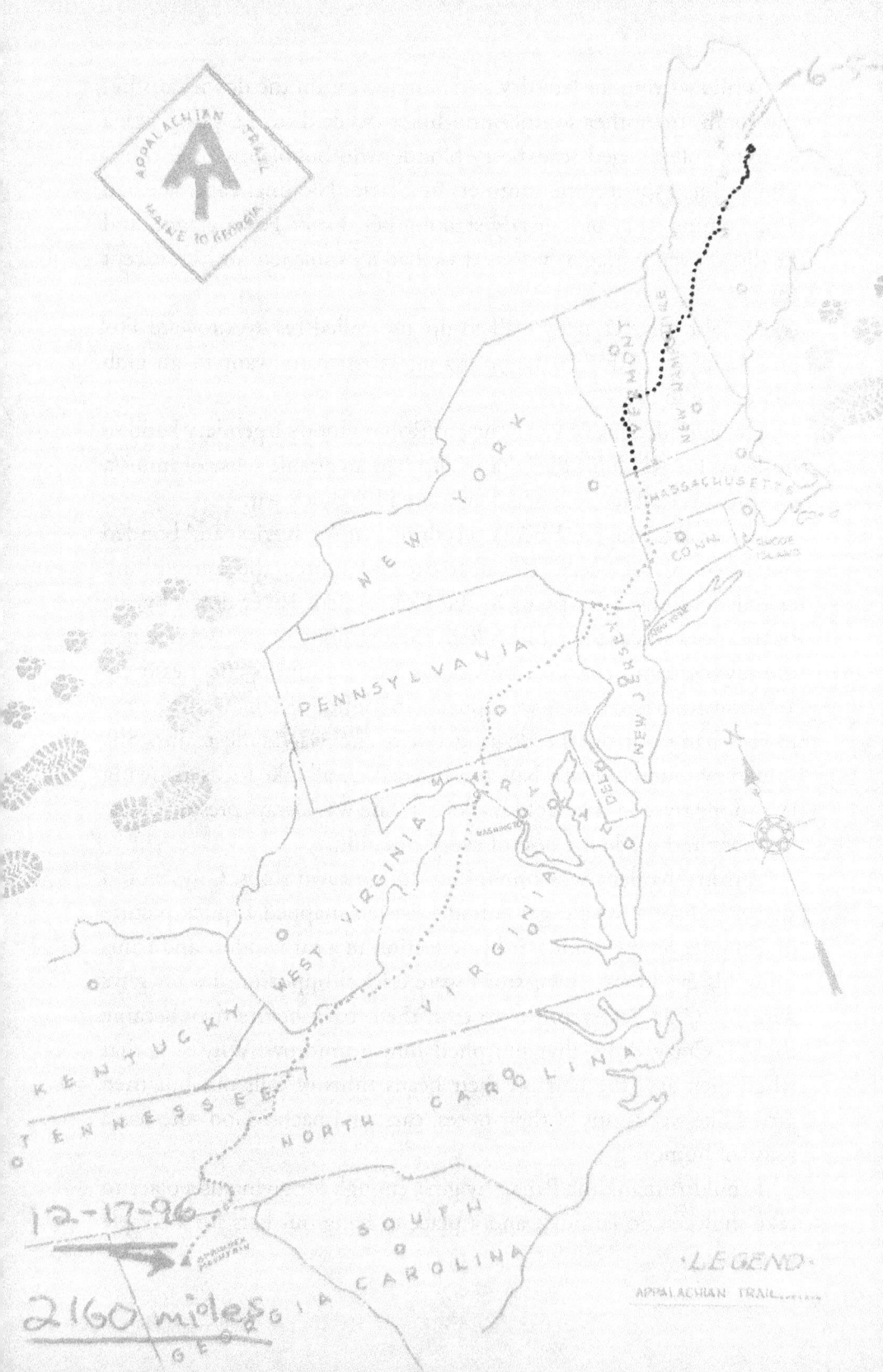

Chapter 12

Vermont

08/03/96

Frequent diners at Dartmouth's Thayer Hall experienced unexpected weight gains, fondly known as the "Thayer Layer." Unphased, we all had the four-dollar AYCE (all you can eat) and headed south with buoyed spirits and boundless energy.

Once on the trail, we had a daunting reality check. The first trail marker south of town indicated that we had seventeen hundred and thirty miles to go, which meant we had only completed four hundred and forty-one miles.

Hope was renewed by a 1987 NoBo thru-hiker's observation in the Wingfoot's handbook that read, "**When you reach Hanover, you've done 80% of the miles, but you still have 50% of the work left.**" As a southbounder, we were beginning to dream of what was possible. Two states down and twelve more to go!

Trail Comraderie

After only eight miles, ominous clouds built into a black tower, and booming thunder reverberated across the sky. Kiana was glued to my side. I think the previous storms may have made her fearful. I quickly set up the tent on a flat spot above Podunk Brook. When I went to filter water, I saw Kiana waiting patiently at the tent's door. She seemed to be trying to seek shelter from the growing crescendo.

"It's going to be okay, Kee! Come on, let's go get a drink, girl."

We headed down to the creek, and she never left my side. We ate dinner inside the tent as the thunder subsided and the rain began in earnest. There is something comforting about having a full belly, a dry shelter, and a warm bed while listening to the rain drum off a tight rainfly. Consciousness relinquished its hold, and slumber enveloped me in a cathartic hug.

08/04/96

Paradox of Diversion

Settling into the rhythm of hiking an eighteen-mile day, mostly in a green tunnel, gave me the time to contemplate the great central questions we all must ask, sooner or later. Questions like—is there a God? Why am I here? What is the purpose of life? Are we here to exist through the storms or to persevere and excel? What happens after death?

I've always been certain of the first question and hadn't really pondered the rest. As far as the last question goes, when we are young and invincible, we don't think to question the inevitable.

Ten hours later, we reached the Wintturi Shelter and set up our tent nearby.

> "The sole cause of man's unhappiness is that he does not know how to stay quietly in his room. The only thing that consoles us for our miseries is diversion, and yet it is the greatest of our miseries."
>
> – BLAISE PASCAL, *The Misery of Man without God*

08/05/96

It was a hot and humid day, and by 8:45 am, I was a sweaty mess and looking forward to a swim with Kee at Kent Pond that evening. After only fourteen and a half miles we were treated to the beautiful cascade of Thundering Brook Falls and nearby Kent Pond. It is one of the most picturesque settings to camp, and we fell asleep listening to the soothing sound of tumbling water.

08/06/96

When I left camp the next morning, I noticed Dr. Slow Jive was already gone. I thought it odd since he wasn't a morning person, but I shrugged it off, thinking he wanted to get a head start so we could end up in the same place that night.

I arrived at the Inn at Long Trail around lunchtime and thought I could hear Dr. Slow Jive's bass laughter reverberating from within the Inn.

I watered Kee, tied her to my pack in the shade, and went in to see what all the excitement was about. Sure enough, I found Dr. Slow Jive bellied up to the bar, surrounded by three northbounders.

L to R: Sweat Hog, Tundra, Dr. Slow Jive, & Napalm

Sweat Hog was wearing a gray hiking shirt; Tundra was wearing a nice striped, button-down "town stop shirt;" and Napalm came ready to party wearing a loud Hawaiian shirt and sunglasses held together with duct tape. I'm not sure how Napalm got his trail name, but rumors were that it had to do with either his ability to toss down cocktails or with a gastrointestinal malfunction. Regardless, the North was doing their best to drink Doc under the table.

I don't think they realized that the Doc was a seasoned competitor, and my money was on him. It was a friendly rivalry, and those boys were doing their best to keep up. As the liquor continued to flow, the three became a highlight reel full of information about what we could expect from the South.

I had a beer with the guys while my three sandwiches were being prepared, and then I went and ate with Kee under a shade tree.

SoBo Band of Brothers Grows

We hiked to the Governor Clement Shelter, and since it was a weekday, we decided to make camp despite the warnings that this shelter was frequently used for parties. Our gamble paid off as Dr. Slow Jive was the last to roll into camp at sunset.

08/07/96

Everyone at some point gets tired of hiking in the "Green Tunnel," But having grown up in the desert, I wasn't accustomed to such abundance of foliage, so I continued in awe as I hiked.

I continued to be impressed with Thunder Snow and Fox as they seemed to enjoy each other's company and love for adventure. We made it to Clarendon Gorge and were able to go for a much-needed swim in the heat of the day. The rock formations at the Gorge were an incredible testament to the power of water. It was a jumbled deposit of car-sized boulders that were polished and dished out, and some had holes that were bored all of the way through.

Kee had been crowding me from behind, which caused me to trip several times. I finally had enough and told her in a stern voice, "Kee! Get in front!"

She gave me a look and then walked away and laid in the bushes about ten feet off the trail. She laid there and stared at me like she

was pouting. It's amazing how human some of her expressions are.

She stayed right there and wouldn't budge, so I walked down the trail while I called her name and whistled for her. I was almost out of sight when she finally gave in and came running. I think I met my match on the stubborn scale.

We reached the Greenwall Shelter, where we met two more southbounders. Fashion, a lean, good-looking guy who had quit his job as an Urban Forester in Iowa City, wanted to test himself while seeking adventure on the famed AT. Out of all of us, he was the most color-coordinated and had all the best hiking equipment. He could have been a model for outdoor gear.

Gretchen, a spunky, curly-headed blonde belied a trusting soul with her stunning blue eyes. She could've been of Scandinavian descent and Viking royalty. She was tough, rugged, and an independent thinker, all qualities of a natural-born leader or man-eater. She invited all southbounders to her mom's house in Manchester for a barbeque, and it was apparent that Fashion was captivated by her charm.

08/08/96

Our band of southbounders had grown to seven, and Kee was doing her best to keep everyone together. She didn't understand that everyone hiked at their own pace. If they didn't, some would not finish. Kee would do her best to double back, check on everyone, and then catch back up. She probably logged double the miles I did daily, but it was her way of checking on her pack. At the end of the day, she would know if somebody was missing and would wait at the perimeter of camp, like a sentry, patiently watching down the trail we had just come from. She was the first to greet any of the stragglers, which always seemed to elevate morale.

Kee's pack was rubbing her raw, and Dr. Slow Jive was kind enough to let me cut some of his closed cell foam sleeping pad off to use as a blanket under her pack. Dr. Slow Jive always tried to come across as the gruff, insensitive, no-bullshit doctor who had seen it all and called it the way he saw it, but I think he had a soft spot for dogs.

About seven miles into our day, the trail crossed the Danby-Landgrove Road, and to our surprise, a Trail Angel was waiting on the tailgate of her truck with a cooler full of ice-cold soda. No one hesitated to drop their packs in a semi-circle around the back of the truck and swap stories with the angel and two northbounders who were already there.

Our Trail Angel, Sally, was a newly married bride hiking the trail with her husband. She had hurt her knee and was taking a support role while her husband was slack-packing a section on that fortuitous day. They had been married on March 4 and their trail name was Mr. & Mrs. H (short for honeymooners).

I can't tell you how wonderful it was to have that cold, carbonated flavor invigorate my palate, especially when it wasn't expected. So, there we sat, talking about the beautiful places and people we had seen, while Kee sacked out in the shade under the tailgate. Somehow, I couldn't help but think that Sam, the adventurous soul who rekindled a passion so long ago in the Bashas' parking lot, would have approved of this impromptu rendezvous. Mrs. H had just added to the legend of the trail.

As soon as we all started putting our packs on, Kee was up and ready to go. Eight miles later, we arrived at Peru Peak Shelter to filter water and grabbed a quick snack before pushing on. Before heading out, I noticed a northbounder settling in the shelter. I went over to make small talk and noticed he had an intricately carved hiking stick. I marveled at its beauty, thinking I was in the presence of a master artisan.

"Did you carve this?"

"Oh no. I went into Manchester to get a few things and when I came out of the store, this stick was lying on my pack with a note that said **the Stick Man carved it**. All the Stick Man asked in return was for the recipient to write him a little letter telling him where his stick ended up."

"That is amazing. You have a work of art there."

"I know," he said. "And I guess it's this eighty-year-old guy who carves these sticks in his spare time; he only does a couple of sticks a year and lays them on the trail to see where they will end up."

"Brother, that is another level of trail magic I have not seen. You are fortunate to have been blessed with such a gift for your journey. Safe travels, my friend."

And with that, we were off to hike another 4.5 miles to Mad Tom Notch before dark, where the luxury of a hand pump promised crystal-clear mountain water for those who could figure out the attached mechanism. I knew we were getting close to town since there was a spring in Dr. Slow Jive's step as we covered 19.2 miles for the day. I was able to get an honorary picture of Dr. Slow Jive, aka Tom, madly pumping water at Mad Tom Notch for everyone. After filling everyone's water containers, Slow Jive rolled his Gortex bivy sack out next to my tent. I shook my head, knowing that his snoring ability was something that legends are made of, and sleep would be contingent on a fresh set of earplugs.

At 2:30 in the morning, one of my earplugs had fallen out. I could hear a freight train rumbling, and the ground was vibrating. I fumbled in the dark for my headlamp frantically searching for the missing earplug, only to find it mid-way down my sleeping bag. Slow Jive could wake Lazarus, and I pitied his future wife. Being bone tired and having both earplugs proved to be a winning solution, and we were still friends in the morning.

Manchester Magic

08/09/96

We only had six miles to Manchester, Vermont, where Gretchen's boasting of her brother's grilling ability had us drooling. Slow Jive couldn't wait and was packed up and gone before the rest of us could shovel down some instant oatmeal gruel and break camp. He turned from Dr. Slow Jive to Mr. Over Drive and was gone in a flash.

We arrived at Gretchen's house early in the day, a beautiful cabin nestled harmoniously into the native landscape. The cozy confines of the home were exemplified as Gretchen's mom, Phyllis, greeted us with open arms. It was apparent that this wasn't her first rodeo as she encouraged everyone to settle in, get showers, and do laundry. Then her boyfriend, Mike, offered to run us into town to resupply while her son Andrew prepped everything for the barbeque. They completely understood the needs of thru-hikers. I later learned that Mike had completed a thru-hike twenty years earlier and graced us with a slide show to prove it.

During the early evening gathering, Dr. Slow Jive pulled a miniature magnetic chess set from his pack and asked if I wanted to play. It had been a while since I had participated in a game, and I quickly lost the first two. I should have known better than to tangle with a guy who carries a chess set on the AT, but it only fueled my competitiveness and our camaraderie.

Andrew knocked it out of the park with his culinary ability, feeding twenty hungry thru-hikers like a seasoned pro.

Leapfrog had us on the edge of our seats, telling tall tales of her being stalked by grizzlies in Glacier, as firelight danced on the faces of her hushed audience. She had grit and proved to be a bundle of positive energy that captivated all of us, especially Fox. I wondered how that might affect the father/son team.

To witness a gathering of trail-hardened thru-hikers and their insatiable appetites was amazing. It was as if everyone's metabolism was in overdrive, and food was being processed and distributed to our muscles before it even had a chance to make it to our lower intestines.

For example, I had two sandwiches, some Vermont cheese and crackers, two beers, and a soda for an appetizer. For dinner, I had two pieces of chicken, two pork chops, a hamburger, two heaping servings of potato salad, two corn on the cob, and three fat slices of ice-cold watermelon. Then, for dessert, a pint of Ben & Jerry's ice cream. We all had such a caloric deficit that we could've been mistaken for a pack of ravenous wolves in a feeding frenzy. None of us ate out of gluttony. We only ate until we were satiated. No one left the table uncomfortable. Andrew never blinked an eye, and all the rave reviews from our hungry hiking coalition only spurred him to grilling greatness. I had never before or since seen anyone as skilled with a set of tongs and a spatula.

Homecooked meals tantalized our taste buds and filled us with appreciation as we savored every meal as if it were a gourmet masterpiece. After a mouthwatering breakfast, it was time to say goodbye. As I was getting ready to strap Kiana's pack on, Phyllis walked into the yard and gave Kee and me a care package for the trail. Kee danced around like a puppy; she could probably smell what was inside. It was some of the grilled protein from last night's fiesta wrapped in tin foil in the shape of a swan. I gently packed it in the top of my pack so it wouldn't be crushed. I thanked Phyllis for sharing her home and letting us get to know her amazing family.

Parting gift of a tin foil swan loaded with barbeque leftovers

I slung my pack on and walked away, moved with emotion as the symbolism of the swan was not lost on me. It represented peace and tranquility found in large quantities on the trail. In literature, the swan symbolizes light, purity, transformation, intuition, and grace. I could only hope that some of those traits would come to pass as I felt the wall of distrust being crumbled by the kindness of strangers.

08/10/96

Leaving the comforts of society and new friends wasn't easy; it tore at me, tried to pull me back in, and tested my resolve to continue.

We only went 2.5 miles and found Fashion and Gretchen hanging out with three northbounders at Spruce Peak Shelter. I decided to call it a day as well. The atmosphere was a little melancholy until I pulled out the tinfoil swan with six pounds of grilled perfection. A school of piranha could not have cleaned the bones any faster. My Great Depression Era Grandmother would have been so proud that we didn't waste anything.

The next day we continued to ease our way back into the rigors of trail life and hiked eleven miles to the top of Stratton Mountain. We climbed the fire tower and were treated to an even better top-of-the-world view than what Benton MacKaye experienced while sitting in a tree and pondering the feasibility of the AT seventy-five years prior, on this very mountain. I remember being very grateful and honored to have walked in the steps of a dreamer with a big vision.

View from Stratton fire tower where Benton MacKaye gazed upon the same landscape while perched in a tree

08/11/96

We stayed at the Stratton Mountain Ski Patrol warming hut and had time to ride the Starship XII gondola down to the village and get some sandwiches from the grocery store for dinner. It was Kiana's first gondola ride, and she took it all in stride. Back at the warming hut, Dr. Slow Jive and I played a couple of chess games while everyone else journaled or checked their gear. He's tough, and I could beat him occasionally, but for the most part, he'd given me a lesson in the game's finer points.

The expansive views of the surrounding majestic mountains were breathtaking. Then we were treated to an amazing top-of-the-world sunset as the night sky was ablaze with deep reddish orange, brilliant orange, fading into yellow. It was a masterpiece of vibrant colors that just made my soul smile.

08/12/96

The best fathers not only give us life, but they also teach us how to live.

Kiana had been moving with a noticeable spring in her step since we left Manchester. Changing her dog food to one with higher protein and fat content made all the difference. The only downside was she had the worst gas, and she always seemed to cozy up to someone in our hiking pack before letting off a silent but deadly volley. I always knew without looking she had claimed another victim when I would hear, "Oh, Kee!!" I couldn't help but chuckle under my breath and be thankful that these friends of mine loved Kee so much that they were willing to suffer a little on her behalf.

Coming off Stratton was easy, and then we had a lot of ups and downs before calling it a 16.3-mile day at Goddard Shelter. It was a great log shelter with a cold spring and an incredible view to the south.

While Thunder Snow was filtering water, Fox let us know that his dad's fifty-fourth birthday was the following day. So, we devised a plan to have Fox distract his dad when we all went into Bennington under the ruse that everyone needed something from the store.

08/13/96

To give Leapfrog's No-Bake Cheesecake time to set up, everyone filtered water, ate dinner, cleaned up, settled in for the evening, and we celebrated at Congdon Camp.

After dinner, Fox gave his dad a birthday card. I marveled that he had been able to pull that off and still keep his dad preoccupied. After reading his card, I saw that Thunder Snow was moved, and his eyelids fluttered a few times to clear the tears. Leapfrog presented him with two small pans of Cheesecake adorned with candles.

He gushed with that southern drawl, "Wow, guys, this is amazing! You didn't get fifty-four candles on there, did you?"

Then his son quipped, "Naw, Pops, no one had room for a fire extinguisher in their packs." The laughter was contagious as Fashion and Gretchen procured two six-packs of beer chilling in the nearby stream. Slow Jive pulled out a pint of Jack, and we toasted a well-lived life and wished him many more.

After things settled down a little, I pulled him aside and said, "I've got one more thing for you, buddy." I pulled a pint of frozen Ben and Jerry's out of my sleeping bag. "This one's for you. You've earned it."

Surprised, he asked, "How in the world did you keep this frozen hiking all the way out here in this heat?"

"I didn't know if it would work, so I had it in a Ziploc bag just in case. But it stands to reason that a sleeping bag is designed to keep you warm; that same insulation can keep things cold."

As he savored the ice cream, he looked at everyone gathered around and said, "I'll never forget this birthday."

I fell asleep knowing that the bond between a father and son had been forged stronger by their shared adventure. I think our dads teach us how to dream, and I drifted off remembering the many adventures I had been on with my dad.

Celebrating Thundersnow's B-day. L–R: Thundersnow, Fox, Leapfrog, Fashion, Gretchen, Dr. Slow Jive. Me in the center with Kee passed out under the table

Chapter 13

Massachusetts

08/14/96

"Who am I?"

While everyone was still sawing logs, I ran down to the creek with Kee, and we went for a quick icy dip. It was a great way to start the day, and it challenged me to never take hot running water for granted.

Slow Jive was still sounding like a bear in deep slumber, so I took the remaining can of beer and duct taped it to a long limber limb and then taped the stout end to the back of his pack so that it ran up and over his pack and dangled in front of him about six feet. Just far enough where he couldn't reach it, but close enough to spur Mr. Over Drive into action. He loved it and hiked some of the day with it on, to the delight of every northbounder we came across.

We crossed the border into Massachusetts and had walked five hundred and eighty-eight miles. We only had one thousand five hundred and eighty-seven miles to go. This trail is no joke. We were again blessed with an expansive view at Eph's Lookout. We gazed upon the immaculate farms in the valley below and marveled at man's ability to tame great swaths of the natural world and still live in harmony.

Dr. Slow Jive/Mr. Overdrive

We hiked the short detour into North Adams to get something cold to drink. I left after downing an ice-cold two-liter of Pepsi, half of a fifteen-inch turkey sub sandwich (Kee gladly ate the other half), and a pint of Ben and Jerry. It was a steep three-mile climb, but we powered to the Wilbur Clearing Lean-to in no time. Everyone settled in for the evening, journaling by headlamp in the fading light. Kee was sitting on the perimeter of camp, waiting, watching our backtrack, and sure enough, in came Dr. Slow Jive, carrying a seven-foot section of a tree at least six inches in diameter. He put one hand on his hip, and in his best Superman pose asked, "Who am I?"

"Who are you?" we all chimed in.

"I'm Ducttape!" He made his way through the middle of camp using the tree as a walking stick. He could've earned an Oscar and may have missed his calling.

That was a slight exaggeration, but I did walk with sticks that were bigger than average so I could get an upper-body workout as well. I also felt that a hardwood walking stick could be used as a defensive weapon if necessary. If the guy who murdered those two girls had the nerve to show up in our camp, there would be hell to pay, and I believe Kee would protect those in her pack.

08/15/96

Turned Away at the Inn

We summited the highest point in Massachusetts, Mt. Greylock, at 3500 feet. On the approach, I was stung by a yellow jacket on my left calf, which made things a little more challenging, as I was trying to make it to the summit in time to wish my brother Greg a "Happy Birthday" before he went to work. While on the phone, I claimed the mountain as Mt. Huber for the day in honor of my brother. It was the best I could do for his birthday at the time.

During the Great Depression, volunteers from the Civilian Conservation Corps built this amazing lodge on the top of the mountain using native rock and old-growth Red Spruce timbers. In 1937, Bascom Lodge opened its doors, originally intended to provide refuge for hearty souls searching for adventure. As a centerpiece of a 12,500-acre wilderness park, the lodge felt like it was inviting me to take in its architectural grandeur, refresh my soul, and nourish my body, but they didn't accept dogs, so we moved on.

Also, on Mt. Greylock was a unique war memorial dedicated to the sons and daughters lost in war by the state of Massachusetts. We lingered, paying our respects, and then climbed to the top of the tower. Kee would not be left behind, so she scrambled up the spiral staircase with us, where the views went on for miles.

The AT goes through the town of Cheshire, Massachusetts. En route is St. Mary of the Assumption Catholic Church, and Father Tom, who's trail name was Father Time. He was an avid hiker and opened the parish hall for hikers free of charge. Everyone wanted to stay, and Father Tom wouldn't budge on his no-dog policy even when I explained that Kee was exhausted. So Kee and I hiked on, searching for a place to lay our heads. Before leaving town, I stopped by the post office to get my food drop and to see if my new hip belts had arrived. They hadn't, so I had to reinforce both belts to the pack frame with more duct tape. I called home, thanked my parents for my food package, and told them where my next town stop would be.

They made sure that I knew Grandpa was doing well and even eating again. That was the boost that I needed to keep going. It was 6:30 in the evening when we crossed the Hoosic River and started climbing. Kee kept trying to turn and herd me back to the rest of the gang. She didn't understand, so I had to leash her to my pack and continue to The Cobbles, a vantage point looking down on the Hoosic River valley and the church that turned us away. I understood why Father Tom stuck to his policy based on a bad experience with a dog in the past. His zero tolerance didn't make it any easier when I knew Kee was tired, and I had to push her to go an extra two miles before we found an adequate place to camp. While I set up the tent, she ate, drank the last of our water, and then passed out as a cool breeze blew over us. She didn't move until the next morning.

08/16/96

The Power of Pears

We were awakened by geese flying down the Hoosic River and a Meadowlark singing in the nearby bushes. It was a beautiful morning, and I was blessed to have spent the night on high ground. We had 2.7 miles to go before I could filter water at Crystal Mountain Campsite, so I quickly broke camp and got us going before the sun started heating the day. At Crystal Mountain, I made sure we both got caught up on our hydration and then had breakfast.

I stopped at a laundromat in Dalton to take care of laundry I couldn't do at the town stop the previous day. Kee slept in the corner of the room and didn't even budge while I ate lunch. I knew she was beyond tired when she didn't attempt to Yogi me.

The difference between begging and a great Yogi is subtle. With one, you must ask. With the other, you position yourself near the person with food and wait patiently while looking nonchalantly in another direction. If that doesn't get the result you are hoping for, then you should look directly into the eyes of the person who has what you would like and then use some kind of Jedi mind trick. Kee was the master of the Yogi, and not many could withstand her powers. I watched people walk up to pet her and then ask me if they could give her something to eat. Day hikers would say, "I think I have packed too much. I need to lighten my load. Do you mind if I give her something?"

Usually, this acknowledgment of one's limitations would happen on steep ascents as they were gasping for air or two miles into a ten-mile day.

"I guess it depends on what you need to offload. She's not a garbage disposal." Then, I would list the things that were not on her diet. "She can't have chicken bones, onions, garlic, or chocolate."

"Fair enough." Then they would pull out an extra pound of sliced deli meat, or a bucket of fried chicken, or a couple of handfuls of footlong Subway sandwiches.

I was always amazed at how much extra people would carry, especially on short day hikes.

I checked Kee's nose after I finished laundry. She was running cool and moist but still not as energetic as usual. It was three miles to the next shelter and designated campsite, so I decided we would walk south and play it by ear.

On our way out of town, walking down Depot Street, I heard laughter off to my right, and then a voice called out from the picnic table in the front yard, "Hey, come on over!"

To my surprise, it was the homeowner, Tom Levardi. Sitting at the table were Fashion and Gretchen and a northbounder. The table was adorned with potted flowers on one end and a bowl of fresh pears and apples as the centerpiece. Soon, a couple more northbounders strolled up, and Tom welcomed the lively banter and stories that ensued. He invited us all to stay and have something to eat. He brought out appetizers, salad, and lasagna for the main course, followed by a mouth-watering dessert of fresh strawberries, vanilla ice cream, topped with whipped cream, and a slice of lemon bread. All he asked for in exchange was for us to sign his register.

I contemplated this man's generosity. *Who is this guy? He's genuinely happy being hospitable to total strangers.*

And then he asked, "If anyone wants to stay, you are more than welcome to camp out in the backyard. You can use the restrooms inside this evening, but I have to leave at 4 am to get to work."

I looked at Kee and said, "What do you think, girl?"

She just gave me that look, and I knew this was just what the doctor ordered. We only had hiked seven miles that day, but the extra rest was what she needed. Plus, having Gretchen and Fashion around also seemed to lift her spirit.

08/17/96

Early the next morning, I heard Tom head off to work, and then I felt the rumble in my stomach. I jumped out of bed to see if he had left a door unlocked. No luck! I broke camp and loaded my pack in record time. When I got to the front yard, I faced a dilemma. Do I go left three hundred yards toward town and a restaurant that might be open for breakfast, or head right five hundred yards to the sanctuary of the forest?

I went right, fighting back the spasms that brisk walking caused. I rose to tip toes at times, my intestines screamed to be relieved, and it became a test of agonizing willpower. Cold sweat broke out on my brow as I struggled to save my dignity. It felt like one of those surreal dreams where you walk into a room with wall-to-wall toilets and realize you must go to the bathroom, but there are no toilets in this nightmare.

After what seemed like a torturous eternity, I ran up a bank, crossed a road, dove into the trees, and threw my pack to the ground. I dug a cat hole and ripped my shorts down just as the dam broke. Squatting there, I vowed I would never underestimate the power of fresh fruit again, but then I heard another low rumble that wasn't coming from me. It grew louder, and it soon became apparent that my personal space was about to be invaded by a jacked-up 4-wheel drive truck rumbling my way. All I could do was wave as two redneck brothers drove by, acknowledging me in all my glory.

Lost and Found

A funny thing happened on my way to Upper Goose Pond. I had stopped to filter water from a crystal-clear creek. As I was pumping water through my Sweet Water filter, I was mesmerized by all the brook trout swimming around actively slurping rising nymphs caught in the surface tension of the slack water eddy. Suddenly, I heard some crashing coming through the trees, and I looked up to see this guy working his way through the dense foliage, bushwacking and plowing through the undergrowth.

He saw me from a distance and then stopped. He yelled, "Hey! Are you on the AT?" "Yeah, are you northbounding?"

"No, I'm southbounding! Are you sure you're on the Tr...?"

Kiana bolted through the woods to greet this person as soon as he started speaking. When she got close, I heard, "Keeee!... Dr. Ducttape?!"

A relieved Dr. Slow Jive crossed the stream, muttering, "There was a split in the trail way back there, and I was following the blazes for a while, then they started growing dimmer and dimmer, and after a while, I was following faded white blotches."

He shook his head in disbelief, then he summed up his predicament, "I realized I had to be on an old section of the AT."

"Well, I'm glad you found your way back, brother." For a brief moment, I envisioned Slow Jive as John Belushi in the movie *Continental Divide* and chuckled to myself.

Kee trotted effortlessly, seemingly happy that some of her pack had been reunited. We finished a twenty-one-mile day and arrived at the Upper Goose Pond Cabin in the early evening. Dr. Slow Jive hustled a game of chess with a northbounder, French Arrow, while I set up my tent at a vacant tent platform.

After rolling out our bedding, I called Kee, "Hey girl, before we eat, you want to go for a swim?"

She cocked her head and perked her ears up. "Race ya!"

We both ran through the trees toward Upper Goose Pond, and when she saw that beautiful glacial pond, she pulled ahead and launched into the brisk water with reckless abandon. When she surfaced, I could've sworn she was smiling. We swam for a while when suddenly she made a beeline for the shore. She shook her coat, picked something up with her mouth, and turned to show me her treasure. It was the blade of a canoe paddle.

"Oh my gosh, Kee. Don't you get tired of playing fetch?" I full well knew the answer before I asked. While we played, a small crowd of kids gathered, and some wanted to take turns throwing the paddle for Kee. One girl couldn't control her enthusiasm and dove in with Kee to retrieve the paddle. Kee was in her glory, playing with kids and swimming.

Kee in her glory

Back at the cabin, Slow Jive and I played a friendly game of chess while Kee made friends with most of the northbounders. I found her hanging out with this big guy named Beorn, who said he was an ex-navy seal and was hiking the trail to clear his head and lose weight. He explained that *Outside Magazine* had done a feature article on him doing the trail, weighing around four hundred pounds. He had lost eighty-ninety pounds last year, and another eighty pounds this year. What surprised me most was his ability to recite poetry with a passionate flare. The AT certainly draws an eccentric crowd. I thought it was interesting that with all the people there, Kee instinctively found the one person who needed some Kee time. She loved the affection that people like Beorn showered on her.

I met another guy with the trail name Fox Trot. He was a ROTC guy straight out of high school and was on the trail to test himself and spread his wings. He said his parents wanted to throw him a party and told him to invite all southbounders to their house in Kent, Connecticut.

I asked him, "Are you sure you know what you're asking? There are eleven of us, including you. There's Thunder Snow and his son Fox, Gretchen and Fashion, Dr. Slow Jive, Leapfrog, Shoofly Pie and Tree Trunk, Me and Kee."

"The more the merrier! My parents are going to love it!"

I couldn't help but like the kid—he reminded me of myself when I was that age.

08/18/96

Next morning we got a late start. The entire camp seemed comatose, so Kee and I went for an invigorating swim. I discovered that with the aid of my earplugs, I had slept through a rowdy party last night. I learned from some irritated campers that the crowd that stayed in the cabin were howling at the moon with a bit of liquid courage from Jim Beam and Jack Daniels. Bull Moose led the vocals and apparently could give Hank Jr. a run for his money.

Fashion even asked them to keep it down and be considerate of the other campers. They told him off, so he packed up at one am and walked away.

As we headed out, Slow Jive told me he had to return to work in South Carolina and would try to get back on the trail eventually. I tried to talk him out of quitting, but he said he was bored and his feet hurt. He wanted to see if he could go to Bosnia or Africa and teach doctors how to be doctors or work with Doctors without Borders. If none of that came to fruition, he said, "I'll 'yellow blaze' (drive) to try to catch up with you guys. Besides, I need a worthy chess partner."

After a couple of challenging climbs and a late start, we only walked 13.3 miles and ended up camping near a small creek by Beartown Mountain Road. We didn't catch up to Fashion and Gretchen, and I wondered how far he had walked to cool off.

08/19/96

After breakfast, Kee was laying out of the way, and watched everyone pack up, and as soon as Thunder Snow and Fox started hoisting their packs to their backs, Kee jumped up and ran over to me, prancing in circles as if to say, "Put my pack on, let's go!" Her joy is infectious. Sometimes, it is a little extra work to have a dog along; it's like having a kid on the trail. I have to constantly worry about where she is, wonder what she is doing, and keep an eye on her all the time. But seeing her excitement makes it all worthwhile.

Kee and I spent most of the day hiking with Thunder Snow and Fox through fertile farmland to Benedict Pond, another glacial pond that beckons hikers to go for a swim on a hot, humid day. Kee whined in anticipation, and I barely got her pack off before she sprinted to the shore and launched in between Gretchen and Fashion.

It felt sooo good to cool off!

None of us relished moving on because we knew the sweat would soak us within minutes once we started hiking again.

We hiked along the rim of Ice Gulch in the shade of the trees, where the ambient temperature was at least ten degrees cooler. We stopped at the Tom Leonard Shelter and filtered some of the sweetest mountain spring water I had ever had out of the bottom of Ice Gulch. It was the simple things that I came to appreciate with heightened anticipation.

While I admired the Tom Leonard Shelter, I noticed a flyer posted on the inside.

ATTENTION

Two female hikers were found dead in the Shenandoah National Park at a backcountry campsite near mile 42 on the Skyline Drive on Saturday, June 1. The case is under intensive investigation as a suspected homicide. As a result of the crime, Shenandoah is increasing patrols in the park. Hikers on the Appalachian Trail are being made aware of the incident and asked to exercise additional caution.

PLEASE REMEMBER:

- It is always advisable to hike in groups of two or more.
- Be sure family or friends are aware of your backcountry itinerary.
- Be cautious of strangers, especially inquisitive ones. Do not share details of your route or planned camping location.
- Do not set up backcountry campsites near roads or developed areas.

Once again, I asked why such senseless acts continued to happen. Do we, as a society, propagate fertile ground for this type of behavior to manifest? Can we do better? I know we must, but I'm unsure how we turn this ship around.

For the next two and a half miles, everyone hiked in silence, with the murders weighing heavy on our minds. When we got to Homes Road in the Housatonic River valley, we all dropped our packs and began swapping trail mix for Power Bars as we collectively decided how far we should push on.

The mosquitoes were thick, and we had eleven miles to get to the next shelter with a creek running next to it. As we contemplated tackling a twenty-two-mile day and finishing in the dark, Mrs. Paul, who had been watching our powwow from her living room window, walked out and said, "You guys look tired. Do you want to pitch your tents on the grass in my yard?"

Everyone's feet were hurting, and my legs were tired. So, when she offered us her yard, I felt like an angel was talking to us. It dawned on me that's how we turn this ship around—random acts of kindness. Little Holy Moments done with love can collectively elevate one's sense of well-being, especially when enduring hardship. We don't always know what people are going through; even a simple, sincere smile can elevate a soul from despair.

Thunder Snow assured her we weren't a bunch of hell-raisers and would be quiet. We all thanked her in unison and quickly set up our tents. As we prepared our evening meals, a northbounder wearing a dress walked up and asked if he could join us.

He set up his tent nearby and I had to ask, "So, why the dress?"

"You like it?"

It was a drab gray, and I scowled. "It's not really my color."

"Drastic times require drastic means. I had enough of the chaffing from my shorts, so I bought the first thing I thought would work at a Thrift Store."

I laughed. "Dude, that's hardcore!"

He didn't care what other people thought of him; his only concern was that he could hike another day.

08/20/96

The mosquitoes were horrendous the next morning. I fed Kee while I broke camp, and we made a hasty retreat down the trail with a cloud of winged bloodsuckers in hot pursuit. For the next eight miles along the Housatonic River, the mosquitoes were so thick we had flashbacks of Maine.

Hiking through the farmland in the river valley, we came across a monument, next to a cornfield, addressing Shay's Rebellion that took place February 27, 1787. The rebellion was an armed uprising where the farmers were about to lose their lands because they couldn't pay the unreasonably high Massachusetts state tax. As a result, states were forced to rethink their enslaving taxation policies. Tax relief came at the cost of four citizens being killed and twenty more wounded during the rebellion. As we walked away from that landmark, the haunting song "Find the Cost of Freedom" by Crosby, Stills, and

Nash played in my head and where they mentioned the cost of freedom being buried in the ground was more poignant than I realized.

The field where a few paid the ultimate price.

Our ongoing battle with mosquitoes suddenly seemed trivial, but we were still thankful they began to thin out the higher we climbed Mount Everett. I have no idea how hot it got that day, but the combined heat and humidity made it a tough climb. All I know is that I kept overheating and had to take several breaks and make sure that Kee and I stayed hydrated. Another big climb up Race Mountain proved to be worth the effort as the trail went over an exposed cliff that opened to a view of a verdant valley below, dotted with lakes. We ended up staying at Bear Rock Falls. The campsite was nestled in a beautiful Hemlock grove with a creek cascading over a cliff's edge, plunging into the valley below. Hiking through the Green Tunnel sure made me appreciate hard-earned views, and the one from Bear Rock Falls did not disappoint. Sleep came easy with the sound of tumbling water and a gentle breeze blowing through the trees.

APPALACHIAN TRAIL
MAINE TO GEORGIA

12-17-96

2160 miles

LEGEND
APPALACHIAN TRAIL

Chapter 14

Connecticut

08/21/96

We left our picturesque campsite early and walked a short distance downhill before we crossed the Massachusetts-Connecticut state line. A sense of accomplishment from walking seven hundred miles welled within each of us and made climbing Bear Mountain a little easier. Bear Mountain is 2316 feet tall and the highest mountain in Connecticut. A massive rock tower was built on the summit more than a century ago. It provided a great viewing platform above the trees. While we cooled off on that enormous rock cairn, the caretaker of Sages Ravine (Spaceman-94 thru-hiker) appeared with a pack full of apples and oranges. I can't begin to tell you what a glorious treat that was. Who in their right mind would pack twenty pounds of fruit up the highest peak in Connecticut? It was trail magic in spades.

Overall, the sixteen-mile day felt like a stroll in the park. We crossed the Iron Bridge over the Housatonic River and walked into Falls Village so Leapfrog could call some folks who had no idea who we were. According to Leapfrog, her sister's teacher had just married the daughter of an elderly couple who lived eleven miles away in Cornwall Bridge, Connecticut. They had never met any of us, not even Leapfrog. But they thought so highly of their son-in-law, who had just married their daughter one week prior to our call, that they were excited to go out of their way to meet all of us.

Charlotte and Denny thought meeting new friends and seeing what was happening on the AT would be a great opportunity. Charlotte was a schoolteacher who taught the underprivileged and students with disabilities. One of her students became a lawyer despite being unable to read or write. Apparently, he learned by listening to tapes; instead of taking written tests, he took them orally. Charlotte and Denny gave us a place to stay, do our laundry, and take hot showers. After everyone was cleaned up, Denny grilled up a couple dozen burgers, and we sat down together and shared a meal of burgers, macaroni salad, and home-grown tomatoes, followed by ice cream for dessert.

08/22/96

FRONT: L-R: Charlette, Kee with new friend.
MIDDLE: Thundersnow, Fashion, Denny   BACK: Gretchen, Leap Frog, and Fox

We were awakened early the next morning to the mouth-watering aroma of sausage and eggs floating through the open kitchen window to our encampment on their back lawn.

While we were breaking camp, I noticed Fox was looking frustrated. I walked over. "What's up, brother?"

"Oh, my dad has his way of doing things, and I've got my way of doing things, and we're just butting heads."

"Hey man, you guys are so alike; it's no wonder there's conflict. You're both pretty independent-minded. I get it. I've been there wanting to spread my wings and fly the roost, but your dad will only be on the trail another fifteen to nineteen days before he has to go back to work. You only have one dad, be patient. Besides, I had a serious talk with your dad the other day about what it meant for him to be hiking the trail with his son. You know what he said?"

I didn't wait for him to answer. "He was so fired up about hiking with you and so proud of how you coordinated this trip. He said it was like a dream come true for him. He even said he's already thought of a book title he'd like to write—*Hiking the AT in My Son's Footsteps.*"

Fox looked like a bearded barbarian, a real rugged individual with a heart of gold. He got a little choked up and had to cover his eyes. I think our talk inspired him to continue with his dad and throttle back on his desire to explore where his feelings for Leapfrog may go. If I were to guess, the father-and-son team would do just fine. I may have to run interference for Fox and hike with Thunder Snow.

We made it to Silver Hill Campsite. It was a fantastic campsite on top of a mountain with a grassy knoll and the luxury of a freshwater pump attached to a wellhead. The water was cold, crystal clear, and absolutely refreshing. Thunder Snow took the time to pump water for Kee before filling his own Nalgene water bottles. The original shelter had burnt down, but there were still picnic tables and a swing to be enjoyed.

We fell asleep to the peaceful serenade of frogs and crickets singing their mating songs.

08/23/96

Fox Trot skipped the Connecticut section of the trail because he had already hiked his home state and wanted to help his parents prepare for the southbound rendezvous. We only had 10.5 miles to walk, and another .8 miles to call Fox Trot from the Kent market pay phone. But first, we had to get up and over Caleb's Peak during the heat of the day. We were all overheating by the time we descended Caleb and walked into a field that had a small stream running through it. Kee jumped in before I could get her pack off. I'm so glad I double-bagged her dog food, or she would have nothing but mush to eat.

Everyone else jumped in after we dropped our packs and stripped off sweaty socks and boots. We could feel our core temperature drop to a comfortable level again as we floated through a school of fish hanging in the shadow of an undercut bank. It wasn't long and that refreshing plunge made us shiver and look forward to getting back on the trail.

I started to heft my pack to my shoulders when I noticed an odd-looking stick on my pack, and then that stick moved just as I was getting ready to brush it off. I had no idea how long this fragile hitchhiker had been tagging along, but after marveling at its stick mimicry camouflage, I relocated it to a nearby bush.

The stick bug or walking stick has an amazing life cycle. Adult stick bugs can regenerate appendages, so they will sacrifice a limb to escape a threat. They also utilize another escape tactic: dropping from a tree or bush to the forest floor, where they blend in with other sticks. Another ingenious survival strategy is when the adults lay eggs that look like seeds. The first frost kills off the adults, but their eggs can survive the winter months and hatch into nymphs in the spring. Newly hatched nymphs climb back into the deciduous foliage, where they spend the next four to six weeks eating leaves before becoming a mature adult resembling a stick or leaf.

As we approached where the AT crossed Highway 341, I was lost in thought, thinking about all the amazing critters and their survival adaptations I had seen when I noticed a bush moving unnaturally to the rhythm of a gentle breeze. The bush exploded as I neared, and a guy with weeds sticking out of his shirt sleeves and the neck of his shirt jumped out, yelling, "Ducttape, Kee, Thunder Snow, Fox!"

Dr. Slow Jive was doing his best to blend in, and he seriously challenged the stick bug for mimicry superiority. True to his word, Slow Jive yellow blazed to catch up but not to rejoin the march south. Instead, he shared a little trail magic with us, which consisted of ice-cold beer and soda. He then gave us a ride into Kent, where we were able to make a call to Fox Trot and get directions. He then drove us to Fox Trot's house and stayed for one more party.

After taking a quick shower and doing my laundry, Fox Trot gave me a ride to a nearby sporting goods store, where I could purchase a Gregory Backpack and officially retire my Jansport external frame pack that was held together with duct tape. It was Friday evening, and Dick, Fox Trot's dad, was getting ready to barbeque hotdogs and hamburgers. It appeared they were running low on drinks, so Slow Jive and I offered to make a beer and soda run. By the time we found a liquor store, dusk was quickly turning dark. We went in and made our purchases, but when we left the parking lot, we looked at each other and he asked, "Do you know how to get back to the house?"

We had grown so used to navigating by landmarks that neither of us had paid attention to street signs. The night sky turned inky black, and nothing looked the same. Neither of us had noticed our hosts' street or address, so we couldn't ask for directions. Fox Trot's phone number was still in my journal, which was in my backpack, at their house. We had never been formally introduced, so looking up their number or address in the phone book was impossible since we didn't know their last name.

We drove in the general direction their home should've been. Nothing looked familiar, so we backtracked to the liquor store and planned to sleep in the truck until first light, knowing we could use the sun to get our directional bearings. Then we could find the familiar landmarks of trees, rocks, and shrubs that we had grown so accustomed to for route finding.

We were just falling asleep around one in the morning when some drunk teenagers walked into the parking lot and started yelling and screaming. From what I could understand, in my sleep-deprived state, was that they had been at a house party nearby, and a guy named Tom was upset at a guy named Ed. Ed had decided to escort Tom's date away from the party, and Tom's ego was bruised. The altercation never escalated past puffed-up chests and vulgar language, so we drove off looking for a tranquil sanctuary to get some shuteye. We planned to start backtracking at first light from the liquor store.

Thick fog settled in as we searched for a peaceful place to crash. The fog had left a slippery glaze on the asphalt, and when we came to a hairpin turn, we slid off the road, and into a tree stump, blowing the left front tire.

Neither of us had our headlamps, so we had to change the tire in the dark. With the headlights on, we had just enough light to install the spare tire and drove into the night until we found a dark side road in the general direction of Fox Trot's house. We slept peacefully from 4:30- 5:30 and woke to the songs of birds. With the morning light, we found our way back within ten minutes, traveling through residential housing tracts where every fourth house was the same, using the shrubs, flowers, and trees to identify Fox Trot's house. Somewhere in the previous seven hundred and twenty miles on the AT, we had transitioned to a more primitive route-finding skill set.

08/24/96

Slow Jive dropped me off, grabbed his pack and hiking boots, bid me goodbye, and said he had to get his passport in order before he went to Angola to teach doctors to be doctors. That was the last adventure I shared with Dr. Slow Jive, and I knew I would miss the caring individual hidden beneath a brash, hard-charging exterior.

After checking in on Kee and getting her fed, I walked into the kitchen where Fox Trot's parents were busy making breakfast for everyone and spilled the beans on our misguided beer and soda run, much to the delight of all. During breakfast, Fox Trot's dad announced that he would be available to run people into town to resupply and then encouraged all eight of us to stick around because they wanted to take us out to dinner. I felt like I was witnessing a modern-day Prodigal Son story where the Father was pulling out all the stops to celebrate the return of his Son.

I don't know if it is the lure of shared struggle on the trail or the deep camaraderie born of adventure that entices people to go out of their way to perform acts of kindness for strangers; maybe it is both, but I do know that the love they had for their son was very moving.

Trail magic at the Woodford's

08/25/96

After another glorious breakfast, we all went swimming in their pool for a couple of hours, and then they shuttled us to the trailhead at noon. All eight of us and our gear were piled into a jeep and a truck. Everyone was quiet, and like me, lost in thought, half listening to the music on the radio. It was hard to say goodbye to our incredible hosts and the luxuries of society, knowing we had more than fourteen hundred miles to go, and like me, they were probably wondering how many of us would make it to Springer Mountain, Georgia. Fox Trot stayed with his family for a couple more days and agreed to meet us on the New York section of the trail.

With the late start, we only hiked nine miles in the heat and humidity and ended up camping under a full moon sky on the confluence of Ten Mile and Housatonic Rivers. Kee waited patiently for me to pitch our tent, and when I asked, "Do you want to go for a swim, girl?" She pranced around in a circle like an excited puppy before we raced through the woods to swim in the Housatonic.

I swear, if I didn't know better, I would think she was bred to be a water dog. I think she enjoyed those refreshing swims more than anyone, and the most reliable way to get her out of the water was to say, "Let's eat!" She would rocket out of the water and be waiting back at camp before I even waded ashore. She would gobble her dinner before I could finish preparing my meal and then watch me eat, using that Jedi mind trick to convince me that I was full and then give her the leftovers.

We fell asleep to the chorus of rushing water, serenading tree frogs, and crickets.

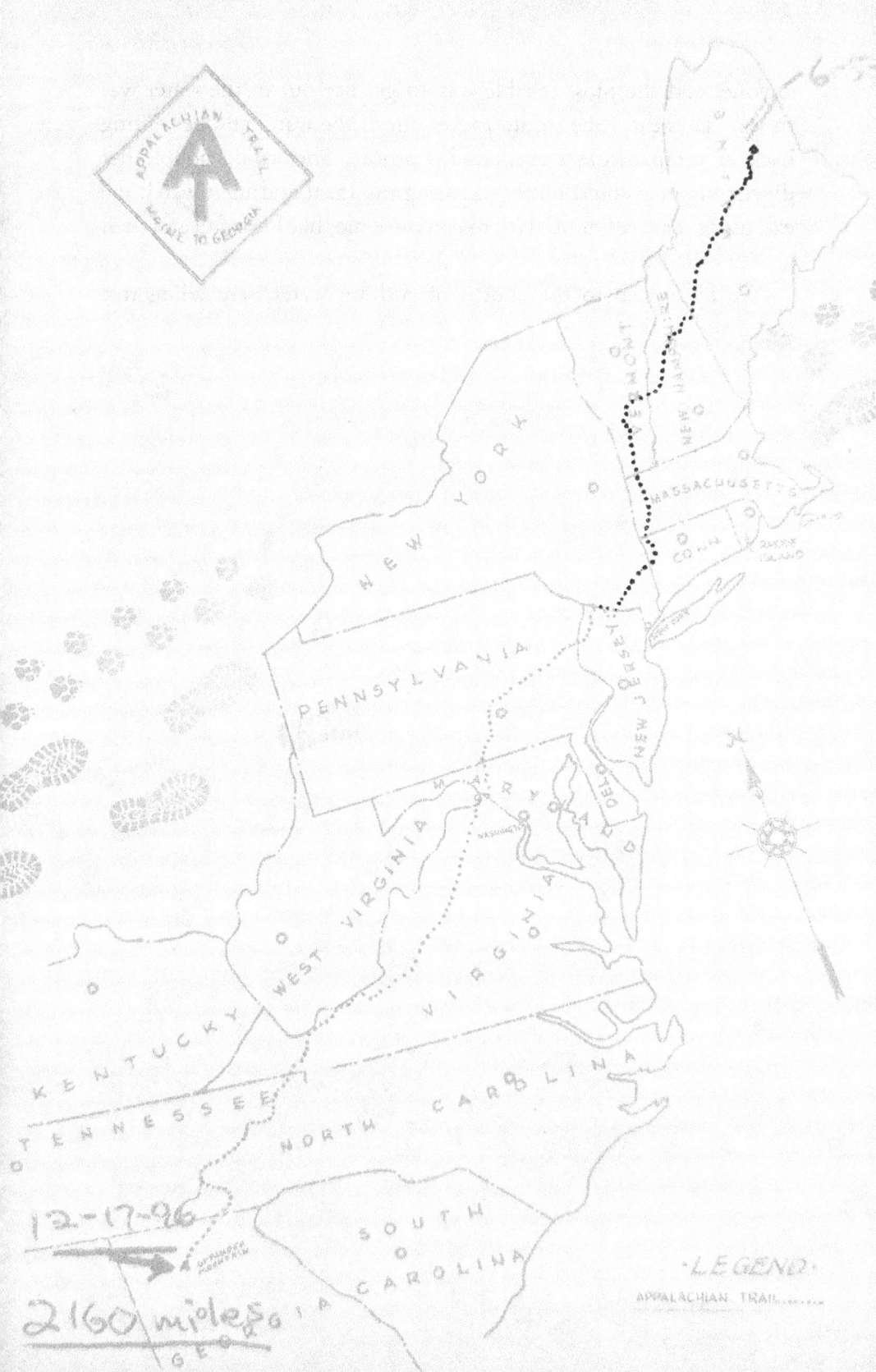

Chapter 15

New York

08/26/96

We awoke to the honking of several flocks of Canada geese. Who needs an alarm clock when we had birds calling to each other as they fly up and down the confluence of the Housatonic and Ten Mile Rivers at 4:30 in the morning? In fact, I was contemplating sending my watch back. The more I was in tune with the rhythms of nature, the more it seemed foolish to have that timepiece strapped to my arm, but I hung on to it not out of necessity but as a reminder of a life full of time constraints and commitments that I had left behind. One day I would let go of the unnecessary stuff in my life.

We made it to the Appalachian Trail Station, a stop on the Metro-North Commuter Railroad that takes you into NYC. We were only ten miles into a planned twenty-mile day, and the lure of the big city was tempting. I could only imagine what adventures would have waited if we hadn't had to wait four and a half hours for the next train. I had visited New York with a friend several years earlier and was amazed the city never seemed to sleep. It buzzed with activity 24/7.

My most memorable encounter happened as I was walking on the sidewalk with a crushing number of people when a tall stranger in high heels caught me staring. He wore patent leather pants, a floral print shirt, and a feathery boa. He caught me off guard when he dipped his head and, looking over his sunglasses, asked, "Honey, what are you looking at?"

With his high heels, he had to be over seven feet tall. "I'm not sure," I said, "But you should be playing basketball!"

He responded with a wry smile, snapping his finger in the air, "Don't knock it until you try it, and if you do, give me a call!"

I had no idea what he was talking about. Confused, I walked away, shaking my head. I later found out he was the ever-flamboyant RuPaul, a drag performer.

A few miles later, we were rewarded by seeing the largest tree on the AT. The Dover Oak is over three hundred years old and more than twenty feet in circumference. I marveled that this majestic tree had not fallen prey to the bite of an axe. I wondered how it had been spared and what it had been witness too—if only it could speak.

After a long, hot day, we camped at the Morgan Stewart Shelter and were rewarded with cold water, hand-pumped from a hundred-year-old well.

08/27/96

Another hot and humid day. I couldn't get enough to drink, even though I drank gallons of water daily just to keep up with my sweat loss. Thunder Snow and I stopped at a little stream to filter water. He was twenty feet upstream from me when I heard, "Oh crap!"

I looked up just in time to see him jump and slip on a moss-covered rock. His feet shot out from under him, he levitated horizontally for a split second before splashing in the deep pool where he was trying to get water. I gave him an 8.0 for style because he had too much splash on entry for anything better. Some guys will go to great lengths to cool off.

It was still early when we reached the RPH Shelter, so we filled water bottles and pressed on. Leapfrog twisted her ankle and went down in a heap. She said she felt something pop and was in a fair amount of pain, but there was no immediate swelling. We decided to lighten her load and divvied up her pack. We had two options: we could go back roughly a mile to the RPH Shelter and let her recover there, or we could walk about a mile and a half to Long Hill Road, and if her ankle got worse, then we would be able to get her to the nearest medical facility. It was unanimous that we would press on, and if needed, we were prepared to carry her.

Before we reached Long Hill Road, we came across Shenandoah Shelter, which wasn't supposed to be open until the 1997 hiking season, but Joe, the caretaker, unlocked the pump so we could refill our Nalgenes. He noticed Leap Frog limping and conceded to let us camp on the grass around the shelter.

While sitting around the picnic table making dinner, Leapfrog called Fox's attention to a tick crawling on his shirt. We immediately self-checked, and then everyone checked the person sitting next to them. Leapfrog took it upon herself to check everyone's head and found two in my hair. Some guys had three or four crawling in their hair. We can only attribute it to the tall grass we had been hiking through, where the ticks were waiting to hitch a ride.

Soft, well-manicured grass is the next best thing to Grandma's feather bed, and we slept with another level of comfort, content that we were tick-free. Thanks, Joe.

08/28/96

By morning, Leapfrog's ankle had slight bruising and minimal swelling. She was able to walk with some discomfort. As a precaution, we distributed the weight of her pack to everyone else and put in eighteen miles before getting off the trail at Old West Point Road and then checked in at the Graymoor Friary, which is the home of Franciscan Friars.

Father George welcomed and showed us around. In the old Friar housing facility, a typical room was barely big enough to contain a chair, a twin bed, a sink, and a small closet with two upper shelves. This simplistic lifestyle allowed them to focus on prayer and walking as brothers alongside those who are lost and in need of God's healing.

Father George went the extra mile to take care of all of us. He ensured those with dogs had a place to camp by the water tower. He let us take showers and do laundry as well.

One of my boots had a delaminating sole, and I used some Shoe Goo Adhesive to make a temporary fix and applied duct tape to keep the sole fastened to the uppers while the glue cured overnight. The repair seemed secure, but I knew I would have to find a boot cobbler soon.

Father George exuded sincere kindness as he listened to our stories of life on the AT while he ate dinner with us. He made sure all twelve of us, northbounders and southbounders, had our fill. He was even there to serve us breakfast before his morning church service. He went out of his way for all of us hikers, wayward men, and anyone who needed to go there for a retreat. Father George was not judgmental but instead radiated an incredibly soothing peace while his eyes pierced our souls.

08/29/96

We crossed the Hudson River on the Bear Mountain Suspension Bridge, which spanned two thousand two hundred and fifty-five feet across the powerful river. We were thankful that we didn't have to ford this one. Most of our group had to stop at Bear Mountain, New York, to resupply. After purchasing food for Kee and me, I spoke with a Bear Mountain Park Ranger to see if he knew about any campsites in the nearby vicinity. He mentioned a great site, and after setting up camp, Thunder Snow, Fox, Leapfrog, Fox Trot, and I hitched the four miles into West Point to see the campus.

The first guy to stop and give us a ride pulled over in a mini work van and stopped on a blind corner in the right lane. He waved for us to get in, and when he realized there were five of us, he turned the van off, took the keys, and unlocked the rear doors, oblivious to oncoming traffic. We all jumped in, and I prayed we weren't going to get hit from behind. The driver couldn't get the vehicle to start, and I began to tense, expecting an impact any minute.

"Oh, of course, the van needs to be in park to start." The driver laughed as the engine roared to life, and we headed down the road. He then proceeded to turn around to talk with us. How he managed to stay between the lines, never mind staying on the road while looking back, was beyond me. He was either an ex-New York cabbie or had eyes in the back of his head. Regardless, it was the longest four-mile ride of my life. Come to find out, he was heading in to work on the phones at West Point's visitor center and may have known these roads like the back of his hand.

The well-manicured lawns on West Point's campus were surrounded by massive Gothic-style buildings that looked like formidable medieval fortresses. There were huge bronze statues of Dwight D. Eisenhower and Douglas MacArthur. The most impressive was a green patinaed copper equestrian statue of George Washington. I had to include a walk onto Michie Stadium field to get a feel of what it would have been like to play there as a visiting player had I accepted Senator John McCain's appointment to the Naval Academy back in high school.

Thunder Snow, a professor of Education at Kennesaw State University, was naturally enamored with the history and striking architecture as well.

08/30/96

As we climbed Bear Mountain, we were able to look down on the mighty Hudson and watch as barges moved up and down the river, looking like toy boats in the expanse of water flowing toward the sea.

During the climb up Bear Mountain, I kept smelling a strong odor of a woman's perfume wafting down on the morning thermals. It was a sharp contrast to what I had grown used to, and I had to ensure I wasn't fantasizing by asking everyone else, "Does anyone else smell perfume?"

Rev was the first to answer, "Oh yeah!"

Everyone else confirmed that I wasn't hallucinating, but the aromatic person was nowhere near. The higher we climbed, the stronger the scent became, luring us on like the singing of sirens in Greek mythology. It was more than an hour of climbing before we overtook a woman hiking with her teenage kids. We chatted briefly out of courtesy but had to quickly move on as the perfume became overbearing and left us nauseated.

This was the first time that I noticed we had reverted to wild ways with sharpened senses that must have been inherent in our predecessors. All of our senses became more acute the longer we were on the trail. There were weeks at a time when my vision was so crisp that I could go without the use of contacts or glasses, which is saying something since my uncorrected vision was 20/225.

From the stone observation tower on top of Bear Mountain to West Mountain Shelter, we were occasionally blessed with a view of the New York City skyline, thirty-four miles away on the eastern horizon. By 8:00 AM, we summited Black Mountain and startled a couple sleeping on a rock face where they had a romantic view of the New York City skyline.

So, they wouldn't think eight thugs were mugging them, I called out, "Good morning! It's going to be a beautiful day!" We all filed around them as they pulled the double sleeping bag tight around their shoulders while keeping a confused and bleary eye on us.

On the downhill side of Black Mountain, Shoofly Pie stepped on some loose gravel on top of a rock, and his foot shot out in front of him. He fell back on his other leg, twisting his leg. I don't know how he didn't blow out his knee, but he got back up, grimaced a little bit, and continued on.

We had just passed the William Brien Memorial Shelter and were climbing Goshen Mountain when yellow jackets swarmed Thunder Snow and me. We never saw their nest as they came boiling out of the grass next to the trail. We bolted as fast as we could with weighted packs. Thunder Snow was the first to cry out a slew of obscenities as they stung the hell out of his right cheekbone. We managed to outrun them, but not before they peppered my right leg. A little farther down the trail, we were still moving on adrenaline when Thunder Snow let out a scream and went down in a heap. I thought a snake had bitten him, but actually the grass had obscured an oak log with a snag waiting to catch an unwary hiker. He was bleeding steadily, and there was a chunk of his hairy hide hanging from the snag.

He looked at me. "What do I do?"

"Your blood is purified; let it bleed until the wound is sanitized.

Scabs are nature's Band-Aids. Then walk it off."

He looked at me like he thought I couldn't be serious but then seemed to realize he had no choice.

We let it bleed until it began to coagulate, then put a makeshift bandage on it, securing it with duct tape to keep it from being torn off.

We made it to the Fingerboard Shelter without any other mishaps. I was setting up my tent when Thunder Snow decided to hike the .5 mile down to Lake Tiorati to purify some drinking water when he realized he had lost his iodine bottle when he fell. I lent him my Sweet Water Purifier and finished setting up camp. While I was feeding Kee, Fox hobbled in with a gash under his left knee, and I had to ask, "Did you get bit by an oak snag about a mile back?"

He looked at me with amazement and asked, "How did you know?"

"Your dad is sporting the same wound in the same location."

"Where is he now?"

"He's down at the lake getting water. I've got to get more water too; I'll check on him."

With that, Kee and I raced down to the lake. Without a full pack, the half mile run seemed like a walk in the park. On the way down, we came around a bend in the trail, and the woods erupted with snorts and breaking branches as a herd of whitetail deer scattered into the brush with their tails raised in alarm.

As soon as Kee caught sight of the lake, she was gone, pulling away from me as if I were running in the other direction. She launched, clearing twenty feet of water before splashing down. A couple of beavers slapped their tails in disapproval as Kee swam in their direction to see if they wanted to play, only to be met with a couple more warning slaps as they dove into the depths of the lake, reappearing a safe distance away. Fish were swirling everywhere, and I so wished I hadn't sent my fishing pole home.

While swimming with Kee, I couldn't help but notice literally hundreds of dragonflies swarming the shoreline. Some were linked in a heart-shaped mating clinch, flying with amazing acrobatic ability. Others skimmed the water's surface, dipped their tails, and deposited eggs. Once hatched, the larva will spend up to two years growing and will go through ten to twelve molts before they are ready to climb out of the water. Once they are the right size, the warming air and increased sunlight of the spring and summer months trigger the larva to climb toward the light and exit from their exoskeleton for the last time, drying their wings and taking to the air with an incredible ability to fly in every direction. This ability to hover, go backward and forward, and change direction makes them an apex aerial insect predator, consuming anything their size and smaller.

Having suffered greatly from the probing proboscis of the pesky mosquito, part of me found satisfaction in knowing that these marvels of nature could consume thirty to a hundred mosquitoes a day. I could only imagine what the prehistoric two-foot fossils were capable of, and I wondered if the creators of the *Predator* movie found inspiration in the dragonfly's life cycle. Before they become masters of the air, they are assassins of the water. They have a hinged lower jaw that can be extended with astonishing speed to snare prey and bring their victims back to their mouth, where they are consumed alive. They can dart through the water to attack with pinpoint accuracy using a form of jet propulsion where they draw water into their rectum, over their gills, and then forcibly expel the water. This enhanced mobility helps them from becoming a meal themselves. The abundance of dragonflies usually indicates good water quality as they are not very tolerant of pollution, which is good to know when filtering water for personal use.

As I waded ashore, it occurred to me that hiking had simplified my life and unencumbered me from the mind-numbing sensory overloads that dominated my real existence. It allowed me to be more present and, therefore, more aware of my surroundings, as if I were seeing for the first time with the eyes of a child the natural wonder that was surrounding me.

08/31/96

A distinct brisk breeze blew through the camp this morning. The next day would be the first day of September, and I wondered if this cool air should trigger a sense of urgency to finish the trail before the weather might hinder backcountry travel. The thought was fleeting as I took in the beauty of Lake Tiorati, glistening in the morning light. I vowed to stay present in the moment and not worry about what tomorrow could bring.

While Kee was making her morning rounds checking on everyone, I read the hiker register. I found an interesting entry from a northbounder bragging about Pappy's Deli and the delectable delights that awaited any hiker willing to walk the .4 miles off the trail. Even Wingfoot's *Thru-Hiker Handbook* validated this claim by quoting "Full Sail and Grommett"–1993, saying Pappy's Deli had "the best grinders on the Trail." As hungry as we always were, the promise was more than we could resist, and our thoughts didn't wander far from the pleasure of filling our bellies with exceptional food during our eleven-mile march toward epicurean delight.

Our mad march to Pappy's was slowed temporarily as we negotiated the Lemon Squeezer in Harriman State Park. Again, my hat was off to the route finders of the Trail. It went between two gigantic boulders that looked like it could've been one massive boulder at one time before splitting in half, giving new meaning to "being between a rock and a hard place." A bit of nostalgia swept over me, knowing that the founders of the AT had squeezed their way through this section with childlike enthusiasm. It was rumored that this natural obstacle had also enticed the adventurous side of Marylin Monroe. While this wasn't on the same scale as the Mahoosuc Notch, it was still a hidden gem that Kee negotiated better than all of us.

Tantalizing our taste buds with Pappy's grinders was a bust, as he was on vacation. Determined not to accept defeat in our search for gastro nirvana, we all decided to walk into town to see if we could find the next best meal. We were stopped by a gentleman working in his garden, who informed us that everything else was closed due to the Labor Day weekend. We couldn't help but notice his vine-ripe tomatoes and asked if we could pay him for some. He refused to take any money as he handed us the most succulent and tasty tomatoes we had bitten into in a long time. He got a great deal of satisfaction watching nine hungry hikers devour his tomatoes until there was only juice dripping off our chins. While we couldn't validate everyone's claim regarding Pappy's grinders, we found something of far greater value—a stranger's generosity.

We made it fifteen miles to the Wildcat Shelter before calling it a day.

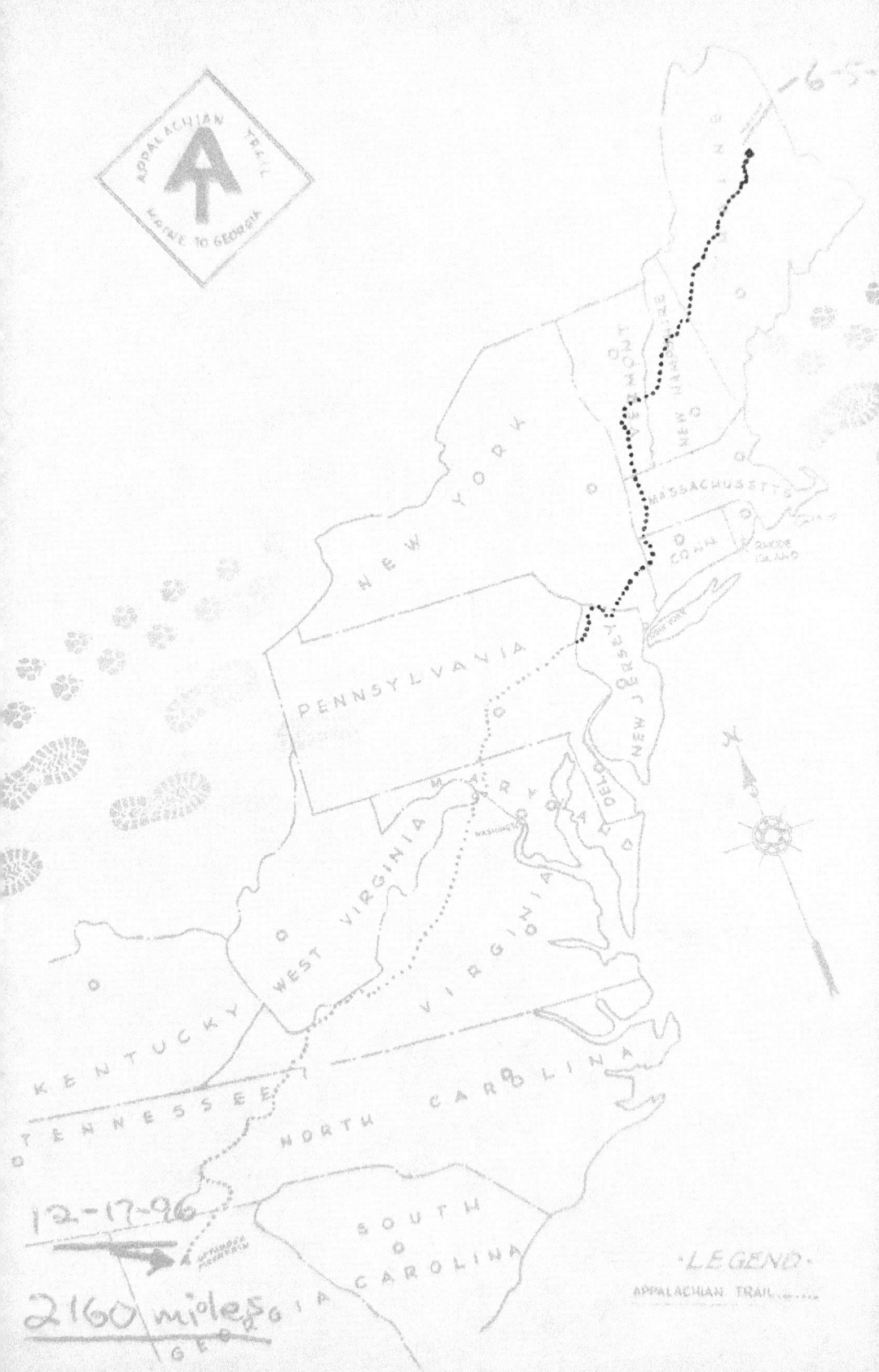

Chapter 16

New Jersey

09/01/96

We hiked the 17.5 miles into Vernon, New Jersey, and officially entered the seventh state on the AT. We found a pay phone, and I got a great picture of everyone waiting in line to call home from a lone public phone. Thunder Snow was the first to call home and let his wife know that he had sixty more miles to go before he reached Delaware Water Gap and would be heading her way.

Waiting to make a call home

I found a cobbler who was kind enough to take my boots on a Sunday and willing to work on them the next day.

We stayed at the Vernon Fireman's Lean-to, which was the fire department's five-bay truck shop.

09/02/96

Everyone pressed on to make it to Delaware Water Gap so they could say goodbye to Thunder Snow when he got off the trail to head back to work as a professor of Education at Kennesaw State University in Georgia. I had to hang back and wait for my boots to be salvaged by the local cobbler/boot guru, but I promised to do my best to catch up. It was Labor Day, and everything in town was closed. I hoped my boots would be waiting for me when the boot repair shop opened Tuesday morning. If they weren't, it would make it almost impossible to catch Thunder Snow and the gang before he left the trail.

Right after the heart-stopping noon alarm went off in the firehouse, a couple of southbounders showed up to fill water bottles and eat lunch. They were a young couple that went by the trail names Rev and Trillium. We made small talk about the adventures we had so far, and then they were gone. For the first time in a long time, I would spend the night alone with Kee at a shelter, and I reminisced about something I had once read. It went something like this:

> *"Sit with animals QUIETLY, and they will show you their HEARTS. Sit with them KINDLY, and they will help you locate YOURS."*
>
> – Ramblings of the Claury

Kee had been sleeping most of the day, and her nose seemed a little warm. I wondered if she was reacting to the bug bite on her back, which had swollen to the size of a golf ball. The cool concrete floor must have felt good. So, we rested, and I promised her we would stop by the veterinarian the next day to ensure she was okay to continue.

09/03/96

The veterinarian checked Kee first thing in the morning and agreed that a spider had caused her wound. He was very reassuring when he said the resulting Seroma would usually resolve on its own and that there was nothing to worry about. He complimented Kee for being in great shape and advised us to continue our hike. Encouraged by the good news, we headed to the Boot Repair Shop. Not only were my soles reattached, but additional padding had been sewn into the heel pocket. They felt like slippers, and once again, I couldn't believe my good fortune in finding a guy that would go the extra mile.

We didn't leave Vernon until 2:30 PM, and the hike was easy until we went through some swampy areas that were abundant with ducks and geese. We came across a massive flock of wild turkeys getting a drink while a whitetail deer was lying in the shadows, in the water to cool off. While the water was a welcome respite from the heat, it also was the breeding ground for mosquitoes, and it wasn't long before I had a merciless cloud of bloodsuckers attacking. We couldn't outrun them. They were relentless, and I was having flashbacks of Maine, so I threw my pack off, dug my Back Woods repellent out of my pack, and sprayed us both down. That held them at bay, and we were able to continue at a more leisurely pace.

We did eleven miles before camping between Oil City Road and N.J. 284.

09/04/96

If I wanted to catch everyone and say goodbye to Thunder Snow, I would have to pull some big days. I had promised Thunder Snow that I would be there for his farewell sendoff. With that goal in mind, I set out to do a twenty-two-mile day.

Thankfully, the Vernie Swamp had bog bridges to walk on, so there was no need to wade. This swamp was loaded with waterfowl, and the chorus of frogs was almost deafening. We walked around a bend in the trail, and the water exploded as a monster whitetail buck launched from his resting spot to a dead run in a split second, disappearing into the thickets. We dared not linger long for fear of the mosquito onslaught.

The only people I ran into that day were a couple of guys from London who were graphic artists and were documenting their trip around the world. They wanted to interview people along the way and highlight all the amazing architecture and natural beauty they encountered. They were filming the High Point Monument, the highest point in Jersey. They planned to hike to Virginia along the Appalachian Trail to give their audience perspective on the rugged beauty hidden along the way. We talked about some of the incredible sights I had seen and the wonderful people I had met on my journey, and it fueled their enthusiasm. At the end of their world tour, they hoped to market it to the folks back in England, emphasizing that we have more in common than what separates us.

I wished them safe travels and good luck on their project. With hope rising, I walked away, wondering if our meeting was more than coincidental.

By the time I closed in on the Gren Anderson Shelter, the liner in my shorts was causing severe chafing on my inner thighs. The kind that made you forget about the pain in your feet and fully understand the sensibility of northbounder in a dress.

I walked up to the Gren Anderson Shelter only to find it packed with young adults from Princeton. They were an outdoor action group that escaped to the woods so the first-year students could mingle with the upperclassmen. They swarmed me with questions about life on the trail, gear choices, hardships endured, and a litany of other questions. They fell in love with Kee, as she was no stranger to working a crowd. Their curiosity was only rivaled by their enthusiasm. Overall, they were a great bunch of guys. One was from El Paso, Texas, and wanted to study law and get into government to help change the world. I admired his youthful vigor and found myself inspired by his desire to be the positive change for the future. He wanted to return to the streets of the Texas ghettos to encourage kids to dream big and realize that an education at an Ivy League school was not out of reach if they wanted a ticket out of poverty.

A recon group packed in all the supplies for their evening meal, and they were gracious enough to give me a bell pepper, which I added to my spaghetti dinner. They also gave me a pint of Ben and Jerry's before I retreated to my tent to clean my chafing wounds. I fell asleep to the sound of them singing the Princeton fight song and many other tunes that were muffled by my earplugs. As I drifted off, a lightness overcame me like a weight had been lifted from my shoulders, knowing that these guys would be future leaders.

09/05/96

I cut out the liner on my shorts and then put a pre-wrap on my thighs, securing it with duct tape.

The hiking was relatively easy at this point. There were a lot of small ups and downs with nothing more than one to five hundred feet of elevation gain or descent. Sweating profusely was unavoidable as the humidity and heat combined to suck the life force out of me. Thankfully, there were plenty of springs and swimming holes along the way.

Do you remember the movie *Stripes*, starring Bill Murray and John Candy? Well, they had a snappy *Do Wah Diddy Diddy* marching song, and I took the liberty to change the verses and incorporate the *Hawaiian Shaka* into the chorus to help pass the time. The Shaka sign means to hang loose, don't worry, or rush. In basketball slang, it was used when someone made an awesome slam dunk. The verses followed a military cadence or "Jody," which is a traditional call-and-response song, and it went something like this:

Call: "Oh, I don't know, but I've been told…"
Response: "The AT is very old."
Chorus: Boom Shaka Laka Boom Shaka Laka Boom

Call: "I've been hiking from Katahdin, Maine…"
Response: "People think I'm incredibly insane."
Chorus: Boom Shaka Laka Boom Shaka Laka Boom

Call: "Black flies and mosquitoes in June…"
Response: "Will make you crazy like a loon."
Chorus: Boom Shaka Laka Boom Shaka Laka Boom

Call: "I've got chafing of the inner thigh…"
Response: "It's so bad I think I'll die."
Chorus: Boom Shaka Laka Boom Shaka Laka Boom

Call: "I've been hiking all day long…"
Response: "Boy, my armpits sure smell strong."
Chorus: Boom Shaka Laka Boom Shaka Laka Boom

Call: "Leapfrog is turning mighty green…"
Response: "Somebody must have peed in her Nalgene."
Chorus: Boom Shaka Laka Boom Shaka Laka Boom

Call: "Ducttape's pack is heavy as hell…"
Response: "How much it weighs, he'll never tell."
Chorus: Boom Shaka Laka Boom Shaka Laka Boom

Call: "Black flies bite, and mosquitoes suck…"
Response: "It only gets worse when you fall in the muck."
Chorus: Boom Shaka Laka Boom Shaka Laka Boom

Call: "All day long, I step on rocks…"
Response: "I pity the fool who smells my socks."
Chorus: Boom Shaka Laka Boom Shaka Laka Boom

The last line was a tribute to the rocky, ankle-turning section I was on, which I had heard was just a warmup for the notorious rocks of PA.

Shortly after filling my Nalgene bottles at Rattlesnake Springs and before I reached Catfish Fire Tower, I had my first bear sighting. He was standing on his hind legs twenty yards off the trail and ripped at a hole in a tree until it was large enough for him to stick his paws in. He scooped out clumps of honeycomb as bees bombarded his head. I could hear him smacking his lips as he swatted at bees stinging his nose. He continued to rip at the tree to get at the hive, unconcerned about our presence or too involved in his effort to notice us. Part of him seemed to want to run from the onslaught, but every paw dripping with honey kept him there. My first thought was that I had to capture this moment on film, but then I noticed the two red ear tags he had. Usually, that meant that they were prone to aggression, and he had probably been relocated. I didn't want to give him an excuse for a third strike, so I quietly moved on, searing the scene in my mind.

Darkness was fast approaching, and I needed to find a level campsite soon. As luck would have it, the trail opened to a small clearing that held a pond with fish jumping everywhere. A campsite on the north end of the pond had a fire ring. I threw my pack down and raced Kee to the water. As we waded in, Kee began to whimper, and my chafed thighs began to burn. I knew something was wrong.

"Kee, get out of the pond!" If I could've walked on water, I would have. At the shoreline, I watched as the fish continued rising, confusing me further about how anything could survive in that water.

Sunset at Sunfish Pond

Exhausted after hiking 25.5 miles, I fed Kee, set up my tent, ate some trail snacks, and passed out to the sound of frogs chirping.

09/06/96

I woke up at 4 AM. The frogs were still singing while I broke camp. I walked to the south end of Sunfish Pond and took a moment to sit on a rock with my pack and lean back against a tree. Attentive with all my senses, I watched a sliver of a moon play hide and seek behind a few scattered clouds. There were a few stars still clinging to the heavens as the horizon brightened, slowly turning to a faint shade of pink. The moonlight was twinkling on the ripples of the water. A cool breeze blew in my face as I listened to the waves gently break on the rocks below and the wind rustle through the trees. A light fog began to rise from the water but then was quickly swept away by the prevailing winds. With her Malamute bloodline, Kee relished this cooling trade wind that blew in from the east and was eager to get going. I lingered for a moment; a peacefulness washed over me and in awe, I tried to take it all in.

We had a buck snort at us as we crossed the outlet of Sunfish Pond. I caught a flash of his antlers with my headlamp before he disappeared into the darkness of the forest. On the northbound approach to the pond, I found some trail signage indicating that Sunfish Pond was the southernmost glacial pond and was highly acidic. Only a few hardy fish could survive, one of which was the Pumpkin Seed Sunfish, and the other was the Yellow Perch. The pond was the result of receding Wisconsin glacier that left a sixty-foot-deep lake on top of Kittatinny Ridge.

The author Bill Bryson attempted a NoBo thru-hike in 1996. He walked eight hundred and seventy miles; we must have just missed each other. He then wrote a humorous book, *A Walk in the Woods*, about his adventure. In it, he wrote, "Sunfish Pond is something of a glorious novelty since nowhere south of here will you find a body of water on a mountaintop." Sunfish Pond is one of the seven wonders of New Jersey.

Signage on the north end of the lake would have been helpful for those who were hiking south.

On my way down to the Gap, we were engulfed by morning fog

coming off the Delaware River. It was so thick at times I could barely see ten feet in front of me. A deer sounded off a warning snort from somewhere on the other side of the veil. My imagination went into overdrive, and the Credence Clearwater Revival song, "Bad Moon Rising," from the movie *American Werewolf in London,* began to play in my head. I heard another snort to my left a little farther down the trail. Then suddenly, a horrendous noise came out of a bush beside me. A grouse ambushed me, nearly hitting my right leg before disappearing into the fog. It was either protecting its brood or making an escape maneuver from a predator. I favored the predator scenario as it meshed perfectly with the song playing in my head. I wondered where the werewolf was.

After a short six-mile hike into Delaware Water Gap, I found the gang at the Presbyterian Church of the Mountain Hostel. Pastor Karen had an amazing, gentle soul and was very welcoming. She insisted that Kee and I settle into the Hostel. She was so warm and caring that I felt as if I was home and could take some time to rest and let my feet and thighs heal. She had such a strong, nurturing pastoral way about her that I felt compelled to ask her how she became a pastor. She said it was a very strong calling from God, and doors were opened when she got out of the way and followed the promptings. Her congregation was incredible, offering to run us to the store, post office, and the Pack Shack Outfitter for those who needed gear or fuel.

Some of her more musically talented members were upstairs rehearsing for the Jazz Fest, a weeklong celebration. We were fortunate enough to catch the last weekend.

After getting a shower, I decided to check on my mail drop while Kee was sleeping next to Fox and Cookie Moose, a northbounder from Maine. I picked up my box addressed to General Delivery, Attention AT Thru-hiker Dr. Ducttape. Then I hustled over to the pay phone across Main Street and called my parents to check on my grandpa's status and let them know where to send the next package. My next call was to the airline to set a tentative date for my flight home. I looked up just in time to see Kee running frantically, looking for me and Cookie Moose running after her.

My heart sank; I hung up on the agent and ran in Kee's direction but was helpless to intercept her as I was on the opposing side of the road. I tried to yell commands for her to stop but over the traffic noise was useless. I darted across the road, dodging traffic, whistling to get her attention. When she heard my whistle, she would stop and look around. I kept running in her direction, and once she zoned in on where my whistles and yells were coming from, she trotted over to me, wagging her tail and dancing in circles as she neared. It looked like she had a smile on her face when I grabbed her and gave her a hug.

We had been together 24/7, and I had no idea how deeply connected she was to me. So, when we went out that night to celebrate Thunder Snow's return to society, I made sure that Kee was tied to my pack outside and could see me through the window at Brownie's Pub. I ordered an extra sandwich for her and checked on her periodically while everyone played pool and listened to music. The band's lead guitarist resembled David Landers, "Squiggman," from the "Lavern and Shirley" show. He was undoubtedly a talented showman with a wide range of music, which he graced us with. As the evening wore on, jazz rolled seamlessly into rock and roll, and he proved to be a master of both genres. Before the evening was over, I got a great picture of Fox and Thunder Snow, the Father and Son team strategizing about their next shot at the pool table.

Toasting Thundersnow

Fox and his dad strategizing

We returned that night and had some cake from the local bakery that Leapfrog had inscribed with "We'll Miss You Thunder Snow!" Then Fox pulled a wrapped package from his mail drop and gave it to his dad. On it was written in bold letters, *"The Hello Martha Kit."* His wife had sent him a grooming kit.

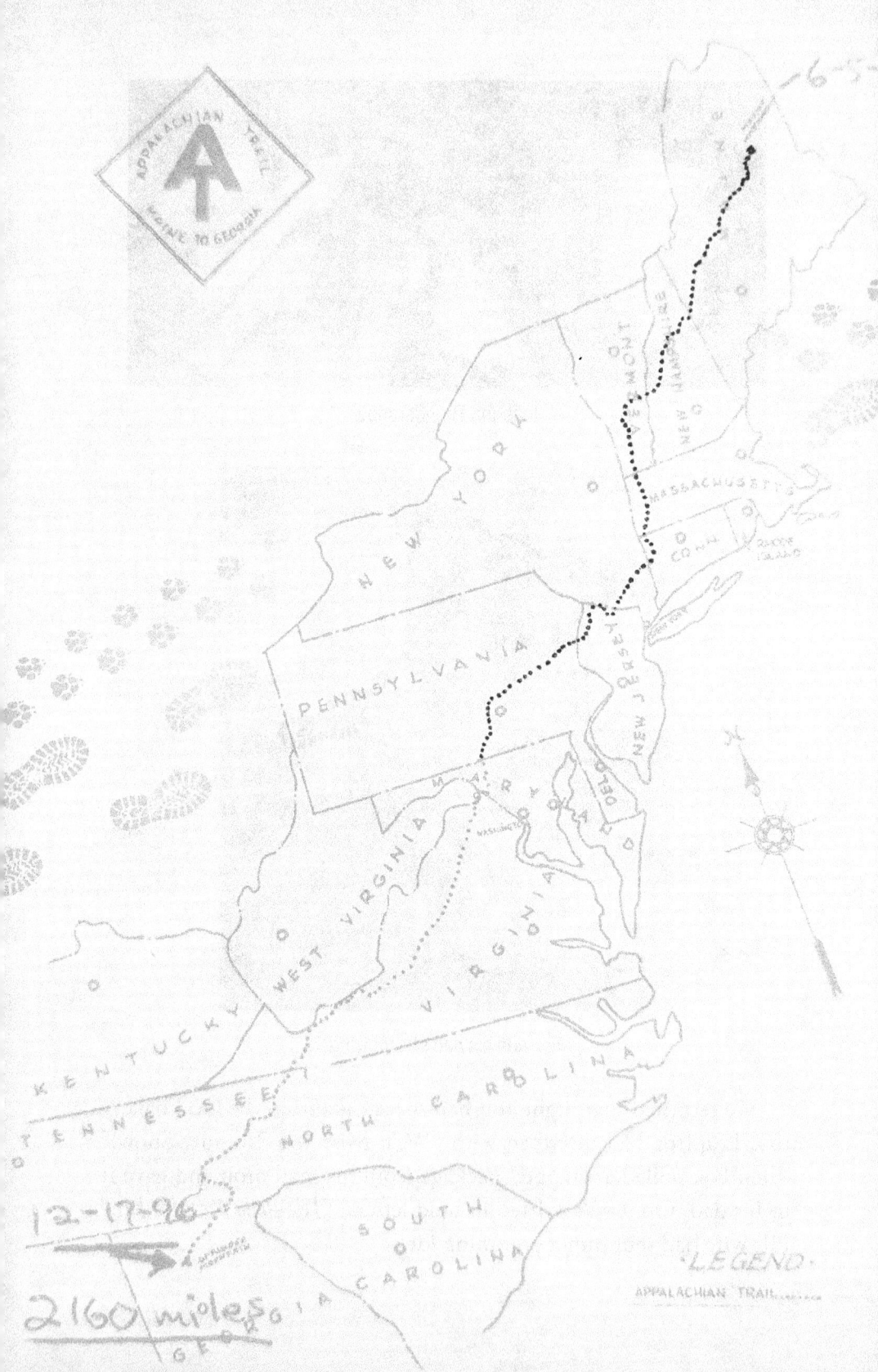

Chapter 17

Pennsylvania

09/07/96

After lunch the next day, sadness hung in the air as the time for goodbye was closing in. Band members were beginning to rehearse upstairs, and to put off the inevitable or get his composure, Thunder Snow walked upstairs to listen to the music. You could hear the song "Moon River" being played and after the lyrics, "Two drifters, off to see the world. There's such a lot of world to see…"

Thunder Snow came back down the stairs with tears trickling down his cheeks and gave his son a final hug goodbye. Wiping his eyes, he hugged everyone else and was gone. It was an honor to witness the love between father and son. Perhaps these moments were the riches that Rene the Kennebec River Master in Maine, had spoken about.

09/08/96

I got a late start and hiked into the night so I could make it twenty miles to the Leroy A. Smith Shelter. A lot of the springs and water sources were dry along the way. I didn't know when we would find water, so I gave Kee my last quart, and we hiked almost five hours before finding the springs at the shelter running cold and clear. I filtered water as fast as I could. It tasted sooo good. I slammed two quarts and started to get the chills as my core temperature dropped. I had to pull Kee off the spring's edge so she wouldn't get sick. I changed into all my dry clothes, including my fleece jacket. I filtered more water before the shivering subsided and drank another gallon and a half to rehydrate. It was not uncommon to drink three to five gallons of water per day, depending on the level of exertion and the heat index. I slowly drank a quart with dinner and another one before going to sleep, thankful we didn't have to hike another three miles to reach the next potential water source. That was worse than two-a-day football practice in the heat of a Phoenix summer, where the coaches would push you until you almost puked before they called for a water break.

09/09/96

It was a cool start to our morning hike, and thankfully so. Kee walked past a timber rattlesnake, stretched out and sunning himself. I almost stepped on it before it coiled up and started to rattle. I stopped long enough to get a quick photo before Kee got too interested.

Pennsylvania rocks! No, seriously, the rocks in Pennsylvania are everywhere, and notorious ankle twisters at the very least. Extreme caution should be heeded in this section, or it could quickly end your hike.

The trail took us through a super fund cleanup site. The stark landscape, where almost everything appeared dead, was shocking. The area was filled with tree skeletons, some standing and some fallen, all caused by a nearby zinc-smelting plant. Decades of unregulated pollution had destroyed everything as far as the eye could see. There was a pond with an EPA sign, warning people not to drink the water and claiming it wasn't safe to filter.

I felt like I was walking through a desolate, post-apocalyptic landscape. Suddenly, I understood viscerally *The Crying Indian* ad that debuted in 1971, drawing attention to the industry's role in pollution. How can we call ourselves an advanced society when we traditionally fail as stewards of this beautiful nation and its resources? I grew up with a father who instilled in us the importance of always leaving an area in the outdoors better than we found it. He was pushing "Leave no Trace" before it was a coined phrase or a growing trend. He required it of us because it was the right thing to do.

Heading down into Lehigh Gap, I paused briefly on a rocky outcrop to shake the last few drops of water from my Nalgene. Thirst would not be slaked. I sat there, taking in the view of the Lehigh River valley, I felt the midday heat radiating off the rocks. It felt like I was in a furnace. As I was getting ready to leave, I heard a multitude of tiny clicking noises. Upon closer inspection, I found a horde of giant black spiders maneuvering from the shadows of the rocks, flanking me in every direction. Was it curiosity, or did they sense my energy lagging due to dehydration? Regardless, I did not stick around to test my hypothesis, but I quickly scanned the rocks for remnants of any ill-fated hikers. My concern would have been elevated had turkey vultures been circling overhead, anticipating an easy meal.

Thirst is a remarkable motivator. The AT Data Book listed a spring on the far side of Lehigh Gap, at least two miles away. With no other option but to keep moving, I scrambled down to the river valley and then up the other side and forced myself to breathe out of my nose so my tongue wouldn't dry out. By the time I reached the spring, I thought my eyes were playing tricks on me, and I was seeing a mirage. There was a large pipe protruding from a cliff gushing cold mountain water. I threw all caution aside and rationalized that clear water gushing from a cliff couldn't be contaminated. I shoved my face into the water, letting it flow over my head as I drank deeply. I could feel it's regenerative power bring me back to life. My senses were no longer dull. With the renewed clarity came the realization that I had broken my rule to always filter my water. Only time would tell if I had gambled correctly.

We walked up to the George W. Outerbridge Shelter and were greeted by the rest of our southbound tramily (trail family). That was the nice thing about hiking with a group: you could hike your own hike, see the things you wanted to see, and by the end of the day, if you hadn't hiked with certain people, you could always catch up on their day's experience around the evening meal.

09/10/96

I stopped for lunch at the Bake Oven Shelter and found the most accurate weather gauge ever. A sign was attached to a tree with a rock strapped to the top of it. The sign read:

WEATHER REPORT

If the Rock is…

Wet - It's Raining

Hot - It's Sunny

Cool - It's Overcast

White - It's Snowing

Moving - It's Windy

Gone - Tornado!

Lunch didn't sit well with me, and my stomach became increasingly upset throughout the rest of the day. Initially, I suspected that I had the stomach flu or possibly food poisoning since it was way too early for the onset of giardia symptoms after drinking the untreated water. The rigors of hiking became increasingly difficult as I lost my appetite, had an upset stomach, and frequent bouts of diarrhea.

It took longer than usual to cover the eighteen miles to Allentown Hiking Shelter. I had to convince myself to embrace the suck. The day was a bit of a blur, but I remember having to hike another half mile down a hill to get water. The climb back up to my tent seemed to take forever. Sleep didn't come easy, and when I did wake to find a more comfortable position, I would see Kee watching me, as if she knew something was wrong.

09/11/96

A couple of miles into the next day's hike, the brothers, Shoofly Pie and Tree Trunk, caught up with me. Shoofly looked at me and asked, "You okay?"

I explained that I was suffering from some stomach issues and was getting dehydrated from my frequent bouts of diarrhea. He promptly dropped his pack and started digging for something.

"I have something for that." He pulled out a bottle of Imodium.

It was just what the doctor ordered, and the symptoms seemed to subside. By mile fourteen, I was feeling well enough to take a moment and enjoy the view from The Pinnacle, which is a big rock platform overlooking the fertile farm country of Hamburg, Pennsylvania. The Delaware Indians once inhabited this beautiful valley before the settlers arrived. I wondered how many of our ancestral native population had sat on this very rock with the same attitude of gratitude for this expansive view of creation. A red tail hawk rode the thermals overhead, hovering above, enjoying the same views.

My daydreaming was disrupted when a naked hiker walked up and remarked how rugged Shoofly looked. Amused, I slung my pack and thought about commenting on how I didn't think it was that cold, but instead, I added to the awkwardness. "He sure is!" Then, I walked away with Tree Trunk, leaving Shoofly to work on his exit strategy out of an uncomfortable situation.

I had never known Shoofly to be at a loss for words, but the deer in a headlight look from him was worth it. We had a good laugh when he caught up moments later.

We made it eighteen miles to Windsor Furnace Shelter despite me having to disappear frequently into the woods, to answer the call of nature. I cannot tell you how often I charged with reckless abandon into the dense undergrowth, seeking privacy to relieve my misery, only to discover that I had brushed up against some poison ivy in my haste. It was becoming apparent that my intestinal ailment wouldn't resolve quickly on its own, so I made plans to get off the trail at Port Clinton and visit the nearest ER.

The brothers suggested that we all get off at Port Clinton and stay at their parents' house in Reading for a barbeque as well. The mention of grilled food was more than any of us could resist, and we all went to bed dreaming about the delectable delights that waited a short six trail miles and a hitchhike away.

09/12/96

The next day's short hike was the longest of the trail for me. My energy level was almost nonexistent, and the day became a test of sheer willpower. I had left Delaware Water Gap with five days of food, but with my loss of appetite, four days of rations remained in my pack. To make matters worse, I was getting a rash from the poison ivy on my arm. Shortly before getting off the trail, we ran into a guy on a day hike. He was a doctor who advised me to wrap the infected area of my arm so that it wouldn't spread. He then proceeded to write me a prescription. I remember thinking what a lucky coincidence it was for our paths to cross on the AT.

On our way into Port Clinton, we ran into the "Quilt Lady." She was making a huge quilt of the Appalachian Trail and wanted all 1996 hikers to sign it with their trail name, real name, and where they're from. I traced Kee's paw on it and signed it for her. The Quilt Lady and her husband were retired, and they loved to help with the needs of hikers. Although I wasn't feeling so hot, meeting the Quilt Lady and her husband lifted my spirits.

After a brief introduction to Shoofly and Tree Trunk's parents, Tom and Nancy, I got a quick shower, and then Tom shuttled me to the nearest emergency department in Reading, where they prescribed Cipro. Then Tom graciously took me to fill my poison ivy prescription, and we made it back in time for dinner. I wished I had more of an appetite. It seemed almost a sacrilege to eat food out of necessity and not to enjoy it like everyone else was.

I called home to check on Grandpa and let everyone know that I was on the road to recovery and that they need not worry. Everyone was excited that Grandpa was eating again and seemed to have more energy throughout the day. After planning to have my next supply box shipped to the Boiling Springs Post Office, ninety-six trail miles away, I thanked my parents and hung up.

My next call was to the Vasque Boot Headquarters in Minnesota. After a brief discussion about how my current boots were not holding up to the rigors of the trail, the customer service rep was super cool and agreed to send me a Glacier mountaineering boot to replace my Alpine boots. She wanted to allow for a week to get them shipped, and we decided that Harper's Ferry in West Virginia, one hundred and ninety-four trail miles away, would be a safe bet so that I wouldn't be waiting for them to arrive.

09/13/96

Shoofly and his dad shuttled everyone to the post office and store. My weakened state forced me to make some hard decisions about trimming my pack weight. I decided to mail my eight-pound Sierra Designs three-man tent to Thunder Snow in Georgia and would keep my ground tarp for emergencies. I knew that if I needed my tent back for the colder months ahead, he could get it to me quickly. From here on out, I would rely solely on the shelters.

With military precision, Shoofly and his dad helped us get our resupply boxes and do any additional shopping we needed for our next leg of the hike. We even went to REI, where Shoofly was able to replace his worn-out boots with a stiffer pair. We were like kids in a candy store, walking through REI, drooling and dreaming, but we were still able to get home in time for Shoofly's dad to prepare his mouth-watering barbeque. To feed eight ravenous hikers with metabolisms on overdrive was no small undertaking. Thankfully, my system responded to the Cipro regimen, and I was able to enjoy the incredible meal. Pound for pound, Fox could consume more than any of us. It was as if food was being converted to energy in such an efficient manner that he was able to continue to eat long after everyone else had stepped away from the table. To Tom and Nancy's credit, their barbeque buffet was not only a labor of love, but it was lip- smacking, delicious, and plentiful.

Tom and Nancy invited their daughter, Sally, and a couple of friends, Shane and Linda, over to join in the feast. After dinner, Sally and Shane tuned their guitars in front of the fireplace in the living room. Sally started off singing a beautiful rendition of "Amazing Grace." She had the voice of an angel, and by the time she sang the first three verses, there was not a dry eye amongst any of us hikers.

Our hosts L to R: Tom, Nancy, and their friends Shane and his wife Linda)

Shane and Sally playing "Amazing Grace"

AMAZING GRACE

How sweet the sound
That saved a wretch like me
I once was lost but now am found
Was blind but now I see

'Twas Grace that taught my heart to fear
And Grace my fears relieved
How precious did that Grace appear
The hour that I first believed

Through many dangers, toils and snares
I have already come
'Tis grace hath brought me safe thus far
And Grace will lead me home

The Lord had promised good to me
His word, my hope, secures
He will my shield and portion be
As long as life endures

Yes, when this flesh and heart shall fail
And mortal life shall cease
I shall possess within the veil
A life of joy and peace

The earth shall soon dissolve like snow
The sun forbear to shine
But God, who called me here below
Will be forever mine

When we've been there ten thousand years
Bright shining as the sun
We've no less days to sing God's praise
Than when we'd first begun.

I don't care how often I hear that song; I never tire of it. But this time, it was incredibly poignant. Sally told us she wanted to join a religious community to discern if she had what it takes to be a nun. I hoped she would find fulfillment in her search to become who God created her to be.

Then Shane, a retired English teacher, took over and lightened the mood with a humorous ditty about "What A Scotsman has Under His Kilt." The song went like this in Shane's best Scottish baritone brogue.

> Oh, a Scotsman in a kilt passed a bar one evening fair; you could tell by the way he walked he had more than his share, he stumbled, and he tumbled; he was drunk, it was plain to see and slipped and fell into the woods where he slept beneath a tree.
>
> **Chorus:** Rum tum tickle um tidy aye, Rum tum tickle I aye
> He slipped off into the woods; he slept beneath a tree.
>
> About that time, two young and tender girls just happened by; one said to the other with a twinkle in her eye, See yonder sleeping Scotsman so young and handsome built, I wonder if it's true what they don't wear beneath their kilt.
>
> **Chorus:** Rum tum tickle um tidy aye, Rum tum tickle I aye
> I wonder if it's true what they don't wear beneath their kilt.
>
> Now they snuck up on the sleeping Scot as quiet as can be and lifted up his kilt about an inch so that they could see, and there they saw a handsome sight beneath his Scottish skirt, 'twas nothing more than God had given him upon his birth.
>
> **Chorus:** Rum tum tickle um tidy aye, Rum tum tickle I aye
> 'twas nothing more than God had given him upon his birth.
>
> Now they stared in great amazement; one said we must be gone, Let's leave a token for our friend before we move along, and so they went and tied a bright blue ribbon, in a bow, around the handsome thing the Scotsman's lifted kilt had shown.

Chorus: Rum tum tickle um tidy aye, Rum tum tickle I aye Around that handsome thing, the Scotsman's lifted kilt had shown.

Now the Scotsman woke to nature's call, and to himself said he, I think I'll go off in the woods so that no one may see. He looked down in great amazement; then he dabbed his eyes. Lad, I don't know where you've been, but I see you've won first prize.

Chorus: Rum tum tickle um tidy aye, Rum tum tickle I aye Lad, I don't know where you've been, but I see you've won first prize.

Shane was just getting warmed up, and he continued to sing into the night with his wry sense of humor and deep voice. Many of the songs he sang were originals, and we all laughed until our sides hurt and our cheeks ached. Laughter is such good medicine.

09/14/96

The next day, Shane took Shoofly, Leapfrog, Fox, and me on a tour of Amish country in Lancaster County while Kee played in the backyard with her new buddy Levi, the family's Black Lab.

Driving through Amish country was like going back in time to another century where life was much simpler but physically more demanding. Come to think of it, I didn't see a single overweight Amish or Mennonite person all day. This simplistic lifestyle was something all of us who had been on the trail for any length of time could relate to.

In Lancaster County, the average family farm was eighty-five acres. It is the most productive non-irrigated land in the United States. There were pristine farms everywhere. They weren't cluttered with junk and looked like they should've been on the cover of a magazine. We saw corn being harvested and loaded onto wagons pulled by draft horses. There were horse-drawn carriages everywhere. Some were fully enclosed carriages with turn signals to make them highway compatible. Striking, Bay-colored Tennessee Walkers seemed to be the horse of choice for pulling some of the finest buggies and carriages I had ever seen. Pride and quality of artistry were everywhere. In any given parking lot, you would likely find an old-world mode of travel, a one-horse carriage tied to a hitching post, next to a modern four hundred horse Mercedes-Benz.

For dinner, we had pizza and leftover barbeque. After dinner, Shoofly gave his brother and Fox Trot a clinic on the game of darts while everyone else retired to their quarters to journal and get packed for the next day's departure.

09/15/96

It's incredible how you can get so attached to people in such a short amount of time. Tom and Nancy reminded me of my parents. Their support for their sons' adventure was spectacular and heartfelt, especially as they said goodbye and wished their boys safe travels. I could only imagine what a parent must go through.

We headed into the woods with Shoofly sporting a new knee brace on his right leg and me still struggling with low energy. We made it fifteen-plus miles to Fort Dietrich Snyder Marker and camped nearby for the night. The marker was the site of a lookout post, built during the French and Indian War, whose sole purpose was "to warn of the approach of enemies."

09/16/96

We walked eight miles to the 501 Shelter and stopped for lunch. It started to rain, and I began to get chilled, so I decided to stay and wait out the rain in my sleeping bag. Shoofly and Tree Trunk chose to push on to the next shelter, and I hoped to catch up later. The brothers were inseparable, and I wished I could share an adventure like this with my brother. Two hours later, I was awakened by two soaked southbound hikers, Rev and Trillium. Had they not shown up, I probably would have slept through the night. The storm was intensifying, and it was a unanimous consensus that we should stay put until the next day. It rained so hard that it sounded like the tin roof would collapse.

09/17/96

I didn't get much sleep that night. The wind was blowing the rain sideways, and I had to relocate to the back of the shelter to keep from being soaked. I woke up feeling like my old self. The Cipro medication was working.

The morning was cold and blustery, the skies were gray, and it was threatening to rain again. This is the type of weather that would kick off the elk rut back home. I missed not hearing the wild, high-lonesome bugles of a backcountry bull in my home state of Colorado. The sound of distant and responding challenge bugles ringing through the crisp mountain air had always stirred something profound within my soul. It was a connection, awakening a zest for life and an appreciation for all things wild that had lain dormant in the recesses of my domesticated DNA.

There was nothing like being able to sneak in on a herd of elk during the heat of the rut and be able to call in the herd bull within ten feet. It was both exhilarating and humbling to watch them destroy a mature tree-sized bush. Throw it over their shoulder and then let out a growling, warning bugle that made the hair on the back of your neck stand on end. I wondered how many of us living in this modern world still had this latent desire to test ourselves and live in harmony with nature and our creator.

I had to get moving if I was going to catch the brothers. Despite the weather, I felt invincible, like a true hiking machine. We passed the William Penn Shelter and had officially hiked one thousand miles. Rev, Trillium, and I gave each other a brief celebratory high five and then continued on. It was starting to feel like we might be able to do this! We called it a day when we caught up to the brothers sheltering from the rain, eighteen miles later, at the Rausch Gap Shelter.

09/18/96

The rain stopped, it was overcast, and a crisp bite was in the air. I could feel the fall season upon us, and the leaves were starting to change, making for perfect hiking conditions.

Holy smokes! I was buzzed by a fighter jet. I guess Fort Indiantown Gap Military Reservation was nearby. Wow, another two fighter jets screamed overhead. It was impressive and better than coffee first thing in the morning. I was glad to be past that bout with giardia, or this flyover would have scared the you-know-what out of me.

I didn't know if I was getting stronger or if this had been an easy section of the AT, but I made it the eighteen miles to Peters Mountain Shelter and still felt like I had something left in the tank.

We had been following another southbounder named Little Buddy for some time, and his humor was often found in the shelter register. His PMS entry was about the **Top Ten Reasons to Visit the Peter Mountain Spring:**

10) *Everything is better after you work for it.*

9) *It's fun to say, be right back! And return an hour later.*

8) *Not enough real climbing on the A.T.*

7) *It's okay, it won't fit on the trail maps cuzz it's blazed really good.*

6) *It will remind you of your favorite slack-packing day.*

5) *Can register at the Doyle Hotel while you are down there.*

4) *It is a good way to break in your new boots.*

3) *Wouldn't have gotten to see the bottom of the mountain otherwise.*

2) *No need to worry about H2O for the hike up.*

1) *The much-respected rocker patch 2000 miler Peter Mountain Shelter.*

It was undoubtedly steep and maybe a third of a mile down to the water source. At the end of the day, I really didn't have a choice if I wanted to stay hydrated. It certainly made me sympathize with those in third-world countries who don't have the convenience of running water and have to carry their water great distances.

PMS was a great shelter that had additional sleeping quarters upstairs. The loft was filled with hikers, so we claimed some first-floor space with our mats and sleeping bags. After we had eaten, Kee curled up and passed out. A couple of hours later, after I cleaned up from dinner, filtered water for the next day, hung food bags, and made some journal entries, I called it a night. This shelter sleeping is going to take some getting used to. It turned into combat, sleeping with Tree Trunk. It seemed that every time I would roll over, Tree Trunk would muscle in on my Therma-rest. I woke up at three o'clock in the morning with Kee restlessly pacing and then standing over me, looking down at me as if she wanted me to get going.

That was the last time I would let Kee go to sleep that early. I was unusually stiff in the morning. I think Tree Trunk continued to hike in his sleep and had completely hijacked my sleeping pad and left me on the floor.

09/19/96

We made it the eleven miles into Duncannon before noon. We were able to find fuel for our stoves at the True Value Hardware store and then grab lunch at a truck stop before the lunch crowds convened. I then went to the pharmacy and renewed my prescription for poison ivy, just as a precautionary measure. We thought about heading to the Doyle for their fifty-cent happy hour beer special, but Tree Trunk, who wasn't of age, wasn't excited about waiting outside with our backpacks. So, we pressed on, climbing until we got to Hawk Rock. On this viewpoint overlooking the town of Duncannon and the Susquehanna River Valley, we had an organic "Kavorka" discussion with Tree Trunk that could've been an episode for Seinfeld.

It started simply enough with us teasing Shoofly about his rugged look, and it somehow evolved into his innate animal magnetism that women found irresistible. Shoofly was a great sport and fell into an impromptu about how the "Kavorka" was such a curse for him.

The discussion ended with us reassuring Shoofly that his "Eau de Trail" was probably strong enough to break the curse. With that, we renamed Hawk Rock to Kavorka Rock in honor of Shoofly's animal magnetism.

It was late evening by the time we got to the Thelma Marks Memorial Shelter, and we didn't want to hike another seven miles in the dark to the next shelter, so we decided to stay despite the senseless murders that happened to a young couple in this very shelter in 1990. We paid our respects to Geoff Hood and Molly LaRue in our own personal ways, vowing that fear would not hold us hostage. It still weighed heavy on me, knowing that they were two people who had the heart to help at-risk youth. Sometimes, it seemed to me that life was unfair, and that evil was winning.

09/20/96

The day's hike was relatively easy. We hiked through some farmland where a dairy cow decided to follow us. Kee was a little unsure of our new hiking partner, but the cow seemed perfectly content to walk along with us. When we reached the far fence, the cow just stood there and watched us walk away. It was almost as if she longed for adventure. Soon after we went through some corn fields where we were swarmed by mosquitoes. In my hurry to outpace the onslaught, I stepped on a stick but when it frantically started squirming, I realized it was a baby copperhead. Poor thing, it didn't have a chance under my size fourteen boot. I'm grateful it wasn't a bigger snake and that it was trapped underfoot before Kee walked by.

Shoofly was having a hell of a time breaking in his new boots. His feet looked like hamburger, and he had blisters on the knuckles of his big toes and the bottoms of most of his other toes. His heels had ruptured blisters almost to the bone. We taped mole skin donuts to the affected areas with duct tape, and he gutted out the twenty-two miles into Boiling Springs on a steady diet of Ibuprofen. His misery made me apprehensive about breaking in new boots that should be waiting for me in one hundred trail miles at Harper's Ferry, West Virginia.

Shoofly and Tree Trunk

I was able to get my mail, but the brothers' package hadn't arrived, so out of necessity we stealth camped on the grass next to a historic Blast Iron Furnace. Shoofly wouldn't openly admit that he was hurting, but his body language spoke volumes about how he had suffered through the day and could push no further. The brothers hoped their resupply box would arrive at the post office the next day.

Camping there was a big mistake. Every hour throughout the night, a train would roll by, blasting its horn. That kind of disruptive sleep will frazzle anyone, and then, to add insult to our stealth campsite, the morning dew was so thick that our sleeping bags were soaked.

In our defense, the 1996 *Thru-Hiker's Handbook* was only in northbound format, so we had to read it backward. From the direction we were hiking, there wasn't any mention that camping wasn't allowed along the AT in the Cumberland Valley. It wasn't until I was waiting in the parking lot for the brothers to finish shopping, that I noticed the "No Camping" advisory. The local AT club and the Appalachian Trail Conference provided a campsite on the southern edge of Boiling Springs through Labor Day, which didn't help us or any of the southbounders behind us.

09/21/96

Their package never showed, so the brothers filed a forwarding slip with the postal clerk to a post office along the trail in West Virginia and hustled to Karns Grocery Store for supplies. They bought extra donuts and chocolate milk, and we feasted in the parking lot before heading out.

The sugar buzz would only get us three or four miles down the trail before we hit the wall. Our lack of sleep didn't help. It took Tree Trunk and me five and a half hours to go twelve miles. In the process, we passed the official halfway marker. It felt great knowing that we had traveled so far, and at the same time, it was daunting knowing the effort it would take to finish.

We waited over an hour before Shoofly limped into the Tagg Run Shelters. When I saw him he looked miserable. "How are your feet doing?"

He clenched his teeth. "They're killing me."

> "The same boiling water that softens the potato hardens the egg. It's about what you're made of, not the circumstances."
>
> – MEL ROBBINS, X (formally Twitter)

There was no doubt in any of our minds that Shoofly was not only rugged, but he was as tough as they come.

Halfway, only 1069 miles to go

Tagg Runn Shelter

That evening while looking for firewood, we came across five skinheads cutting down trees and chopping them into firewood. Their camp was just down the hill from the shelter we were at.

It was a star-filled night, and after I cleaned up from dinner, I joined the others around a crackling fire, mesmerized by the flames licking at the darkness of the night.

I had been asleep three hours when I was awakened by loud howling from the skinhead camp. I don't know what they were celebrating, but their shouting contest kept getting louder and louder until they all must have passed out around one in the morning. I fell into another deep sleep only to be awakened at 3:30 am by the steady pounding of rain on the shelter roof. Disoriented, I sprang out of bed and hurried into the downpour to retrieve my clothes that had been drying on the clothesline.

09/22/96

I would not sacrifice my sleeping clothes to hike in so I knew I would be starting my day in cold, wet clothes; not that it mattered much, it was still sprinkling.

Just as we were getting ready to head out, the skinhead camp erupted in gunfire. It sounded like 9mm semi-automatic handgun rounds being shot as fast as they could pull the trigger. Then, there was a short hesitation. We assumed they dropped a clip to load again. Then, they continued rapid gunfire. We all yelled to let them know we were just uphill from them. Everything from their camp went quiet, and it was as if they were shocked that people were nearby.

We took the opportunity to hustle down the trail.

We did less than eight miles because Shoofly was suffering and needed a short day to heal. We all stayed at the Ironmaster Mansion Hostel in Pine Grove Furnace State Park. The furnace was used for smelting iron ore, aka pig iron, which was then forged into wrought iron, wood-burning stoves, kettles, and whatever else could turn a good profit.

Supposedly, Martha and George Washington stayed here back in the day. James, one of the guys who managed the place, was kind enough to show us around. He gave us a little historical tour of how the Underground Railroad used the mansion to harbor fugitive slaves. The mansion was only thirty miles north of the Mason-Dixon line. James showed us a secret passageway, in a first-floor closet under the stairs, where they would hide all the slaves that had escaped. There was a jail cell in the cellar where the bounty hunters, oblivious to the secret passageway, would keep their prisoners until they could expedite them back to the South. I marveled at the courage of those who ran this covert operation under the noses of the bounty hunters and simultaneously felt disgust for what the bounty hunters would do for money. I found solace in knowing that people like Harriet Tubman, known as the Moses of her people, were selflessly dedicated to freedom, even risking personal peril at being caught.

To decompress from the weight of our history reminder, Tree Trunk and I played lawn chess while Shoofly went to the dormitory room at the hostel to nurse his wounds. The chess game was built in 1990 by a Carlisle Eagle Scout named Chad Bassett, and I thought it was ironic that another Eagle Scout was here to enjoy this game with me. From my perspective as a builder, Chad did a fantastic job, but more importantly, he helped renew my hope in today's youth and tomorrow's future.

Thanks James!

09/23/96

We may have had a Ward Leonard sighting at Tom's Run Shelter. Ward "Spooky Boy" Leonard was famous for hiking the trail ten times and infamously notorious for his anti-social behavior. We had just finished lunch and were heading down the trail when this northbounder came barreling by.

As he approached, I called out, "Hello!"

He didn't wave but held his hand up to block us from seeing his face. He never looked at us as he blew by, only to disappear into the shelter we had just vacated. Besides that, it was an uneventful day, leaving plenty of time to think and ponder. After ten miles, we called it a day at the Birch Run Shelters to make sure Shoofly's feet would be ready for bigger miles in the upcoming days.

There was an interesting entry in the shelter register that read, **"DON'T BOTHER ME, JUST LEAVE ME ALONE!!!!!"** I guessed the author was the guy we encountered at Tom's Run.

The brothers and I finished the day sitting around a crackling fire, mesmerized by the flickering light, each lost in his thoughts while listening to the increasing crescendo of the last cicadas of the season.

Campfire Comraderie — Shoofly, me, and Tree Trunk

09/24/96

I saw a couple of catfish on the trail during my morning hike. That was highly unusual, especially since I hadn't seen a lake nearby. The biggest fish was half eaten and must have been there for some time since there were five turkey vultures perched in the trees directly above, waiting to grab an easy meal. I must have taken a little too long inspecting the carcasses, or these vultures weren't the patient kind as they all took to wing in unison and sounded like a Huey helicopter taking off.

Shortly after the catfish sighting, I ran into several bow hunters in a tree stand. They came down as I walked by, so I stopped to see how they were doing.

One of them said, "We just got here at ten o'clock and haven't seen anything."

I grinned. "I've seen all kinds of signs and quite a few deer on my hike this morning." I wished them good luck and thought, *They better get up a little earlier if they want to be successful.*

I stopped at the Quarry Gap Shelters for lunch and read some of the more recent entries in the register. Magoo and Blue Noodle, a southbound father and son team, had stayed at the shelter a few nights before when a visitor came and looked around at 12:45 am. When they woke in the morning, there was no one there. Their visitor had hiked off into the night, leaving them wondering if they had even seen him at all. Chances were it was the same guy that we had seen the previous day.

To our surprise, we came across about twenty kids decked out in military attire, marching in unison toward us. They were clean-shaven and sporting crew cuts. They were very courteous; they stepped aside and addressed me as sir. I was a little caught off guard and spoke briefly with one of the leaders as the kids marched down the trail. He told me they were with the Abraxas Youth and Family Services reform program for at-risk youth.

"All of our kids go through extensive background checks, and they are allowed to go on treks once they are deemed ready, willing, and safe."

I shook his hand. "Keep making a difference, brother."

I walked away, honored to have seen kids who knew they had a second chance and were excited about their futures.

It had been overcast and sprinkling on and off all day. As I was getting close to the Tumbling Run Shelter, I could hear what sounded like raindrops hitting the dry leaves on the forest floor all around me. I didn't think anything of it until one of them landed pretty close to me, and it wasn't the color of rain. It was white! I stopped and looked around. There were white bird droppings raining down on me. Frozen in my tracks, I looked into the bushes and trees and saw they were alive with swarms of little blackbirds. They were feeding on remnant berries in the bushes and insects in the trees. I must have lingered a little too long, making them nervous, and causing them to take off in waves that sounded like wind blowing briskly through the leaves.

There was nowhere to hide from the ensuing bird bombs. I didn't dare tilt my head back to look up. Instead, I watched them swarm through the trees in front of me like locusts. It was as if they moved as one living being, contracting and expanding, moving with surprising speed and precision. They never collided with one another or the tangled forest canopy through which they flew. I have witnessed some incredible team sporting events where the athletes work together to near perfection. While those moments in human history are spectacular, they fail to match the harmonious movement displayed here. Then, like smoke in the wind, they were gone. When the last of them had disappeared, I ripped my pack off to assess the damage. I never felt anything hit me, but I still ran my fingers through my hair, half expecting to find a fresh mess. Miraculously, Kee and I never suffered the humiliation of a uric acid bird baptism. Apparently, the birds were courteous enough to swerve to either side of our position before regrouping after they passed us. Wouldn't it be something if we as humans could work together with a fraction of the unity that the birds of the air were capable of? Some would say it is impossible, like unicorns pissing rainbows. I think we can do better; at least, we must try.

I ran into Pilgrim at the Tumbling Run Shelters. It was still early enough, and I could've gone on to the next shelter, but I decided to stay and visit while I waited for the brothers. I told Pilgrim that this would be a true test for Shoofly to see if he was healthy enough to put in some big miles. An hour and a half later, the brothers came rolling in, and Pilgrim and I gave them a standing ovation. We had a great visit with Pilgrim, and according to him, he was the last northbounder we would see. He had been hiking the AT off and on for over twenty-five years and had a wealth of pertinent trail knowledge.

At 8:30, we saw a bright light working toward us cutting through the pitch-black night. Somebody was coming up spot lighting both sides of the trail and then shining up into the trees. I don't know if they were coon hunting or poaching for deer. Since I didn't hear any dogs, I assumed the latter. We couldn't be sure what their intent was, so we flashed our headlamps at them, and they immediately turned their spotlight off and disappeared.

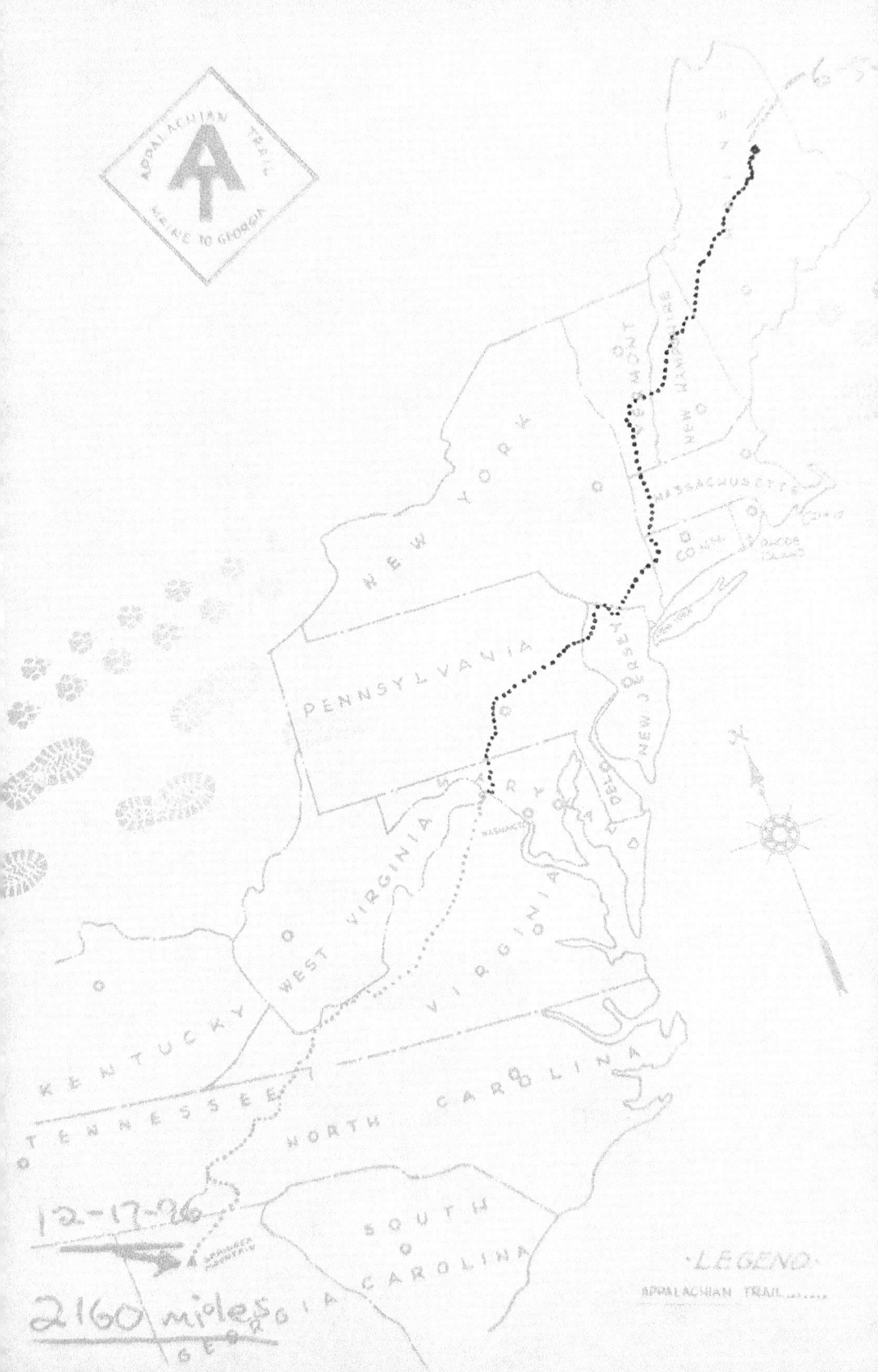

Chapter 18

Maryland

09/25/96

I was hiking along mid-morning, lost in thought when an unusually vibrant green leaf on the trail caught my eye. The leaf was twitching erratically, so I stopped long enough to look closer. I had never seen a katydid before, and I marveled at its ingenious mimicry until I realized it was missing a wing and its head was partially chewed off. There was a saboteur in our midst who was not fooled by the katydid's realistic leaf impersonation. A scan of the overhead branches revealed a three-inch praying mantis waiting for me to move on before he finished his meal.

We would soon be crossing the Mason-Dixon line. It wasn't just another milestone for us; it was a historical reminder that represented

"Originally, Charles Mason and Jeremiah Dixon, a couple of English surveyors, were called in to settle a land grant boundary dispute between Maryland and Pennsylvania in 1763. Legislation in the form of the Missouri Compromise would ban slavery north of the line in 1820. In April of 1861, the Civil War began. In our nation's bloodiest war, three hundred and sixty thousand, two hundred and twenty-two Union soldiers would die defending the right that all persons be free. Two hundred and fifty-eight thousand Confederate soldiers died defending a way of life and protesting government overreach." - **history.com** the division of fractured ideology amongst the colonies.

We caught up with Rev and Trillium as we neared the Mason-Dixon line. Rev's apprehension was apparent.

"Rev, what has you so worked up?"

He looked at me and chuckled. "Listen, I'm just a little nervous that these Southerners are going to know I'm a Yank."

I scoffed at the thought that anyone would harbor such anxiety in today's day and age, but there was a degree of sincerity in his statement that left me wondering if there wasn't some resentment still lingering in the southern shadows of the Mason-Dixon line.

We stopped at Pen Mar Park to fill our water bottles and have lunch at the pavilion. There was a soda machine nearby, so I walked over to see what the selections were, and this guy named Gary walked over to make small talk about the trail. He must have sensed that I didn't have any loose change to buy a soda, and he handed me fifty cents.

At first, I shrugged my shoulders and politely declined. "Thanks, but I don't need it."

He smiled. "Get what you want."

It felt awkward to take his offer, but I relented. I savored that sweet, carbonated flavor as if it were the first my mouth had ever experienced. Sheer joy must have radiated from me because when I opened my eyes, Gary was smiling back as if he had gotten just as much pleasure watching me enjoy that drink. It donned on me that for Grace to flow, there needs to be a recipient. If I had let my pride get in the way, that magical moment would not have happened.

"Brother, that was the best A&W Root Beer I have ever tasted!"

He smiled, wished me good luck with my adventure, and walked away.

This may seem like a simple gesture, but for me, it was another act of trail magic that continued to erode at the foundation of my distrust in humanity.

As I reflected on the kindness of strangers, I walked over to the scenic viewpoint. Views on the AT are hard-earned because of the dense foliage that encases you in a green tunnel that sometimes felt claustrophobic, especially after enjoying the vast vistas out west. I admired the view, probably more than most. I looked down at a small town nestled in the valley below, surrounded by beautiful, well-manicured farms. While trying to absorb the beauty of the place, I came across a placard that spoke to my soul.

> **"How can one behold all that is about him and not think of the Creator."**

I personally don't think it is possible to immerse yourself in creation, undistracted and present in the moment, and not walk with awe and amazement.

We made it twenty miles to Hemlock Hill Campground and Shelter. Shoofly was getting healthier by the mile, and Tree Trunk was still the invincible youth. Rev and Trillium seemed to be at odds the farther south we went. She didn't seem to be enjoying the journey and was tired of the rigors of the trail. Watching this play out was a reminder of what can transpire when two people are not equally invested and passionate about the same goal.

09/26/96

A crisp bite to the morning's air made me wish I was already in Harper's Ferry, where my fleece jacket and beanie awaited me in my mail drop. The green tunnel transformed into brilliant fall colors on the upper reaches of the mountains. I felt like I was walking into the most exquisite painting.

Fall was beginning to show herself with masterful self-portraits. Northbounders followed spring north, but we got to chase autumn's vibrant colors south. I found great delight in walking amongst the brilliant colors and smelling the pungent, earthy aroma of rotting flora. The only thing missing from this autumn setting was the wild call of elk bugles and the crack of herd bull antlers, locking in an ancient fight for dominance, echoing across distant valleys. Elk would not set foot in the Mountain State until December 2016.

I came across a clear opening cut for a power line that afforded an unobstructed view of the sky. A shadow passed over my head, and I looked up to see a hawk and a peregrine falcon soaring on the thermals, apparently hunting. Farther above an opportunistic vulture was effortlessly riding the thermals, watching, and following the raptors.

I wondered if dinner bells didn't go off for the vultures in this area when they spotted hunting raptors. I watched with envy at the grace with which they flew—circling, diving, and then climbing to soar once again to watch with ever-vigilant eyes. Oh, how I longed to be able to fly like these birds of the sky, seemingly free of the grasp of gravity. I wished I could have spent more time to see if they were successful, but the trail beckoned me to see what waited around the next bend.

I ran into a ridge runner, Thurston Griggs, who, at the spry age of eighty, covered the entire Maryland section of the AT. He was in incredible shape and hiked twelve miles a day. He used to teach history at the University of Maryland and was also a physics administrator. He impressed me so much with his sharp wit and the fitness level of someone thirty years younger, I had to get a picture of him with Kee. There must be something radically beneficial to one's overall well-being from outdoor activities like hiking.

We had another twenty-mile day before we stopped at Crampton Gap Shelter right before dark. The days were getting shorter, and I had to hustle to get dinner ready, so Kee and I could have a headlight meal.

80-year-old Maryland Ridge Runner, Thurston Griggs

12-17-96

2160 miles

·LEGEND·
APPALACHIAN TRAIL ....

Chapter 19

West Virginia

09/27/96

    We had an eleven-mile hike to Harper's Ferry, and the primary motivation for the day was an all-you-can-eat Pizza Hut buffet in the neighboring town of Charles Town. It seemed that the farther we walked, the hungrier we were. Snacking in between meals only provided momentary relief, and we were forced to ignore our most basic instinct. With hunger gnawing at our subconscious, the thought of a feast set before hungry hikers provoked everyone to walk with renewed purpose. The excitement was elevated for me because I would be getting a supply box from home, and the letters from loved ones were more important than food.

    The brothers and I stopped a few miles before the Weverton Cliffs vantage point for a quick snack break. While we were sitting there, a swarm of hundreds of black birds flew through the trees with the sound of a great wind. The flock split, and they flew to each side of us and then regrouped into one massive flowing unit, flying through the dense forest with amazing agility. Then, they were gone. In the silent vacuum, we watched with awe as they disappeared to the south.

    We crossed the Potomac on a six-hundred-foot pedestrian footbridge built by the National Park Service in 1987. Then, we went to the Appalachian Trail Conference headquarters, where Jean Cashin, information specialist extraordinaire, immediately greeted us. She took a Polaroid picture of each of us and put it in a book, documenting the day we came through, along with our trail name, contact information, and official southbound number. After formally registering with the AT conference, we walked out onto the lawn and were greeted by the Appalachian Trail's first Thru-Hiker, Earl Shafer. He completed the entire trail in 1948, and it felt like we were in the presence of humble greatness.

Only after hiking over one thousand miles could we begin to appreciate how tough Earl was. He certainly didn't have the luxury of being able to weather a storm in one of the two hundred and fifty plus backcountry shelters. Even at age seventy-seven, he looked fit enough to hike big miles. He wrote a book, *Walking with Spring*; his trail journal is in the Smithsonian. He was a rock star in the hiking community, but you would never know it as he posed patiently for his photo to be taken with each of us.

Earl Shaffer

Our next stop was to the post office for my mail drop and hopefully my new boots. True to their word, Vasque had sent me my replacement boots. I took my Alpine boots off at the post office and sent them back to customer service. In their defense, the Alpine boot that I chose to start with needed to be more heavy duty to handle my starting physical weight, along with my pack weight and the ruggedness of the trail. The Vasque Glacier mountaineering boots were sturdier than my original Vasque Alpine hiking boots. They had full-grain uppers and were crampon-compatible. They were a great fit, but I dreaded breaking them in. There would be no slow, casual time for this; I could only hope I could break them in before they broke me.

With cavalier determination, I laced them up and headed to the Cliffside Hotel with thoughts about how decadent a hot shower would be. I have to confess that in my pre-trail life, I had taken the luxury of hot running water for granted. Now, it seemed to activate heightened senses, where you could feel tantalizing rivulets of water running across your skin, and the warmth was something that every cell rejoiced in.

Kee and I called it an early night. As she lay snoring on the floor, I was in bed reading through my mail. My sister Jennifer and her husband Dave wrote me about their most recent adventure at the 1996 Summer Olympics in Atlanta. She spoke about the beauty of having people from around the world and the palpable comradery. She wrote about seeing Michael Johnson win the 400m wearing his iconic gold Nike running shoes and watching Carl Lewis take gold in the long jump. She penned about her favorite moments, such as when Michael cried when he received his medal and how Carl got emotional as well. She mentioned seeing President Clinton at the women's gymnastics event and how it got started late because of all the extra security. Then, she mentioned the bombing at Centennial Park and how they were fortunate not to have had any events to watch that night. They had been there the previous two nights and were horrified to be watching the news the night it happened. Two people were killed, and one hundred and eleven people were injured.

She finished by saying that they bought some Astronaut food while in Atlanta and thought that I would appreciate how lightweight it was and get a kick out of eating a real Astronaut meal.

I lay there with mixed emotions. A competitive pride grew in me as I rejoiced in Michael's and Carl's hard-earned success. Elation was followed by gratitude that my family was safe. But, I had a sick visceral feeling after reading about the bombing. It weighed heavy on me knowing that someone could perpetrate such a senseless act of violence against their fellow man. I tried to bury the negative emotions so I could get to sleep, having convinced myself there was nothing I could do. Sleep did not come easy.

09/28/96

After an all-you-can-eat breakfast, I went back to my room to sort and pack my additional warm clothing and food. I oiled my new boots, hoping to ease the break-in process. Then Kee and I went for a walk around town. After a few miles, my feet began to hurt, so I went back to my room to doctor the hotspots with moleskin and duct tape.

I called home to check in and see how everyone was doing. My parents were always so happy when I called and were eager to hear about life on the trail. After filling them in and planning for my next mail drop, I asked, "How's Grandpa?"

"He's doing all right," said my dad. "He has his good days, and then he has his bad."

Before I could ask for clarification, he continued, "He had trouble getting up and getting to the bathroom the other day, and he wet himself."

"Oh no! How did he handle it?"

"He's pretty embarrassed, especially when I had to bathe him. This getting old isn't easy."

"I can only imagine. I'm sure his pride took a hit on that one. Dad, I feel like I'm running out of time to see him before…"

"Rick, there is nothing you can do."

There was an awkward silence as he struggled to find the words, but none came.

Tears welled up in my eyes as we said our goodbyes. It was difficult to hear the pain in my dad's voice, knowing that my grandpa's failing body was excruciating for Dad as well.

I called my aunt's house to speak with my grandpa, but he was sleeping, and my aunt thought it best that he got his rest.

Later that evening, the rain began in earnest, but we didn't let that keep us from finding comfort in a buffet at Pizza Hut in Charles Town. While the pizza was good, the salad bar was spectacular. We were all beginning to crave fresh vegetables and fruit at the cellular level. The look on the manager's face was priceless as he watched five hungry hikers clean out the pizza and salad bar twice. We left him shaking his head in astonishment, like we were human locusts, as his cooks scrambled to restock the bar.

Chapter 20

Virginia

09/29/96

    The rain hadn't let up, so we waited, hoping the weather would break. After a rest day, we were all getting antsy and wanted to get back on the trail. Staying another day in town was not an option for me; I needed the healing rhythm of walking into the classroom of silence.

    We left the comforts of town after lunch and hiked into the rain and fog. Shoofly was still having problems with his boots and was slowly dropping behind. His brother stayed with him, hiking in silent support. My heavy pack forced my foot to splay wider than my boots would allow, and I developed new sore spots and blisters on my fifth metatarsals. My ankle bone was also getting roughed up by the metal eyelet rivets. It was raining too hard to stop and make field adjustments on my boots, so I tried to make it eight and a half miles to the David Lesser Memorial Shelter before my feet turned to hamburger.

    The sun had dropped below the horizon, and with it, the temperature plummeted. The rain was on the verge of turning to sleet, and the fog was so thick that the light from my headlamp blinded me. I had to shine my light from waist level to be able to see in front of me. I wondered if I may have passed the shelter. I knew I had to be close.

I began to second-guess my decision to hike without my tent. Perhaps it had taken me longer to hike the short distance to the shelter because my boots made every step torturous. Panic began to rob me of clear thinking. I had nearly convinced myself that I had gone too far and somehow missed the shelter in the fog, but I was reluctant to turn back, fearing that I hadn't gone far enough, so I pressed on to make sure.

I was on the verge of calling it quits for the day and had decided to take my chances weathering the storm curled up with Kee under my tarp, when I rounded a bend, and my light caught a ghostly silhouette of a shelter before it disappeared in the swirling fog. At first, I thought I was hallucinating, but decided I had better investigate to be sure. It was as if I was walking blind and had to rely on my internal compass to navigate through the disorienting swirl. I almost bumped into it before I saw it again.

Unfortunately, the shelter was packed with six medical students from Georgetown University. I must have had a disappointed look as one of the students yelled, "Hey, we'll make room. There's no sense in hiking in this weather."

"Are you sure?"

"Absolutely."

I threw my pack down and tore off my boots to assess the damage to my feet. I quickly patched all the blisters with a moleskin donut and duct tape. I taped a double moleskin donut to the inside of my boot where the rivet was digging into my ankle bone and then wrapped all pre-blister hotspots with duct tape.

The brothers still hadn't shown up, so I laced my boots, looked at Kee, and said, "Let's go get 'em."

As we headed into the soup, Kee's ears perked up. I could hear voices in the darkness, and then I saw the fog glowing at waist height. I called out, "Hey, over here!"

In unison, they replied, "Ducttape?"

"Good to see you boys."

Kee was just as happy and greeted the brothers and Rev by prancing around and wagging her tail in circles. It looked as if she had a smile on her face.

That night, with ten people and a dog, we joked that if anyone wanted to roll over, to signal so we could all roll at the same time. If empathy and humor are necessary to succeed in the medical field, these students were Rock Stars.

09/30/96

After breakfast, we wished the students good luck with their studies and started walking in the rain. Before we got too far down the trail, I called out behind me, "Rev, where's Trillium?"

"Oh, she's tired of the oatmeal, so she decided to leave the trail."

I chuckled. "Is that code for she's tired of you or the weather?"

He just smiled sheepishly, and we hiked on.

Ten miles into the hike, we reached Snickers Gap. We were so cold by then that we went into Horseshoe Curve restaurant to warm up, and the aroma of grilled burgers was more than we could take. It was two burgers apiece, a double order of fries, and a coke before we returned to the trail. We were always running on a caloric deficit, and this by no means satisfied our appetites.

While walking along the pavement, I spotted a baby rattlesnake stretched out, trying to warm itself. I moved it with my sticks to the edge of the road so it wouldn't get run over, and it managed to coil up and strike a couple of times at me while Kee walked behind me indifferent to the snake's attitude. Sometimes, our best intentions can be misinterpreted.

My boots were getting the best of me after mile fourteen. Shoofly and I didn't think it wise to push another seven miles to the next shelter, so we settled in at the Sam Moore Shelter and decided to give our feet a break and do some sightseeing in D.C

10/01/6

Shoofly and I limped our way into Linden, Virginia. My feet were hurting, but Shoofly's feet looked like hamburger. He had put a couple hundred miles on his boots and said they were beginning to feel comfortable; he just needed to let his feet heal. Tree Trunk was never far from his brother's side, and it seemed that Shoofly gained strength from his presence, or maybe he didn't want to let him down.

Honestly, I didn't know how he was still walking.

Rev kept waiting for us, even though he needed to pick up his supply box before the post office closed. We made it there with minutes to spare. We rented a car and drove forty-five miles to Shoofly and Tree Trunk's cousin's house in Fairfax, Virginia.

10/02/96

Rev had lived in DC for four years, so he was our designated tour guide. Not surprising, our first stop was to eat a steak lunch at the Inter-American Development Bank. Once our hanger (hunger and anger) was under control, we went to the Capitol Building and were able to see Republican John Linder's office in the House of Representatives. He wasn't in, so we headed over to the Senate and Rev's friend, David Baldwin, took us on a tour of the Senate House while they were still in session. We watched from the balcony as the leaders of our great country followed protocol in addressing the Presiding Officer, who in turn would recognize the Senator, and then the Senator would speak.

I would have loved to stick around to see what went into getting something passed, but there was so much more to see in a short amount of time. We drove by the White House, where there were a bunch of media trucks out front waiting to get footage of President Clinton's meeting with Israeli Prime Minister Benjamin Netanyahu and the President of the Palestinian Authority, Yasser Arafat. The two-day summit was intended to resolve their differences. In hindsight, they may have needed more than two days to overcome their differences and learn to play nice. It's been nearly thirty years since that Summit, and they are not any closer to getting along. Until we quit looking for worldly solutions to spiritual problems, the violence in the Middle East will continue to repeat like Groundhog Day until they learn to love God and love one another. In the meantime, we can all learn from the mistakes of those who lash out in anger and hate. When will humankind finally be both human and kind?

We then went to National Geographic Society Headquarters, and I spoke with Peter Miller, Senior Assistant Editor of Expeditions.

While he loved my pitch for my book idea, he politely declined my story. He insisted they were looking for professional writers if they were to do a profile on America. Especially after dealing with Peter Jenkin's *Walk Across America* book. He said, "It was an editorial nightmare."

In Peter's defense, I told him it may have been a little extra work on their end, but the book gave great insight into what makes America great. He did say they would be interested in doing something if I continued across America and for me to drop him a letter. With that, he gave me his card. I shook his hand, thanked him for his time, and walked away, contemplating, *I have some work to do.*

We then went to the Washington Monument and Lincoln Memorial because that's what tourists do. They were magnificent monuments that deserved to be viewed in a way that allowed the significance of what they represented to resonate. To that point, I will return someday.

On the way back to the cousin's house, we rehashed the day's events, and I took some gentle ribbing about being shot down by the Senior Assistant Editor at National Geographic.

10/03/96

Five miles into the next day's hike, we were greeted by signs on a post that read:

ENTERING RESTRICTED BREEDING CENTER
NATIONAL ZOOLOGICAL PARK

Pets on Leash

No Camping

No Fires

Stay on Trail

No Trespassing

Violators will be Eaten

It was the last mandate on the sign that caught our attention. The National Zoo compound fence parallels the trail for a while, and we were able to see an impressive Ibex buck that had already undergone a dramatic transformation from his light brown summer coat to a deep chocolate brown winter coat, signifying to the does that he was ready for the rut.

We stayed at the Tom Floyd Wayside Shelter, the last shelter before Shenandoah National Park. We listened to the wind sigh through the trees, sleep came easy.

10/04/96

The fall colors were beginning to peak, and we were almost giddy with anticipation as we started the one hundred and one-mile section of the AT that winds through Shenandoah. Some say this is the Yellowstone of the East. I have never witnessed firsthand the vibrant fall colors of these eastern hardwoods. Something in the air felt like magic as we walked into the morning stillness of the most incredible landscape painting, where the crisp air had a certain bite and the organic, earthy aroma enveloped me. We found ourselves breathing deeply, and our senses never tired of this encompassing beauty. We walked in silent gratitude and fell into a dawn to dusk rhythm, making a crucible of self-reflection inevitable.

> Look deep into nature, and then you will understand everything better.
>
> – ALBERT EINSTEIN

"Brother, you don't seem like a preacher, so what does Rev stand for?"

"Reverence."

"I like it. It's appropriate."

We made the 23.5 miles to Pass Mountain Hut, and my boot pain threatened to steal my gratitude. I have never popped so much aspirin in my entire life.

10/05/96

I read the trail journal in the morning, and it seemed we were gaining on Magoo and Blue Noodle, a father/son southbound team. I couldn't wait to catch them to find out how they got their trail names.

Rev's zipper thermometer was holding steady at thirty-four degrees. In an effort to pare my pack weight down, my gloves made the extravagant list of things I didn't need, so I used an extra pair of socks until the day warmed up.

Shoofly was walking with a less pronounced limp every day, and I could only speculate that he dodged infection and was slowly healing.

The sun was shining, backlighting the canopy, and creating a fiery glow in the tunnel we were now walking in. We emerged at Mary's Rock and paused to climb to the top, soaking in the expansive views. Kee wanted to join us and was smart enough to wait for our help in scaling the rocks. I don't know what it is, but rocks have a way of bringing out the kid in us. We couldn't' help but smile until we called it a day at Rock Springs Hut.

Mary's Rock

10/06/96

We had become so ingrained with the rhythms of nature that there was no need for alarms, and there hadn't been a need since we started. The singing of birds woke us every day before the morning light. Sometimes, Kee's internal alarm clock kicked in before the birds woke. Some mornings I was awakened by Kee's insistent stare. If that didn't get the response that she wanted, then a full-face wash would ensue. The more I protested, the more thorough the face wash would be. She loved our morning ritual. She ate while I prepared my breakfast. After a quick cleanup, I would load my pack while she pranced around in circles, then she stood next to her pack, waiting for me to strap it on.

We stopped briefly at the Big Meadows Wayside Area because Rev insisted he had to make a phone call. He sauntered back to our group with a big smile and said, "Fellas, my brother Tim has agreed to meet us at Hightop Hut with steak and all the fixins."

Shoofly, Tree Trunk, and I responded in unison, "Really?"

Like Pavlov's dogs, we hiked with purpose for twenty-four miles through the aftermath of Hurricanes Bertha and Fran. Both hurricanes were merciless when they tore through the Shenandoah, creating the trail's largest jungle gym. Great swaths of trees were uprooted or sheared off and piled as high as a one-story building in places. The devastation was immense, and had it not been for a trail maintenance crew that cleared the trail ahead of us, our progress would have been limited. For the last couple of hours, our discussions turned to food and our unbelievable cravings. Our food fantasies helped take my mind off my incessant foot pain. Our daydreaming became a reality as Rev's brother, Tim, and three of Rev's buddies packed a cooler full of steak and beer along with backpacks brimming with bread, corn on the cob, potatoes, cans of baked beans, and all the spices to enhance a barbeque.

L–R: Shoofly, Terry, Rev, Shawn, Me, Kee, and David

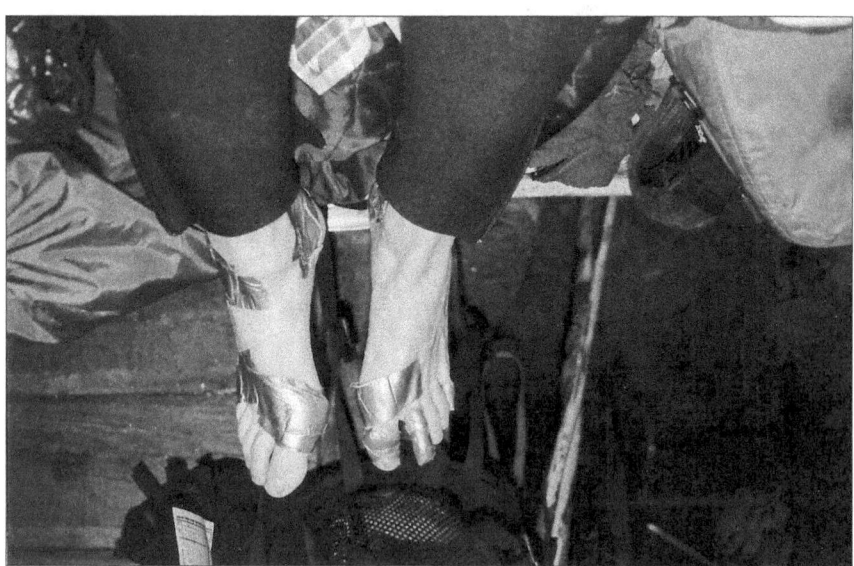

After one hundred and twelve miles, my feet were losing the battle with my new boots. By the time I finished taping the sore spots, it looked like I had silver slippers on. Whatever it took, I was determined to break these boots in.

We sat around the fire, sharing stories of the trail with our four new friends, Tim, Terry, Shawn, and David. Tim was attending the University of North Carolina at Chapel Hill, and Rev's buddies had attended American University and were full of authentic ambition to positively impact society. Their passion was uplifting and "wicked cool" to witness. The camaraderie born of that fireside chat led me to believe these young men would make a difference in public service.

10/07/96

We made great time during the day but were constantly reminded of the violence that blew through here in the preceding months. Stout trees had their tops sheared off as if they were merely toothpicks. Visions ran through my mind of violent and raw forces of nature that had ripped through the landscape and turned everything into mayhem and chaos. My pulse quickened, and visions of my ordeal on Wildcat Mountain played in my head as I walked through the aftermath of fury unleashed, knowing that this would have been a deadly dance through hell as well.

As we walked along, the sound of chainsaws grew louder and louder. We caught up with the trail crew and thanked them for all their hard work. They had made incredible headway on what seemed like an impossible task, and they had no idea how far the tangled mess would continue. The day was still young, so instead of backtracking, we forged ahead, climbing and crawling through the jungle for several miles until we reached the Kissing Tree.

Somehow, the Kissing Tree escaped unscathed. It looked like two trees with separate trunks, three feet in diameter, that were growing so close together that they could've been mistaken for the same tree. The trunks continued to grow apart, but at about ten feet up, they were united by a shared branch, about a third the size of their trunk. It looked like they were kissing. Kee and I posed for a self-portrait, and she planted a sloppy kiss on my cheek as if she understood the tree's significance. I sometimes wondered just how much she understood.

We finally caught Magoo and Blue Noodle at Brown's Gap on Skyline Drive. They were the father and son team from Kentucky

that we had been following for months. At first glance, they looked like seasoned mountain men who had grown up in the backwoods of Appalachia. Both sported magnificent beards, but Magoo's showed patches of silver seniority. He was a retired Kentucky State Trooper, and Blue Noodle had just graduated from the Air Force Academy in Colorado Springs with a degree in computer science. They had a laid-back and unassuming presence about them, combined with an affable southern drawl that quickly disarmed the worst of Rev's concerns. Kee, on the other hand, loved them immediately.

Sunset from Blackrock Hut-Shenendoah

The sun had just dipped below the horizon, and the sky lit up with fiery colors as we gathered around the table and prepared our dinners in reverent silence. It was a glorious end to our day at Blackrock Hut. It felt like we knew Magoo and Blue Noodle personally after reading their register entries at each shelter during the last five hundred miles. Since they never penned this information, I had to ask, "Hey guys, how did you end up with your trail names?"

Magoo and Blue Noodle

Magoo replied with self-deprecating humor, "I've been told I look like the cartoon character, Mr. Magoo. So, I went with it, and it stuck."

"I guess if you squint, I can see the resemblance," I joked. "How about you, Blue Noodle?"

"Well, it's interesting. When other hikers see you boil starchy noodles in water treated with iodine, you end up with a catchy trail name."

We all chuckled while we ate with the aid of headlamps, but Rev's laugh lingered a little longer than everyone else's. Magoo and Blue Noodle seemed to sense something was amiss.

I jumped in. "Don't worry about him. He's usually a lot more talkative. He's just apprehensive about meeting some good ol' southern boys."

Blue Noodle looked puzzled. "What do you mean?"

Rev responded sheepishly by quoting historical facts and his genuine concern that the Rebel spirit was still alive and well, south of the Mason-Dixon line.

"Really?" Magoo glanced at his son, and from that moment on, the father and son team seemed determined to put his fears to rest.

10/08/96

We woke to the sounds of birds chirping in the predawn darkness. The stars were still shining brightly, and it looked like we were in for perfect hiking weather. Since everyone walked at different speeds, we agreed to meet at Waynesboro, twenty miles down the trail.

Shortly after we crossed the southern boundary of Shenandoah National Park, we saw a rather unusual growth on a large white oak tree. This proud tree displayed a well-endowed low-hanging branch that resembled a part of the male anatomy. To say there was mild envy from the hiking crowd would have been an understatement.

We continued through crimson fields of sumac shrubs with deep red flowers as the skies grayed and it began to mist. We crossed Beagle Gap and climbed Bear Den Mountain. The cool air felt invigorating, and we climbed with ease. Shoofly was leading and setting

a good pace when we neared the summit. The trail traversed over a large rock outcropping. Without slowing, we moved across the rocks, and then suddenly, where the rock slabs canted noticeably to the right, I stepped on a patch of the mist-laden moss, and it gave way. In an instant, my feet shot out from under me, and I catapulted over the jagged edges. I sliced my left calf and landed on my feet five feet below. I opened the wound to gauge the severity and could see the round muscle fibers about an inch deep on the lateral side of my left calf. It ended near my tibia, and looked like a surgeon's scalpel had cut me. I scanned the rocks, and at eye level, I found the culprit with fresh hide and hair clinging to it. I let it bleed to self-cleanse the wound site, wrapped it with gauze, and secured it with duct tape. Then I finished the five-mile hike into Waynesboro.

I purchased butterfly bandages and Peroxide before meeting everyone at the local Deluxe Budget Motel. After getting cleaned up and butterflying my wound together, we all went out to eat, and Magoo dropped a bombshell on us.

"Guys, I'm getting off the trail."

We were all surprised and I asked, "What? Why?"

Blue Noodle nodded his head, knowing what his dad was going to say.

"Yeah, I'm missing my wife something fierce, and I need to go see her, but I don't want to miss hiking with you guys, so if anybody wants to see what southern hospitality is all about, you're more than welcome to come with us to Kentucky. You don't have to answer tonight, but if you could let me know in the morning so I know what size rental car to get, that would be great."

I knew that the brothers had to catch a flight in Georgia and would have to keep going. So, I tossed and turned all night contemplating whether to push on with Shoofly and Tree Trunk or embark on a side adventure. I had an open-ended return flight that allowed me to adjust my departure date without penalty. The decision was difficult, especially since I had hiked over four hundred miles with the brothers, and they felt like family to me.

10/09/96

Kentucky Detour

By morning, Rev was sure he wanted to go, and the lure of Southern hospitality was more than I could resist. I knew a few days rest would help my body heal, but when the brothers walked toward the trail in the rain, it was still hard for me to watch.

On the ten-hour ride to Mayfield, we swapped hardship and highlighted trail stories, along with our reasons for wanting to hike the trail.

Blue Noodle was quick to start it off when he recalled, "We went on a family vacation to Great Smoky Mountain National Park when I was about twelve years old. We parked at Clingman's Dome parking lot, and when I hopped out of the car, I saw a sign for the Appalachian Trail. Dad thought we might take a thirty-minute day hike, so he asked a Park Ranger, 'How far does the trail go?'"

"Maine," said the Park Ranger.

"Ever since then, I always thought it would be cool to hike the AT. It was a huge bonus that our life circumstances allowed it also to be a father-son trip."

I smiled, understanding fully the power of a father's influence to plant seeds and nurture his son's dreams.

We were all in agreement that the black flies of Maine were at the top of our hardship list, followed by countless days of walking in the rain.

Then Magoo chimed in, "After Stacy (Blue Noodle) asked me to join him on the hike, I trained by doing stadiums at the local school for two to three months, and I was still humbled in the hundred-mile wilderness. I was terribly overweight, and the self-doubt crept in like a black cloud, but I lost twenty-nine pounds in ten days. It left me feeling like I was slowing my son down, possibly keeping him from finishing by his target date or even finishing at all. In hindsight, I should have done the stadium workout with a weighted pack."

Stacy quickly added, "Yeah, but you did it, Dad!"

"I couldn't have done it without you picking me back up when I was down. Remember that day after leaving Carter Notch Hut, we started climbing Wildcat Mountain, and I hit the wall? I sat down on a rock and started crying, I was so disappointed in myself, and I knew I was slowing you down, but you came up to me and said, 'Don't worry about it, Dad, we're in this together."

Stacy nodded. "We were there for each other. You helped me when I was having a bad day as well."

To keep it from getting too sappy, I said, "Man, I thought you were going to tell me it was worse than when you walked ten miles to school barefoot in the snow, and it was uphill."

Rev jumped in, "It was uphill both ways."

It was easy to see it was tough on Magoo to admit his mortality, especially after being the "Man" that everybody counted on as a State Trooper. He had his right knee surgically fixed before starting the trail, and you could hear the disappointment in his voice when he told us his left knee was giving him problems off and on. It had almost forced him off the trail at the Graymoor Friary in New York. Father John was kind enough to take him to the hospital in Peekskill, where the doctors diagnosed that he had torn something in his knee. So, they gave him a knee brace and a bottle of 800mg Ibuprofen, and Father John let him stay for another five days at the friary before Magoo attempted to hike. He made it a little over three miles to Peekskill and decided that he couldn't go on. He and his son got a room, divided up their gear, and arranged for Magoo to catch the bus the next day. The next morning, his knee felt fine, and he was able to continue on for another five hundred and fifty miles to Waynesboro, Virginia.

Had that sequence of events not happened, I was sure that Rev, Kee, and I would not have been sitting in a rental car with two southern boys, heading to Kentucky to experience some Southern hospitality.

We were all in agreement that the number one highlight of our hike was the people we met along the way and how the trail had a way of humbling us and gave everyone ample time for self- reflection. Magoo (aka Gary) was the most contemplative of our bunch.

I'm not sure if his heightened musings were a result of Father Time knocking on the door, but the countless moments of trail magic they had experienced along the way had gradually eroded the distrust he had from seeing the worst in people in over twenty years of service. He'd grown accustomed to those who weren't nice. He was suspicious of everyone, especially those who were nice, thinking they wanted something in return, that is, until he hiked the trail. He was quick to share the story, which erased his suspicions and made him choose to find the good in humanity.

"My wife Jan met us in Manchester Center, Vermont, at the Zion Episcopal Church Hostel. We were walking around town when this guy, Charles Fisher, walked up and asked where we were staying. When we told him, he insisted we stay at his house instead. He opened his house to us and then left, telling us to make ourselves at home. The fridge was fully stocked. He even left credit cards on the counter, and as a retired detective, it blew my mind that someone could be so trusting with strangers. He didn't return home until we were leaving four days later."

Jan, Gary, and their dog, Rip

We all agreed there was something special about the people along the trail.

With all the stories and lively banter, it didn't feel like a ten-hour drive. It felt like I had known these guys for much longer than two weeks and when we pulled into the driveway, Gary's wife, Jan, welcomed us like family. Even Kee was welcomed by their golden retriever, Rip, and their Scottish Terrier, Mac.

10/10/96

We left Kee and Rip in the yard playing tug-o-war with a stick, and we went to Emma's Restaurant for breakfast. When we walked in, Rev (Brian) was nervous and wide-eyed. We were surrounded by a bunch of good old boys wearing bib overalls and britches (Levis).

In an effort to fit in, Brian ordered biscuits and gravy for the first time ever.

The waitress looked at Brian like he was an oddity and definitely not from these parts.

Gary quickly jumped in and salvaged the moment, "Brian, you have to have a little southern flare and swagger in your delivery if you want to blend in," he chuckled.

Brian reordered with an Oscar-worthy southern drawl and had our waitress smiling from ear to ear.

The next stop was the local barbershop, and Gary pulled us aside before we walked in. "Beware of the guy nicknamed Dubber because he'll talk till the cows come home."

Well, as luck of the draw would have it, my turn came up, and the only chair available was one in the far back corner, Dubber's. He gave me a haircut and a beard trim. He got so carried away talking that my beard all but disappeared, and I had a bald spot on my right jawline, but he was funny as all get out. Listening to his animated speech made me think he had a future as a stand-up comic. I left that shop feeling like I had just gotten a crash course on Southern linguistics.

Jan had some honey-do projects around the house that needed some attention. So, Gary and Stacy insisted that we go sightseeing in their Toyota pickup while they worked on the house. Before we left,

Gary gave Brian a camo trucker hat to help him become one with his inner redneck and then gave him some helpful hints to help him survive if he had a run-in with any of the good ol' boys.

Brian was a good sport and, without blinking, went into character, with a thick southern drawl, "I reckon I can talk my way out of anything, like, for instance, if I get in a pickle, I'll give them a crazy-eyed stare and say, I'll tell you what, if you don't hush your mouth, I reckon I'm fixin' to whoop your ass!"

We all laughed at Brian's bravado. Somebody had been soaking up the friendly barbershop banter like a sponge. Brian was a student of people.

We had just started cruising down Main Street when Brian rolled down the passenger window and started screaming like a wild man.

I was shocked. "What are you doing?"

Still in character he answered. "I'm practicing my Kentucky Wildcat call."

I pulled into the nearest fast-food restaurant, hoping the food would distract him. "Dude, people are going to think we're either drunk or crazy."

He just laughed.

After lunch, we found a pay phone and called our loved ones. I wasn't able to get through. The phone just rang and rang; nobody answered at my parents' house or my aunt's. It was tough not knowing how things were going back home. I didn't want to run up a phone bill at Gary and Jan's house, so I resolved to try again the next time I came across a pay phone.

We found our way back to the house just in time to go to Massac Kountry Kitchen in Long Oak, just outside Paducah, Kentucky. Gary wanted us to experience what Southern cuisine was all about, and on the way there, we took a driving tour of some of the most expansive and beautiful thoroughbred ranches I had ever seen. The horses that roamed those pristine pastures were magnificent.

We had an amazing seafood buffet, and we got our money's worth in true hiker fashion. Everything was fried except for the baked chicken. I couldn't get enough of the Po'boys, shrimp, and frog legs.

It is true that frog legs indeed taste like chicken. I can't tell you how nice it was to be able to eat whatever I wanted and not worry about putting on weight. It was as if I had regained the metabolism of my youth when weight gain was next to impossible.

10/11/96

We went to Emma's again for breakfast, and this time, Brian was sporting his camo trucker cap and had his laid-back game face on. Like a seasoned actor, Brian was relaxed and ordered biscuits and gravy with a side of grits and bacon. The waitress from the previous day commended him on his transition to the south side while we all chuckled at his believable performance. He was a natural, and I wondered what his future held: lawyer or actor?

Sparks Elementary

Next, we went to Jan's fifth-grade class at Sparks Elementary to give a talk and demonstration on backpacking.

Gary gave us a pep talk on the way. "This is a neat age for them because they still think things are cool, and they're not too cool to listen."

We knocked on the classroom door, and Jan opened it. "Class, we have some special guests here who are backpacking on the Appalachian Trail. Does anyone know how long the Appalachian Trail is?"

No one answered as we filed in. All eyes were glued on the four bearded men and a dog walking to the head of the class. Magoo, the official spokesperson for our group, was dressed in sweats and his Air Force Academy sweatshirt. Blue Noodle was wearing a fully loaded pack and carrying his hiking sticks. Rev was wearing his hiker's best town stop clothing. I walked in with Kee wearing her fully loaded pack.

Gary started it off. "The Appalachian Trail is two thousand one hundred and seventy miles long. Does anyone know how many states it goes through?"

Crickets, you could have heard a pin drop as Kee took it upon herself to walk the aisle between the desks to greet the kids.

I called her back to the front and held her there so Gary could continue.

Gary started again, "Let me back up here. The cool thing about hiking on a long trail is that you will eventually get a trail name. Mine is Magoo, Stacy's is Blue Noodle, Brian's is Rev, Rick's is Dr. Ducttape, and of course his faithful dog, Kiana."

He went on to talk about the fourteen states we would be walking through, the mountains we had climbed, the 100-Mile Wilderness, the animals: bears, moose, deer, rattlesnakes. We had experienced the pesky black flies of Maine, and the most important, the people and the trail magic along the way.

Blue Noodle was next. He explained how he got his trail name, and the kids loved that story.

He said, "This is my backpack, and it helps me carry everything I need to survive out in the woods."

He then pulled out his stove, water filter, first aid kit, food bag with samples of what we ate, sleeping bag, and Therma-a-Rest sleeping pad. He explained how to use the stove and water filter and what temperature the sleeping bag was rated for, and then he asked, "Has anyone ever slept on a sleeping pad before?"

One kid raised his hand.

Blue Noodle inflated the pad, then explained how it was the first layer of defense against the cold ground and was very comfortable. He laid it on the floor. "Would anyone like to try it out?"

Hands shot up everywhere.

Blue Noodle chose one eager boy to come up and lay down on the pad and Blue Noodle asked, "Is it comfortable?"

The boy nodded.

Blue Noodle reached in his pocket. "Okay, now let me put this set of keys under the pad, and let's see if you can feel them."

With a sour look on his face, the boy shook his head and then added, "But this thing stinks!"

I jumped in to deflect. "I got my trail name because I fixed a lot of things with duct tape, including my leg when I cut it on some sharp rocks."

While showing them my duct tape dressing, I noticed that the majority of the class had already shifted their attention to Kee, so I transitioned to introducing Kiana.

"Kee is half-Alaskan Malamute and half-German shepherd. She carries her food in her pack."

I could see the tension building, so I said, "She's super friendly. Would anybody like to come up and meet her?"

Every hand in the room shot up.

"All right, come on up."

They all gathered around, and I could tell Kee was in her glory when one of the kids blurted out, "Does she do any tricks?"

"Sure. Ask her to sit. Now say 'High five' while you hold your hand up like this."

To everyone's excitement, Kee reached up and slapped the kid's hand.

"Now, someone step up to her and say, 'Glad to meet you,' while you hold out your hand like you want to shake her paw."

This little girl got down on her knees, held out her hand, and said, "Glad to meet you, Kee!"

Kee put her right paw in the girl's hand, and they shook, looking into each other's eyes. It was pure magic; the excited kids started firing off questions faster than I could answer.

Back in the car, Gary commented, "That went pretty well."

I nodded. "Brother, I had no idea you were such an eloquent speaker; you may have a future in public speaking or at least figure prominently in your local Toast Masters."

"Yeah, but Kee stole that show."

Stacy and Brian agreed, and chuckling, Brian said, "Yeah, she did."

I just smiled, beaming with pride for my girl.

We got in the car, and Gary asked, "Hey, do you guys mind going to the nursing home so Stacy and I can visit my mom?"

Brian was quick to respond, "Hell no, let's go!" He let out his version of the Kentucky Wildcat scream.

Gary and Stacy turned to look at each other with wide eyes. They seemed to be asking without saying, "What was that?"

I just shook my head and laughed as Brian explained while still in character.

Heritage Manor

When we walked into the nursing home, it became apparent that Gary and Stacy were not strangers to this facility. The staff knew them on a first name basis and let him know that his mom, Jessie, could be found in the dining room. Jessie was wheelchair-bound, and Kee walked up and stood next to her. She stroked Kee's head and neck while we introduced ourselves and made small talk.

Brian and I excused ourselves so the guys could have some private time with Jessie. We were heading out the door when Kee veered off and walked across the room toward two ladies in wheelchairs who were sitting next to the farthest table.

Kee walked up to each of them, and they bent over to cuddle Kee. They both petted her as tears streamed down their cheeks. They kept their faces at Kee's level, and she gave each of them a face wash until all of their tears were gone. They were both smiling as they related fond memories of their own pets long ago. We said goodbye, and I knew Kee had just made their day.

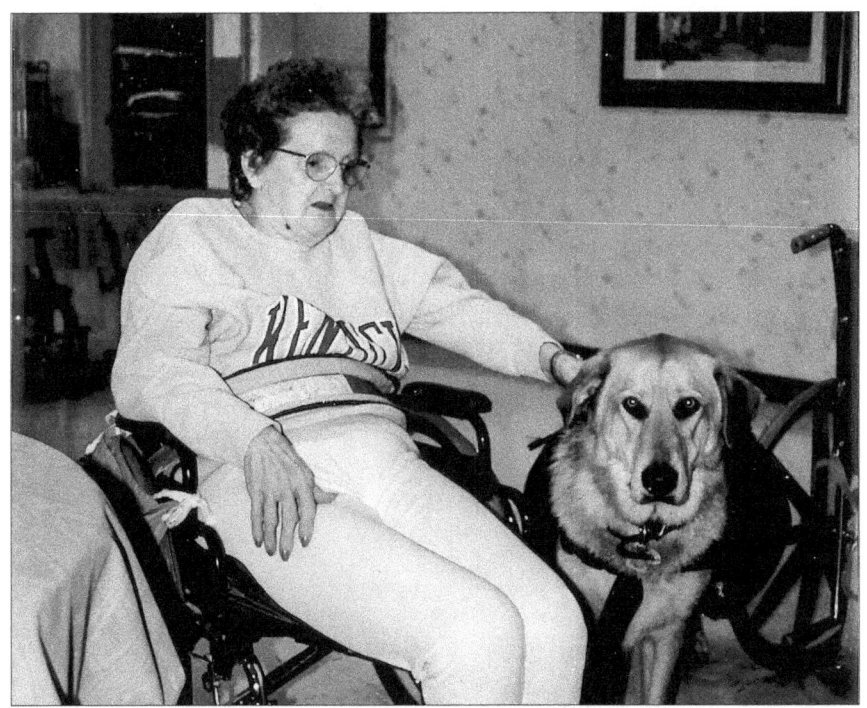

Jessie & Kee

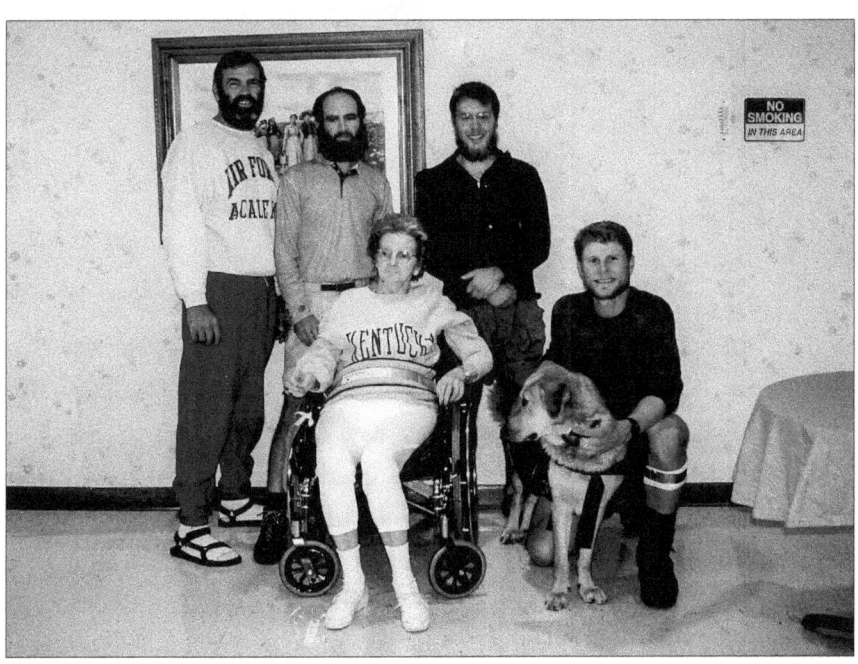

We ran into a young man named Brian in the hall, who was also wheelchair-bound from a stroke. His wrists were strapped to the arms of the chair, so he couldn't pet Kee even if he wanted to. Kee rested her head on his hand and watched him as we spoke. Brian had the most incredible, upbeat disposition I have ever witnessed from someone facing a lifetime strapped to a chair. I had Rev snap a picture of us because I never wanted to forget that amazing guy and his indomitable positive spirit.

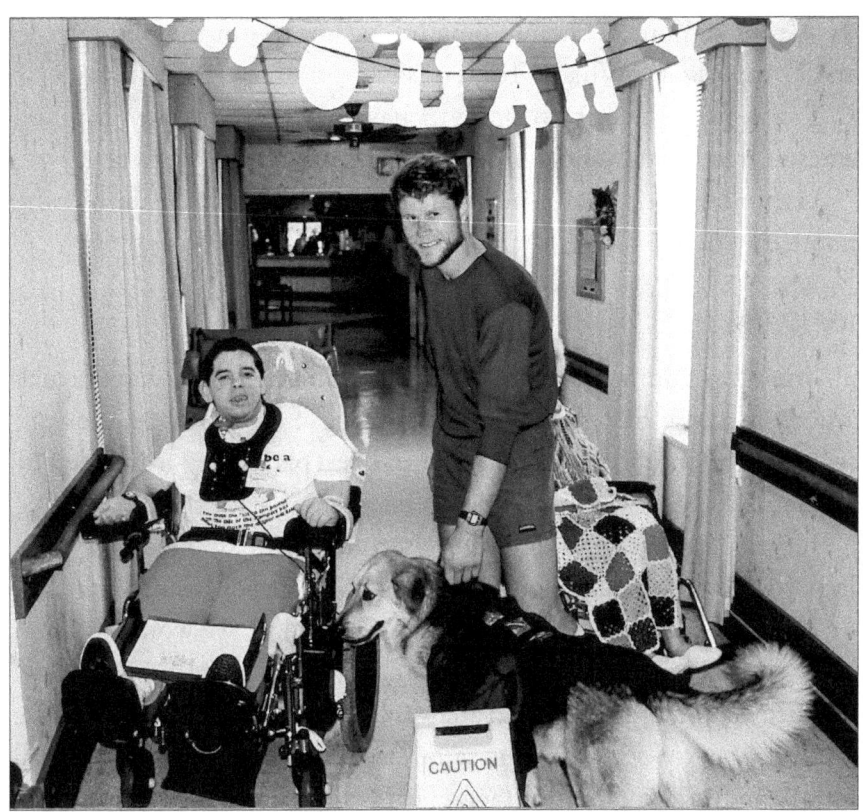

My hero-Brian

We said goodbye to Brian, and it felt like we were walking on clouds down the long hallway when a guy rolled around the far corner in his wheelchair and started yelling profanities at us and questioning why there was an expletive dog in the building. I panicked, thinking that maybe we weren't supposed to have a dog inside.

He then yelled at us, "Get the hell out of here," and then acted like he was going to unbuckle his safety belt, yelling, "I'm going to kick your ass!"

A nurse chased him around the corner, and when she saw the shocked look on our faces, she said, laughing, "Don't worry about him; he's harmless; he just has Tourette's."

We could overhear him telling the nurse, "You just can't trust that kinda man, with his beard and all."

We walked out of the building to decompress in the parking lot, and Brian asked, "What is Tourette's?"

I shrugged. "I don't know, but I have never been cussed out and emasculated in such short order in my life; that was impressive."

Gary and Stacy had a hearty laugh at our grand finale nursing home experience.

10/12/96

The boy's comment about Stacy's sleeping pad must have struck a nerve because first thing in the morning, he was out in the yard spraying and scrubbing it while Rip and Kee played tug-o-war nearby with a stick. Mac was just happy to be hanging with the big dogs.

It was Scott's, aka Bear, twenty-second birthday. He's Gary and Jan's youngest son, and I just had to ask how he got his nickname.

"Well," Gary said., "When he was a young kid, we would ask him to do something, and if he didn't want to do it, he would just growl at us. It came in pretty handy later on when he was in school because there were two Scotts with the same last name, and it was easy to call him Bear and the other kid Scott. It just kinda stuck with him ever since."

Bear was recently married and a pre-med student, waiting to see how he did on his entrance tests for med school. As busy as he was, he still made time for his family, and they were determined to make his day special. We went to Kentucky Lake on the Tennessee River and let Rip and Kee play in the water. Then we went to nearby Hematite Lake for a grilled burgers and hotdogs picnic, where Kee taught Rip how to properly Yogi from Jan.

We finished the day with homemade ice cream, and everyone sang Happy Birthday to Bear. Seeing the authentic love this family had for one another was beautiful, and I found myself missing my family even more.

Rip and Kee having fun with the Smith boys on Kentucky Lake

Celebrating Scott's B-day

10/13/96

Everything in Mayfield shut down on Sunday, so working people could attend church and be with their families. There were no restaurants or grocery stores open, and somehow, they managed not only to survive but thrive. It reminded me of the early days I worked in the grocery business. Initially, we were closed on Sundays and the major holidays of Thanksgiving, Christmas, and Easter. Then, we were told that we had to sacrifice our Sundays to remain competitive. Then corporate greed steamrolled Thanksgiving. Eventually, there was a push to stay open round the clock to maximize profits. Initially, people were upset but were willing to sacrifice for the company's well-being and to save their jobs. The greed was slow and methodical, as it pulled people away from the one day a week they had for God and family. People eventually accepted the changes as simply the cost of doing business, and then those who followed didn't think to question them because they had never known any other way. Busyness is a catalyst toward the erosion of the family unit.

We walked into The Church of Christ, Gary and Jan's parish. We were welcomed despite our hiking attire. It seemed they didn't notice how underdressed we were but were genuinely excited that we were there. The service was similar to what I had grown up with, and then they had a Bible study afterward, which I thought was a nice bonus. The people of the Bible belt take their relationship with God seriously, and I found it refreshing. I quietly hoped corporate greed didn't find its way here.

That evening, Jan's extended family gathered for a wonderful pot roast dinner. Her mom's peach cobbler was absolutely the best I had ever eaten. The perfect finale to a day filled with quality family time.

Kee working her Jedi Yogi trick on Blue Noodle

10/14/96

In anticipation of the colder weather, we were sure to encounter, we all headed to Hooper's Outdoor Center where a pair of beautiful chocolate labs greeted us. I picked up a couple of Smart Wool socks and a closed cell sleeping pad for Kiana so she wouldn't have to sleep on a cold shelter platform.

After our shopping spree, Gary said we had to go to the airport to pick up Jan's brother, Wayne. Well, Wayne happened to be a pilot working on getting his thousand hours of airtime and wanted to know if we wanted to take a ride in his aerobatic biplane, the Skybolt. Rev and I both had a turn going up, and it was exhilarating. After strapping the parachute on and squeezing into the front cockpit, Gary closed the canopy, and we were off. It hadn't been long ago when I wished I could fly like the hawk and falcon I had seen soaring with the greatest of ease while back on the trail. We made a couple of loop-to-loops, then some barrel rolls, and finished with a Hammerhead maneuver where we rocketed straight up. We pulled about four G's, climbing until we stalled and were weightless for a brief second, did a hundred- and eighty-degree pivot, before diving back down toward the earth.

Synchronicity?

10/15/96

During the ride back to the trail, Gary confided in us about an event that happened early in his career that changed the trajectory of his life. He was only twenty-three, and with five minutes left on his shift, he decided to check US 45 for drunk drivers coming from the nearby county where alcohol was legal. The bars and liquor stores were doing a booming weekend business just over the county line. So, instead of parking in his driveway, he made one more trip at one a.m. to the county line to make sure there were no drunk drivers on the road and to prevent being called out to investigate a fatal accident.

Gary explained, "There was a pursuit that ended with me head down in a road ditch and the driver sitting on my chest beating, choking, and bashing my head into the ground while his passenger was kicking my head with his sharp-toed boots. I was on the verge of passing out when I heard the driver's wife yelling from the road above."

"Get him! Get him!" she screamed.

"I had resigned myself to the inevitable, that this night, in this place would be where my life would end. All I could think about was my wife and four-year-old son that I would leave behind. My decision to make one more trip to the county line seemed to be a terrible decision, and I couldn't help but think I was going to hell for the way I had been living. Then a Good Samaritan happened on the scene with his wife, and they talked the guys down."

> "Hiking. I don't like either the word or the thing. People ought to saunter in the mountains, not hike! Do you know the origin of the word 'saunter?' It's a beautiful word. Away back in the Middle Ages, people used to go on pilgrimages to the Holy Land, and when people in the villages through which they passed asked where they were going, they would reply, 'A la Sainte Terre,' 'To the Holy Land.' And so, they became known as Sainte-terre-ers or saunterers. Now these mountains are our Holy Land, and we ought to saunter through them reverently, not 'hike' through them."
>
> – JOHN MUIR, *John of the Mountains: The Unpublished Journals of John Muir*

He ended by saying, "Seemingly small decisions can make monumental differences, both good and bad. My life would have been so different, both good and bad if I had gone to bed that night."

Stunned, I marveled that our paths had crossed, and even more, at the gift of second chances.

Emotions on the ride back to the trail were a melancholy mix that transitioned to excitement as we got closer to the trail. I couldn't help but feel that I had stepped back in time and visited the fictional Mayberry R.F.D. with all its lovable characters from the "Andy Taylor" show. Now, as thoughts turned to getting back on the trail and letting in the quiet, I knew I had the privilege of walking the trail with a modern-day version of Sheriff Taylor and his grown son.

I phoned home from the hotel, got Mom and Dad caught up on my experience in Kentucky, and had them send my next supply package to Troutville, Virginia, one hundred and twenty-eight trail miles away. I breathed easy once I found out that Grandpa was doing better than most expected and seemed to have gotten a second wind.

10/16/96

Fitness reality check

We got a late start and hiked until dark. We had a couple of big climbs today and I was reminded of how soft I had gotten every time my legs and glutes cramped. The hiking was made even more treacherous as the leaves began to fall, covering ankle-twisting rocks and holes in the trail. The dark of night closed in on us quickly, and we didn't know how much farther it was to Maupin Field Shelter, so we decided to bivy out on the trail. The five of us spread out on the trail, head to toe. Kee loved her new Z-rest sleeping pad and was quite protective of it once I laid it out for her. She softly growled if anyone pretended to commandeer her pad. Once everyone had settled in and turned their headlamps off, we all said goodnight to each other, and it felt like a scene out of the TV series the "Waltons."

Sleep came easy as I breathed in the pleasant earthy aroma of freshly disturbed soil. It soon became apparent that the nocturnal night shift also favored the trail. The mice were really active on this section of the trail. I could hear the pitter-patter of little feet as they scampered over my sleeping bag. I thought it would be a long night with all the mouse activity until I felt a sudden but silent whoosh of air pass over me. The mice disappeared as two Great Horned Owls settled into the tree above us and called back and forth to each other.

Initially, I was thankful for the reprieve in the mouse activity but was forced to reconsider our good fortune because we didn't get much sleep that night as the two owls continued to hoot the night away. Their calls awoke something in me that had me reveling in the sheer wildness of the moment. At some point in the early morning, while the sky was still pitch black, I felt something walk over me. It moved silently, and had it not been for a hoof or paw lightly dragging across my sleeping bag, I wouldn't have known it was there. In the morning light, I could not find any track on either side of the trail that would tell me who had moved under the cover of darkness with such stealth. I did see bent and broken blades of grass that were the only indicator that something had moved through the area before disappearing into the forest.

10/17/96

We awoke to an amazing view of the Tye River Valley and the looming presence of the Priest Mountain that we would never have seen had we continued on to the next shelter. I was a little stiff that morning. It's incredible how quickly you can get out of trail shape. From the sound of everyone grunting and groaning as they got ready, I was not the only one out of shape. The colors were spectacular when you followed the autumn season south. The Blue Ridge Mountains looked like they were on fire; it was a great time to be sauntering.

We crossed the Tye River on a wooden suspension bridge, and the sunlight lit up the canopy, illuminating the many hues of yellow, gold, orange, and red. It made them look like they were glowing, radiating the cheerful colors of fall, and inviting us to venture into God's creation and the classroom of silence. With the silence came acute awareness.

Kee leading the way across the Tye River

There was something very soothing about walking next to a gurgling spring that gushed from the side of a mountain. Maybe I've never really paid attention before, but the sweet sounds of this mountain music had me pondering the very essence of this life-sustaining force. Kee seemed to share my appreciation as she gulped water from the stream's edge.

There was a price to be paid for taking a week off, and as expected, those debts came due. A storm front was moving in, and as the day warmed up, the humidity climbed, eliminating the cooling effect of evaporating sweat. We couldn't take in enough fluids to ease the muscle cramps we suffered with as we climbed Priest Mountain, but we pressed on, knowing Rev's brother, Tim, would meet us at the Priest Shelter with the promise of a mountain barbeque.

My legs felt like lead going up and over the Priest. We had climbed over a mile in elevation with all the mountains we had summited for the day. In the last four miles, we had climbed about thirty-five hundred feet, making it one of the more grueling hikes on the trail. I definitely hit the wall; my legs felt like anchors, and I had just enough energy to get a fire going at the Priest Shelter when Tim appeared like a mirage coming from the south, greeting us with his deep, gravelly voice that sounded more like a grizzly growling. "Anybody hungry?"

His greeting was music to our ears and had us all smiling as he unloaded a pack full of huge Idaho Russets and marinated steaks, enough to feed a small army. We feasted on steak and potatoes grilled over an open fire until nothing was left.

Tim planned on hiking some of the trail with his brother, so by the night's end, we all agreed that Tim's trail name should be "Grizz." He was a legend for us, the kind that any reputable mountain man of old would have aspired to be.

Tim AKA Grizz sporting a fashionable duct tape fix on his glasses

Virginia | 317

10/18/96

At thirty-eight hundred and forty feet in elevation, the trees had dropped most of their leaves and afforded us a spectacular sunrise. As the sun peeked over the horizon, the sky lit up like it was on fire, backlighting the mostly naked trees before us. We all watched, lost in thought, sipping our morning coffee, captivated by the moment's glory, knowing that another storm was coming as if this were the weather report on the morning news.

On brisk mornings, it took me a little longer than everyone else to get moving down the trail. Kee was in her element on these cool mornings and insisted on playing fetch before I could strap her pack on. We played for a while, just a guy and his dog, on the side of the Priest, in the Blue Ridge Mountains. It made me smile to see her zest for life, and a part of me wanted to linger in the moment, but we had a storm brewing, so I asked Kee, "You ready to load up, girl?"

Just like other mornings, she walked over to her pack and waited for me to strap it on with the stick still in her mouth. With a distinct bounce in her gait, she carried the stick as if it were a trophy for the next mile before dropping it.

There was a sharp bite in the air as the wind picked up, and by the time we crossed over Main Top Mountain, the heavens opened up. The rain increased in intensity as the clouds closed in and thunder rolled through the gray veil, making it impossible to see anything from Spy Rock. Confederate soldiers used this dome-shaped rock to gather intel on the movements of the Union troops during the Civil War. Someday, I hoped to come back and see for myself what those men were able to see from this formation over one hundred years ago.

We had only hiked seven miles in driving rain when we came across a packed Seeley-Woodworth Shelter where six guys and a dog named Licker had settled in for the evening. Not wanting to crowd everyone, I briefly considered forging on. It was a calculated risk as the temperature dropped, and it was another ten miles to the next shelter. Fortunately, everyone graciously made room for Kee and me.

Hart, his dog Licker, and Jacob were the only section hikers brave enough to be out in this weather. No one seemed to mind having two wet dogs in the shelter, and Kee and Licker bonded immediately after their ritualistic sniffing of one another.

Jacob had been the first to arrive at the shelter and was able to do some house cleaning before we arrived. He even waxed poetically in the ledger:

"Inn of the Mouse, a family of four.
They lived in a hole, in a corner by the floor.
Momma tripped the trap first, but Junior got it the worst,
Now you only have to sleep with two more."

He even had them displayed on the firepit with their respective trap as proof. We all slept a little easier, knowing there were not as many mice scurrying through the night trying to scavenge food or something to line their winter nests.

Jacob, the poetic mouse slayer

10/19/96

No vacancies at the Seeley-Woodworth Shelter

We woke up to a mostly naked forest. The night's wind and rain had knocked off all but the most stubborn leaves, and the remnant few didn't stand much chance of making it through the day buffeted by the stiff, cold wind. But the sun shone bright and disarmed the thermal drain of the wind. It seemed like a typical Colorado autumn day, and I felt at home on the Priest.

As Grizz headed north back to his car, we continued south, and Rev turned to watch his brother disappear into the woods.

I felt his pain and said, "Hey man, it's not goodbye; it's until we meet again."

Rev nodded in agreement and added with brotherly pride, "I know. He's just such a good guy."

With that, we continued walking south, each of us lost in thought. It was obvious that moments with loved ones could be fleeting and should never be taken for granted.

Going up and over Tar Jacket Ridge and Cold Mountain, we walked over extensive bald sections with stunning views, but we were exposed to bone chilling cold winds.

By the time we had walked the fourteen miles to the US 60 intersection of the AT, Grizz was waiting for us with hot sub sandwiches and some ice beers to wash them down with. Hiking up Brown Mountain with a slight buzz helped tame my boot pain. Grizz decided to stay one more night with us at Brown Mountain Creek Shelter before heading back to school at the University of North Carolina, Chapel Hill.

10/20/96

I found it curious that while everyone else was packing up after breakfast, Magoo and Blue Noodle would disappear into the woods. They were so nonchalant about it that I didn't give it much thought and focused mostly on getting Kee and me ready for the day. Rev said goodbye to his brother and seemed a little melancholy, so Kee and I headed out so he could hike alone and sort things out.

From Brown Mountain, we could see Pedlar Reservoir nestled in the valley below, with the colors of autumn vibrantly reflecting on the edges of its mirror-like surface. With the temperatures nearing fifty degrees, it seemed to beckon us to go for a swim. We hiked down toward the dam wading through ankle-deep leaves as more floated lazily to the ground. My thoughts drifted to the golden glow of trembling Quaking Aspen trees, or more fondly known as quakies. They flanked the sides of jagged mountains in my home state. This section of the Blue Ridge Mountains, with epic mountaintop views, vibrant autumn colors, crystal clear mountain streams, waterfalls, and lakes, was stunning and reminded me of home. This exhilarating section was a true-Blue Ridge Beauty worth walking again, especially this time of the year!

Unfortunately, Lynchburg, Virginia's drinking water comes from Pedlar Reservoir. No Fishing and No Swimming signs were posted near the water's edge. So, we soaked in the aesthetic beauty of this tranquil lake and then walked on.

I had not seen another person all morning until Kee and I came around a bend in the trail, and I caught some movement off to the side. Camouflaged from head to toe, two hunters greeted us. They were super cool guys, and before I departed, I asked, "Can you guys do me a favor? I have a buddy coming up behind me who is from Massachusetts, and he's a little nervous about being south of the Mason-Dixon Line. Do you think you could ham it up and give him a reason to be nervous?"

Wide grins spread across their faces. "Oh, absolutely. That'll be fun."

I walked on, chuckling to myself, *If that doesn't snap him out of his funk from saying goodbye to his brother, I don't know what will!*

All the ups and downs were taking a toll on Magoo. His knees were bothering him, and the downhills were chewing up his little toes. He told us he had been harboring thoughts about getting off the trail and going home to his wife. Before he made the decision to throw in the towel, we tried to elevate his heel with some shims, which should pull his toes back into the wider toe box section of his boot. The fix seemed to help, but it may have been a little too late to save his hike.

After an eighteen-mile day, my left knee began to hurt from all the downhills, and Magoo was suffering when we rolled into John's Hollow Shelter. In a moment of desperate brilliance, Magoo put his boots in a nearby creek to let them soak overnight. He said he hoped that would soften his boots.

At the shelter, we caught up with Captain Morgan, a Florida chef who didn't skimp when it came to packing mouthwatering culinary delights. It was pure torture watching him heat up a meat lasagna, and he paired it with a bottle of cabernet sauvignon. The scent was heavenly, causing involuntary salivation amongst any hiker with a nose. We all had a severe case of lasagna envy, and I wished I had put more forethought into my meal planning. The Captain had pre-made all of his meals, then freeze-dried everything. He preserved the nutrient value and flavor better than any commercially dehydrated foods.

Later that evening, Rev came strolling into camp, "Ducttape!" He had a huge smile on his face. "You got me! I was walking along, totally minding my own business, lost in thought, when a couple of guys in camo stepped into the trail, blocking my passage. Then, they asked me what the password was. I freaked! I threw up both hands and told them 'Listen guys, I'm just a poor thru-hiker, I don't have any money.' They let me squirm for a bit before they started laughing. One of them said, 'Your buddy put us up to this. Have a great day.'"

Preconceived beliefs are often born of fear or anger, and this was just another reminder that we needed to look a little deeper before we judged a book by its cover.

Laughter is such good medicine.

10/21/96

I think I twisted my knee a couple of days back when I stepped on a rock hidden under a thick blanket of leaves. More hiking only aggravated it, and I had little choice but to wrap it in an Ace bandage and keep moving. If anything, this knee pain helped me empathize with Magoo. I think this last stretch would either make or break him. We could only hope that his boots would conform to his feet and ease his pain.

We hiked to the top of Bluff Mountain and were rewarded with expansive views and a very sobering concrete memorial with an embedded bronze plaque.

> **THIS IS THE EXACT SPOT, LITTLE OTTIE CLINE POWELL'S BODY WAS FOUND APRIL 5, 1891, AFTER STRAYING FROM TOWER HILL SCHOOL HOUSE NOV. 9, A DISTANCE OF 7 MILES. AGE 4 YEARS, 11 MONTHS.**

Hikers had adorned this sacred site with wildflowers, various personal effects, and a stuffed doll. After paying our respects, we walked away with new perspectives, reluctant to complain about aches and pains.

Looking down at the James River from Fuller's Rocks was breathtaking. I could only imagine what early settlers would have thought about this fertile country that spread as far as the eye could see.

The next ten miles in the James River Face Wilderness did not disappoint with its big mountains and tough climbs. As soon as we crossed the James River and started up Matt's Creek drainage, small stands of old-growth forests greeted us. There was something very regal being in the presence of these magnificent trees. These testaments to fortitude humbled me as I walked amongst them. The diverse splendor of these southern hardwoods, like chestnut oak, yellow pine, hickory, northern red oak, basswood, and tulip poplar, to name a few, needed to be experienced to fully appreciate. The fertile abundance was astounding.

When we started the walk up to the Thunder Hill Shelter, the shadows grew long. We were met by a large group coming in from the south. One of their leaders greeted us. "You guys take the shelter, and our guys will set up their tents."

"Thanks!" I noticed one of the boys had broken a support on his external frame pack. "Do you want me to fix that?"

"Yeah, that would be great."

"Awesome. Set it on the picnic table. Let's find a stick to use as splint."

We duct taped the stick to the broken upright. It probably made it stronger than before. "Thanks, mister."

"You're welcome. We're a little less formal out here on the trail; you can call me Ducttape."

While eight boys of varying ages scrambled to find the perfect flat tent site, I had an opportunity to talk with the leaders. They were working for Elk Hill, and this group of boys had earned the right to go backpacking in the woods.

"What's Elk Hill?"

"It's a nonprofit started by Buford Scott, a Richmond businessman. He donated his three-hundred-and-fifty-acre farm to help serve children in need so that they could benefit from the beauty of nature. Some of these kids have never been in the woods before."

I smiled while part of my heart melted. I gave them all high fives. "I'm so proud of you guys for giving these boys a chance before they turned to a life of crime. Keep making a difference."

The boys from Elk Hill

The magic of Duct Tape

10/22/96

We were fortunate to get to climb the Apple Orchard Mountain. At four thousand two hundred and twenty-five feet, it's the highest mountain south of Mount Moosilauke in New Hampshire. Near the summit, we walked along some unique rock formations and hiked under "The Guillotine," a huge boulder wedged fifteen feet above us between two massive, sheer rock slabs. Soon, we found ourselves traversing a windswept highland bald. These were an anomaly; they were grassy meadows found on ridgetops where trees would normally grow.

There were many theories about what caused the Balds on ridgelines, below the tree line of surrounding mountains. The most realistic was that they were cleared for grazing livestock and harvesting the grasses. While we were more exposed, the breathtaking views left us feeling like we were on top of the world. We looked down on creation, seeing its beauty from a perspective only a few had witnessed.

As we neared the Bobblets Gap Shelter, we came across the granddaddy of Black Rat snakes sunning himself. He was close to three feet long and incredibly camera-shy. He slithered off the trail and down the hill with amazing speed. I had to run to catch him and bring him back up so I could have a wide-eyed Rev snap a photo before releasing him. I had to admit this snake was rather sinister looking, but by the looks of that glossy, black constrictor, we shouldn't have any mouse issues at this shelter.

It was a warm day, and we had sucked down the last of our water with four miles left to go on a twenty-two-mile day. A cold mountain spring was flowing next to the shelter, and we drank deeply, like our lives depended on it.

The Bobblets Gap Shelter was one of the cleanest we had stayed in, and we didn't have to share it with any hungry rodents.

10/23/96

We had just finished breakfast and were loading up when a coon dog came into camp. He was wearing three different collars; each one had an antenna, and the collar with the longest antenna was for long-range tracking. He didn't seem like he quite knew what to think about Kee's pack. But he fell in love with Kee and followed us for a couple of miles. He eventually got sidetracked probably by the scent of a coon and disappeared into the forest.

Kee waiting patiently for me to break camp

Kiana getting strapped into her pack at Bobblets Gap Shelter

Kee making friends with the local Coon dog

Trying to teach old dogs new tricks

The morning air had a definite bite, and the temperature seemed to drop fast. Before long, we were walking amongst the clouds. For most of the day, visibility was, at best, one hundred feet or less. Out of necessity to stay warm, we kept moving. My gloves and rain pants were waiting for me in my Troutville maildrop, and I was looking forward to the luxury of wearing them once again.

There was a distinct disadvantage to being the first one down the trail. Besides breaking all the spider webs, I may have just sucked down a spider. I could feel its legs tickling the back of my throat as I tried to gag it back up, but it wasn't working. So, I swallowed and chased it with a swig of water, hoping my stomach acid would finish it off before it could bite me. Maybe it wasn't a poisonous spider after all. Note to self: Try not to breathe so deeply on these uphills.

Well, we tried to cross a creek with Kee in the lead. She stepped on what looked like a rock covered with a blanket of leaves but there was no bottom. She went completely under on this slow-moving section of the creek where the leaves were so thick that it looked like solid ground. She bounded to the other side, shook off, then gave me a look as if to say, "your turn, let's go!"

It took some prodding with my hiking sticks to find solid footing to cross on. I was glad she was in the lead on this one, or I would have been soaked to my waist and forced to stop and dry my clothes over a fire on that cold and blustery day.

I stopped and chatted with an elderly lady who was sipping hot tea and living at Fullhardt Knob Shelter. She had a tarp wall set up in the shelter that both gave her privacy and helped keep the heat in. She was very soft-spoken and just as sweet as could be. I asked her if she needed anything, and she politely said she didn't. She was living as simply as we were, but I still worried about her with the brunt of winter looming in the not-so-distant future. She didn't seem concerned, and I didn't know whether to think she was naïve or that this wasn't her first rodeo.

We almost ran headlong into a couple of turkeys walking in our direction. We came around a bend and suddenly, the two birds were just as startled as we were. I could have reached out and grabbed one of them when they exploded into the air. They made an incredible racket. It was impressive that such a big bird could take flight so quickly.

We had just stepped out of the woods and were prepared to walk to the post office when Ray Fisher pulled over in his truck. "You guys need a ride?"

He not only gave us a ride to the Troutville post office, but he gave me a pep talk, encouraging me to write about our adventure. "You should write these stories down, cause guys like me love to read 'em, we just can't do them anymore cause life gets in the way."

Ray waited for us to sort through our mailboxes and then gave us a ride to the Best Western Lodge, where we met up with Magoo and Blue Noodle. Initially, we had intended to get showers at the truck stop, but they were six bucks, and for ten dollars each, we could get a shower and a heated room with a TV. You would have thought we had won a million bucks.

Ray Fischer

Rev and I getting our mail drops from home

10/24/96

I found a pay phone and called a cobbler in Roanoke to see if he could make some modifications to my boots. He wasn't able to get to them any time soon, so I kept running duct tape on my feet and hoped that I would find someone in the next town stop who could fix the heel pockets and sew a donut pad over the right speed hook rivet that was ravaging my ankle bone.

My next call was to Mom and Dad. I thanked them for all the extra food items they had added, especially the beef jerky and homemade pumpkin iced cookies. The letters of encouragement from everyone back home were very uplifting. Then I asked how Grandpa was doing.

Dad said, "We just left Aunt Annie's, and he's sleeping. He's been sleeping a lot lately. Try him again on your next town stop. Love you son, hang in there."

"Love you too."

A nagging hunger implored all of us to pay the "all you can eat" Pizza Hut a visit. To eat hot food until you were full seemed almost decadent.

We finished the night watching the Yankees battle the Braves. The Yankees narrowly escaped with a 1–0 victory.

10/25/96

After a zero-day, Kee pranced around, excited to put the pack on and get going. She looked very stylish with her blaze orange vest attached to her pack. It's deer season, and I was worried that a hunter could mistake her bushy tail for that of a whitetail deer.

Rev and I ran into a couple of female day hikers doing the twelve-mile roundtrip to Tinker Cliffs. One of them asked, "Are you a thru-hiker?"

"I'm attempting a thru-hike. A lot can happen between here and Springer Mountain."

Unphased, the boldest lady smiled and approached. "Can I touch a real thru-hiker? If I didn't have so many obligations and had the time and money, I would do this in a heartbeat."

"Well, if you ever get the chance, I don't think you will regret it. Enjoy your hike. Kee! Come on, girl, we have a long way to go if we're going to be home for Christmas."

As soon as we were out of earshot, Rev said, "Ducttape, I was getting a little nervous back there."

"I think they were harmless, but yeah, it was a little awkward. I never knew hiking was such an enviable pastime."

We walked through an apple orchard when a herd of about sixteen goats caught sight of us. They surrounded us and began licking our legs as if we were walking salt blocks. My guess was that this wasn't their first nonconsensual interaction with hikers. It was almost a sensory overload to have that many tongues licking my legs.

We caught up to Magoo and Blue Noodle at Tinker Cliffs, and I got them to pose for a photo near the precarious cliff edge. My heart jumped as Magoo's new grippy boots caused him to stumble, just feet from falling to a certain death. He was able to grab a tree before doing the Tinker Cliff plunge. The far-reaching views of fertile green fields nestled at the base of tree-covered mountains that still clung to remnant fall colors were as tranquil and breathtaking as they come.

Shelters have always been first come and first served, and by the time we reached the Campbell Shelter, it was overcrowded with a group celebrating a family reunion. So, we bivouacked about fifty yards away next to a college-age couple, Bryon and Susan. Bryon was a political science major and planned to do the trail after graduating in 1998.

A few members from the reunion came over to apologize for commandeering the entire shelter and brought cookies, Kool-Aid mix, and sodas up to our site as an olive branch. The Perpetual Hiker and the Umbrella Lady left the sodas behind, with stickers indicating that they were for thru-hikers or anyone who had been on the trail for three consecutive weeks. Once again, kindness prevailed, and we all shared stories around the campfire, which only seemed to fuel Bryon and Susan's wide-eyed enthusiasm, fanning their desire for adventure. I truly hoped that our chance meeting helped encourage him to follow his dream.

10/26/96

We broke camp in a light rain, wished Bryon and Susan good luck, and were on the trail before there was any sign of life at the shelter.

By the time we reached McAfee Knob, the rain had stopped, but there was still a thin layer of gray clouds blocking the sun. We had a hazy view of the peaceful farming community nestled in the valley below. This picturesque setting had a few cows dotting the lush, green pastures adjacent to Christmas tree farms.

McAfee Knob

We were the only ones at this iconic site that looked like a massive, anvil-shaped granite rock jutting out into the skyline. It was one of the most photographed spots on the AT that captured the danger and rugged beauty of the trail in one image. Finding willing subjects for a photo shoot didn't take much arm-twisting. Of the many photos I took, my favorite was the group shot of Magoo, Blue Noodle, Rev, Kee, and I perched on the edge of McAfee Knob. Rev later titled the photo "The Wild Bunch."

We popped out of the woods to cross VA Route 311 and were met by Byron and Susan, who offered to haul off our trash and give us a ride into Catawba to get something to eat. Byron mentioned that The Homeplace Restaurant had heaping family-style meals of fried chicken, roast beef, and country ham.

McAfee Knob

The Wild Bunch-Rev, Magoo, Blue Noodle, Kee & me on McAffee Knob.
True adventurers and a better bunch of guys you would be hard pressed to find

I was game. "You got my attention at 'heaping' let's go!"

We all piled into his vehicle and headed into town only to discover that The Homeplace didn't open until 4 p.m. We settled on the Catawba General Store, where we found some amazing deli sandwiches that curbed our hungry hiker appetites.

Once again, I was humbled, this time by a young couple whose enthusiasm was contagious.

After lunch, we hiked in the rain for another seven and a half miles and opted to bivouac near a small stream about a mile before Dragon's Tooth so we could summit the next day in good weather.

Rev and I couldn't shake the thought of those heaping plates of food at The Homeplace Restaurant, so we hiked a mile back out to County Road 785, hoping to hitch a ride. Apparently, CR 785 doesn't get a lot of traffic in foul weather, and the motorists that did pass us showed no interest in picking up a couple of soaking-wet hikers. So, with tails tucked, we hiked back to camp and made dinner. My freeze-dried beef stroganoff, compliments of Mom and Dad, was tasty but not as filling as I had hoped. We were all looking forward to the AYCE Pizza Hut in Pearisburg, which was about sixty-four trail miles away.

10/27/96

Sunday morning was brisk, and while we were packing up, the father and son team disappeared into the woods. Neither Rev nor I wanted to infringe on their privacy, so we waited for a while and then decided to hike on without them, hoping to see them again sometime during the day or at the Niday Shelter eighteen miles away.

Rev and I were the first ones to the Dragon's Tooth rock formation. I'd learned that hiking the AT forces you to revert back to your childhood wonder and sense of adventure. So, unencumbered by the busyness of societal norms, we climbed that rugged crag because it was there, tempting and challenging us to find a new perspective from the summit. It was still overcast, and the views were limited, but it was still fun.

It was still morning when we came across a tightly stretched barbed wire fence. While I was fumbling with the gate, Kee walked a short distance to a section of fence that was down. She walked on the post, being careful not to step on the tacked barbed wire. She then gave me an impatient look as if to say, "Are you through messing with that gate?"

I was beginning to think she was too smart to be a dog. I swear, it's uncanny how her expressions had taken on human characteristics. Just the other day, I was distracted watching a baseball game at our hotel room when she came over and put her paw on my leg.

Dragon's Tooth

Once she had my attention, she walked over to the door, looked at it, and then at me to make sure I knew she wanted to go outside. Sometimes, I thought she got frustrated with me if I didn't feed her according to her internal clock. She would come up and sit in front of me and then sigh, exhaling enough air to cause her lips to flap. Once she had my attention, she would go over to her pack with her food and wait patiently.

Rev had been so proud of his heat exchanger, and I got to listen to his dissertation on the many benefits of owning such a unit. After his sales pitch, I felt compelled to rename his heat exchanger the "mini atom splitter" or the "portable nuclear fission reactor." Seriously, when he got off the trail, he should get into marketing.

We met an Indiana Hoosier going by the trail name Felix at the Niday Shelter. He's a good 'ole boy and a bit of a smart ass with all of his smack talk. I couldn't help but like him because he reminded me of some of the guys I used to play ball with. The feeling must have been mutual, as he'd decided to hike with us for a while and had unofficially adopted us as his trail buddies.

10/28/96

We had been climbing for almost three miles and were finally on a ridge south of Niday Shelter. As we climbed over the last rise, a huge whitetail buck exploded from the bushes not ten feet from us. The cool breeze blowing in our faces helped conceal our approach from this magnificent creature. With a snort, he whirled, and the last thing we saw was his white tail when he charged into the forest, disappearing within seconds like a ghost.

We walked on the spine of Sinking Mountain on some huge rock slabs that were tilted just enough to be very slippery with all the rain we'd had. Every one of us had, at some point, slipped and slid down the rock face, only to be ensnared by the waiting briars. Rev had the most graceful slide. He was able to stay upright and ski down the rock, narrowly missing a briar patch. It was an excellent recovery, especially for a guy with a history of going down hard. One look at his bent trekking poles would tell the story of how many times they had been body slammed. Once we were off the ridge, the hazards continued as we waded through ankle-deep leaves. Blue Noodle hooked a hidden root with his boot. He pitched headfirst, downhill and into the leaves off the side of the trail. Hiking poles went everywhere. He came up smiling, and I would have given him a perfect ten for form if he had come up with a mouthful of leaves.

We walked through some of the most incredible stands of

Mountain Laurel. I could only imagine how beautiful this stretch would be when they bloomed. They are native evergreen shrubs, but some of these were at least fifteen feet tall, the size of most trees. The fertile diversity of these eastern hardwoods continued to impress me.

Before calling it a day at War Spur Shelter, I went to the creek to filter water. I came across a small copperhead snake hiding in the rocks and leaves. Thankfully, it was cool enough to hinder his movement. With all the cold weather we had been having, I was a little surprised to be bombarded by a swarm of diehard mosquitoes.

10/29/96

In the morning, I woke up to what looked like a forest fire on the eastern horizon. The flaming reds, yellows, and oranges were low on the skyline, backlighting the dark, naked trees of the forest. I was almost finished with breakfast before a fiery orb peeked above where sky meets earth. I never tire of seeing those spectacular sunrises in all their grandeur. With the morning light, I spied a War Spur neighbor hanging from the tall grass beside the sleeping platform. It was a giant black and yellow spider, the likes of which I had never seen. Magoo was quick to point out that they were harmless, and their bites weren't any worse than a bee's sting.

"Good to know and with the cooling weather, we should probably be a little more diligent about checking our boots before we put them on in the morning."

I had a big push to get to Rice Field Shelter, 24.4 miles away. I wanted to be at the cobbler in Pearisburg the following day before he closed at noon.

When I left the Mountain Lake Wilderness Area, I almost stumbled upon a turkey hunter sitting on the side of the trail about a half mile north of Bailey Gap Shelter. He was a good old boy dressed in overalls, a Levi's shirt, and an old pair of well-worn boots.

"How's the hunting?"

Obviously surprised to see someone else in the woods, he stood up and spit a wad of tobacco on the trail. "Where are you coming from?"

"Well, I've been hiking from Maine."

He pushed his camouflage hat back, gave me an incredulous look, and said, "That's a long way. I hiked about fifty miles of the AT when I was in the Boy Scouts, and I had a homemade pack that wore a big ol' sore on my back. I had enough of that, but I still like to get out here and go hunting." He spit one more time.

> "Many men go fishing all of their lives without knowing that it is not fish they are after."
> – HENRY DAVID THOREAU

"Well, I'll let you get back to it, but so that you know, another four guys will be coming down the trail shortly. Have a great day."

It turned out to be a beautiful day. The sun was shining, and the sky was blue. Kee and I were walking along the calming waters of Stony Creek, which was a beautiful, crystal-clear trout stream. Kee was trotting ahead of me while I walked and tried to count the fish swimming in the slack water. I sure wished I had my fishing pole.

Suddenly, Kee disappeared.

Somebody had laid some logs across a washed-out section of the trail, and all the leaf coverage made it look like a solid bridge. She fell through the gaps but popped right back out, hardly missing a stride.

I yelled at her, "That a girl. Good job, Kee!" Wagging her tail, she waited for me on the other side. She is so athletic; nothing fazed that girl. I probably would have broken my leg.

We entered Peter's Mountain Wilderness in the Jefferson National Park. I took some extra time to photograph a magnificent sunset, trying to steady my shot between gusts of wind. We drained the last of our water a couple of hours before arriving at the Rice Field Shelter, just as twilight faded to dark. I changed the batteries on my light, grabbed my water bottles, and headed down a blue-blazed side trail, where a spring was located about one third of a mile away. When it felt like I should have been near the spring, I slowed my pace to listen for running water.

Nothing.

So, I kept going downhill until I came across a power line clear-cut. I could smell pizza wafting up from the town somewhere below.

As tempting as it was to follow those glorious odors, I turned around and headed back up the trail. I hadn't gone twenty paces when the bulb on my light blew out. It was so dark; I couldn't have changed the bulb even if I had a spare. I let my eyes adjust to the darkness and followed the trail back up. I came across a turnoff with a very faint blaze on a tree. I immediately thought I had found the trail to the spring, so I followed it, and continued until it eventually petered out.

Clouds were moving in, and the night was turning black as coal, especially in that dense section of the forest. I couldn't find the trail I had been following. So, I told Kee, "Girl, I don't think we'll find that water tonight. We better get back to the shelter before it gets much colder."

I knew the shelter and the AT were somewhere above us; so, we started bushwacking. I eventually cut a faint fire road that I followed until I could see a silhouette of the privy and the shelter nearby. I fed Kee, as relief washed over me, knowing it would have been a miserable night if we had not found the shelter. She sure makes that dog food sound tasty as she gulped it down.

Rice Field Shelter

With the aid of a Bic lighter from my cooking kit, I cleaned up the best I could with my emergency stash of towelettes. I set my Therma Rest sleeping pad next to Kee's and slipped into the warming confines of my North Face sleeping bag, then took my contacts out.

"Good night, Kee. I'll find water in the morning."

10/30/96

I woke up with my tongue sticking to the roof of my mouth. It was the worst case of cotton mouth I had ever experienced, and that's saying a lot, having grown up in the desert around Phoenix. It was imperative that I found water soon, but I had to wait for the morning light before I started my search. I lay there waiting, listening to Kee snore, and I realized my legs hurt. When I checked them, they looked like I had been in a catfight during the night. With the adrenaline surging through my body while bushwhacking, I hadn't even noticed they were badly scratched and torn.

The dark of night began to give way to shades of gray. I noticed some dark images slowly moving in the meadow in front of us. Kee was awake now, and she and I watched as the images morphed into a herd of deer calmly grazing, oblivious to our presence.

Kee couldn't take being a casual observer. She launched from our sleeping platform and hit the ground running.

"Kee! Stop!"

She did, and we watched them prance across the meadow with their tails held high, until they disappeared into the woods.

I laced up my boots. "Good girl. Now, let's go find that water."

Everything was so damp, and with the growing light, I discovered why. I had been sleeping in a cloud all night. It was starting to drizzle as we headed down the blue-blazed trail. I found the spring; it wasn't much more than a trickle. I couldn't even hear it. I had to dig a hole in the silted spring to create a reservoir from which to filter. Kee drank her fill as I mixed powdered Gatorade in my first bottle and drank deeply, savoring the cool refreshment like never before. Each gulp lifted my spirits, and gratitude washed over me as my energy level rose.

Back at the shelter, as I packed the last of my gear, the wind picked up, and the temperature dropped. I needed to hustle and get off that exposed ridge. I leaned into the wind as I walked and came across two log poles in the shape of a rudimentary cross, lashed together with rope. It was planted in the ground overlooking the valley below. That wretched cross, a reminder of humanity's worst day culminating in treachery, brutality, and what man was capable of. Simultaneously, a lesson in selfless love.

Approaching the Cross

When I got close, the details were barely discernable against the gray cloudy background. I walked past it, following the trail down toward the valley. I turned to admire that old rustic cross and was shocked, as a beam of light suddenly pierced through the clouds illuminating it. Amazed, I fumbled with my camera, trying to capture the photo before it disappeared. Some would rationalize that it was a mere coincidence. Still, the probability of having one shaft of light, as far as the eye could see in every direction, break through the clouds and illuminate only that cross at the exact moment that I happened to be there, and turned to get a second look, seemed astronomical, if not improbable.

Looking back at that Rugged Cross

In awe, I gave thanks to whoever had gone out of their way to put that beacon of hope on this ridge. I walked down the trail a couple of hundred yards and looked back up the hill one last time to see that rugged cross barely discernable in the haze of the clouds. I took one more panoramic photo and couldn't help but feel blessed to be in this place and on this journey. It felt like the eyes of my heart were opening.

> "Not to us, O Lord, be the glory, but to your name."
> ~ Psalm 115 (NKJV)

It was mid-morning when we hiked lower into the valley, and it seemed the sun was finally going to make an appearance from behind the gray curtain. The skies began to clear halfway down the ridge, and the shining sun felt magical on my face.

Things were looking up. Pearisburg was a quaint little town nestled in the sprawling farming valley below. I was making good time and hoped to arrive at Mutter's Shoe Repair before he closed for the day.

Kee and I crossed the bridge over the New River, which was supposedly the second-oldest river in the world. The Nile holds claim to being the oldest river. Midway across the bridge, I was dismayed to find a wayward beaver who had met his demise and was as flat as his paddle tail. I wondered what had provoked him to wander halfway across the bridge before he met his untimely fate. Most people don't give it much thought, but for me, I felt it's pain. It seemed to be such a tragic and unnecessary loss.

We arrived at the cobbler's with plenty of time to spare. Mr. Mutter, a kind and elderly gentleman, promised he would have my boots ready for me by the next morning.

Mr. Mutter, my hero!

I stopped at the AYCE (all you can eat) Pizza Hut lunch buffet before meeting with the guys at the Rendezvous Motel. It was incredible how preeminent the thought of food, driven by incessant hunger, dominates life on the trail.

10/31/96

The staff at the Rendezvous were super friendly and even went out of their way to lend us their van so we could finish all our running around.

True to his word, Mr. Mutter repaired my boots as I had requested. He sewed some extra padding in the heel pockets, to stabilize that part of my foot. He even put a padded donut over the speed lace rivet. When I put those boots on, it felt like I had a custom fit. He even went the extra mile and waterproofed them as well. I couldn't even imagine what it's going to be like to walk without constant pain.

A lady in the post office, at our next stop, gave Magoo and Blue Noodle ten dollars to buy lunch.

"I'm envious of your hike," she said. "My husband won't let me do a thru-hike."

Next, we went to the hardware store for more stove fuel and a headlamp. The grocery store was our next-to-last stop, and I got enough supplies to get me another ninety miles down the trail. Finally, we made it to Pizza Hut for their $3.99 lunch buffet. Four hungry hikers were like locusts at an all-you-can-eat establishment. I had two heaping plates of salad, one and a half large pizzas, a large bowl of peaches, a large bowl of pears, and a bowl of chocolate pudding. While this might seem gluttonous, it felt like we were only beginning to fill the tank. I think the manager was also shocked at how ravenous we were; he and his staff scrambled to keep pizzas coming and fill the salad bar for the lunch rush hour. Our waitress, Rose, was the sweetest lady who didn't seem fazed by our hunger. If anything, she made it her mission to ensure we had our fill. As we were getting ready to leave, she gave us a box of matches with an image of a local natural bridge and said, "If you ever get back this way, that bridge is must-see."

We thanked her, and on our way out, I noticed the manager give an accentuated sigh of relief.

Still a little hungry, Rev and I headed to Dairy Queen while Magoo and Blue Noodle went to the motel to pack. We both had a banana split and shared a dozen Dilly bars. On our way back to the motel, we stopped at the grocery store and bought three Ben & Jerry's pints.

I intended to eat one and pack the other for an after-dinner snack, but none made it back to the motel.

It was hard to leave the friendly hospitality of that town, especially when the AT was the crucible that jolted you back into reality, refining through hardship and toil. The struggle began on the first climb out of town, where blood needed for muscles was busy contending with a full stomach. With our late departure, we only made it eight miles to Doc's Knob Shelter.

11/01/96

We woke up to a cold rain. There wasn't much of a breeze, and this storm appeared to be a slow-moving soaker. We walked in silence. Magoo and Blue Noodle led us into the storm. Rev walked with a methodical determination ahead of me, and Kee and I took up the rear. Kee followed on my heels; she seemed reluctant to lead. We walked for hours before stopping for a mid-morning snack. I dropped my pack, and when Kee approached, her pack was missing.

For hours, we backtracked, searching the underbrush on both sides of the trail to no avail. We were getting hypothermic, and I had to call off the search. Frustrated, I now knew what it must be like to have kids. Sure, I felt frustration and disappointment because she lost her pack, but my love for that dog outweighed any potential delays or the price of a new pack.

Despite the rain threatening to turn to snow, none of us wanted to stay at the Wapiti Shelter, where Randall Lee Smith killed two social workers in 1981. It felt like sacred ground, so we paid our respects to those who had been slain and forged on. We were completely oblivious that Randall had been released thirty-five days earlier on September 26 for good behavior, after only serving fifteen years of a thirty-year sentence.

Getting to Trent's Grocery on State Highway 606 was a cold, wet slog. We walked into the store and were hit with the tantalizing smells of grilled foods. The lure of hot food was more than we could take. Like moths drawn to a flame, we made our way over to the deli and placed our orders. The owners, Jim and Sherry Miller, welcomed us.

Warming up with Jim and Sherry

Sherry told us, "You guys stay inside as long as you need to thaw out. Enjoy your meal."

While waiting for our food to be prepared, I bought a twenty-pound bag of dog food and fed Kiana, who was waiting patiently outside.

We sat down in the dining area next to a bunch of locals and listened to a hunting highlight reel of boastful stories and possible lies while we ate. Some of them spoke so fast in that southern slang that it was hard for me to understand. It was as if they were talking in code or another language altogether. What I could decipher was that everyone had gotten their turkeys, and they were excitedly talking about the sighting of a monster buck down in a nearby "holler." That deer's ability to elude and disappear into thin air held legendary status for the men in that room.

A state trooper walked in, grabbed a cup of coffee, and joined the roundtable discussion. "I sure hope crow season is opening soon." Then added with an air of frustration, "A bunch of crows pecked my baby ducks to death, and the momma duck flew off without protecting them."

Before anyone could offer a consoling comment, a truck pulled into the parking lot with its horn blaring, and everyone filed outside to see what all the ruckus was about. Three guys in Camo jumped out of the cab and waved everyone over to look at what was in the truck bed. There were three turkeys, all were fine specimens, but the largest was sporting a ten-inch beard and two-inch spurs on the inside of its legs just above its feet. They were sharp enough to do serious damage.

While everyone congratulated the successful hunters, I slipped away to make several phone calls while Rev disappeared into the store. My first call was to Jandd Mountaineering to order another pack for Kiana and arrange to have it shipped sixty-three trail miles away to Atkins, Virginia. While on the phone, I couldn't shake the feeling that I was being watched. I turned around to see a tan van full of Mennonite women turn their heads forward in unison, all except one brazen soul, who flashed a smile and waved. I smiled and waved back; thoughts of converting to the Mennonite religion briefly flashed through my mind.

My next call was to check on my grandpa, only to find he was sleeping peacefully, so I asked my aunt to give him a hug for me when he woke.

Rev emerged confidently from the store, wearing a blaze orange vest that complimented his swash-buckling pirate ensemble.

Hunters stopping for fuel and to swap stories

The evening shadows were getting long, so we camped in the field adjacent to the store. We were beside the RV campers and between the fresh cow pies. I pulled an old rusty gun barrel from the ground where I set my tent. It wasn't the most idyllic site to hang our hats for the night, but for tired hikers, it worked perfectly.

11/02/96

We broke camp and were waiting at the front door for the store to open by seven a.m. I washed three ham, egg, and biscuit sandwiches down with a cup of coffee and grabbed a couple of Danish pastries for the road, but they didn't make it past the end of the parking lot.

Kee was officially slack packing this section without her pack. I had ten pounds of her food in my pack, and Rev was kind enough to take the remaining five pounds.

Sounds of shotgun blasts surrounded us as we ducked into the forest, on the trail once again. It sounded like a miniature war going on around us. The first AT sign we saw had suffered a close-range peppering of buckshot. I'd been a hunter my whole life, and seeing the wanton disregard for property dismayed me. Where was the challenge? There's no skill needed to shoot a sign.

Blue Noodle & Magoo at Kimberling Creek

The hunting activity calmed down by the middle of the day, and we made it seventeen miles without ever seeing a hunter until we camped along Kimberling Creek near VA-612. In a pullout next to the backcountry road were a couple of coon hunters stepping out of their camp trailer to get their dogs ready for the night hunt. All of their dogs had long-range GPS tracking collars with a range of ten miles.

I walked over to their camp. I met John and Jesse and after brief introductions, I said, "I've been hunting all my life, and I can't say I know anything about coon hunting."

"Thar ain't nothing to it, jest gotta have some good dawgs," said John.

His buddy Jesse added, "These egg-eating coons will put a hurt on wild turkeys. They been cleaning out my chickens too."

"We're fixin' to put these dawgs in the woods if you want to stick around for a bit. It shouldn't be long before they're on to a coon."

"Sure, I'd love to see how your dogs' work."

"We'll run them over into the next holler so as not to disturb you boys tonight."

"I appreciate that."

"Cut 'em, Cut 'em loose, Jess!"

We listened intently as the dogs ran into the woods, searching for something worth hunting.

It wasn't ten minutes before Jesse exclaimed, "That dog struck!"

With that, they grabbed their 22-caliber rifles and disappeared into the woods in the direction of their baying hounds. Their headlamps bobbed and weaved as they worked their way up the ridge and dropped out of sight.

Back at camp, we were all cooking dinner around the campfire. Suddenly, Kee jumped up and began barking at the darkness. I was startled because that was the first time I had ever heard Kee bark. I turned in the direction she was looking and saw a guy with a gun standing next to a tree, where our circle of light faded to dark.

Busted, he stepped forward into the light, stammering, "I, I, I just wanted to see if you were skinning out a deer."

I grabbed Kee and yelled over her barking, "It's not a good idea to sneak into a camp unannounced, especially during hunting season."

He apologized. "I, I, I, was just out squirrel hunting, and I saw your fire, so, so, so, I thought I'd come on over and see if you were skinning out a deer…"

He was obviously nervous and kept repeating himself while trying to tell us his life story. There was something off about him as Kee never took her eyes off him, and the fur on the back of her neck didn't relax until he walked away.

11/03/96

I had ice crystals on the inside of my rainfly in the morning. I don't know how cold it got during the night, but all my water bottles and my water filter were frozen. My toothpaste was solid, and my boots were blocks of ice. All the mountain laurel leaves were wilted as the night's blitzkrieg frost overwhelmed the resilient evergreen.

After breaking camp, Magoo and Blue Noodle disappeared into the woods, so Rev and I walked over to the coon hunter's camp to see how they did while Kee polished off her breakfast.

They had gotten a couple more coons that night and had them displayed, along with the previous night's bounty, on the hood of their truck and brush guard. John and Jesse were looking a little tired, so I snapped a picture of them posing with their raccoons, then Rev and I thanked them for being the most courteous coon hunters we had ever met.

The previous day's sweat-soaked back pads on our packs were like blocks of ice. It felt like we were strapping on rudimentary cryonic therapy packs to aid in the recovery of sore muscles. According to research, cold plunging increases the concentration of dopamine, which can lead to a sense of well-being and improved moods. That being said, the initial experience, combined with freezing temperatures, made for an uncomfortable start to our day. The heat from our effort softened both packs and boots within an hour.

As we neared Jenkins Shelter, we could hear the sweet sound of flute music coming from inside. To our surprise, Mary was a lone northbound hiker who had gotten a late start on the trail and was going to go as far as the weather permitted. After brief introductions, I asked her if she knew how to play "Amazing Grace." Without hesitating, she played a beautiful rendition suitable for a Sunday evening service in the mountains of Appalachia.

John and Jesse after hunting all night

11/04/96

The bite of winter was getting colder every day. While Kee was unphased, I worried that winter was coming with a vengeance. As we packed for the day, apprehension was apparent on Mary's face. Then, as we were ready to go our separate ways, she asked, "Do you guys mind if I hike with you?"

We all felt that was the safest option for her and unanimously gave her the trail name, "Wrong Way."

We ran into our first hunter on his way into his deer stand. Kee was the first to spot him sneaking along in the morning shadows of the trail, and she alerted us with another round of uncharacteristic barking. Embarrassed that we may have blown his morning hunt, I apologized and wished him luck before he disappeared into the forest.

We stopped and got water at the Chestnut Knob Shelter Spring. The view from the shelter toward Burke's Garden was breathtaking. Burke's Garden was a stunning farming valley that looked like it was carved out of a mountaintop and had earned the name "God's Thumbprint." It was easy to see the artist in the artwork. This was one of those vistas that left me smiling with gratitude.

We were hiking on a bald along an incredible ridge just south of Chestnut Knob, and the three hundred-and sixty-degree views of the rugged mountains from which we had come and where we were heading left me in awe at the vast distance we still needed to travel along the spine of the Appalachians.

Coming down off the Grassy Balds, we ran into a skunk. While it wasn't the first one we had come across, it was the first skunk that refused to get off the trail as we approached. Kee was behind me and tried to pass by to play with that smelly cat. I grabbed Kee by the collar as she brushed past, narrowly averting a catastrophe. The skunk started getting nervous and began stomping its hind feet and turned around with its tail raised as a last warning. Kee, Rev, and I cautiously backed out of the potential spray zone before the skunk jumped into the weeds adjacent to the trail. We gave it a wide birth in case it was waiting in ambush.

The guys decided to camp near a stream, and I pushed on another three miles to the Knot Maul Shelter to set myself up for a leisurely fourteen-mile day to the Atkins Post Office before they closed. I could only hope that Kiana's pack would be waiting for us. After saying goodbye to everyone, Kee and I were walking along a small feeder stream to Lick Creek when a kingfisher flew by in a hurry. He suddenly stopped, hovered momentarily, dove into the water, and reappeared with a small fish. He flew with astonishing speed down the river and disappeared around the bend with amazing agility. I'd never seen a kingfisher before, and seeing one in action was impressive.

Hiking in the "void" between hiking groups can be exhilarating, liberating, and unsettling at the same time. Hiking solo allows you to focus on moving through the woods with intent. Heightened senses, tuned in to the harmonious sounds of nature and the concentric circles of activity, can alert the listener to something amiss by the excited cries of a bird, the chastising chatter of a squirrel, or the sudden snort of a startled deer.

Listening could be like reading a book, where the struggle for survival was fraught with peril from predators who reigned supreme. That stark cycle of life becomes a reality when you hear a distressed cry become muffled and then suddenly silenced. Even though I rejoiced in the submersive experience of hiking alone, part of me missed the camaraderie of hiking with the guys. It would take a monumental effort to catch up with Shoofly and Tree Trunk, who were about a week ahead of me. While I loved challenging myself, I was unwilling to miss out on the beauty that seemed to abound around every bend in the trail because of my haste. I think we are hardwired to be communal beings, and I found myself wanting to postpone my departure flight so that I could share the magic of the trail as it unfolded.

Shortly before the Knot Maul Shelter, I climbed a five-hundred-foot ridge just in time to see a fantastic sunset. As an orange ball of fire settled onto the horizon, it backlit the wispy clouds overhead, illuminating them with enough color and depth that they took on the shape of sand dunes in the sky. Mere mortals would be hard-pressed to capture such beauty on canvas.

We made it nineteen miles to Knot Maul Shelter. The shelter got its name from the practice of early pioneers utilizing the dense tree knots or burls in the area to make mauls or hammers. It's interesting that different environmental stresses on a tree force it to grow stronger appendages, the same way adversity only makes us stronger.

Just when I thought Kee and I had the shelter all to ourselves, a hunter walked up with a duct tape patch on his jacket that made me smile, prompting me to comment, "I can see you are a believer in duct tape."

He laughed, and we talked about the many uses of duct tape. Mark Smith was a local from Bluefield, Virginia. He was the epitome of a mountain man. He grew up exploring these mountains, and hunting was second nature to him. It felt like I was talking with a modern-day Daniel Boone, and a part of me was envious that he was able to roam at a very early age in one of the most magical places in America.

11/05/96

Kee and I left Mark at the shelter and were hiking along a ridge as the sun peeked over the horizon, illuminating the surrounding mountaintops as far as the eye could see. I found myself singing without a care in the world John Denver's "Country Roads."

"Almost heaven, West Virginia

Blue Ridge Mountains, Shenandoah River"

Where it seemed life reverted to a simpler existence. I have always loved John Denver's music and to walk through these ancient mountains in Virginia, only brought his song to life.

For the first time, I understood the meaning of those lyrics with my heart.

Kee and I passed the O'Lystery Community Pavilion Area, a great place to stop for a picnic if you were driving through the area. We made a quick detour to fill up my water bottles from the spigot at Mr. Bruce's house. The water had a distinct sulfur taste, and my system protested the incursion. I burped eggs for miles. The only thing that made the rotten egg taste palatable was that it was flavored with the taste of Snickers.

We climbed up Big Walker Mountain, and it looked like someone had gotten a deer up above and had been dragging it downhill. With all the tufts of fur left on the jagged rocks of the trail, I would be

Kiana without her pack, waiting patiently at Knot Maul Shelter

surprised if there was anything left to skin. I had to keep a vigilant eye out for the gut pile, so Kee wasn't tempted to roll in it or grab a quick snack. We never found it, but Kee found a blood-covered acorn and trotted off with her prized possession. She tried to keep it out of sight like a kid who had just been caught sneaking from the cookie jar.

When we dropped down off the ridge, we walked into a verdant valley toward a couple of farms below, complete with barns and silos, surrounded by the Blue Ridge Mountains. It felt like we were walking into a postcard with the sound of cows mooing. Those farmers had the most pristine pastoral setting with a gurgling brook running through their fields. I marveled at their good fortune for having found such an idyllic property. My daydreaming about owning such a beautiful property someday was shattered when Kee proudly trotted by with something sticking out of her mouth.

"Hey, what do you have in your mouth?"

She looked at me and then sped up.

"Stop!" I said firmly. "Donde vas?" Sandrine had always spoken Spanish or French to Kee, and Kee quickly looked at me as if she were surprised. "Drop it!"

She dropped it and stood over it like it was a prized possession. It was a stiff, rotten piece of deer hide that I could smell before I got to her. "Leave it. Don't even think about licking me."

She trotted off with a smirk as if she understood everything I had said.

I stopped at the Village Motel in Rural Retreat, Virginia, to get my mail drop. By the time I sorted through it and got Kee's pack fitted to her, the guys showed up. It didn't take much arm-twisting to convince me to share a room with them. The lure of running hot water, aka a shower, was more tempting than I could stand.

11/06/96

We started early in the morning, so I couldn't call home and thank everyone for the birthday wishes. Bless her heart; Mom did what Moms do and snuck some beef jerky and dried fruit into my prepackaged mailbox.

> "It is only with the heart that one can see rightly, what is essential is invisible to the eye."
>
> – ANTONE DE SAINT-EXUPÉRY, *The Little Prince*

We hiked about three miles before we came across a pay phone near the one-room schoolhouse of The Settlers Museum. It was still too early to make a call out west, so we took a self-guided tour of the 1890 farm. The farmhouse wasn't open, so we settled for peeking in through the windows. Nearby, the 1894

Lindamood School House was unlocked. So, we got some pictures of what it might have been like back in the day when a teacher would teach eighteen to twenty-five students, grades 1-7, for $30 a month. Their only heat was from a mandatory wood stove in the center of the room. Rev and Kee waited on the front deck of the schoolhouse while I made the hardest phone call of my life.

Lindamood School House

I called Mom and Dad to thank them for the birthday wishes and the extra goodies. After the usual birthday pleasantries, we spoke briefly about the trail and where to send the next mail drop. Then, with a tightness in my chest, I asked about what was weighing heavy on all our minds, "How's Grandpa?"

Dad grew unusually quiet as he struggled for words.

Mom jumped in. "Son, Grandpa is bedridden and isn't long for this world."

My dad's voice was riddled with emotion. "Yeah, I asked him last week who he was most anxious to see, and he said his mom. You can try calling him, but he's been sleeping for days without waking."

It was hard for me to hear the pain in my parents' voices, but to feel my dad's heart breaking almost dropped me to my knees. I told them I loved them, then hung up, took a deep breath, and called my Aunt Annie.

"Hello?"

"Aunt Annie, this is Rick. How are you holding up?"

"We're hanging in there."

I wasn't surprised by her comment. She was a born caregiver, one of the most selfless human beings I'd ever known.

"How's Grandpa?"

"I'll go check."

I could hear another phone being picked up.

Aunt Annie said, "Rick, he's awake! It's almost as if he's been waiting for your call. Here he is."

"Grandpa?"

"Yes."

"Hey, this is Rick. I'm out on the Appalachian Trail and just wanted to tell you how much I love you."

"I love you." His voice cracked, and I heard him sniffle. His big heart was breaking as we both knew this was goodbye. He struggled for air as he tried to say something else, then went into a coughing death rattle that shook me to the core. After what seemed like an eternity, he regained his composure.

Panicked that I was running out of time, I blurted, "Grandpa, thank you for being my number one fan and showing up to all my football and basketball games. Thanks for taking us kids out fishing when no one else wanted to. We sure had some good times out on your boat."

His last words were barely audible, "I'm proud…finish…" He began choking again, and my Aunt Annie got back on the phone.

I had so much more I wanted to tell him, but somehow, I think he knew how honored I was to be his grandson. "Tell him I'm going to finish this trail in his honor. Please give him and Grandma a hug for me and tell them I love them."

"Will do, Rick. Love you! Bye."

Those were the last words I ever heard him speak. Colon cancer snatched an amazing man from this world; he breathed his last the very next morning.

It's a little ironic that, of all days, the sun was shining, and we were hiking in shorts and t-shirts. The sun's rays warmed my face as I sauntered, reflecting on all the good times we'd had at Grandma and Grandpa's house over the years. Countless Sundays, Thanksgiving, Christmas, and Easter gatherings were almost always at their house, surrounded by the buzz of conversations, cousins playing, and hearty laughter that frequently filled the air and blended with the aroma of Grandma's mouthwatering creations.

Despite the relative chaos of a big family, there was always an overwhelming sense of love and belonging. Grandpa would always take time to show those interested in what he was working on in his shop. The guy could fix anything. His ingenuity was born out of necessity, honed by depression era frugality.

On Sunday evenings, we would all pile into the TV room and watch the latest episode of "Mutual of Omaha's Wild Kingdom," followed by a Disney show. It never ceased to amaze me to see so many people packed into that room. Grandpa would be in the center of it all, with a couple of the youngest grandkids snuggled in his arms, watching his favorite show with a twinkle in his eye. He was the richest old guy I'd ever known.

I was emotionally drained, and hiking was extremely difficult. My legs felt like lead. At times, I didn't think I could go any farther. As I pushed on, it felt like my legs were no longer attached, and I was floating along the trail. I wrestled with pangs of guilt for not being there with Grandpa. Thoughts crept into my mind about going home to be with family, but then I remembered my promise. I forged on in silence, fighting my inner demons. Rev honored my need for silence and walked quietly behind me with an empathy born of his own loss. His grandma had died four days before the start of his AT adventure. I wouldn't have known he was there if it wasn't for the rustling leaves behind me. Anguish flowed freely from my eyes as I struggled with mortality and the crushing pain of loss.

I don't remember much about our climbs over Glade Mountain and Brushy Mountain other than it was a struggle to keep moving. We dropped down from the mountains and walked up to the Mount Rodgers National Recreation Area (NRA) headquarters, where we found it closed for the day. While we filled our water bottles, I noticed a flyer from Misty Hills Diner on the bulletin board advertising a ten-piece chicken dinner with free delivery. We couldn't get to the pay phone quick enough to place our order. Our meal showed up remarkably fast, and we feasted on chicken, mashed potatoes with gravy, corn, and biscuits. It was the perfect comfort food to lift our spirits.

With renewed energy, we climbed to the top of the next ridge just in time to witness the setting sun illuminate the building clouds and turn them into an eruption of fiery colors. A gentle breeze blew the leaves, and the lyrics from "Dust in the Wind" by Kansas played in my mind. We paused to take it all in. I silently thanked God for the gift of my grandfather and asked him to take good care of him.

Rev broke the silence. "That sunset is for you."

Waving goodbye. It was then that I became a Thru Hiker

It was at that moment that I became a thru-hiker. Nothing, absolutely nothing, would stop me from honoring my grandpa. I would crawl if I had to. Looking west, toward home, I waved a last goodbye, wishing my grandpa safe travels, and then we walked into the night.

We walked for miles in the dark; two brothers lost in thought until a beacon of light from a lone campfire danced in the distance. Like moths to a flame, we were drawn from the darkness and found Magoo, Blue Noodle, and Wrong Way camped at the south fork of the Holston River. We had a coon dog wander into camp and hang out with Kee for a while before disappearing again. The owners showed up looking for their dog about a half hour later, only to realize that he was heading back over the mountain from which they came once we pointed them in the direction he departed. I found it curious that Kee didn't get excited about these guys coming into camp even though one of them was packing a .357, which I thought was a bit much for coon hunting.

The sky had cleared, and we could see stars twinkling in the vastness of the midnight sky. I fell asleep wondering what it would be like when my grandpa was reunited with his mom and the Creator of this stunning place in which we live.

11/07/96

During the morning, we hiked for four miles on the lee side of a ridge, and we could hear the winds howling through the trees above. At times we could see the tree tops dancing wildly. It was unseasonably warm that day, and we worked up a good sweat as we crested the top. The wind buffeted us, chilling us to the bone, and promising to bring cooler temperatures along with icy rain once again.

The farther south we hiked, I began to understand what the mythical "green tunnel" was that the northbounders spoke of as we hiked through the rhododendron thickets near Comers Creek. Those evergreen shrubs were so thick they blocked any chance of seeing sky or sun. We got a taste of this up north, where the trees grew so dense that I wondered if I would ever see the sky again. Vistas were often thwarted on hard-earned summits by impenetrable foliage. The fertile soils of the Appalachian Mountains are unparalleled.

We walked down a set of stairs and crossed Comers Creek on a footbridge, I couldn't help being in awe of the herculean efforts trail crews go through to maintain this jewel of a trail. We headed into the Louis Fork Wilderness Area of the Jefferson National Forest, which is home to Mount Rodgers, the highest mountain in Virginia.

We walked for the pure joy of walking, and we encountered a most unusual growth on a tree. It was a burl about three feet in diameter that sloped down from the main trunk and was curiously shaped like a human nose; it even had two holes strategically located to make it anatomically correct. Humor sure helps heal a broken heart.

After eighteen miles, we walked into the Old Orchard Shelter, and Rev was looking a little tired. I can't say that I blame him. Hiking in the cold could take a toll. After dinner, Wrong Way played some haunting melodies that stirred my soul, similar to the way Native American flute music had a calming, meditative sound that made one's mind transcend beyond thoughts and worries.

Wrong Way playing Amazing Grace

The Old Orchard was a small shelter, and with the addition of another hiker, Elmo, we were packed like sardines. There was no room for Kee, but she didn't seem to mind sleeping on the ground in front of the shelter. We fell asleep to the soothing sounds of wind blowing through the trees. Around 11:30, the rain began with a flash of lightning that could be seen through closed eyelids. The booming thunder that immediately followed woke us all. The crack was still ringing in our ears when Kee plopped down between Rev and me, then flopped her head over on top of mine and started snoring. It made me smile, knowing she sought refuge from the storm and cuddled up to me.

By morning, she had muscled Rev off his Therma-Rest pad and slept peacefully, unlike Rev who had been fighting a fever through the night and hadn't gotten more than a few hours' sleep.

11/08/96

It continued to drizzle on my birthday. I slept with my hiking clothes, water bottles, and water filter at the foot of my sleeping bag so they wouldn't freeze. My toothpaste was frozen, so I kept it in my jacket's breast pocket and hoped I could brush my teeth later.

Magoo's knees were bothering him, Rev was feverish, and it didn't look like the weather was going to break. We were forced to decide to take a zero day and run the risk of running out of food before getting to Damascus or press on. With the weather worsening, it didn't seem likely we could go the twenty-two miles up and over Mount Rodgers to Lost Mountain Shelter. We had to make it at least eleven miles to the Thomas Knob Shelter on top of Mount Rodgers.

The rain was coming down hard. On the steeper sections of the trail, it felt like we were running class four whitewater. It was nearly knee-deep in some of the bigger pools. We could've run canoes through that section. If I had a fly rod with me, I would've broken it out just for the photo op.

As we entered Grayson Highlands State Park, the rain slowed to a light mist. We hadn't traveled far on the grassy section when a couple of feral ponies magically appeared from the distant gray clouds.

They couldn't have been more than three feet tall at the withers. The more daring of the two came over and worked each of us for a handout, then stopped nose to nose with Kee who may have just met her match in these adorable little ponies' innate "Yogi" ability.

Feral pony of the Grayson Highlands State Park

Kee making friends

We left the ponies behind and continued our climb toward Mount Rodgers's summit. The mist turned to a drizzle, and then it became a steady rain, which turned to stinging sleet the higher we climbed. Eventually, it turned to snow as we neared the shelter, and Blue Noodle had the biggest, burliest, frozen beard of all of us. If there had been an award for the best "Frozen Mountain Man Beard," it would've been his. Thomas Knob Shelter was at an elevation of five thousand four hundred feet and was nearly two hundred feet higher than any mountain we had climbed so far. While these mountains do not reach the lofty altitudes of the 14'ers, (58, fourteen thousand plus foot peaks in Colorado) back home, there was a surprising amount of climbing to be done because you began most ascents from a lower elevation in the Gaps. While we didn't have to deal with oxygen deprivation or altitude sickness, climbing to the summit in inclement weather was still challenging.

After everyone settled into the shelter, to rally the troops, I broke out my astronaut pizza and ice cream, divided them up, and then had a brief birthday celebration before calling it a night. Our Mount Rodgers pizza bash fell short of filling our caloric deficit. While the pizza and the ice cream were digestible, I sympathized with our astronauts. They must be a pretty tough breed to be able to eat this stuff on a daily basis. I couldn't imagine that we sent the best of our best into space with food that a chef at a soup kitchen wouldn't serve. I think someone scammed my sister, but it was the thought that counted.

Thomas Knob had a sleeping loft upstairs. The stairs were too steep to get Kiana up safely, so we were the only ones to sleep on the lower level. Before everyone drifted to sleep, Magoo called out, "Does anyone know the chorus to the *Hee Haw* show?"

Blue Noodle and I were the only ones old enough to be familiar with it.

I yelled back up. "Are you kidding? That was one of my dad's favorite shows when I was growing up."

I don't think Rev and Wrong Way had ever been exposed to it, and Elmo just thought we were crazy, but they were all good sports as Magoo rehearsed the chorus with everyone.

Magoo started it off with his best deep southern twang, "Now we get along, my life was real sunny, but only one thing would ruin our fun. I know you love me, but you worship money, and you got mad when I offered you none."

Everyone joined in, "Where oh where are you tonight? Why did you leave me here all alone? I searched the world over and thought I found true love, you met another and 'pfsff' you was gone."

The laughter that echoed through that shell of a hut was great medicine. With that, we took a scene out of the *Waltons*, calling out to each other, "Goodnight, Magoo, goodnight Blue Noodle, goodnight Rev, goodnight Wrong Way, goodnight Elmo, good night Ducttape, goodnight Kee." It couldn't have been more fitting, as the *Waltons* was a TV series about a Depression-era family that lived on a fictional Walton Mountain in the Blue Ridge Mountains.

The temperature plummeted throughout the night, and the wind took on a life of its own, blowing snow sideways into the shelter. I have never experienced such a bone-chilling cold as I did that night. The wet cold of those eastern mountains will penetrate to your core. Even Kee was uncomfortable and paced most of the night. When I tried to pull her in close to share body heat, she growled at me.

I shivered, and I began to think about Jack London's book *To Build a Fire* and the dire consequences that were paid. I knew I would have to work fast before my shivering became uncontrollable and my stinging fingers went numb. It was too windy to set up my tent, so I ripped my tarp out of my pack, threw it over my sleeping bag, and secured it underneath me to keep it from blowing away. Then I got my faithful Whisper-lite stove fired up while sheltered under the tarp and began boiling a pot of water. It took longer than usual to get it to boil, and it took every bit of that time to thaw my fingers to the point where they just stung. I poured the scalding water into my Nalgene and shoved it between my thighs. The heat warmed my femoral arteries, and I could feel the warmth travel down my legs to my feet. Warmth slowly invaded my abdomen, and a feeling of well-being came with it. This must be what heroin addicts feel when they inject their drug of choice, and it courses through their system. I drank the warm water and boiled some more. Kee seemed to sense she wouldn't be snuggling with a cadaver and joined me under the tarp.

As the weather threw everything she had at us, I pulled Kee close as the Gordon Lightfoot song, "Wreck of Edmund Fitzgerald," played in my head. Especially poignant were the haunting lyrics when he sang about the witch of November and had me asking where the love of God goes when time seems to stand still.

For me, time seemed to crawl with each artic blast as well.

11/09/96

I woke in the morning, thankful that the worst was over and glad to find that no one had suffered from the last stages of hypothermia, called hypothermic paradoxical undressing. That would have been embarrassing. The new day held promise of warmer temperatures. Everything that I had hanging to dry during the night was flash-frozen. My hiking socks were stiff as a board. My shirt could've doubled as a sword. My boots were blocks of ice, and trying to lace them up was futile. But with daylight came renewed hope and a sense of urgency to get off that mountain.

Coldest night of the AT

Thankfully, I kept enough water in my pan to make a hot meal. It took at least ten minutes to thaw the water. Had I left it in my Nalgene, I would have had to go without. We put on frozen boots and tucked the laces inside, hoping they would thaw enough to tie. We slung our frozen packs with frozen clothes, lashed to the outside, and headed into a dazzling winter wonderland. Everything had a coat of ice on it. The trees and bushes were encased in a white tomb, waiting for thawing temperatures. The smaller branches were brittle, and when we brushed up against them, they shattered like they were made of glass. Rev, Wrong Way, Kee, and I took the .4-mile blue-blazed side trail to the summit where, at 10:15, I claimed Mount Rodgers to be Mount John C. Huber, posthumously for the day, to honor a great man. The cold began to seep in, so we didn't linger.

As we descended from the summit, we were briefly treated to a sliver of light that appeared underneath a dark gray bank of clouds and above the distant horizon, illuminating the peaks of the Smokies to the south. The view was a brief tease of what lay ahead. Then, just as quickly, the curtain closed, and it began snowing again. Wind-blown snow blasted our exposed faces, forcing us to march with purpose.

Everyone hiked at their own pace, so when I got to a couple of stream crossings, I waited, out of an abundance of caution, for Rev and Wrong Way to catch up. It was still cold enough that an errant step and an icy plunge would mean certain trouble. We crossed one at a time with great care until we were all safely across. Farther down the trail, we saw a yellow message in the snow. It was written in cursive longhand, with a flair toward artistic calligraphy. The author was attentive enough to dot his i's and cross his t's while signing his first and last name, leaving Wrong Way to claim, "That's not fair! I don't have that equipment."

It was even more impressive when he added "was here" and added an exclamation mark.

It wasn't long before we came across another message scratched into the snow alongside the trail that read: "Crash Site," with an arrow pointing downslope to a snow drift with an impression of a backpack, a head, and a hiking stick. Our first backpacker snow angel was large enough to belong to Magoo, which we verified once we caught up to them.

We pushed through twelve miles of snow before stopping early at the Lost Mountain Shelter. It seemed prudent, and the general consensus was to get a hot meal and settle in for another cold night instead of hiking another seven miles to the next shelter. We all set our tents up in the shelter to help minimize our heat loss. Wrong Way suffered the previous night, even though she was in the protected loft, so I let Kee sleep in Wrong Way's tent. Their shared body heat proved to make the night more tolerable.

11/10/96

We got another four inches of snow on top of the previous day's accumulation. The winds were not as stiff, and the cold didn't penetrate my core. It was still wet and cold, and sheltering inside our tents made sleeping easier. Empty Nalgenes stuffed down the collar of my boots kept the uppers from freezing too small to slip my foot into. I could then pull the bottles out of my boot, fill them with boiling water, then slide them back into my boots. It felt like a day at the spa, sliding your foot into a semi-warm boot, only to be shocked back into reality when your toes settled into the still-frozen toe box, forcing you to ignore and override. Once the water was lukewarm, you could drink it to warm your core. Little things like this paid great dividends and started the day off right.

Magoo and Blue Noodle were moving a little slow that morning, and as the rest of us headed out, they promised they would catch us by Damascus. My guess was they would see us sooner because Rev was still feverish, and the sixteen miles into town would be a struggle. It was imperative that we got him out of the weather soon. We'd been hiking along The Virginia Creeper Trail, which was part of the AT. It was a section of the trail with a gentle grade and part of the Rails to Trails system.

It was 12:15 when I finally saw my shadow for the first time in days. With all the recent rain and snow, Laurel Creek was roaring down below and seemed to be getting louder with every mile we walked. Talking without shouting was futile, so we walked in silence, lulled into a contemplative state by the sounds of rushing water. It continued to snow lightly, but our spirits were given a boost as we kept going down that repurposed rail bed and passed a seventeen-hundred-mile trail marker, signifying that the State of Virginia would soon be a memory.

We saw our first snowplow on Highway 58 as we stopped at the picnic table to take a snack break and let Rev rest. He said he was feeling like he was going to throw up or pass out. To make matters worse, his back was locking up from an earlier slip and fall. Hitchhiking into Damascus was never an option that he entertained. So, with steeled determination, he walked the last mile into town with Kee by his side as if she sensed that he was struggling. Wrong Way, and I walked close by to make sure he didn't collapse. The AT had a way of testing one's resolve, and it amazed me how far people were capable of pushing themselves past preconceived limitations.

Magoo and Blue Noodle caught us on the last mile into town, and we all agreed to meet at "The Place," a nearby hostel behind the Methodist Church. They were in the process of winterizing the building but decided to let us stay there so Rev could get some much-needed rest. They had already turned the heat off, and despite expecting a record-breaking cold front, they assured us the water wouldn't be turned off until we got our showers. For a two-dollar donation, they were the best hot showers we'd had in a while.

After everyone cleaned up, we celebrated my birthday at Quincy's. We shared a couple of pitchers of beer, and I had a large steak sandwich and a large pizza myself. To my surprise, everyone pitched in and bought my dinner. As I looked around the table, I was able to see past hardened exteriors and see genuine, kindred souls singing out-of-tune birthday wishes. I couldn't help but smile.

It got down to eighteen degrees that night, and I could see my breath in the blue room where we slept. Regardless, we rejoiced because we had full stomachs and were sheltered from the wind.

11/11/96 Monday & Veterans Day

Veterans Day, and the post office was closed. None of us would be getting our much-needed mail drops. Rev was in his warmest winter clothing and buried in his sleeping bag, silently shivering. Magoo, Blue Noodle, and I went to the store to get some food and medicine for Rev while Wrong Way stayed back to journal and keep an eye on Rev. I could be wrong, but I think she was kind of sweet on him. Regardless, she was a genuine caring person who was as tough as they come, and we're all thankful that she had decided to hike the "wrong way." Grandma Gatewood would have been proud of her mettle.

Magoo, Blue Noodle, Kee, and I went to Mount Rodger's Outfitters to get some additional cold weather gear and a pump assembly for my water purifier. There, we met Damascus Dave, the owner, and a class of 1990 thru-hiker. He was a spry individual who sported the white hair and beard of a seasoned person who had seen a thing or two. He carried an air of confidence when he spoke, and his self-assurance was born from experience. After a brief introduction, he told me, "You don't have to leave your dog tied up outside, bring her in."

I was grateful for his kindness, as Kee made herself at home and melted onto the carpet under the table while we poured through Dave's thru-hike scrapbook and his trail ledger book with all the north and southbound entries for the year.

On our way out, I asked Dave about a Mount Ranier banner hanging on the wall with all the framed maps, and he said, "Yeah, I climbed Ranier, but it pales in comparison to what you guys are doing. Good luck."

Craving a hot meal, our next stop was Quincy's, and as luck would have it, they were running half-price specials every Monday in November. It was like manna from heaven, and we feasted as only hungry hikers could.

More southbounders had rolled into "The Place," and we gathered around an electric heater in the kitchen. We shared stories over some hot pizzas from Quincy's. It was an honor to meet guys who were total strangers and simultaneously brothers with a shared passion for the trail. They had been reading our register entries for months at shelters along the way and were excited to finally meet the authors. It was a humbling experience to know that mere musings, scratched on remote registers, could connect people in such a way.

11/12/96

Rev wasn't improving, and Blue Noodle was also beginning to feel the energy-sucking grasp of the flu. Even so, we all rallied to retrieve our mail drops and reconvened at the hostel to sort our packages. Kee danced around the room when I showed her the "Old Roy" dog treats that my sister, Cindy, snuck into the box. They smelled good enough for human consumption, but I held off because Kee relished them like a kid in a candy store, and it made me smile to see her so happy.

The trip to the post office was very taxing on Rev, and while we discussed amongst ourselves the necessity of getting a hotel room for the guys to recover in, some of the church members came walking through, making final notes on what needed to be done to shut the hostel down.

One of the ladies came over and said, "I'm sorry, but I couldn't help overhearing about your situation. Don't spend your money there. Let me show you where this lady named Kay lives; she'll welcome you in, all five of you, including your dog."

Fortune continued to smile as Kay welcomed us into her home. As I walked up the steps to her front porch, I couldn't help but notice a collection of heart-shaped rocks displayed on the side of the steps and around the porch columns. Kay had made it her mission to welcome sojourning thru-hikers. She gave us a tour of her house and insisted we settle into the two empty bedrooms upstairs. Then she told us, "Make yourselves at home; you have full rein of the kitchen. Stay as long as you need to." She asked for nothing in return. It wasn't until later that we discovered she was a gourmet cook and worked as a pastry chef at the Bristol Country Club. She was also a gourmet columnist for one of the local papers. To say we ate well would have been an understatement.

11/13 thru 11/15/96

It took three more days before the guys were well enough to travel. This unexpected delay forced me to reschedule my flight home to December 15. I would have to average almost 16.5 miles per day for twenty-eight days if I were to make it to the visitor's center at Amicalola Falls State Park, four hundred and sixty miles away. That would give me a buffer of two days to get to the airport. In a perfect world, it sounded more than doable.

On our last day at Kay's, we all pitched in and cleaned the inside of her house and rain gutters before taking her out to eat at an Oriental Buffet for dinner.

> If you feel pain, you're alive. If you feel other people's pain, you're a human being.
> – LEO TOLSTOY

APPALACHIAN TRAIL
MAINE TO GEORGIA

12-17-96
2160 miles

·LEGEND·
APPALACHIAN TRAIL........

Chapter 21

Tennessee

11/16/96

In an effort to leave no trace, we stripped the beds, did laundry, made the beds, and washed the breakfast dishes before Kay walked us through town to the forest edge and gave us all hugs. She was in tears as we all gave her a parting gift of cash for her amazing hospitality. The words of Rene, the Kennebec River Master, rang true as we went our separate ways; we hadn't been looking for gold or silver, but what we did find left us far richer than before. Kay's trail name is "Queen of Hearts."

Kay the "Queen of Hearts"

Damascus certainly lived up to its reputation as the friendliest town on the trail. The lure of the trail was barely strong enough to break the genuine bonds of small-town America.

Blue Noodle, Wrong Way, Magoo, Me, Kiana, and Rev.

With our late start, we only made it ten miles to the Abingdon Gap Shelter. The ledger was filled with hiker entries bemoaning a biblical mouse infestation. It was getting late, and another eight miles separated us from the next shelter, so we chose to disregard the warnings and stay the night. After all, hikers have been known to spin some pretty big yarns, not unlike a fisherman boasting about the one that got away. With a false sense of bravado, we all hung our food bags, boots, and packs up high in case all the reports were accurate. We settled in for the night with sleeping bags drawn tight around our faces to keep the night's chill from creeping in. We could hear the shelter coming to life as soon as it was dark enough not to see. Wrong Way was the first to shine a light on the hanging food bags. To her horror, her bag looked alive, with mice swarming it. She sprang out of her sleeping bag with a lightning-quick intensity and served up a backhand that sent one of the mice sailing while the rest scattered. Those mice should have known better than to mess with an ex-competitive tennis player.

Sometime during the night, Wrong Way was awakened by mice tugging on her hair, probably looking for nesting material.

I had a rough night's sleep not because of the mice, but because the guy next to me, Ed, a section hiker, kept talking in his sleep. Even earplugs were no match for his nonsensical rantings.

11/17/96

We awakened in the predawn hours to prepare meals and pack for the day. It was then that I discovered that my food bag had been infiltrated. There was a small entrance hole and a shredded bagel bag with only crumbs left as evidence of the three bagels' demise.

I was sitting next to Rev when he began stirring his favorite maple and brown sugar oatmeal into boiling water. He started eating it after it had cooled sufficiently. He only realized something was amiss after the light from his headlamp illuminated his steaming meal. "Hmm, I have clumps of brown sugar in my oatmeal."

At that very moment, the first rays of sun peaked over the horizon, backlighting Rev's water bag hanging from a rafter at the front of the shelter, exposing some shadowy figures floating in the water. I yelled, "Rev! Stop eating! Don't eat anymore!" Pointing at his water bag, I said, "Look at your water bag!"

"Is that…Is that a tail?" he asked, knowing the answer before he spoke.

Wrong Way and Blue Noodle jumped up, untied the bag, and pulled out seven *mice*-cicles. Wrong Way laid them out in the snow execution style while I grabbed my camera and asked, "Rev, how long did you boil that water?"

"At least five minutes."

"You should be okay. If anything, you just got a little extra roughage with your meal!" I said, not wanting to raise any alarms.

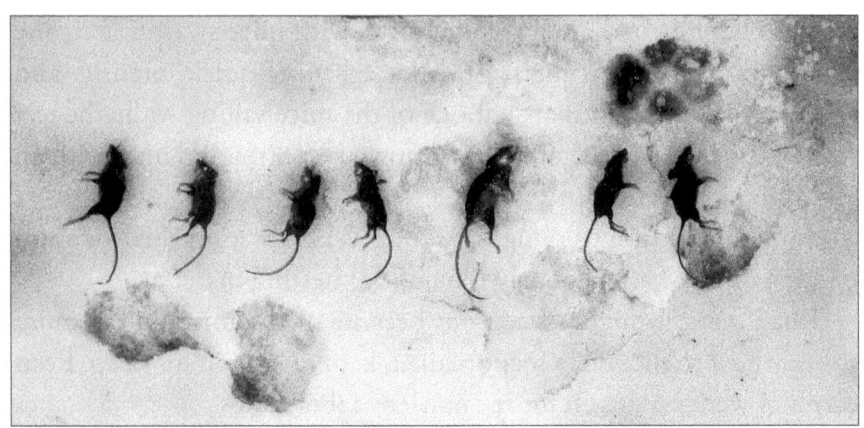

Mice-cicles

I sure hope your stomach acid finishes anything that may have survived the boiling water, I thought to myself. I didn't know if hantavirus was an issue out east, like in Colorado and Arizona, but I vowed to keep a close eye on him. It was a ten-mile backtrack to Damascus and just under five miles south to Shady Valley, Tennessee. I hoped that if Rev needed medical attention, we would know by the time we got to Shady Valley.

> "When I was a boy, my father was so ignorant I could hardly stand to have him around. But when I got to be 21, I was astonished at how much the old man had learned in seven years." **- MARK TWAIN**

Once it was apparent that Rev had a cast iron stomach like a coyote, we motored down the trail while Magoo and Blue Noodle lingered at the shelter. I thought it was great that they took the time to hike together and seemed to really enjoy it. Fond memories of shared times with my dad would always come to mind. I wondered if Blue Noodle went through a stage in life similar to what I went through with my dad, which was summed up by a famous author's comical quip.

Isn't it ironic that as we get older, our dads get smarter!

We made it sixteen miles to Iron Mountain Shelter and found Little Buddy's ditty in the register. It was dedicated to Boota and the Spirit of Saint Louis Crew, with specific directions for singing it to the tune of "King of Pain" by The Police. It went like this:

King of Slack

Refrain: "Got that little red pouch on the waist today, no cumbersome pack to get into the way.

Got the cigarette, soda, candy bars, and lunch; they're hiking the whole thing going both ways at once…

Verse: I stood on the trail out in the pouring rain; they blew by me just like a hurricane. I wondered how come these guys could be so quick, then I realized, no packs. Well, what a bunch of goobers, king of slack, king of slack, they'll always be the king of slack, they'll always be the king of slack."

~ **Little Buddy**

Not to be outdone, Leapfrog, Shoofly Pie, and Tree Trunk jumped into the fray with a trail jingle of their own. It went to the tune of "Isn't it Ironic" by Alanis Morissette.

"It's a black fly, and you're too late.
It's hiking to the post office two minutes too late.
It's like losing your spoon and having to eat with your knife.
It's like getting to Springer and getting a real life.
Isn't it ironic, don't you think? A little too ironic, and yeah,
I really do think it's like rain for the third straight day.
It's like leaving town when you'd rather stay.
It's like ten more miles when your feet really ache.
Are these ticks on my legs or chiggers?"

~ **Leapfrog, Shoofly Pie, and Tree Trunk**

It's painfully obvious these guys had too much time on their hands.

11/18/96

Sleep was intermittent last night, thanks to the high volume of mice scurrying about looking for something to fill their bellies and insulate their nests. Wrong Way's hair was a popular target throughout the night. There seemed to be insufficient natural predators around Iron Mountain Shelter to keep the mouse population in check.

On top of that, there were a bunch of hound dogs that treed a coon and continued to bay from midnight until six, never moving from that tree to our south. I didn't think it was possible to carry on for that long and not lose your voice.

We had been hiking for hours in the rain, and it was beginning to make us question our sanity and our ambitious plans of doing a twenty-one-mile day. We ran into a bear hunter before we got to Watauga Lake Shelter. He warned us, "There's a lot of bar around here. There was a couple o' locals that tried to outrun a bar; one climbed a tree, and the other didn't make it up the tree in time and ended up gettin' his leg chewed up pretty bad."

We thanked him for the heads-up and walked a short distance to the Watauga Shelter, only to find similar warnings from other hikers in the register regarding bear activity. It didn't matter; we were spent after walking all day in the rain on very little sleep. I changed into dry clothes, made some hot chocolate, leaned back onto my backpack, and took a couple of big swigs of that warming beverage, and that was the last I remember. I was jolted back to consciousness by everyone's laughter. They claimed I was snoring instantly, but everyone knows I don't snore. Exhaustion sure makes for blissful slumber.

11/19/96

We had a two thousand-foot climb first thing. It was better than coffee. We got part of the way up and were treated to a postcard view of Lake Watauga. Iconic fishing holes, with timber-lined shores, the lake was one of the most picturesque I'd seen in a long time. It seemed to call to me to fish her banks, but I would have to save that for another trip.

Another overcast day, but with friendlier gray skies, a welcome change from the angry black skies of days past. The recent rain had washed the forest clean, and we breathed in deep the pungent scent of pine. We climbed into the clouds as we ascended Pond Mountain, and it began to mist on us as we traversed across Pond Flats. We walked past trees that had been shredded at shoulder height by a rut-crazed buck, which only added to the gratitude we felt for being able to walk through wild places.

We hiked down out of the clouds and eventually found ourselves walking into the Laurel Fork Gorge, rimmed with rhododendrons. The ruggedness of this place reminded me of Oak Creek Canyon in Arizona, minus the red rocks. As a transplanted desert rat, I'm fascinated by clear running water, and the cascading beauty of Laurel Falls is magical. Again, my hat is off to the creators of this trail and their ability to locate it through areas that allowed for a sense of discovery and left me wanting to know what was around the next bend.

After sixteen miles, Kee seemed to be struggling, so she and I stopped at Moreland Gap Shelter while everyone else continued for another five miles to camp along Laurel Fork. It was uncharacteristic for Kee not to wolf down her food and be the first to Yogi me for my leftovers. Tonight was different; she was uninterested in food and drank very little. Instead, she walked right by her food bag to the front of the sleeping deck, sat on her haunches, and looked into the darkness, like a sentry, in the direction everyone else had gone. She watched for nearly an hour while I made dinner, ate, and cleaned up. I settled in for the night to journal. I looked up at Kee still sitting in the same place.

"Kee, they're not coming. We'll catch them tomorrow. Come lay down, girl." I patted her sleeping pad. "You need to rest."

She walked back, flopped down on her mat, and was snoring within minutes. I left her food bag next to her in case her appetite returned during the night. Not only was she exhausted, but I think she was missing the rest of her pack. She woke at midnight and gobbled her food like the Kiana of old. She did her three spin moves and then laid down next to me. Finally, I could drift off into a deep slumber, knowing she would be okay.

11/20/96

I was jolted awake by the screech of a barn owl at 4:30 am. I lay there for the next hour, listening to him make his rounds, screeching as he passed by. Ironically, we didn't have any mouse issues at that shelter.

I finally rolled over to nudge Kee, saying, "Hey, girl, we have to get moving if we are going to catch everyone."

She sprang out of bed as if she understood. She gobbled down the last of her five-pound Ziploc bag of food and worked me for last night's leftovers with those big brown eyes. She ate another pound of spaghetti along with a can of tuna and finally seemed content as she went over to her pack and waited. When I picked it up, she did her happy dance, spinning in circles. After securing her pack, she bolted down the trail, and I had to yell, "Hey, wait for me!"

She stopped, turned, and cocked her head impatiently. Smiling, I slung my pack and hustled after her. "Yeah, girl. We're back!"

It was a glorious day; the sun was shining, the sky was blue, and there were nonthreatening wispy cirrus clouds in the distance. My step was light as I rejoiced in our health, giving thanks for our ability to walk with ease through some of the most stunning landscapes my eyes had ever seen, just a guy and his dog.

We had a three hundred-foot climb first thing that morning and were rewarded with a beautiful sunrise along with great views of the fog-filled valleys below. We watched a feral dog chase a herd of deer across the trail and down into the hollow, barking in hot pursuit. I could tell where the deer circled wide and were running up the hollow by following the sound of that baying dog. It wasn't long, and they came charging back across the trail with their tongues hanging. Out west, a dog that harassed wildlife or livestock would have been shot. I hoped the deer had the stamina to outrun that dog and still have the energy reserves to make it through the winter.

I love getting an early start. Especially this time of year when I don't have to deal with industrious spiders shooting a constant barrage of webs across the trail, which always seemed to be at face height. Mornings are always so peaceful as nature's day shift begins to wake up. As we walked through the rhododendron forest, the ground sounded hollow, and each step sounded like the beat of a drum. When I was settling into the rhythmic beat of my footsteps, the serenity of the morning was shattered when we rounded a bend in the trail, and a covey of grouse exploded from underfoot. Nature's version of a double shot of espresso is guaranteed to quicken your pulse.

We caught up to everyone as they were breaking camp, and boy, was Kee excited to see them. We walked down verdant valleys toward US19E, we caught glimpses of Roan Mountain, a five-mile-long ridgetop, looming in the distance. I loved climbing the grassy Balds of Hump Mountain. The expansive views to the north gave me a sense of accomplishment, only to be humbled as I looked south at the Roan rising above everything else I had worked to climb. A sense of scale can be lost in landscape photos, so I took some pictures of our group traversing Hump Mountain for perspective, and they appeared as ants in the grandeur of it all.

The father and son team traversing Hump Mountain

Kee and I did over twenty-two miles before stopping for the day at Overmountain Shelter. She didn't seem tired as she quickly gobbled her food and pranced around camp to see what everyone was cooking.

According to Wingfoot, this old barn with a loft upstairs was used in the movie *Winter People*, which starred Kurt Russell, Kelly McGillis, and Lloyd Bridges. While I hadn't seen the movie, I'd always been a fan of Kurt Russell, especially after his role as Wyatt Earp in *Tombstone*. Kelley McGillis was incredible in the movie *Top Gun*. We were all enamored about spending the night in such a cool place with some action figure history.

11/21/96

It was cold, and I could see my breath in the morning air. We were awakened by two bucks battling in the meadow below us. The rattle and crack of antlers were close, but a thick wall of gray fog veiled them. They must have been equally matched, as neither seemed to admit defeat.

Kee sat on the perimeter of our visibility, listening to the chaos while we packed for the day. The fight for breeding rights continued for at least a half hour, moving to our left, then crashing through the brush to our right before it went silent once again.

It was cold enough that Rev's feet pained him enough to say something. Blue Noodle selflessly cradled Rev's feet under his fleece jacket next to his skin until he regained feeling again. The image of a bearded mountain man jumping to ease the suffering of his brother was seared in my memory.

It started to mist on us when we climbed up to the Balds on our way to the top of Roan Mountain. There wasn't any lightning or thunder as we traversed the grassy ridge Bald, but the wind buffeted us mercilessly as the clouds screamed past with startling speed. I would have preferred to have witnessed the views from this lofty place on a clear day, but I found it exhilarating to be hiking in the clouds once again. We were like ghost hikers, disappearing and reappearing from each other's sight as we leaned into the prevailing winds.

We stopped at the Roan High Knob Shelter, the highest on the trail at six thousand two hundred and eighty-five feet, to get out of the wind and rain. We ate lunch but couldn't stay for long as the temperature continued to drop. We headed down the trail and the rain turned to hail. The clouds enveloped us, and we were witness to the formation of rime ice on the windward side of all branches. It grew steadily and transformed the forest into a winter wonderland. We walked for another six miles through a white tunnel before stopping at Clyde Smith Shelter. On some of the steeper sections, our footing broke loose, and if we kept our center of balance forward, we could ski the hill until our boots gained traction. Once we got our footing, we had to be ready to run, or we would do a face plant. If we were leaning too far back when our feet slid, our feet would shoot out from under us, and we would hit the deck, butt-sliding to an eventual stop. While it was great fun, switchbacks would have made it safer and minimized erosion.

We surprised a massive flock of turkeys at the blue blaze intersection to Clyde Smith Shelter. Turkeys flew everywhere, and the ensuing pandemonium sounded like a helicopter taking off next to us.

Someone left a can of cat food at the shelter, and Rev, in a show of bravado, popped the top and chowed down. Indeed, a hiker's appetite knows no bounds.

11/22/96

It was four degrees and already feeling warmer than yesterday.

We were obsessed with thoughts of past Thanksgiving feasts surrounded by family. We talked about family traditions and wondered what this Thanksgiving would bring. We talked about how glorious a Swanson frozen turkey dinner would be. We hiked, we drooled, and then we fantasized some more.

Some would complain about the PUDs (pointless ups and downs) in this section of the trail. I would have to argue that these ups and downs represent just how rugged the mountains of Tennessee are. If you were to bypass or skirt the peaks, you would never be able to appreciate how challenging the Volunteer State is. I don't think the trail founders intended to minimize our authentic backcountry experience.

We stopped briefly at the Cherry Gap Shelter to gnaw on frozen snacks. Nobody took the time to heat anything. Instead, we kept moving to stay warm. I'd resorted to storing my Nalgenes upside down so that when I needed a drink, I could unscrew the lid and have only a thin layer of ice to break through.

We traversed a frozen grassy Bald called the Beauty Spot, where the rime ice was up to two inches thick on the occasional shrub and T-post. It was 1 p.m. before my mustache started to thaw. Blue Noodle had the best frozen beard of the day, with his dad coming in a close second. As we dropped down from the Beauty Spot, gusts of wind broke off the rime ice and gave the appearance that it was snowing. An icy rain began to fall as we dropped in elevation toward the Indian Grave Gap. The wet leaves and exposed roots were as slippery as an ice rink with a fifteen- to twenty-degree grade. Still, I reminded myself that the worst day of hiking is better than the best day of working.

Blue Noodle — best frozen beard award

It took us less than eight hours to do twenty-one miles. As we settled into Curley Gap Shelter, I noticed that Magoo was walking gingerly. He tried to hide the pain and refused to complain, instead he chose to ignore and override as long as he could. We all wondered how long he would last while silently willing him to endure.

Steam rose from our pots as we cooked our separate dinners, and our breath looked like smokey tendrils rising past our headlamp's beam of light, that clouded our vision with every exhale. To make light of our misery, we all joined in singing the chorus of the *Hee Haw* song:

"Where oh where are you tonight? Why did you leave me here all alone? I searched the world over and thought I found true love, but you met another, and pfft, you were gone."

I thought the shelter's acoustics were spectacular with the cinder block construction, but Wrong Way's eyeball roll and the shake of her head indicated she thought Rev, at the very least, may have been suffering long-term adverse effects from the mouse poop oatmeal.

We were awakened by the sound of coon dogs hot on a scent nearby. They were stationary for a short while, baying up a tree, until we heard the crack of a 22-caliber rifle. The dogs went silent after the eighth shot.

11/23/96

It was a cold night, and the brisk wind turned that cinder block shelter into a walk-in freezer. Kee was restless most of the night, getting up multiple times to reposition. She would do her spin move and then flop down next to me, each time a little closer, until she was plastered to my side. However, the extra heat was greatly appreciated.

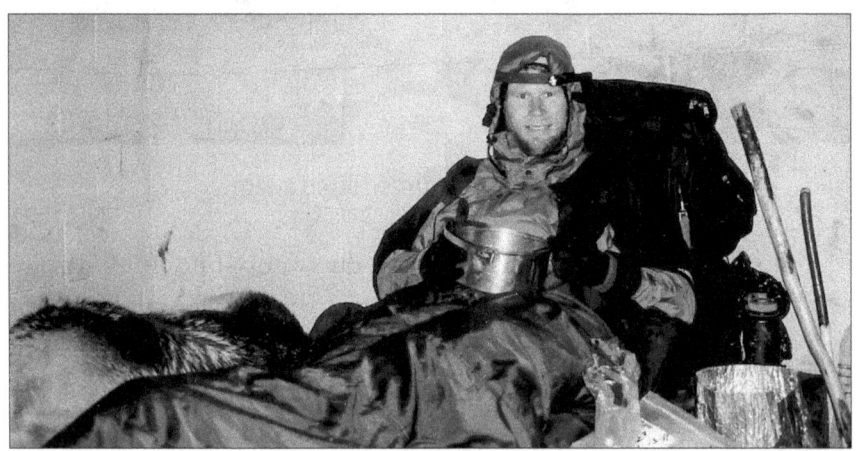

Cold night at Curly Gap Shelter

Kee and I were the first to cross the Nolichucky River on the Chestoa Bridge. Nolichucky is Cherokee, meaning "rushing waters," and has class three to four rapids for rafting enthusiasts. They should have added Uwoduhi (u-woe-doo-hee), meaning beautiful, to the Nolichucky name. Unfortunately, they were not running trips this late, or I would have been tempted to float that river.

I grew up watching Disney shows every Sunday evening. Back then, they ran a series on Davy Crockett that captured my imagination. Walking in the same backcountry as "The King of the Wild Frontier" left me feeling nostalgic about a simpler time, and I wondered if our conservation efforts as stewards of this great nation would have made him proud.

We had just started crossing the Chestoa Bridge when a vehicle approached from behind. I stuck out my thumb, and the driver immediately pulled over and said, "Hop in! Where do you need to go?"

I climbed in. "Post office." I wondered if my hitchhiking technique had somehow miraculously improved.

I had just finished sorting through my mail drop when Rev and Wrong Way showed up with a similar hitching success story. A successful father and son team showed up in a brand-new Ford Explorer driven by Anna Fanor, who seemed impervious to smelly hikers. As soon as Magoo and Blue Noodle got their box, she shuttled them to the Maytag laundromat, where they sorted their mail while doing laundry.

As they drove away, another guy came over. "Hey, I've got a truck. You guys need to go anywhere; just let me know."

I told him, "We're going to be another ten minutes getting everything sorted."

"No problem. I've got some running around to do; I'll be back in ten or fifteen minutes. You let me know where you need to go."

Soon after, we loaded three packs, Kee, and me, in the back and drove to the laundromat. Once we were done with laundry, we all headed across the street to Kentucky Fried Chicken, where they had an all-you-can-eat buffet. The colonel's original recipe never tasted so good; we all agreed we had died and gone to heaven. Shortly after we had finished, Anna swung by to shuttle all of us to the Erwin Motel and, in a neighborly fashion, recommended a quaint little restaurant/ice cream parlor.

Magoo's youngest son, Scott, arrived that evening to hike the next several days with his dad and brother.

11/24/96 Sunday

We had been packed and ready to go for a while but hadn't heard much movement from the Magoo family next door. I attributed it to the storm that was heading our way, and nobody was excited about leaving the comforts of town. It was midmorning before we headed out the door, and we decided to grab an early lunch at the diner that Anna suggested. It was like we had walked onto the set of Arnold's Diner on the TV show, *Happy Days*. I half expected the Fonz to come strolling in with his hair slicked back, looking cool in 501 jeans, a white t-shirt, and his black leather jacket. He would make his entrance and utter his catchphrase "aaaaay" as if to announce that the king of cool had arrived. While we didn't have any Fonzie types make a grand entrance, we were surrounded by friendly locals.

> 'Tis strange—but true, for truth is always strange; stranger than fiction; if it could be told, how much would novels gain by the exchange!
>
> – LORD BRYON'S *DON JUAN* (1823)

A father and his daughter sat in the booth next to us, and on the other side of us, a table of guys dressed in jeans and flannel shirts. They were ribbing each other about the upcoming deer season and questioning each other's woodsman and hunter skills. One guy upped the ante and asked, "So, what kind of seasoning do you prefer in your tag soup?"

The guy closest to our table leaned over and said, "Don't mind these guys. It's like this every season. Where are you guys from?"

After brief introductions, he pointed to a framed black and white photo on the wall behind him. "You guys ever heard the story about 'Murdering Mary' the elephant that was hung nearby?"

Another guy at his table piped in, "Oh boy, Doc's at it again. It's story time."

I felt like I was listening to a modern-day Davy Crockett spinning a yarn about some outlandish event.

He continued, "Well, boys, back in the day, the Sparks Circus came to town, and they decided to promote the circus by parading their animals down Mainstreet. Their big attraction was a five-ton Asian elephant named Mary. She had an inexperienced trainer on her back, who two days prior had been a bellhop. When Mary caught sight of a large piece of watermelon lying alongside the road, she bolted for the tasty snack, catching the trainer off guard. Irritated, he forgot all his training about treating the animals humanely, and he jabbed Mary in the lower jaw with a metal prod to get her to drop the tasty treat. Apparently, he hit her in an abscessed tooth area, and she reacted violently. Mary grabbed the trainer with her trunk, throwing him into a nearby drink stand. Enraged, she charged and stomped on his head, killing him instantly. And as they say, the rest is history."

Sure enough, the picture on the wall showed Mary hanging by a chain from an enormous rail yard crane.

Erwin, Tennessee, rivals Damascus for the friendliest trail town we have come across, and the blood lust of generations past should not be held against them.

The climb out of town was steep but offered views of a shrinking Nolichucky River. I couldn't help but ponder that tragic tale of Mary the Elephant, and how the crowd started chanting, "Kill the elephant," and a mob mentality quickly ensued. I wondered if humankind had learned anything from our checkered past. I wondered if Mary's story would cause people to take stewardship of this land and its animals to heart as if our very lives relied on it.

> "Human beings, while capable of the worst, are also capable of rising above themselves, choosing again what is good, and making a new start, despite their mental and social conditioning."
> – POPE FRANCIS, *On Care of Our Common Home*

My mental musings were abbreviated as we crested the summit and were met with the full fury of the incoming storm. We leaned into the wind, tuning an ear for the sudden crack of a toppling tree. Our late start and the force of the storm forced us to seek shelter at the No Business Knob Shelter instead of continuing on another eleven miles to Bald Mountain Shelter. While it was a short day, it was just what Scott needed to give him a taste of what he was in for.

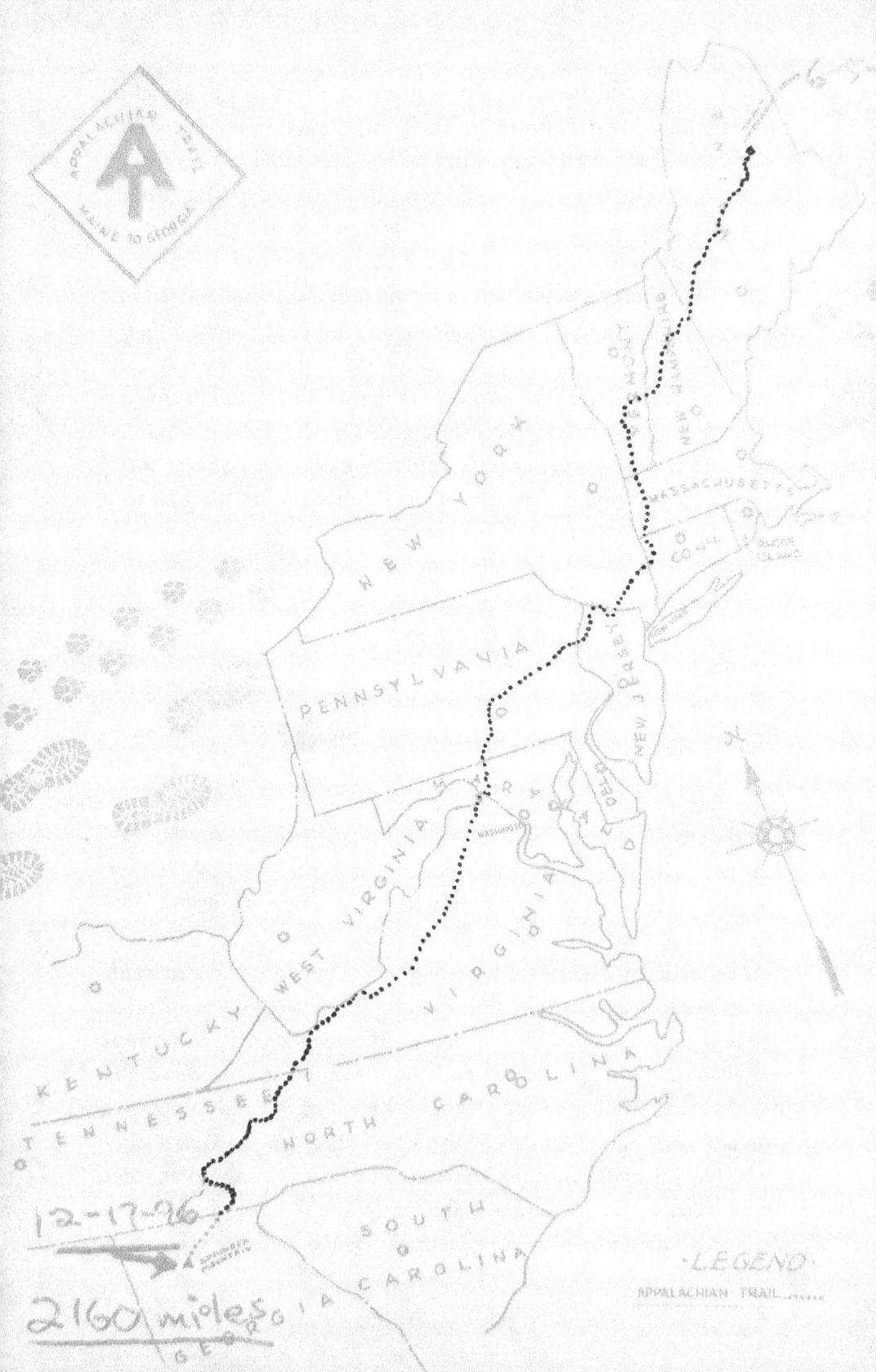

Chapter 22

North Carolina

11/25 & 26/96

Over the next two days, we hiked forty-one miles in a steady downpour, and I couldn't break out the voice recorder or camera during the day. We might as well have been walking at night as there were no views to be seen. Part of me wanted to wait out the storm so I didn't miss anything, but the pressure of finishing before Christmas propelled us ever forward. By the time Kee and I had eaten dinner, I had just enough energy to crawl into my sleeping bag at Hogback Ridge and Little Laurel Shelters. I called goodnight to everyone and then slipped into unconscious bliss.

11/27/96

I woke up in the predawn hours to see a brilliant full moon illuminating dark silhouettes of a deciduous forest void of its crown. The trees' naked forms were cloaked in the finest crystals that glowed with regal radiance and adorned the outline of every branch in luminous beauty.

Witnessing such peaceful grandeur made my heart rejoice like I was a child on Christmas morning who sneaked a peek at our beautifully adorned tree before everyone else awoke. It felt like Christmas had come early as the clearing skies held hope for a new day. The temperature must have dropped into the teens during the night, but I slept so hard I didn't recall being cold. With the morning light the trees appeared as a dazzling winter wonderland, and we hiked into the white tunnel to the sound of woodpeckers hammering wood.

For twenty miles, we were blessed to walk under blue skies on our way into Hot Springs, North Carolina. At times, we could see Roan Mountain to the north, slowly getting smaller, as we got teasing glimpses of Clingman's Dome, eighty trail miles to the south, and the highest point on the entire AT.

I thought I had walked into a four-wheel drive convention along the meadows of Mill Ridge. There were four-wheel drive vehicles of every make and model, new and used. Some didn't seem to have their first scratch, while others looked like they were on their last leg. There was even an encampment of miscellaneous RVs. The coolest one was an old school bus with camouflage paint that helped it blend in with the surrounding hardwoods. A mountain of a man sat in a camp chair alongside the bus, cleaning or trimming his nails with a pocketknife. He eyed me uncertainly as Kee and I approached.

I put him at ease when I said, "Nice paint job on your bus."

He smiled, and his wife came out, decked out in camo. We made small talk about hunting deer. I wished them luck and headed down the trail.

As I walked, I reflected on the conversation. *Had I not seen her walk out of the bus, blending into the bus perfectly, I would've been hard-pressed to notice her if she didn't move.*

We pushed hard to get to the post office before they closed for the day since they would be closed the following day for Thanksgiving.

Feeling pressured to meet my deadline with the airlines, I was tempted to continue hiking after securing my mail drop, but my trail family (aka tramily) talked me into spending Thanksgiving with them. So, the seven of us (Magoo, Blue Noodle, Bear, Rev, Wrong Way, Kee, and I), along with another hiker, Joe from Chicago, and his buddy, packed into the Ramsey's Apartment. We had high hopes of finding a last-minute fresh turkey or at least enough chickens, along with all the side dishes to cook in the full kitchen the next day.

We were determined to make it a Thanksgiving to remember, even if we had to settle for frozen dinners.

11/28/96

Bear left to be with his family for the holiday, and as we all hugged him goodbye, he gave us some words of affirmation. "Guys, that was harder than two-a-day football practices. Thanks for letting me tag along."

Joe from Chicago must have felt especially frisky that morning as he walked over to my pack and eyed it up and down. He'd been following us for a while and yellow-blazed to catch up with the folks he had been reading about for months in the shelter registers.

"What do you think, Joe? Do you want to swap packs for the day?"

"How much does it weigh?"

"I don't know, but I just topped it off with my food drop yesterday, and it has some extra clothing and dog food. Give it a try."

He gave it a mighty heft, set it on his knee, and deftly shouldered it like a seasoned hiker. It was a sight to behold, as the pack was almost as big as he was. His herculean effort earned him the trail name "Spiderman."

On our way to Ricker's Grocery to see what was available for our feast, we stopped by the AT Center and found the legend Dan "Wingfoot" Bruce at work in his office. Wingfoot had hiked the trail seven times and knew it better than most. His handbook was invaluable on our journey. We talked for an hour about the trail, and it was apparent that Dan "The Man—Wingfoot" Bruce was doing what he loved. Rev, Spiderman, and I shook his hand and thanked him for being the real deal. He was as genuine as they come.

Our recon to Ricker's Grocery was not promising, and as we headed back to the apartment to report our findings, a lady pulled into the parking lot and asked, "Can I interest you guys in a Thanksgiving dinner?" Apparently, word got around in that small town, and she just happened to be in the neighborhood.

I think we all had to pick our jaws up off the ground before one of us asked, "Really? There's seven of us."

"Absolutely, we'd love to have you. I'm Debbie, where are you guys staying?"

"At the Ramsey's Apartments."

"Perfect!" said Debbie. "I'll have a van from our church pick you up at three."

I thought, *Oh boy, what are we getting ourselves into?*

My stomach quickly overrode any concerns I had about being proselytized.

Pandemonium nearly broke out in the apartment as we rejoiced in our good fortune. We all loaded into the van at the appointed hour and traveled twenty miles to the Presbyterian church hall in Marshal, where thirteen incredible volunteers greeted us.

I don't know why I thought they were going to hit us over the head with Bibles, but I couldn't have been farther from the truth. These people went out of their way to serve us and share with us the most incredible Thanksgiving feast we could have hoped for. Turkey, mashed potatoes and gravy, dressing, green beans, cranberry salad, and a tossed salad were all part of this mouthwatering meal. Then, just when we thought it wasn't possible to be blessed any further, they brought out dessert. The pumpkin, apple, and chocolate pies and an endless supply of peanut butter cookies were as good as my grandma's. But it went further than that; they were all so genuine and caring. We were treated as sojourners, and they listened intently to our stories. While I couldn't get to know everyone, I was blessed to talk at length with Art and Lilly, who had lived in Boulder, Colorado, for twenty years and shared a passion for hiking. Also, Susan and her daughter Lindsey, who exuded their love for one another in a way that was palpable. Lindsey reminded me of my baby sister, Cindy, with her boundless energy, infectious smile, and can-do attitude. She had great aspirations of being an FBI agent one day, and I believe she had the integrity it would take. Last but not least, we would never have met such kindred souls without Debbie spearheading that gathering. At the night's end, they ensured we all had a to-go bag of leftovers. When I asked Debbie what she was going to do with the ham bone, explaining that my dog was back at the apartment, she said, "Well, I was going to make soup out of it, but you take it to Kee."

Sharing a Thanksgiving feast with some of the Marshal Presbyterian parishioners.

A gathering of kindred souls.

The last vestiges of my religious prejudicial walls crumbled that night over a shared meal and the kindness of strangers. We have so much more in common than what separates us.

Kee did her happy dance and worked on that ham bone until it was polished clean.

11/29/96

Heading out of Hot Springs, we faced forty-six hundred feet of vertical climbing in the next fourteen miles. Along the way, we came across hillsides that looked like they had been freshly plowed under by feral hogs. Out of an abundance of caution, I kept Kee close in case we ran into a herd of swine. I wasn't sure how dangerous those feral hogs could be, but I knew javelina in Arizona could quickly disembowel a dog.

Everyone was struggling with heavy packs coming out of town, especially Magoo. Initially, I thought he was falling behind because he wasn't fueling enough, so I left a Power Bar with his name on it dangling from a tree, with duct tape, at chest height. He thanked me when he valiantly hobbled into Roaring Fork Shelter later that evening.

The four amigos getting ready to leave Hot Springs, NC.

11/30/96

We were five miles into the day's journey and traversing across the summit of Max Patch (el: 4629), an exposed grassy bald. The wind screamed up there, and we were forced to lean into it to stay upright. The clouds flew by and gave us a startling visual of how fast the wind was actually blowing. Every so often, there would be a break in the clouds, and we were rewarded with stunning views of the valleys below, surrounded by rugged mountains. There was something very exhilarating and sanctifying being in the presence of such beauty. The wind seemed to purge my very soul of all negativities. It truly felt like I was living my authentic life.

We did less than twelve miles before stopping at Groundhog Creek Shelter. We hoped the shorter day would help Magoo and his knees. He tried to hide the pain from us, but the grimace on his face was deeply drawn. We knew he pushed on so he wouldn't let his son down but couldn't help but wonder how much more he could endure.

12/01/96

The previous short day seemed to have helped Magoo, so we set out for Cosby Knob Shelter 17.5 miles away while Magoo and Blue Noodle hung back and promised to catch up later. I began to detect a pattern of them getting a late start every Sunday morning, but I hadn't bothered to inquire about it.

There was a break in the weather, so we stopped and had lunch along a swollen Pigeon River. The traffic along I-40 looked like a parking lot, and we didn't find out until later from a stranded motorist waiting to get on the on-ramp that the recent five inches of rain had caused a rockslide.

I tried to call the various services to get Kee shuttled around the Smokies, but it seemed that some of them had already shut down for the season and were on vacation or weren't answering phone calls. The reality that my hike could end at the northern boundary of the Great Smokey Mountain National Park or, at the very least, force me to skip the Smokies, weighed heavy on me. In a "Hail Mary" attempt to find a solution, I called my buddy Mike Pomeranz, who worked for a news station in Knoxville, Tennessee. Unfortunately, my morning call woke Mike up after he had a late night at work. I could decipher from his sleep-deprived delirium that he had two dogs, and it would be at least a couple of hours before he could get to me. I told him, "Look, brother, you sound exhausted. I don't think it's safe for you to be driving, and besides, traffic is at a standstill here. Thanks, but I'll figure something out."

There were no Park Rangers around to ask for advice or alternatives, and it didn't look like hitching would be an option from any of the stranded motorists. The I-40 was literally a parking lot, so I signed in the park register along with everyone else. While it felt like I was trying to smuggle Kee into the Garden of Eden, I didn't know what else to do. So, I kept her on a tight leash and minimized her impact by burying her waste. I prepared myself mentally to receive a fine from the first Park Ranger we came across, but I also hoped for a bit of grace, considering the circumstances.

Heavy dark clouds closed in on the mountains above us as we headed into the park, and we came across a massive pile of fresh bear scat within the first half mile. I started to second-guess my decision.

We did close to seven thousand feet of elevation gain for the day, and most of it came in the last seven miles from Davenport Gap Shelter to Cosby Knob Shelter. That section gave me flashbacks of climbing the Priest, even though it wasn't nearly as steep. The final ascent and all the ups and downs wreaked havoc on Magoo's failing knees. We had been hiking in a constant downpour most of the day, but as we prepared our dinner, the skies finally cleared and exposed a brilliant star-studded sky that seemed so close, it seemed like I could reach out and touch them.

12/02/96

Magoo hadn't improved by morning, and he decided he needed to end his journey. His decision was both self-sacrificing and self-preservation. He washed down a large dose of ibuprofen, said goodbye, and walked away without his pack. With his arm around his son's supportive shoulders, I knew the pain he was bearing ran much deeper than physical limitations. He never looked back, and I know all of us felt his pain. Even Kee seemed to worry as she watched Magoo and Blue Noodle disappear down the trail. Only the love for a kindred soul, a brother from a different mother, can hurt like that.

Our ranks were dwindling.

We lost Tapeworm in Damascus, Cookie Moose in Erwin, Spiderman in Boiling Springs, and now Magoo's decision left us wondering who was next. A lot could happen in the last two hundred and twenty-six miles, but Magoo's decision gave his son the best shot at finishing before Christmas.

Blue Noodle walked his dad to Cosby Campground and returned to the shelter to retrieve both packs. In the meantime, Magoo called a church in Gatlinburg, and they sent someone to pick them up and bring them into town, where they waited a day for Magoo's wife to come for him. For the first time, Blue Noodle found himself hiking solo, trying to catch up with the rest of us. He struggled with loneliness but found solitude in the sanctuary of silence.

Rev, Wrong Way, Kee, and I hiked for hours in silence under a clear blue sky, lost in thought about losing part of our family. The warmth of the sun's rays and stunning views melted the melancholy of loss. With each rhythmic step, we gained renewed purpose and were once again focused on the present.

We crossed Mt. Guyot (second highest in the Smokies, fourth highest in the eastern United States) and Mt. Chapman, then traversed the rocky cliffs of The Sawteeth, where the ridgeline was only a couple of feet wide in places, dropping precipitously on both sides. Stunning views of the surrounding mountains and Charlie's Bunion could be seen from the spine of The Sawteeth. The previous days rain had turned Sawteeth Ridge to ice, and we were extra cautious so we wouldn't slip at an inopportune time. We were forced to scramble down the leeward side of the ridgeline to seek shelter from the cold winds, where we basked in the last of the evening sun as we grabbed a quick snack. At dusk, we reached Charlie's Bunion, a treeless rock formation that earned its name in 1929 when Horace Kephart, an early campaigner for the national park designation, noticed that the formation resembled his friend's inflamed foot malady and promised to name that prominent Precambrian point in his honor.

Views on the Appalachian Trail are hard-earned, and the panoramic vistas of undulating mountains, from our perch on Charlie's Bunion, for as far as the eye could see, made my heart leap for joy. We spent some time on the Bunion with reverent gratitude for those who had the foresight to make the Great Smokey Mountain National Park a reality. I captured the silhouette of a backpacker, who stood on the Bunion at twilight, gazing over a vast American landscape.

Charlie's Bunion

We slipped and slid down an icy trail on our way to Icewater Spring Shelter. Exhausted after twenty-one frozen miles, we slung our packs into the shelter just in time to witness another glorious sunset as the western sky erupted into a fireball of color.

12/03/96

Rev lost his footing on a couple of the frozen downhill sections; he took some jarring falls and wrenched his back. As long as he kept moving, it didn't bother him at first, but he would stiffen up overnight. He was unusually quiet in the morning and obviously in a great deal of pain as he hobbled to the privy. He didn't return for quite some time, and we contemplated drawing straws to see who would go on a search and rescue mission. Before we mobilized, he hobbled and shuffled his way back to the shelter. He never complained, but the tears running down his face gave him away.

He popped 800mg of vitamin I (ibuprofen) with his breakfast and waited for the numbing effect. He declined our offers to offload some of his pack weight, and with gritted determination, he shouldered his pack as if his life depended on it. Wrong Way took the lead, and I walked in the sweep position. I followed close enough not to rush him but near enough to catch him if he fell. He shuffled, and wobbled from side to side, and swung each leg forward with an ensuing grunt. The steady dosing of Ibuprofen did not seem to take the edge off. After I watched him struggle mile after agonizing mile, I didn't dare mention the blister forming on my own heel.

A light smokey haze hung in the distant mountain tops. Their rugged beauty reminded me of Colorado mountain ranges, minus the jagged peaks of my home state. We hadn't seen another person for days, and it was starting to feel like we had the Smokies to ourselves. Near Newfound Gap, we ran into three people from Germany hiking in cowboy boots, John Wayne style. They were shocked when they learned we had hiked so far and clamored to get pictures with us.

We walked across the parking lot at Newfound Gap and were mobbed by tourists jumping out of their cars to eagerly ask us questions as if we were some rare mountain people who had just stepped into civilization for the first time.

The questions came from every direction, "What kind of animals have you seen? Any bears? What do you eat? How long in between shelters is it? Do you take a bath? How long do you go between baths?..." Their enthusiasm was a sensory overload like I'd never experienced. We patiently fielded their questions and then made a beeline for the far side of the parking lot as a tour bus pulled up.

Before we could find refuge in the woods, some nimble silver hairs intercepted us. They waved and called out, "Excuse me!" The same questions ensued. One sweet lady stated, "I'm very envious of you!" Another chimed in, "If only I were forty or fifty years younger."

"Believe it or not," I said. "I've seen people in their eighties who climbed mountains with the best of us."

"Really?" the same lady questioned with a glimmer of hope at the possibility.

"Absolutely," I said. "I just witnessed you sprint across the parking lot. You can do this, even if you do a little at a time. You got this, Sister!"

At the parking lot's edge, I turned and pointed to her one more time, pumped my fist in the air, and yelled, "Just do it. You'll never regret it!"

They continued to watch us as we headed into the woods and slowly disappeared. Wrong Way and I throttled back to accommodate Rev's AT shuffle.

We moved slowly through the woods, and it allowed us to creep within spitting distance of a herd of peacefully grazing deer, out of earshot from the parking lot noise. Once again, we transcended into the peaceful tranquility of nature, and I realized that we had come to prefer the simple serenity of walking in a masterpiece of exquisite beauty that revealed a divine artist.

We reached Clingman's Dome, the highest peak on the Appalachian Trail. The viewpoint on the summit was from an impressive concrete structure that looked like it was inspired by the futuristic design of one of my childhood cartoon shows, *The Jetsons*. We walked the spiral walkway to the circular viewing deck and were blasted by arctic air that was quick to get our attention. Kee's ears were blown straight out, and it looked like she was ready to take flight. We could see for a hundred miles in every direction.

Rev took shelter on the leeward side of the center column and pulled a cell phone out of his pack, which looked like it weighed at least two pounds. He didn't want to burden us with his physical limitations and tried to find one of his friends to hike the last two hundred miles with him. It was a big request that was complicated by the winter season. I can't say that I blamed them for not being able to get away, especially since it was cold enough to freeze our water purifiers. That made it a challenge to get clean drinking water. Even my Polar Pure Iodine was frozen, and I had to keep it in the chest pocket of my jacket if I wanted to disinfect my water.

Rev's "Hail Mary" phone call was to no avail, so we trudged cautiously south with the western sky exploding into a blood-red sunset when we arrived at Siler's Bald Shelter. Our 15.5 miles pushed Rev to the limit, and I wasn't sure how much more he could take.

12/04/96

Despite dropping almost twelve hundred feet in elevation from Clingman's Dome, everything was still frozen in the morning. My camera and voice recorder refused to work under those conditions. There wasn't an outhouse at Siler's Bald, so we were forced to dig into the frozen ground at least a football field's distance from the shelter. That may have been the coldest bowel movement of my life, and I hurried for fear of frostbite.

I offered to walk sweep as Rev and Wrong Way headed out. Kee and I weren't four miles into the day when we found Rev and Wrong Way stopped in the trail. Rev was finished. He wasn't able to push any farther.

"That's it, you've tortured yourself enough! We're going to divvy up your pack." I half expected my mule-headed brother to resist, but there was no more fight left in him. We took at least twenty pounds from his pack. I took his tent, sleeping bag, stove, and cooking kit. Wrong Way took his extra clothes. Kee even took a few things. The lightened load helped, but he said he still felt as if he was being stabbed in the back with a searing hot knife. Calling Search and Rescue was not an option he was willing to entertain.

When we crossed the summit of Rocky Top, I couldn't help but break into singing the chorus of the *Rocky Top* song. I'm sure my rendition wasn't in perfect pitch, and I couldn't be certain if Rev's smile was indicative of him being transported beyond his pain by my singing or if it was his way of acknowledging his ability to endure another level of agony. Regardless, we were able to distract him enough to get to Russell Field Shelter for a 14.3-mile day.

With reverent awe, we watched a golden globe of fire nestled between two hills slowly set. Sometimes, it felt like we had reverted to our prehistoric roots, and the setting sun was a form of entertainment that resonated on a very existential level. Even more bizarre was that this setting sun gave me a sense of déjà vu until I realized this scene was one I had consistently drawn in my childhood. Seeing it in real life was spectacular!

12/05/96

I woke up to an incredible windstorm. The gusts sounded like a train roaring by. I kept an eye out for falling branches as I went to filter water from the sporadic gushing spring. It flowed with tremendous force, then slowed, emitting a sucking sound that sounded eerily like the breathing of Darth Vader. On my way back to the shelter, I heard an ear-piercing scream.

When Rev woke up, he tried to move his legs and was jolted with another stabbing sensation. He refused to end his hike by calling Search and Rescue. He was such a purist that I had to convince him there was no shame in hiking with a light pack. We took more weight from him and hoped he could make it to Fontana Dam, where we would reassess his condition. I don't know that I had ever met a more stubborn idealist in my life.

For the last three days we were blessed to have the Smokies primarily to ourselves. We endured frigid temperatures that were made tolerable by clear, sunny skies. But the winds brought gray skies that seemed to back up against the Smokies, slowly building, and growing darker and more menacing as we walked the 12.4 miles to Fontana Dam.

We were taking a break someplace between Doe Knob and Birch Spring Shelter when a massive whitetail buck sneaked through the forest with his nose to the ground like a bloodhound tracking scent, totally oblivious to our presence. I figured he was making a beeline for a late estrus doe.

After passing Birch Spring Shelter, the skies unleashed a raw fury, and we were pelted with quarter-sized hail. Undeterred, we continued on with one goal: get to Fontana Dam. The hail turned to rain as we dropped in elevation. I forged ahead to deposit my heavy load at the dam and then headed back to check on Rev. To my surprise, Blue Noodle was with them. He had made a herculean effort to catch us, and he almost suffered a trail-ending calamity in his hurry. He had reached Clingman's Dome Observatory, where the handrail and walkway were encased in ice. He cautiously made his way up the spiral walkway and took a selfie (before selfies were a thing). He nearly made it to the bottom of the walkway when he suddenly slipped, and the first thing that hit was his head. He said he saw stars and then remembered wondering how long it was going to be before someone found him if he lost consciousness. I think it was that thought and the ensuing surge of adrenaline that may have saved his life and kept him moving. Hiking in the winter is no joke; hiking solo only increases the risk exponentially.

Our tramily was united once again when we crossed Fontana Dam during a brief reprieve from the rain, and we stopped at the Fontana Dam Shelter. It was donated by Papa Smurf of 1993 and, incredulously, had running water in the bathrooms, which earned it the high praise of being called the "Fontana Hilton."

Rev shuffled to a urinal and had to steady himself with his hiking sticks while he relieved himself. That pretty well solidified in my mind that Rev could no longer kick the can down the road and needed to see a doctor immediately. It didn't take too much arm-twisting before he relented. We made a call to Jeff Hoch at the Fontana Motel, and he agreed to come and get us while we waited out the storm at the visitor's center. In the short time it took Jeff to get to us, Rev had stiffened up so bad he couldn't put any pressure on his right leg. We had to carry him to the truck and load him up. Jeff was kind enough to shuttle us the ninety-five miles to Asheville, North Carolina, where Rev spent the rest of the day getting X-rays. The emergency department doctor said he saw no bulging disks or fractures. He diagnosed Rev with intense muscle spasms and prescribed some muscle relaxers and pain medication. The consensus was to get the muscles locked down to relax so his spine would realign naturally. Rev could not make a rational decision and just wanted to sleep, so we checked into a Holiday Inn and waited for his head to clear. He was in less pain once the cobwebs had vacated, but still struggled to walk. He wanted to get a second opinion the next day to make sure there wasn't any nerve damage or a ruptured disk.

12/06/96

The second doctor confirmed the initial diagnosis and gave him some stretches to do along with the medication, suggesting that it was going to take some time and that he needed to be patient. None of us knew how long it was going to take before Rev was well enough to hike again, but Blue Noodle and Wrong Way didn't have any immediate conflicts that required them to finish in the near future. On the other hand, I was scheduled to fly home on the morning of the fifteenth and knew it would be impossible to get back to the trail from Asheville, hike one hundred and seventy miles, and get to the airport on time. I called the airlines, hoping that they would understand the extenuating circumstances. To my relief, they had an opening on a midday flight on the eighteenth, with the next available flight after Christmas. I locked it in and steeled myself to say goodbye to my tough-as-nails tramily.

Kee had been cooped up in the hotel room while we were at the hospital, so I took her for a walk behind the hotel to stretch her legs and get some fresh air. I let her off leash so she could sniff around and be a dog. She wandered across what looked like a subdivision road to explore the forest on the other side when I heard a noise and saw a transit bus barreling our way a couple of hills away. I called for her, and she ignored me. She had that selective hearing going due to being cooped up in a room for most of the day. I ran out into the road and tried to get her, but she thought I was playing a game with her, so she ran off, staying just out of reach.

I lunged, caught her, and pulled her off the road just as the transit bus flew by. I looked up to the sound of screeching tires. The driver of a truck was trying to pass the bus. He went partially off the road in his reckless hurry and would have creamed us had he not slammed on the brakes and veered back behind the bus. That close call made me wonder if I had been in the woods too long and lost my urban survival instincts.

12/07/96

After one last all-you-can-eat breakfast with everyone, we said our goodbyes, and then Kee and I hitched the ninety-five miles back to the trail. Hitchhiking isn't the most efficient means to travel. Still, if you're patient and open to meeting people that fate brings your way, it can be an opportunity to rendezvous with some fascinating and genuine people. It seemed that I had just stuck my thumb out, and a sweet couple named Jim and Mary Lou picked us up. During the ride, our conversation focused mostly on their curiosity about life on the trail. After I told them what the Kennebec River Master said about finding riches greater than gold and silver, they informed me that there were gemstones and rubies found in the surrounding mountains between Ashville and Fontana, and one ruby found by a fishing guide was worth millions.

Before they dropped me off at the Fontana Hilton, they shared that they were members of a rural Charismatic Protestant church that danced with snakes as part of their religious beliefs. They said they danced with copperheads, water moccasins, and rattlesnakes. They favored rattlesnakes because they gave off the most pleasing sound and did it to prove their faith in God. They quoted Mark 16:18 as the reason they trusted their very lives to the will of God.

While snake handling as a profession of faith seemed a bit extreme, almost like you were tempting God to care for you despite the bad choices you made, a part of me wanted to witness this ritual, but I had a deadline to meet. I'm not sure if my hitching technique had improved that much in the course of two thousand miles or if Kee was the impetus that tugged on people's heartstrings. Regardless, it was another experience that helped me believe in the basic goodness of people.

It was Saturday night, and Kee and I had the Fontana Hilton to ourselves. After hiking for a while, the days and nights tend to mimic the rhythm of nature. I found that I never needed an alarm clock if I went to sleep within an hour of nightfall because I could rely on the birds to consistently wake me an hour before sunrise. I could get six solid hours of sleep in the summer and in the winter at least eight hours. This wasn't average sleep; it was the deep, restorative sleep of your youth, and this night was no different until I was startled awake by Kee's barking.

Sometime after ten o'clock, a guy named Hooper came in looking for a place to lay his head. Hooper, who supposedly hiked the trail in 1992, 1993, and 1994, said he had just left Waynesboro, Virginia, and came here to get a good night's sleep. At the time, I thought it was a bit odd that he had left the confines of civilization to find rest. It wasn't long before my weary bunkmate was snoring, reaching a crescendo that rivaled Magoo's. Desperation forced me to rip into my pack, hoping to find a fresh pair of earplugs in my hygiene kit. I fell back asleep as the foam swelled in my ear canals, effectively muffling the nocturnal nightmare to tolerable levels.

12/08/96

Kee and I woke the next morning, got ready for the day and were gone while Hooper continued to sleep as if he hadn't slept for days.

The trail wound around Fontana Reservoir for a distance, affording us some spectacular glimpses of its two hundred and thirty-eight miles of pristine shoreline. The waters glistened with the morning sunrise. Light waves lapped at the shore with a steady rhythm that enveloped me in a peacefulness that only comes from being present in the moment. The shore was so steep in places that people had opted to moor their floating cabins in sheltered coves. I marveled at the lengths people would go to find their sanctuaries. I don't blame them, for it is as essential as air itself.

12/09/96

The weather was so intense that night it seemed improbable that the Brown Fork Gap Shelter could withstand the ferocious onslaught of screaming winds. My hat was off to those who constructed that log shelter. From a structural perspective that building scoffed at nature's worst. There was never a shudder or any indication that we were about to be blown off the mountain.

We woke up to find everything had been flash-frozen overnight, and it felt like we had slept in a walk-in freezer. My camera's and recorder's batteries were so cold they refused to work. But the early dawn's light promised clear skies and a warming sun, simple things that buoyed my spirit.

The shallow spring was icy cold, and to my surprise, several bright orange newts were lying in the bottom sediment. Newts can secrete a potent neurotoxin called tetrodotoxin, which can cause muscle paralysis. I assumed they wouldn't secrete the toxins unless threatened, but I chose to filter my water upstream to be safe.

There were a lot of ups and downs as the trail took us over the tops of countless little mountains. The wind was screaming on the top of Cheoah Bald, and I had to duck down on the leeward side of the mountain to let my mustache and beard thaw while refueling to keep warm. The view from my five thousand and sixty-two-foot perch was awe-inspiring. Spread out before me was an ocean of mountaintops as far as I could see. Some places had low-lying clouds or fog with mountains jutting up through the white veil. They looked like islands in the sky. It was humbling to know that I still had one hundred and forty miles to go through this rugged terrain. I could only imagine how beautiful camping on Cheoah Bald must have been in the spring, summer, and fall.

Kee and I had dropped at least one thousand feet in elevation as we walked along the Cheoah ridge, where we could occasionally glimpse the Nantahala River in the valley far below. We had a long way to go before we crossed the Nantahala, and then we had to climb the far mountains that I had to look up at in order to see their summit from the ridge where we were hiking. It made me smile to think the trail's creators had successfully challenged us in all capacities.

Before we reached the Nantahala River basin, we came across another hillside that had been completely ravaged by wild boars rooting for food. This invasive species would consume roots, tubers, fungi, burrowing animals such as small mammals, reptiles, amphibians, and insects. No stone was left unturned as they hunted indiscriminately, leaving an entire hillside barren. If left unchecked, I could only imagine how much damage these four-legged locusts would cause in an ecosystem.

Nestled at the base of towering mountains, the Nantahala is appropriately named as it means the land of the noonday sun. As we crossed the river, we saw that the Nantahala Outdoor Center, primarily a commercial whitewater outfitter, was vacant and looked like they had closed down for the season. Kayak gates were still strung out in the icy water, leading me to believe some hearty souls were braving the frigid waters to train for competitions.

Darkness came early in the land of the noonday sun, so we tented out on a flat grassy section above the A. Rufus Morgan Shelter. Hiking solo was both liberating and lonely, especially at the end of the day when fellow adventurers would share stories over a hot meal around a crackling fire. Kee seemed to sense my sadness. She walked over, laid down next to me, and rested her head on my lap.

12/10/96

Something moving quickly through the crunchy leaves outside my tent awakened me in the predawn hour. By the time I had gained consciousness and unzipped my tent to catch a glimpse, it had disappeared around a bend, heading up the trail in the direction I would go. I quickly broke camp, fed Kee, and grabbed some quick snacks hoping to see what had been in such a hurry on this frosty morning.

Kee and I were closing in on the summit of Wesser Bald when suddenly I saw a flash of movement through the trees above us. It was running fast down the trail wearing a blue jacket and sporting a blue beanie. It looked like a character from *The Smurfs*. The runner closed the distance quickly, nimble footed like a deer, moving through the woods as if for the sheer joy of running. The poetry in motion gradually stopped, and I was stunned by her natural beauty and radiant smile.

Her name was Becky Barth. We talked for over an hour like long lost kindred souls. She loved to run the six miles to the top of Wesser Bald, climb the tower to watch the sunrise, then run back down to the Nantahala Outdoor Center, where she was a kayak/canoe instructor. She had a client to get to that morning, and I had a trail to finish. I watched her go, and she glanced back with a smile and waved a last goodbye. I had not seen another person for days, and crossing paths with another adventurous soul who radiated beauty and kindness was a true blessing. I climbed the tower at the summit, where the views were endless, and the Nantahala could be seen snaking through the far valleys.

The Goddess of Wesser Bald would haunt me for a long time.

Eleven miles later, I came across Wayah Bald, originally named by the Cherokees, meaning wolf. It had a rock observatory built by the Civilian Conservation Corps, and the view from an elevation of five thousand three hundred and forty-two feet was spectacular. The views validated what was possible if you consistently put one foot in front of the other. Looking back to the north, I could see the Smokies and found it very humbling to know that I had come so far through such rugged terrain.

The leaves were so deep that I kept tripping on hidden rocks and roots. I fell twice today. Once, I tripped on a rock and did a face plant in the leaves, and the second time, I snagged my toe under a hidden root while going downhill, causing me to stumble four or five steps before making a saving grab on a small pine tree before I went over the edge.

I was hiking up Siler Bald from Wayah Gap when I noticed the scent of cooking food being carried in the cooling downward thermals. I pulled into the Siler Bald Shelter after a tough 22-mile day and was pleasantly surprised to find four camp counselors preparing a feast over an open fire. When I walked up, they were pulling baked potatoes, wrapped in tin foil, off the grill.

Tim, the group leader, asked, "Are you hungry? We brought extra, hoping we would run into a thru-hiker."

"I seem to always be hungry, but I have my own food." I pulled Kee's food out of her pack and fed her.

He handed me the biggest potato I'd ever seen. "We have plenty."

It was at least ten inches long and weighed close to three pounds. He loaded it with butter, cheese, sour cream, chives, and bacon bits and then stepped back and gave the other leaders a look as if to say, "*Watch this.*"

I couldn't believe my good fortune, so I exclaimed while shaking my head in disbelief, "That thing is a monster!" I savored every bit as if it was my last meal.

Like a gracious host, Tim gave me that all-approving look as if he understood the depth of my gratitude and cheerfully offered, "We have chicken shish kabobs for the next course."

Grilled chicken and vegetables had never tasted so good. Over the course of the evening, we shared adventure stories, and I was impressed that Tim, Michelle, Shawn, and Brent were leading ten teenage girls on a three-day vision quest. All the girls were isolated in different pockets of the forest. This was their opportunity to disconnect from the busyness of life and be completely present in the moment. Being present in the moment meant allowing themselves to pay attention to details, using all of their senses to help them elevate their awareness of their surroundings. They were encouraged to journal their experiences, dreams, and what really mattered to them. The leaders would make their rounds periodically to check on the girls, and the hope was that this form of asceticism and contemplative thinking would give them a deeper connection with their creator and a renewed sense of purpose. Once again, I was blessed to see these young adults from Hidden Lake Village trying to make a difference in this world!

12/11/96

The morning was shrouded in fog, and it was drizzling. I broke camp and ate breakfast on the trail so I wouldn't wake anyone. It had been drizzling all day, and with every wind gust, we were drenched by a cascading waterfall of moisture blown from every tree and shrub soaked from the day's steady mist. The higher I climbed; visibility was reduced to ten yards at best. I wondered how the Vision Quest girls were holding up. Hopes of a view on top of Albert Mountain were squashed as the clouds continued to thicken.

I entered the southern Nantahala Wilderness and encountered a bunch of insect collectors that the Forest Service had set out to try and figure out what was killing the trees in this area. They were little green log cabin structures made out of tin and filled with a sticky substance. They had been out since May and were packed with a wide assortment of bugs. I sure hoped they were able to isolate which bugs were responsible for the carnage.

I hiked that last section through the stark skeletal remains of a once vibrant forest while slogging through a moisture-laden cloud, made for an eerie, dreary end to the day. On a positive note, we made it the nineteen-plus miles to Carter Gap Shelter just as it began to pour. The clouds were so thick I couldn't see the far wall of the shelter. I was so hungry, but still intent on making my spaghetti dinner, I didn't realize that there was condensation glistening on the interior walls.

Every cell in my body wanted me to crawl into my sleeping bag and fall asleep, then I realized I would be soaked by morning if I did. Instead, I had to set up my tent in the shelter, hoping my rainfly would stave off this new threat for potential hypothermia.

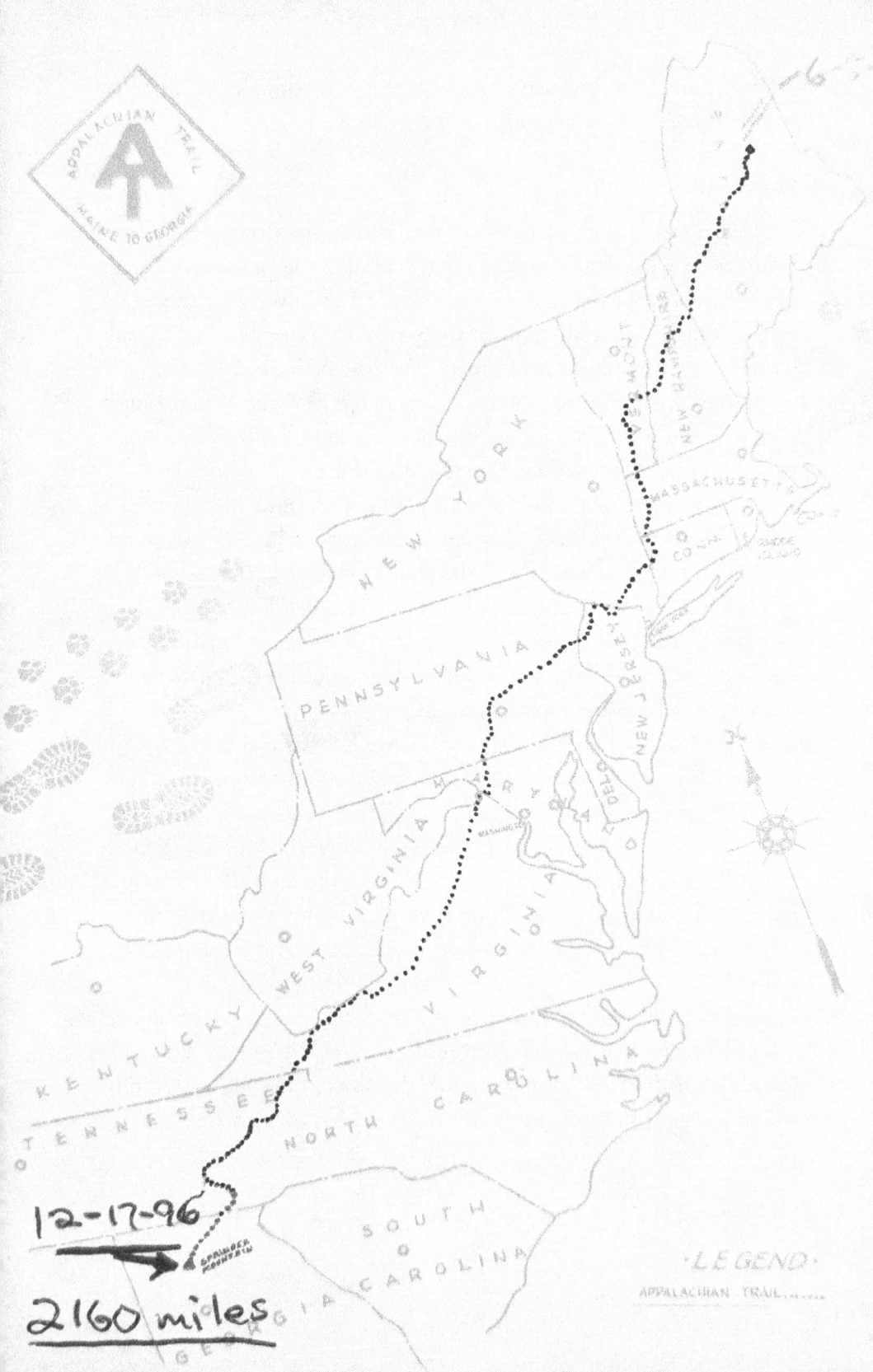

Chapter 23

Georgia

12/12/96

    Six a.m., it was still raining, and the night sky was black as coal. I unzipped my tent and peeked out; mice scattered when the light from my headlamp lit the deck. The clouds dissipated from inside the shelter, but the interior walls still shimmered with moisture. I could see my breath in my dimming light. The near-freezing temperature was sucking the life out of my batteries, so I doused my light to conserve them. Not long after I woke up, a pervasive hunger provoked me to get breakfast going, but I only had a few sips of water left so I had to search for the spring in the rain. I turned my light on once again, and the advancing mice scurried to the dark recesses of the shelter. Kee still slept peacefully through it all, so I retreated to my tent and ate dry oatmeal in the dark, washing it down with the last of my water. I waited for the salvation of morning's light to chase the marauding mice to their hidden lairs.

    The air was so full of moisture that my damp clothes from yesterday didn't have a chance to dry overnight. There was nothing like putting on cold, wet clothes in the chilly morning hours. It was better than coffee and forced you to keep moving to stay warm.

    It quit raining as I neared Beech Gap, where I ran into a hunter. We talked in hushed whispers, not wanting to spook any nearby deer.

Ironically, John had just been hunting elk in the Gunnison area of Colorado. While we shared hunting stories, Kee suddenly got really excited while sniffing a nearby log and then began rubbing her neck on the log.

John said, "Oh, it's probably a little fox piss she's getting all excited over. You may want to stop her before she gets covered in it, otherwise she's going to stink to high heaven."

Too late. She had a very distinct odor, and for the first time on the trail, I prayed for rain. We climbed Standing Indian Mountain in a light mist that was barely noticeable, but while on the summit, the rain came down so hard it felt like we were getting pressure washed. It was warm enough that I hiked in shorts and my North Face rain jacket. I would overheat whenever I climbed, even with my rain jacket's pit zips (armpit vents) open. At times I would pull the rain hood back so I could quickly dump some heat. We ducked into the Standing Indian Shelter for a quick break and to refuel. We didn't stay long because the rain was blowing sideways, and we were still getting soaked in the back of the shelter. Note to self:

Be careful what you pray for!

I decided to continue on another 4.9 miles to Muskrat Creek Shelter and assess how we felt then. A little south of Muskrat Creek Shelter was a blue-blazed trail that took us a short distance to a cliff band called Raven Rock. I bet the view would be incredible on a clear day, but the surrounding mountain peaks were hidden in the clouds, and the valley was blurred by rain. We found the mangled parts and pieces of an old plane wreck. It was hard to imagine that anyone could have survived the scattered trail of twisted metal. Kee seemed impervious to the rain, and the cooler weather only invigorated her, so we pushed on another 7.3 miles before we were chased into Plumb Orchard Shelter by thunder and lightning. Despite having gaiters on, my feet were soaked, and I had to dump at least a half pint of water out of my boots and then squeeze another half pint out of my socks.

We hiked most of the day in the rain, and I couldn't get a picture of an ancient, twisted, and gnarled oak tree that stood on the North Carolina and Georgia border. That old tree had seen some tough times. The first ten feet of its trunk lay on the ground before it grew skyward, with crooked branches growing in every direction. It had survived everything that Mother Nature had thrown at it and proudly stood as a testament to fortitude. It had character born of tribulation. If only it could talk.

After dinner, I snuggled up in my cozy cocoon of a sleeping bag, listening to it rain, and Kee walked over, did her three spins, and plopped down next to me, laying her head on my legs. I rejoiced that she didn't smell like fox urine anymore and then I began to reflect on my day. We had seen more grouse that day than on the entire rest of the trail. Every mile seemed to hold numerous grouse clucking alongside the trail while others exploded from underfoot. After one trailside explosion of grouse, we came across a black newt moving quickly through the leaves as if his very life depended on it. He was missing part of his tail, and the raw nub left me to speculate that our presence had saved him from the feeding miniature Velociraptors. It was not long before the constant drumming of the rain lulled me into a fitful slumber.

12/13/96

I was abruptly awakened by the whistle shriek of a barred owl on an early morning flyby. After hearing that screech, I bolted upright and fumbled for my headlamp, thinking I had just heard a big cat make a kill in front of the shelter. I flipped my light on as my imagination ran wild until a barred owl proceeded to hoot the morning away in a nearby tree. Kee raised one eyebrow and looked sleepily at me as if asking, "What's all the excitement about?" The rain slowed, and I hoped that it would clear by morning light, so I lingered in the warmth of my sleeping bag and listened as the rain continued to fall softly and the owl's call of the wild reverberated through the shelter's opening. I could only imagine how the owl's calling would send any remaining mice scurrying for cover. I didn't see any telltale evidence of rodent activity, and it was apparent that this apex predator controlled the mouse population at this shelter.

The rising sun silenced the vocal night crew. With only fifteen miles to do today, I watched from the confines of my sleeping bag as a golden glow down on the horizon began to illuminate the intermittent clouds, a pink hue surrounded by blue sky. The day crew became more vocal with the light of day as a red-crested pileated woodpecker started hammering a nearby tree and then stopped briefly to emit a crazy-sounding laugh of a call before drilling once again into the hardwood with a force that made my head hurt. Chickadees and nuthatches were busy working the surrounding trees and shrubs in constant motion, flitting here and there with amazing agility. Little brown finches hopped along, scouring the forest floor. Two crows soared above, calling to each other as they flew above the treetops. I saw a solo duck whistle by in a southerly direction as if he had been left behind and was frantic to catch up with the rest of the flock.

I watched in amazement at the simple complexities of life in the natural world. Man, did I love it out here!

The promise of a sunny day made it easier to put on wet clothes with high hopes that the sun would dry everything out at some point. Kee and I hiked the entire day under sunny skies and mild temperatures. Optimal days like this made it impossible to walk without a smile and a spring in my step.

I was conflicted when I stopped at Tray Mountain Shelter. Part of me wanted to hike another eight miles to Blue Mountain Shelter, but another part of me didn't want it to end. Patience won out over rushing to the finale, the southern terminus of the Appalachian Trail, on Springer Mountain. I chose to squeeze every last magical moment out of the AT.

That night, Kee and I watched a fantastic meteor shower. Streaks of white light rained down toward earth, and it humbled me to be in the presence of such grandeur. Kee seemed to sense my melancholy and approached me from behind, resting her head on my shoulder. Together, we stared into the night sky. Words were not necessary.

I fell asleep to the Eagles' song "Seven Bridges Road" playing in my head, substituting Appalachian Trail for Seven Bridges Road.

There are stars in the southern sky Southward as you go

There is moonlight and moss in the trees Down the Appalachian Trail

Especially poignant were the lyrics where they sang about loving in a tame way and loving you wild. Then when you get right down to it, if the AT were capable of human emotions, it is exactly what you would experience while hiking along the rugged peaks of a mountain range that is approximately 480 million years old.

I wish my tramily were here to sing with me. With a great deal of imagination, we could have harmonized like the Eagles.

12/14/96

It was so warm, I hiked in shorts and a t-shirt. Every step was filled with gratitude. The hiking was easy, and I was able to reflect with a deep appreciation for the gift of the Appalachian Trail.

The panoramic view from Tray Mountain was amazing. I was able to look back to the north and see Standing Indian Mountain and the view of what I would have seen if it had been clear when I stood on that summit. I could also see Blood Mountain to the south, the highest mountain I had to climb in Georgia.

I still struggled with the thought of hiking on to Whitley Gap Shelter. Part of me wanted to continue simply because it felt so good to move through the woods with ease. I had to force myself to saunter these last days, soaking the surrounding beauty into my soul as if my days were numbered; in a way they were.

12/15/96

I was awakened by a mouse running across my face, followed by a barred owl hooting just outside Low Gap Shelter. I wondered if my startled reaction, when I swatted at something that had already vanished into the dark recesses at the back of the shelter, had made the owl abandon his scampering meal.

Kee had been eating like a hungry hiker and finished the last of her dog food last night, then worked me for part of my meal. I made eight packages of Maple/Brown Sugar oatmeal for breakfast and split it with Kee. I hadn't worried about calorie counts since the 100-Mile Wilderness in Maine. Instead, I ate until I was not hungry and still lost weight.

Early this morning, we found ourselves walking amongst giants. The White Oak Stamp Area was a large flat section in the Blue Ridge Mountains and was home to an old-growth red oak forest. Back home, our scrub oaks were much smaller than their eastern cousins but still produced a bumper crop of acorns favored by turkey, bear, and deer. After talking with numerous hunters south of the Mason-Dixon line, I found the general consensus was that animals preferred the acorns from the White oak because they dropped earlier and had less tannin in them, which made them less bitter. The tannin in the acorns of the red oak made them less desirable but helped preserve them so they lasted longer on the ground, which helped ensure there was an additional food source on the menu during the late season and winter months.

My main objective for the day was to secure more food for Kee before she cleaned me out of my limited supplies. We hustled into Neels Gap to allow for a twenty-eight-mile roundtrip contingency hitchhike into Blairsville if we couldn't find anything at the Walasi-Yi Center. The trail goes through the Walasi-Yi Center, pronounced Wa La See Yee, which in Cherokee means "place of the great frog." This frog, according to Native American legend, was a sentinel that stood guard over nearby Blood Mountain. According to the *Thru-Hiker's Handbook*, the center had a hostel and backpacking store with a grocery store section. I dropped my pack near the front water fountain and tied Kee to it before heading into the store. As I wandered the small grocery section, Elane, one of the clerks, approached me. "Can I help you find something?"

"My dog has been eating like a horse, and I'd like to get enough dog food to get us to Springer."

"We don't carry dog food but wait here."

While I waited, a lady walked toward me. Her name tag read Dorothy. "Hi, I can see you're thru-hiking. Why don't you help yourself to a soda?"

About that time, Elane returned with a plastic bag filled with two pounds of dog food from her personal stash. When I offered to pay for everything, they said almost in unison, "You don't owe us anything."

"Here's some Christmas brownies," Dorothy smiled. "Merry Christmas!"

As much as I wanted to devour those brownies, I said, "Thank you. I'm going to save this for my last meal on the trail. Merry Christmas!"

I walked out the door like I was walking on clouds, only to find my loyal hiking partner waiting patiently by my pack. To my surprise, an anonymous person had ventured past my guard dog and placed a navel orange on my pack. This, too, would be a part of my last meal.

There was something much bigger than us that united us all. Despite all the bad things that happen, there really were a lot of good people doing good things out there.

From the Center at Neels Gap, I had one last climb up Blood Mountain, the highest mountain in Georgia at four thousand four hundred and fifty-eight feet. It was an easy stroll compared to what I had done, but I was intrigued by how this mountain got its name. Supposedly, a battle between the Creeks and Cherokees was so fierce the mountain ran red with their blood. As I walked through the forest, I imagined Indians adorned in war paint, sneaking through the woods silently on moccasin feet, brandishing tomahawks, war clubs, knives, and bows. As I visualized the brutality and carnage that must have ensued to earn the mountain such a name, I wondered why it started. I thought about my childhood when, as a curious child, I put red ants with black ants in a jar and waited to see what would happen. To my surprise, nothing happened; they coexisted until I stirred them up with a stick. It was then that they viciously tore into each other, while some of them covertly snuck up the stick and then up my arm, biting me as they escaped the mayhem I had created. In my hurry to rid myself of this source of pain, I knocked over the jar, effectively ending my experiment as the surviving ants went their separate ways. I wondered who had stirred the stick on this mountain and every war humanity had fought.

Kee and I cowboy camped alongside a small stream between Granny Top Mountain and Big Cedar Mountain. After dinner, I gathered a nice pile of leaves and laid my sleeping pad on it. It was the softest bed I had slept on in a long time. I drifted off to sleep, listening to the bubbling stream and a breeze lightly blowing through the pines.

Cowboy camp

12/16/96

I woke in a dark silhouette forest with the eastern sky gradually erupting into a dazzling array of colors. The horizon was a fiery orange that faded to yellow, then pinks, blues, and purple as my eyes climbed higher into the overcast sky. I observed the morning sky for my weather report. The color of the clouds, the speed with which they moved, temperature drops, and dancing treetops were all indicators that rain gear would be needed at some point during the day. Red sky at night, shepherd's delight. Red sky in the morning, shepherd's warning. Great, it looks like another storm is moving in. I started this journey getting slammed by a storm on Katahdin, and it would only be appropriate to finish in a storm.

I walked the two miles into the town of Suches, population one hundred and fifty, to get my last mail drop, mainly consisting of dog food and letters from home. On the way in, I noticed that a log home on thirteen acres with a barn adjacent to a lake was listed for $93,000. A similar property back home, in 1996, would have commanded well into the seven-figure range.

Walking forced me to pay attention to my surroundings, and I found it interesting that the inherent vices within a community could be found alongside the road, discarded amongst the grass and shrubs. On that two-mile stretch, I counted one hundred and sixty-four empty beer cans on the way into town. Seeing this triggered a latent sadness that had been festering for a long time. If you walk along any road, you will find the closer you are to town, the higher the concentration of roadside trash will be. This was especially true around big cities. I'd watched with a heavy heart every time I returned to Phoenix to visit family, where it seemed the roadside refuse reached monumental proportions. Sometimes, it could feel like I was driving through a landfill where the cactus, mesquite, and palo verde trees were adorned with trash. Entire desert ecosystems were being polluted. My intent wasn't to rail on people's ignorance, but at some point, we had to quit living like locusts and begin to care enough about the environment in which we live to say, ENOUGH! We can't let our kids inherit such squalor.

> "Man is the most insane species. He worships an invisible God and destroys a visible Nature. Unaware that this Nature he's destroying is this God he's worshiping."
> ~ HUBERT REEVES, Canadian-French Astrophysicist

I was on my way out of town when a blue Mazda light-duty pickup heading into town slowed, then flipped a U-turn. The driver, Roger Belangor, yelled out the passenger window with a southern drawl, "Hey, you need a ride?" Roger had been on his way into town to get antibiotics for his wife but, for some reason, felt compelled to give a stranger a ride. My guess was that his wife's need wasn't an emergency. Even though he was on a mission, he made time to check on me, and I hadn't asked for help by sticking out my thumb. His example of putting other's needs before his own was the backbone of

American culture. I could only imagine how great this nation would be if we spent more time lifting our brothers and sisters up, respecting that our differences were what make us great!

Roger Belanger

After an easy nineteen miles, I stopped at Stover Creek Shelter to reflect. I thought how incredible it must have been for my northbound friends to have been lured on by the looming majesty of Katahdin, whose rugged features would gain clarity with each step. I had chosen to hike in a southerly direction, knowing that Katahdin would be the most rugged and closest semblance to my beloved Rockies. It was my way of eating dessert before the main meal. While Springer Mountain was somewhat anticlimactic compared to the summit of Katahdin, there was no less sense of accomplishment.

Tears ran freely down my face as I did an end-of-trail review. The beauty through which I traveled and the kind souls I had met along the way flashed past my mind's eye. I wanted to believe that life on the Appalachian Trail was a microcosm of society. I had set out to find the good in humanity and had been blessed abundantly. However, part of me still entertained the thought of walking across America to work with National Geographic, documenting the goodness inherent to this country.

12/17/96

I woke up literally in a cloud, still conflicted about what I would tell my parents when I made my final call from the pay phone at Amicalola Falls Visitor Center. I had 10.6 miles to figure it out. I stopped at Springer Mountain Shelter to weigh the pros and cons in my head if I walked across America.

PROS	CONS
1. Work with Nat. Geo.	1. Miss Christmas with family
2. Physically capable	2. Running low on funds
3. Find a job	3. Walking along roads
4. Adventure continues	
5. Meet great people	
6. See beautiful places	

From Springer Shelter, it was an uneventful four hundred and seventy-five steps to the official end of the trail on Springer Mountain. I entered my last impromptu thoughts in the register. It read:

> "I go home penniless as can be, but I am far richer than before since I hiked the A.T. I've never hiked so far and felt so free as I did when I hiked the A.T.
>
> The beauty I have seen, the friends I have met, and oh, don't forget the shelter comaraderie! All to be found on the A.T.
>
> Even though the end is sad to see, I know this incredible journey will live on in memory... All because I have hiked the A.T.
>
> Congrats South Bounders, and good luck, '97 North Bounders!"

As I set up to photograph the trail's end, it dawned on me that had we been northbound, my final summit pictures wouldn't have included Kee, because dogs weren't allowed in Baxter State Park, let alone Mount Katahdin. Perhaps it was just meant to be.

Kee seemed to understand the enormity of what we were celebrating as we gave each other a congratulatory high-five. After a brief celebration, I packed up my camera gear, and we headed down the approach trail. Just as I was feeling a slight melancholy about not standing on Katahdin, my soul was renewed with the sounds of the tumbling waters of Amicalola Falls. For a transplanted desert rat, water represented the essence of life and renewal. To see this magnificent waterfall, cascading crystal clear, at the end of my journey couldn't have been better scripted. Looking up at that beautiful waterfall, my heart was whole, and my soul overflowed with gratitude.

The AT, with all of its twists and turns, reveals a path of discovery along the spine of the Appalachians. These mountains, some of the oldest in the world, hold secrets of hidden treasures as old as time that appeal to curious and adventurous souls alike. It's hard to describe what hiking two thousand one hundred and sixty miles will do for you. But, on a trail with over four hundred and sixty-four thousand, five hundred feet of elevation change, which is nearly ninety miles, or enough to have summited Mount Everest sixteen times from sea level to summit, it will give you a sense of accomplishment at the very least. So, if you pay attention to the people you meet as you walk approximately five million steps through countless beautiful landscapes, you may find yourself reconnecting with the Creator in such a way that all your senses rejoice. I was born for this!

My first call from the visitor center pay phone was to my parents. As I waited for them to answer, I rehearsed how I would tell them that I would continue walking across America. They answered, "Hello?"

"Mom, Dad, we did it! I'm calling from the Amicalola Falls Visitor Center."

There was a lot of cheering on the other end of the line, and then my dad, choked with emotion, said, "We're proud of you, son!"

Springer Mountain-southern terminus of the AT

Celebratory high five

That hit me hard. I think every child loves to hear those words of affirmation, no matter their age. But what made those words even sweeter was that we worked together to make this shared adventure happen.

Just as I was going to tell them about the next leg of my journey, my mom interjected, "Son, we can't wait to see you for Christmas!"

I folded. Somehow, I couldn't bring myself to deny the woman who gave me life, that simple gift.

> "Until one has loved an animal, a part of one's soul remains unawakened."
>
> ~ANATOLE FRANCE, French poet

My next call was to Thunder Snow. Despite being almost two hours away in Athens, Georgia, he insisted I call him. Dr. Randy Elmore answered with as much enthusiasm as my parents, saying in that congenial southern drawl, "Ducttape! We've been waiting for your call. We'll be there in two hours."

I hung up the phone and looked at Kee, who was waiting patiently.

"It's the end of the trail, old girl. Let's go celebrate." With that, I pulled out my food bag and spread out our bounty on a picnic table, most of which represented the kindness of strangers toward a sojourner and his dog.

I was especially grateful for the guy on the rock and our encounter on Franconia Ridge. Had our paths not crossed, I would never have experienced the full healing power of the trail and the goodness in the people I met along the way. The song "Angels Among Us" by Alabama played through my mind as I came to terms with the enormity of what I had experienced. The AT was like a refiner's fire, stripping me of what I thought was important, forcing me to eliminate what I thought was necessary.

Thunder Snow and his son, Fox, picked us up and took us back to their home, where Thunder Snow's wife, Martha, found it humorous that we continued to address each other by our trail names. She was so good-natured about it, and her hospitality spoke volumes about the love that nurtured that family.

End of the Trail with Fox and Thundersnow

Fox, me, Martha and Thundersnow, the recipient of the "Hello Martha Kit"

Chapter 24

Reentry

BY MID-MORNING THE NEXT DAY, Kee and I were on a flight to Denver. We arrived at DIA late in the evening, and I rushed to find Kee waiting anxiously in her kennel at the baggage claim desk. She was so happy to see me. After being on the trail for so long, I could only imagine what a sensory overload flying was for her. She showed signs of distress, so after collecting my pack from the baggage carousel, I let her out of her kennel, and she calmed immediately once she was by my side. While we waited for my sister to pick us up, a lady and her kids made a beeline toward us and asked, "Do you mind if my kids pet your dog?"

> "Dogs do more for us than we can see. They help us know ourselves, and they bring us together."
> – SCOTT HAMMOND, *Finding Caleb*

"What do you think, Kee?" Before I could finish asking the question, Kee was up and wagging her tail at the end of her leash. She was in her glory with those kids loving on her.

With her kids occupied, the woman turned her attention to me and said, "I can tell you have been on a journey."

Part of me wondered if I looked like a wide-eyed wild man struggling to transition back into society. I had a much deeper appreciation of what the character Tarzan must have endured when he first encountered civilization. Telling my story helped transition me back to the calming realm of the trail, where I'd found something greater than silver and gold.

My sister walked by as I was finishing the highlight reel of my journey. I called out to her, "Hey, Sis!"

She did a double take, recognizing my voice but not recognizing me. "Rick? Oh my gosh, I didn't recognize you!" she said as she rushed in to hug me. It was then that I knew I had made the right decision. My sister could light up a room, and when she pulled back to take another look at me, she was smiling with a steady stream of tears running down her cheeks. She looked away and spotted Kee, dropped to one knee while Kee spun in circles. Then, she moved in to give my sister a face wash while wagging her tail excitedly, happy to be reunited with her pack.

I turned to the lady to explain, "I guess that's what happens when you lose sixty pounds and grow a beard."

Her jaw dropped and she just looked at me, her eyes wide for what seemed an eternity before she said, "You need to tell your story!"

I smiled and said, "Maybe someday." Prior to the trail, I probably wouldn't have noticed what a gift it was that our paths had crossed.

I can't tell you how great it was to see my sister, and it seemed that time had scarcely passed before we arrived at our home in Edwards three and a half hours later. My best friends, Dan and Gary, aka "Bomba," greeted me like a long-lost brother. Gary exclaimed, "Holy crap, you're shredded!" I took it as code for, "You look like a POW." We talked into the early morning hours, feeding off of each other's energy, happy to be reunited.

Two days later, Dan, Cindy, Kee, and I headed to Phoenix for Christmas, while Gary went to Upstate New York to be with his mother and extended family. Shortly after arriving in the Valley of the Sun, my eyes began burning, and I could smell the stench from all the air pollution, and the back of my throat gradually became more irritated. Growing up, it never seemed to bother me. I wondered how long it would take me to desensitize or if I really wanted to.

While it was a bit overwhelming to jump right into a big family gathering and all the chaos that ensued with almost forty people, it

My brother from another mother, Dan Schons,
and me, (60 lbs lighter), holding my faithful companion Kiana.

was also what I needed to help assimilate back into the real world. As soon as my brother-in-law saw me, he joked, saying, "Call the FBI, we found the Unabomber!" My sisters were gentler and said I looked more like Wolfman Jack, a legendary radio disk jockey. We grew up listening to his larger-than-life personality. You have to love family. Then to top it off, my sweet grandma refused to hug me, even though she knew who I was. Even my grandma was not impervious to harboring a deep-seated mistrust for men with beards. I had no idea where this latent judgment came from, but I was determined to help sway her opinion with a big Huber hug. She squirmed and laughed sheepishly as I rubbed my soft beard on her face. When I shaved that night for my grandma, I wondered if she was susceptible to judging a book by its cover, even when she knew the content by heart; how could people whom others had wounded be expected to shower the offender with grace and kindness that does not come easy once we are betrayed. Hate and anger breed hate and anger. We will only break our cyclical destructive nature when we recognize that we are all created in His image. Recognition of each other's sacred spirit has to take precedence over money, power, and self. We will have to collectively roll up our sleeves and help our neighbors, family, friends, and associates, be the person that God created them to be. We can start it with random acts of kindness, aka "Holy Moments," done with genuine Love. Until we learn this lesson, we will continue to reap what we sow.

> "I imagine when we die and finally see God, we will not say, 'Lord, I could never have guessed how beautiful you are.' We will not say that. Rather, we will say, 'So it was you all along. Everyone I ever loved; it was you. Everyone who ever loved me, it was you. Everything decent or fine that ever happened to me, everything that made me reach out and try to do better was you all along." - C. S. LEWIS

Christmas with my grandma and all my relatives was chaotic love, but it provided the energy boost I needed to decompress and try to assimilate back into society. After welcoming the New Year in, we returned to the outdoor recreation mecca of the Vail Valley. Our condo was located near the Eagle River, nestled between the I-70 corridor and Highway 6. I hadn't anticipated how sensitive I had become to noise pollution. The constant barrage of eighteen-wheelers barreling down the interstate was driving me mad. Desperation set in after three nights of no sleep, so I grabbed Kee and my sleeping bag and drove down to the boat launch area in a snowstorm. I backed my truck down to the water's edge, dropped my tailgate, and crawled into my camper shell. Buried deep in my sleeping bag, with Kee next to me, I wondered if I would ever get accustomed to societal norms or continue to prefer

Bearded Huber Hug for Grandma

living on the wild side. I fell into a deep slumber with the sounds of the Eagle River drowning out the noise of the modern world.

If our purpose in life is to love our neighbor and help one another along the way, then the AT truly represents what society should strive to achieve. If the AT is a microcosm of society, then there is HOPE.

Like ants stirred in a jar, constant conflict only leads to further division. Treating each other with respect and kindness seems easy for some. Others say it is impossible for us to work together at a unified level anymore. They call themselves realists and insist that to think otherwise would be too Pollyannish, like Unicorns pissing Rainbows. That type of defeatist attitude is what has gotten us into this mess in the first place. We have to try! Better yet, we are all called to love one another regardless of race, social status, economic standing, or political party. How we treat one another will directly determine the future of our nation and our world. It will require

> "Ultimately, there are two ways to live life—as if there are no miracles or as if everything is!"
> – ALBERT EINSTEIN

civility of tongue and intent, especially from those in leadership positions. The Golden Rule must be adhered to. We are all created in his image. How you treat one another, especially your opponents, is how you treat your Creator. Let's break the cycle and say no to discord and chaos. Let us choose to unify and lift up our brothers and sisters without robbing them of their dignity, to help one another be the best that God created each of us to be.

Epilogue

Jacob of 1996 sent me a letter informing me that Fashion, Gretchen, and Little Wing finished on 12-07-96. The Fox, Leapfrog, Shoofly Pie, and Tree Trunk finished on 12-09-96. Little Buddy finished 12-10-96, as did I Don't Know. Silver Toe signed the register but didn't date it. Captain Morgan finished along with Lost Sheep and Tuna on 12-15-96. Mr. Brown, Travis Walker, and Tigger finished sometime after Kee and me on 12-17-96.

I was happy but not surprised to hear that Rev and Blue Noodle finished three days after me. They celebrated on Springer Mountain with Rev's brother, Grizz, and the Noodle's dad, Magoo. Magoo would later finish the trail in 1998, but what impressed me most about that father-son team during their '96 hike was their disappearing act every Sunday. Come to find out, they had been packing a Bible with them, and their Sunday mornings began with some scripture readings and then a service that reflected their faith and love for one another. A love that could weather any storm.

Thunder Snow sectioned hiked the remainder of the trail and finished ten years later. He was doggedly persistent!

Dr. Slow Jive regretted leaving the trail, but he did spend two months in Angola, Africa, before returning home and starting his practice.

Wingfoot's stats:

~ 3500 Northbounders started, and only 250 finished.
~ 250 Southbounders started, 170 quit by the Kennebec River in Maine, 70 made it to Harper's Ferry, and only 30 finished. It was a record year for southbounders!
~ Only two dogs finished.

Dear Reader,

THANK YOU for taking this journey with me. I realize that you are in one of three camps. The first is the believers, those who are sure there is more to this existence. The second is the fence-sitters, those who are not sure and uncomfortable being decisive one way or the other. Then, some are adamant that God doesn't exist. I hope that whatever camp you find yourself in, this book will give you the courage to look deeper and make a lasting difference in your life and those around you. Like it or not, we will all have to come to terms with our decisions when we die.

If you ever want to test yourself to truly know yourself, the AT can be the crucible that helps you step through the fire.

Do you have the courage to step out of the madness and enter the sanctuary of silence?

Love has given you the gift of free will—use it wisely! Don't wait to die to learn to live!

Vaya con Dios!

Rick Huber

Ducttape 1996 AT thru-hiker and his faithful dog, Kiana

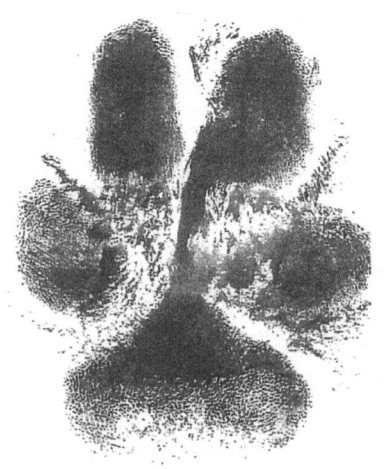

Acknowledgments

I WOULD LIKE TO THANK Richard Paul Evans and his team at Author Ready for their invaluable help in transforming a dream into reality. I consider myself very fortunate to have "discovered" Richard's books in an impromptu visit to a Barnes and Noble in Brookfield, WI. I credit his assistant Diane Glad for bringing us together at a writer's retreat, where I would witness Rick's passion for writing and helping newbies craft their stories into a book. It was contagious! Thank you, Rick, for reigniting that spark again.

Debbie Ihler Rasmussen, author/editor who's seasoned advice and helpful enthusiasm was exactly what this rookie author needed.

Kim Autrey, copy editor extraordinaire, thank you for your keen eye and belief in this story, it gave wind to my sails.

Francine Platt with Eden Graphics, thank you for your caring attention to detail on my book cover and interior design.

A special thanks to Professor Paul Pavich for coming out of retirement to share your expertise. You have a special gift for making people "Happy, Happy!"

Lastly, a big thanks to my loving wife for transcribing my audio recordings and reading through my rough draft with unflinching resolve to help get this work published.

Life tends to throw curve balls and sometimes we are forced to shelve our dreams. I don't think it is mere coincidence that fate would have our paths cross and it is with enormous gratitude that I thank each of you for your participation in this journey.

– RICHARD L HUBER

For more information, to order books, or join the mailing list please visit my website, where you can also find additional photos and color images. I hope they add to the adventure as you read this book.

AuthorRichardHuber.com

www.ingramcontent.com/pod-product-compliance
Lightning Source LLC
Chambersburg PA
CBHW060448030426
42337CB00015B/1518